THE
JAPANESE

D0958982

THE
JAPANESE

Edwin O. Reischauer

CHARLES E. TUTTLE COMPANY
Suido 1-chome, 2-6, Bunkyo-ku, Tokyo

This edition for sale in Japan only

Published by the Charles E. Tuttle Company, Inc.
of Rutland, Vermont and Tokyo, Japan
with editorial offices at
Suido 1-chome, 2-6, Bunkyo-ku, Tokyo, Japan
by special arrangement with
Harvard University Press, Cambridge, Massachusetts

First Tuttle edition, 1978
Twentieth printing, 1980

0230-000435-4615
PRINTED IN JAPAN

Preface

THE RIVER of history flows fast in Japan, and each bend reveals the country in a new light. The time is ripe for a reappraisal of Japan from the perspective of the late 1970s. In the past I have attempted in various works to outline this flow or to describe the conditions of life, social organization, motivating ideas, and international relations of the Japanese people. In the several editions of *The United States and Japan*, for example, I wrote of them as they followed the road to war, as they responded to the wrenching reforms of the American occupation, and as they reacted to their own brilliant postwar economic success. All these phases of recent history, however, are receding into the past and are merging with a much longer tradition that helps shape what the Japanese are today and may be in the future. The time has come to take a fresh look at Japan and the Japanese from our present vantage point.

In viewing Japan from the perspective of the late 1970s, however, I have tried to avoid a close concentration on the present situation for fear that emphasis on current issues might distract our attention from the more fundamental and lasting aspects of the picture that can give us better insights into what Japan may be in the future. I have thus sought to achieve a wide focus on contemporary Japan as seen in the light of its whole past experience. Naturally the basic facts about the past do not change, and in describing these I may at places have unconsciously fallen into the same phraseology I used in earlier books. But even these unchanging facts often appear in a new light when viewed from a new point in time. This book thus is not merely an updating of my previous writings.

In coverage, in structure, and to a large extent in ideas, it is an entirely new book—in other words, a fresh attempt to depict what the Japanese are like today and how Japan fits into the contemporary world.

Japan and the Japanese form so large and diverse a subject that not all aspects can be treated in a book of this size, even in cursory form. I should point out that I do not attempt to deal with the fascinating detail of life in Japan, except to illustrate broader points. Nor do I go into the great esthetic achievements of the Japanese, except as elements in their cultural development and social patterns. Nor have I attempted to analyze Japan's remarkable economic growth, except as part of its general historical evolution and to show how business fits into society and how Japan's economic development has determined its position in the world. All these other important aspects of the story are well covered in more specialized works. Instead, I have concentrated on the social organization and values of the Japanese, on their political system, and on their relationship with the outside world.

In writing this book I have, of course, drawn facts and also interpretations from the writings of a vast number of Japanese and foreign scholars and authors. It would be quite impossible to list even the most important of them, because they would number in the hundreds. But I do wish to express my indebtedness to all my colleagues who have advanced the study of Japan so greatly. I also wish specifically to thank a few colleagues and friends for reading the manuscript of this book and giving me valuable corrections and comments. Albert M. Craig, Ezra Vogel, Hiroaki Fujii, and my wife, Haru Matsukata Reischauer, kindly rendered this service on the whole work, and Henry Rosovsky, Nathaniel B. Thayer, and David Titus on certain sections. I am also indebted to Nancy Harrison for endless aid in the production of the manuscript.

Contents

SOCIETY

POLITICS

JAPAN
AND THE WORLD

THE SETTING

PART ONE

This remote hamlet on an island in the Inland Sea is typical of Japan's crowded countryside. The valleys are crammed with irrigated fields. The hills are covered with dry fields. The houses are packed close together. A few old-fashioned, high-peaked thatch roofs can be seen among the more common tile roofs. (*Japan National Tourist Organization*)

The Land

1 ⊥⁄

THE JAPANESE, like all peoples, have been shaped in large part by the land in which they live. Its location, climate, and natural endowments are unchangeable facts that have set limits to their development and helped give it specific direction. In our study of the Japanese, therefore, we shall start with this geographic setting.

Most people think of Japan as a small country. Even the Japanese have this idea firmly in mind. And small it is if seen on a world map—a mere fringe of scraggly islands off the east coast of the great continental land mass of Eurasia, looking outward to the vast sweep of the Pacific Ocean. It is certainly dwarfed by its near neighbors, China and the Soviet Union, and by the two North American colossi, the United States and Canada, which face it across the Pacific. But size is a relative matter. Japan would look far different if lined up against the lands of Western Europe. It is less revealing to say that Japan is smaller than California or could be lost in a Siberian province than to point out that it is considerably larger than Italy and half again the size of the United Kingdom. For Americans the best comparison, both in terms of terrain and population, might be to New York, New Jersey, Pennsylvania, and all of New England, minus Maine.

National size can be measured in various ways, and square mileage is certainly not the most important of these. In fact, it can be very misleading. A thousand square miles in Antarctica, Greenland, or even New Guinea are not to be equated with ten square miles on the lower Rhine or in the rich agricultural lands of Illinois. The vast stretches of terrain that separate the mineral resources of Siberia, Alaska, or the Canadian north-

3

west from more habitable regions are economic liabilities rather than assets.

A more meaningful measure of a nation's size is by population. In this category, there are four giants—China and India, with their populations each soaring toward the billion mark, and the Soviet Union and the United States, which through historic accident had the chance to expand over vast continental domains and in the process developed populations well over two hundred millions. Indonesia and Brazil have the geographic spread to achieve in time the giant class. Indonesia passed Japan in population a few years ago, and Brazil is in the process of doing so now. But Japan comes next, ranking seventh in the world and far ahead of the major countries of Western Europe, which were considered the great powers of the world not long ago. As far back as the early seventeenth century, Japan had around twenty-five million inhabitants, considerably more than the population of France, which was then the largest country of Europe, and several times the size of England. Today it has a population of around 115 million. (It was close to 112 million in the most recent census at the end of 1975.) This means that Japan has roughly twice the population of each of the Western European big four—West Germany, the United Kingdom, Italy, and France.

Another important measure of a country's size is its productive power, or GNP (Gross National Product), which is the multiple of its exploited resources, its population, and, most important, their skills. In this category Japan is one of the giants, ranking number three in the world, only behind the two superpowers, the United States and the Soviet Union. It is well ahead of the great nations of Western Europe and is advancing on the Soviet Union, despite the more than two to one edge of the latter in population and the sixty to one advantage it has in area. (Let me note as an aside that the omission of specific figures for GNP and the like here and elsewhere in this book is deliberate. Nothing is less memorable than an outdated statistic. Most numbers move quickly toward oblivion in the present age of rapid population and economic growth, magnified in the latter case by galloping inflation. I have preferred for the most part to stick to broad numerical generalizations and comparative ratios, which are less likely to become rapidly out of date.)

We are so conditioned to judge size only by our conventional maps that it may be useful to insert at this point two other types of map. In the one, the size of countries is drawn proportionately to their populations, in the

THE LAND

other to their GNP. I first devised maps of this sort in 1964 in order to point out to the Japanese, who were still suffering from a gross underestimation of their country following their defeat in World War II, that Japan was indeed a relatively large country. The maps on pages 6 and 7 are based on revisions of these earlier ones made in 1974, by which time Japan had grown to be an economic giant.

Taken together these two maps tell a great deal about the world as a whole, as well as about the relative size of Japan. Much of the population of the world can be seen to be concentrated in China, the Indian subcontinent, Indonesia, and some of the other developing nations, whereas its productive power is overwhelmingly bunched in the industrialized nations of Europe, North America, and Japan. The details of these maps will change over time. Already the sudden upsurge of oil prices that started in 1973 has much expanded the GNP of the oil-rich lands of the Middle East. But the basic imbalance between the industrialized rich and the populous but nonindustrialized poor nations will remain and probably grow worse. On the whole, it is the poor nations that are increasing fastest in population and the rich in GNP. Herein lies perhaps the most intractable of all international problems.

DESPITE its largeness by some measurements, Japan is actually a smaller country in geographic size than the figures on square miles would suggest. The whole country is so mountainous that less than a fifth of it is level enough to permit agriculture or other economic exploitation, other than forestry, mining, or hydroelectric power. Belgium and the Netherlands have a higher ratio of people to total land area than does Japan, but figured on the basis of habitable land Japan is much more crowded than either of them. In fact, with the exception of city states like Hong Kong and Singapore, Japan has by far the highest density of both population and production per square mile of habitable land of any country in the world.

The mountains of Japan are almost uniformly precipitous, being relatively young, but in most parts of the country they are to be measured only in hundreds or a few thousands of feet. Most of Japan is made up of long stretches of forest-covered hills interlaced with narrow valleys that form slim strips of agriculture and habitation. Here and there, active or extinct volcanic cones rise much higher, and in the central part of

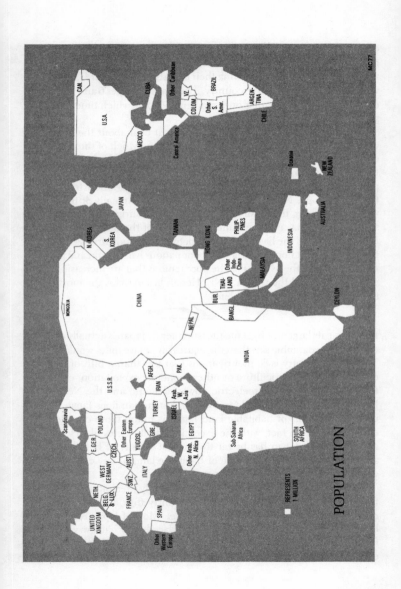

POPULATION

■ REPRESENTS 1 MILLION

MC77

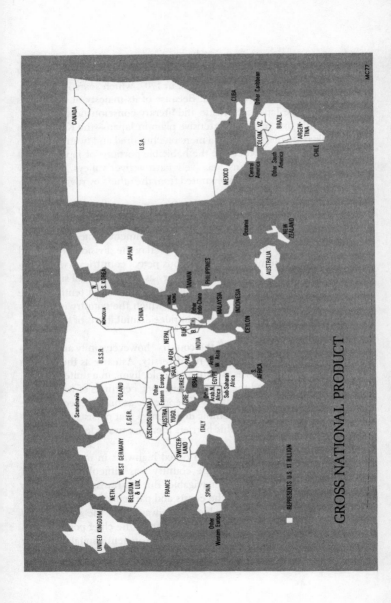

GROSS NATIONAL PRODUCT

■ REPRESENTS U.S. $1 BILLION

MC77

Honshu there are several ranges, collectively known as the Japanese Alps, which attain heights of around 10,000 feet. In this region also is Mount Fuji, a perfect volcanic cone, last active in 1707, which soars 12,389 feet, on one side straight out of the sea. Because of its majesty, it has always been much in the Japanese artistic and literary consciousness.

There is only one relatively extensive plain in Japan—the Kanto Plain around Tokyo—which stretches a mere one hundred and twenty miles in its longest dimension. Otherwise the habitable portions of Japan consist of small seacoast flood plains, relatively narrow river valleys, and a few basins in the mountains, each separated from the others by rugged hills or impassable mountains.

The division of the country into many small units of terrain has been conducive to local separatism and may have contributed to the development of a decentralized, feudal pattern of government in medieval times. These topographical divisions certainly underlay the division of the land in antiquity into a number of autonomous petty "countries," which became institutionalized by the eighth century as the traditional sixty-eight provinces of Japan. It is significant that more than nine tenths of the borders of the forty-seven prefectures into which the country is now divided still follow precisely the mountain ridge delimitations of these early provinces.

Despite the natural division of the country, however, unity and homogeneity characterize the Japanese, not diversity. As early as the seventh century, they saw themselves as a single people, living in a united nation. This has always remained the ideal, despite long centuries of feudal divisions. Today few if any large masses of people are as homogeneous as the Japanese. There is little of the ethnic divisiveness that persists in the British Isles, even though geographic barriers there are much less formidable than in Japan.

Until the building of railroads and paved highways in modern times, communication by land within the country was difficult. Only short stretches of any of the rivers are navigable. But sea transport has always been relatively easy around all the coasts and particularly on the beautiful, island-studded Inland Sea, which has always been the great central artery of the western half of Japan. Leading from the chief point of contact with the continent in north Kyushu to the ancient capital district at the eastern end of the Inland Sea, it was the main axis for much of Japan's early history.

Mt. Fuji, seen from the modern superhighway which skirts the southern coast of Honshu from Tokyo to Nagoya. This whole stretch of coast is today a virtual strip city, except where broken by fingers of mountains plunging down to the sea. At places the superhighway, local roads, the older national railway, and the New Main Line (*Shinkansen*) are all crowded close together, but at this point the railways are out of sight in tunnels. (*Sekai Bunka Photo*)

Agricultural people everywhere have developed a close attachment to the soil that has nourished them, but among the Japanese there is in addition to this universal feeling a particularly strong awareness of the beauties of nature. No part of Japan is more than seventy miles from the sea, and mountains are within view almost everywhere. With ample rainfall, the whole country is luxuriantly green and wooded, and the play of the seasons brings wondrous variety. The earliest Japanese literature shows a keen appreciation of the beauties of seascapes, mountains, and wooded dells, and today Japanese are avid visitors to renowned beauty spots, sometimes all but destroying them in their enthusiasm. In addition to peerless Fuji, there are the famous "three landscapes of Japan" (*Nihon sankei*)—Miyajima, a temple island in the Inland Sea near Hiroshima, Ama-no-hashidate, or "Bridge of Heaven," a pine-covered sandspit on the Japan Sea coast north of Kyoto, and Matsushima, a cluster of picturesque pine-clad islands in a bay near the city of Sendai in northern Japan. Most localities in Japan are likely to have their own three or eight landscapes, and there are thousands of other beauty spots and hot spring resorts, as well as innumerable less known places of beauty.

Unlike the grandeur of the American West, the scale of Japan's natural beauty is for the most part small and intimate. This smallness of scale has perhaps lent itself to the Japanese effort to capture and preserve nature in small bits, as in their miniaturized gardens. The chief exceptions to the smallness of scale are the high mountains of central Japan and the longer vistas of the northern island of Hokkaido. Not fully absorbed into Japan until the latter part of the nineteenth century, Hokkaido has stretches of landscape as well as a thinness of population more reminiscent of North America.

Ironically, the Japanese, for all their love of nature, have done as much as any people to defile it. This may have been inevitable in a country with the highest levels of population and production per habitable square mile. Beautiful green hills have been hacked down for factory or living sites and to provide fill for land recovered from the sea. More distant mountains have disappeared behind industrial smog. Urban blight sprawls across much of the agricultural countryside. Mountains have been defaced by so-called "skyline drives" to accommodate the city tourist. Renowned beauty spots are half buried in hotels, restaurants, and trinket shops. But the greater part of Japan today is thinly populated, and anywhere off the beaten track it remains a land of great natural charm and beauty.

JAPAN'S dense population and rate of production per habitable square mile can in part be explained by the climate, which contrasts quite sharply with that of Europe. Where European agriculture is limited by dry summers in the south and cool summers in the north, Japan has both hot summer weather and ample rainfall, which comes for the most part during the growing season from early spring to early autumn. This has permitted a much more intensive form of agriculture than in Europe, with consequently heavier agricultural populations.

THE LAND

The climate of Japan is more easily comparable to that of the east coast of North America than with Europe. That is because the relationships between land masses, oceans, and prevailing winds in and around Japan show similarities to the American east coast but contrast with those of the west coast and Europe. A general idea of Japanese temperatures and climate can be gained by superimposing the Japanese islands on a map of the east coast of North America at the same latitudes. The four main islands of Japan will be seen to stretch from northern Maine, or Montreal in Canada, almost to the Gulf of Mexico. Okinawa (the Ryukyu Islands) is in the latitude of Florida, and the Kurile Islands, which Japan lost to the Soviet Union after World War II, parallel Newfoundland. The bulk of metropolitan Japan, however, lies at the level of North Carolina.

Miyajima, literally meaning "the island of the shrine," is one of the "three landscapes of Japan" (*Nihon sankei*). Located a few miles west of the city of Hiroshima in the beautiful Inland Sea, it is properly known as Itsukushima. In the foreground are votive stone lanterns; in the middle distance a *torii*, the gateway to all Shinto shrines (its unique placement in the sea has necessitated the untypical buttresses); and in the background the hilly main island of Honshu, with Hiroshima just out of sight to the right. (*Consulate General of Japan*, N.Y.)

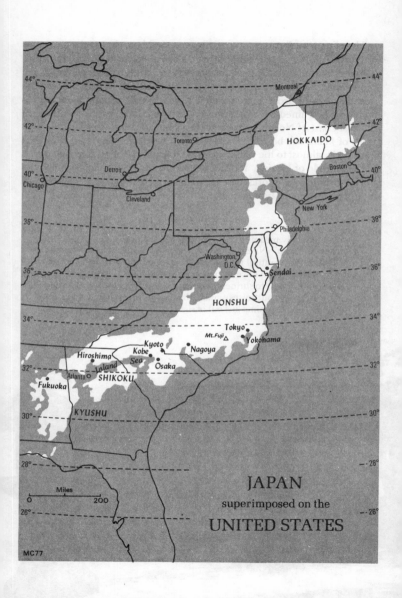

JAPAN
superimposed on the
UNITED STATES

MC77

THE LAND

Since Japan is not part of the continental land mass but lies some hundreds of miles off shore, it has a somewhat more oceanic climate, with less severe heat in summer and cold in winter, than do parallel latitudes along our east coast. There is also more precipitation, ranging roughly from around 40 to 120 inches per year. Late autumn and winter are relatively dry, with long stretches of delightful sunny weather in most parts of Japan. This is because during the colder months high pressures build up over frigid Siberia and Mongolia, causing cold, dry winds to flow outward from the continent.

There is one major exception to this rule, however. The winter winds from Siberia pick up considerable moisture from the Japan Sea and dump this in the form of snow as they cross the central mountainous backbone of Honshu. It is the same phenomenon as the "snow shadow" on the eastern shores of the Great Lakes in North America, only on a much larger scale. As a result, the northwestern coastal regions of Honshu have prodigious winter snows, giving a ground cover of five or six feet in many areas—the heaviest snowfall in the world for any region that has a dense population.

The contrast can be striking between deep snow and gloom on one side of the mountainous backbone of northern Japan and sunshine and bare ground on the other, sometimes only a few miles apart by railway tunnel. These conditions, together with the concentration of all the great cities on the Pacific side of the islands, have given a certain sense of resentment if not inferiority to the residents of what they themselves call the "backside of Japan" (Ura Nihon). In contrast, the peninsulas that jut into the Pacific on Japan's south coast have a particularly benign, almost subtropical climate, thanks to the Japan Current (or Black Current, Kuroshio, as the Japanese call it), which bathes that coast in much the same way as the Gulf Stream sweeps up the southeast coast of the United States.

Except for Hokkaido, the growing season in most of Japan averages between two hundred and two hundred and sixty days, but the period of oppressive summer heat is relatively short, usually lasting only from early July to early September. However, during this period it is indeed oppressive, not so much because of very high temperatures as because of excessively high humidity.

Winters are not very severe, but they can be quite uncomfortable if one does not have adequate heating, which was the prevailing situation in Japan until only a few years ago. Except for the north and the higher mountains, temperatures rarely go down more than a few degrees below freezing, but in most parts of Japan they do dip during the night below freezing for a month or two in the winter, and snow does fall at least occasionally in all parts of Japan except Okinawa. Since winter temperatures are not severe enough to kill sheltered humans, the premodern Japanese, like other peoples living in comparable climatic zones, developed heating systems that only lessened the rigors of winter a little. Traditionally the construction of their houses was light and drafty, more fitted to admit cooling breezes in summer than to keep out the frost of winter. The chief heating device was a charcoal brazier, or hibachi, where one could warm one's wrists for supposed circulation of the heated blood throughout the body, though in some farmhouses one could warm one's feet in a sunken heating pit, or *kotatsu*. A nightly scalding bath would bring real warmth from then until bedtime, and in the middle of the day glorious winter sunshine might heat up the house to tolerable levels for a short while. A good southern exposure was therefore important. Today, though central heating is still rare in private homes, electric, gas, or oil heaters have replaced the old charcoal brazier and together with more solid house construction make winter living more tolerable. But for most Japanese, winter still means heavy long underwear.

Summer and winter, thus, can be unpleasant in Japan, but they are not extreme and are relatively brief. The remaining eight months of the year are very pleasant. The four seasons are clearly differentiated and, unlike the eastern half of the United States, quite regular in their slow progression of temperature changes.

Japan's climate is typically temperate, as befits its latitude, and contrasts with the tropics, where the growing season is year round and temperatures make a relatively slow pace of life advisable. To survive the colder months, food surplusses have always had to be built up by hard, concentrated work during the more productive parts of the year, and daytime rest periods or a leisurely work pace have not seemed necessary to escape the midday heat. The same is true for Japan's East Asian neighbors in Korea and China. Such climatic conditions may lie behind the fact that the people of all three of these countries are noted for their hard work and unflagging energy. Simple necessity at first, reenforced over the centuries by well established custom and insistent moral precept, seems to have produced among the Japanese and their neighbors in East Asia what may be the most deeply ingrained work ethic in the whole world and what undoubtedly is a salient characteristic and great asset of the peoples of this part of the globe.

One outstanding feature of Japanese weather is the series of great cyclonic storms, called typhoons, which devastate parts of the country in late summer and early autumn. These are identical in nature with the hurricanes that occasionally ravage the east coast of the United States, both being products of the same general relationship between land and water at comparable latitudes. Typhoons, however, strike Japan with somewhat greater frequency and usually with more destructiveness to life and property, since the greater part of the Japanese population is concentrated on the seacoasts of southwestern Japan where the typhoons first come ashore.

Typhoons have accustomed the Japanese to expect natural catastrophes and accept them with stoic resilience. This sort of fatalism might even be called the "typhoon mentality," but it has been fostered by other natural disasters as well. Volcanic eruptions sometimes occur, since a large part of the Japanese chain is the product of volcanic action, and there are many active volcanoes. The largest, Asama, devastated hundreds of square miles of central Honshu in 1783. There are also numerous fault lines throughout the islands, and destructive earthquakes are commonplace. Tokyo and its port of Yokohama were in large part leveled by fires resulting from a great earthquake that struck at noon on September 1, 1923, leaving some 130,000 persons dead. Since Edo, as Tokyo was formerly called, had been periodically hit by severe earthquakes, there is a popular belief that it is likely to be visited by a devastating earthquake every sixty years or so. In any case, the Japanese have a fatalistic acceptance of nature's awesome might, as well as a great capacity to dig themselves out after such catastrophes and start afresh.

Agriculture and Natural Resources

2

BETWEEN the ever present mountains and the sprawling cities, only some 15 percent of Japan's land area is under cultivation. The soils of Japan, moreover, are on the whole not very fertile. Nonetheless, a relatively long growing season, plentiful rainfall, unlimited hard work, and high agricultural skills have made it a very productive country despite its narrow geographic base.

Knowledge of agriculture appeared quite late in Japan—only two or three centuries before the time of Christ. Whereas dry millet, growing in unirrigated fields, was a characteristic farm product of early North China, the original homeland of most of East Asian civilization, the form of agriculture that came to Japan was wet-field rice cultivation, which seems to have originated somewhere to the south of ancient China. By the second century A.D. it was practiced in Japan in its essentially modern form in small dike-surrounded, water-filled plots of land, fed by an intricate man-made system of small waterways. Seedlings normally are grown in dense profusion in special seed beds and later transplanted to the main fields by hand, though recently machines have been developed for this task. Transplanting assures more uniform growth in the main fields and also frees them longer for the maturation of winter crops in the warmer parts of Japan where double cropping is possible.

In the small flood plains and narrow valleys of Japan, this sort of agriculture did not require the massive water control efforts needed to harness the destructive forces and agricultural potential of great river systems. Large-scale water-control projects in Egypt, Mesopotamia, and

16

North China are thought by some to have contributed to the development of mass, authoritarian societies in these regions. In Japan, however, what was needed was close cooperation over the sharing of water resources between smaller groups. It may not be far fetched to speculate that such cooperative efforts over the centuries have contributed to the notable Japanese penchant for group identification and group action.

Irrigated rice cultivation, as practiced in Japan, demands enormous amounts of labor, but it produces much higher yields per acre than the dry-field wheat farming of the West. As much of the land as possible has been converted into irrigated rice paddies. Natural marshes and swamps have been carefully drained, diked, and turned into productive areas. Elsewhere rice fields follow each stream or rivulet almost to its source and, where water is available, ascend the hillsides in man-made terraces. Unirrigated dry fields for other crops stretch still higher up the slopes or wherever water cannot be made to flow. Rice can be grown as far north as the western half of Hokkaido, and roughly 40 percent of the total agricultural area is devoted to wet-field rice.

The productivity of the land has been further increased by double cropping wherever possible, usually between summer rice and various winter grains or vegetables. This sort of double cropping can be practiced in the half of Japan southwest of a line running from a little north of Tokyo to the west coast of Honshu north of Kyoto.

As a result of intensive wet-field rice cultivation and double cropping, Japan, like the rest of East Asia, has supported since antiquity much heavier concentrations of population than the drier or colder lands of West Asia and Europe. At least since Roman times China alone has equaled or outdistanced the population of all of Europe, and the Japanese population as long as three centuries ago had grown well beyond that of European states of comparable size. Thus the Japanese have been living together for many centuries in much larger and more concentrated masses than have Westerners. These conditions may have helped develop their propensities for group action and their skills in group organization.

JAPANESE agricultural methods, involving as they do an immense amount of labor, seem relatively primitive when compared with the large-scale, highly mechanized agriculture of the United States. Japanese agriculture is not very productive per man-hour, but it is extremely productive per acre—perhaps the most productive in the whole world in these terms. For example, Japanese rice yields per acre are two to four times those of Southeast and South Asia, having passed the current levels of these southern lands centuries ago. This emphasis on productivity per acre rather than per hand is understandable because Japan for hundreds of years has been richer in people than in land. As a result, some ninety times as many people work a square mile of arable land as in the United States and more than five times as many as even in Germany.

Japanese agriculture, however, is very efficient and even scientific in its own way. Almost every square foot of tillable land is exploited as fully as possible. The rice seedlings or other crops are planted in careful straight rows that fill every square inch of space. The soil is carefully tilled to a depth of one or two feet, in earlier times by the long-bladed hoe of East Asia. The fields are meticulously weeded, and fertilizers are used in abundance. Originally these were organic materials, including until shortly after the end of World War II night soil from the urban areas, which was as malodorous as it was economically beneficial. More recently night soil has virtually dropped out of use, and the Japanese farmer has come to depend largely on chemical fertilizers, which he applies lavishly. He also makes extensive use of vinyl coverings to form a type of simple greenhouse for vegetables.

Even before modern times Japanese agriculture had become self-consciously "scientific," and many treatises on improved seeds and the best agricultural methods were written by eighteenth century farmers. Virtually all the suitable agricultural land had been put under cultivation (except in Hokkaido which remained a largely undeveloped border land), and both the government and farmers sought by every means to increase production. Thus, the population of around thirty million with which Japan entered the nineteenth century was perhaps almost the maximum that could be supported by the country as it then existed—an isolated, pre-industrial land with only very limited agricultural terrain.

The opening of Japan to world trade in the middle of the nineteenth century and the centralization and modernization of its government dramatically changed the situation, permitting a surge forward in agricultural production. In fact, much of Japan's political modernization and industrial growth in the late nineteenth century was financed by surplusses produced in agriculture. Advanced agricultural techniques now could spread more rapidly from more progressive areas to backward regions; cheap transportation by steamships and then railroads made possible a greater regional specialization of crops; Hokkaido came under the plow; eventually government agricultural institutes made available more modern scientific agricultural knowledge; and in the twentieth century Manchurian soy bean cakes and other sources of foreign fertilizers became available. Population growth, however, outdistanced agricultural production, and by the beginning of the twentieth century Japan had developed a deficit of almost 20 percent in its food supply.

Following World War II, a rush of new technology brought another leap in agricultural productivity. Chemical fertilizers, which were already widely used, became available in even greater quantity, and mechanization at last came to agriculture, permitting a sharp decline in the farming population. In the depressed conditions of the early postwar years, close to half the Japanese remained engaged in agriculture, but thereafter the percentage declined drastically. At present only about 15 percent of Japanese live in farming households, and few of these devote themselves exclusively to agriculture. The great majority combine seasonal work on the ancestral farm with other employment elsewhere. The result is a widespread pattern of women and old people running the farms, while the younger men and often younger women as well work in the city or commute to nearby factories, offices, or stores. Thus considerably less than 15 percent of Japanese labor now goes into agriculture, and the figure is likely to decline to well under 10 percent.

The pattern of mechanization in Japanese agriculture is far different from that of the United States or most of the West. In Hokkaido the size of farms is relatively large, though still very small by American standards, but elsewhere in Japan farms average only about two and a half acres, or about one hectare, the unit the Japanese themselves now use. A further drop in farm population may produce in time a consolidation of farm holdings, but this has not yet started on a significant scale. In any case, regardless of the amount of land the individual farmer cultivates, terrain factors make most of the rice paddies and dry fields of Japan extremely small, better measured in square yards than in acres or hectares. They simply do not permit the use of great combines or large tractors. Instead the Japanese employ small, hand-fed threshing machines and what they call the *mame* or bean tractor, which is of a size midway between a lawnmower and an American tractor.

The postwar surge in agriculture resulted in annual new records of rice

Preparing a rice paddy for transplanting rice shoots. The smallness of the fields facilitates irrigation. In the background three women and a man are transplanting shoots in the traditional backbreaking way, but recently machines have been developed for this purpose. The cultivator in the foreground is typical of the small size of Japanese "bean" tractors. (*Embassy of Japan*)

production. Since per capita consumption of rice was declining at the same time, because higher living standards permitted a more varied diet, the Japanese, to their own amazement, suddenly found themselves for the first time in several decades, not with a deficit in rice, but with surplusses. But with a population almost four times the Malthusian limit that had been reached in the eighteenth century, the Japanese now faced an even greater deficit in food of almost 30 percent, or over half if one counts in imported feed grains used in domestic meat production.

Such shortages of food make the Japanese anxious, particularly under present conditions of perceived worldwide deficiencies. This anxiety, together with political sensitivity to the farm vote and a desire to avoid upsetting social changes in rural areas, has induced the government to continue to put emphasis on agriculture, even though it is much less productive per capita than most other forms of economic activity, contributes less than 5 percent to the total GNP, and keeps food prices much higher in Japan than on the world market. For example, American rice identical to that produced in Japan could be unloaded in Japanese ports at half the cost of domestic rice. To keep Japanese agriculture from being swamped by cheaper foreign produce, agricultural imports are strictly controlled, and the government keeps raising the price of rice to artificially high levels in order to maintain production and help farm families keep up with the rapid general rise in living standards. On the other hand, most farmers cling to the land, not just out of their traditional devotion to it but also because, in the land-short, industrialized country that Japan has become, land prices have shot up astronomically, far beyond their agricultural value.

In the early postwar years, when food was extremely short in Japan and the whole economy was half dead, hungry people tried to grow crops among the ruins of the cities and on any other scrap of unutilized land. Such desperate efforts have long since been abandoned, but the search for more food over the centuries has led to permanent terracing far up the sides of hills and the carving out of minuscule fields a few feet wide, deep in small mountain valleys. Some of the more uneconomic bits of farm land will undoubtedly drop out of use in time—in fact some already have—and the sprawling cities will continue to eat up surrounding tracts of the most productive agricultural acreage. But the Japanese will probably attempt to maintain their present degree of self-sufficiency in food. The resulting economic drag of an inefficiently small-scale agriculture will probably be offset in their minds by the insurance value and psychological satisfaction of not being almost totally dependent on foreign sources for food.

THE DIET and cuisine of the Japanese have been strongly influenced by the nature of their agriculture. Rice has always been the staple food and until recent times was eaten in large quantities at all three meals each day. In fact, the word for cooked rice (*gohan*) is also the word for meal. Sake, the chief traditional alcoholic beverage, is made from rice by a brewing process that gives it an alcoholic content of 15 to 20 percent—a trifle stronger than most wine. All land that could be brought under irrigation, almost regardless of the effort required to do so, has been devoted to rice cultivation. Nonirrigable fields are devoted to dry-field crops of other grains, vegetables, and justly renowned fruit, including most of the temperate zone varieties as well as a great abundance of Mandarin oranges.

Of the total land area of Japan, only 2.5 percent, largely in the colder north, is pasture land used for the less efficient production of food through animal husbandry. In the past, cattle were used to haul carts or plow fields but not for food. Their relative scarcity together with the Buddhist prejudice against the taking of animal life made the Japanese for most of their history nonmeat eaters. They obtained their protein instead from the fish that abound in the waters which bathe the whole country and from the versatile soy bean, which is now largely imported from the United States and is used to make soy sauce (*shoyu*), fermented bean paste (*miso*), and bean curd (*tofu*).

The traditional Japanese cuisine is simple and fairly bland, especially when compared with the world-famous cooking of the Chinese. Polished white rice, uncontaminated by sauces or condiments, is not just the belly filler in a traditional Japanese meal but also the most highly prized component. Large mouthfuls of rice are alternated with small bites of fish, vegetables, or pickles. Where the Chinese banquet consists of a series of rich dishes combining a great variety of tastes, the Japanese banquet is made up of a number of small servings of individual things—a few slices of raw fish (*sashimi*), a pickle, a simple vegetable, and the like—all artistically served, often with more obvious attraction to the eye than to the palate. Chinese cooking is an overwhelming gustatory experience; traditional Japanese cooking appeals more to delicate tastes and to esthetic charm.

Of course, like everything else in Japan, eating habits have been changing rapidly in recent decades. Per capita consumption of rice has declined as the Japanese developed more catholic tastes. Cheap imported wheat is baked into excellent European-style bread, which is commonly substituted for rice at breakfast. Meat, either imported or produced from imported feed grains, has become a significant part of the modern diet, though per capita consumption remains less than a fifth that of Americans. The Japanese have even taken to dairy products, which until recently were anathema to all East Asians. Even sake is gradually yielding place to excellent German-type beer, Scotch-type whiskey, and other Western beverages.

The Japanese enjoy a wide variety of noodle dishes; Chinese styles of cooking and a broad range of Western dishes are all very popular. They have also developed a number of specialty dishes which are quite unlike their traditional cuisine and perhaps for that very reason have achieved a degree of international fame. Among these are sukiyaki, a beef dish said to have been invented by iconoclastic medical students in the mid-nineteenth century, tempura, or deep-fried prawns, thought by some to have been borrowed in the sixteenth century from the Portuguese, and entirely new dishes, such as the table-top beef cookery developed since World War II. Japanese beef is known for its excellence, attributed by popular myth to beer mash and massage, though a more plausible explanation may be the fact that the animals are often stall raised and lack a range or even pasture lands in which to toughen their muscles.

The traditional Japanese diet of rice, vegetables, and fish, which contrasts with the heavy consumption of meat and fat in the West, would be almost a perfect health diet if the Japanese did not insist on polishing the nutritious bran off their rice. This diet may account in part for the low Japanese incidence of heart disease as compared with Americans. On the other hand, something about it, possibly the polished rice, may produce the high rate of stomach cancer in Japan. In earlier days the diet was perhaps too austere for optimum childhood growth. Since World War II, Japanese children have increased several inches in height and many pounds in weight. Part of the increased height may be attributed to the straightening out of legs, as Japanese sit less on the floor and more on chairs, but, like the weight, it may be chiefly due to a richer diet, which now includes dairy products and more meat and bread. Young Japanese today are quite visibly a bigger breed than their ancestors, and fat children, which formerly were never encountered, have become a commonplace sight.

———— ⚓ ————

JAPAN'S meager supply of arable land is not offset by any other great natural riches. Water is the only resource with which it is well endowed. Plentiful rainfall makes possible its intensive agriculture and produces a dense forest cover on two thirds of the area. Much of this forest land is now scientifically planted for maximum growth. As a result, Japan, despite its small size, ranks relatively high among the wood producing nations of the world, though the yield meets less than half its own voracious appetite for pulp for industry and lumber for its private housing. Traditionally almost all Japanese buildings were constructed of wood, since stone or brick structures were extremely vulnerable to earthquakes, and even now most private homes and small shops are of wooden construction. The small but precipitously descending rivers of Japan are also a significant source of hydroelectric power. Despite almost full exploitation, however, water power supplies only a little over 5 percent of Japan's present gargantuan consumption of energy and is constantly sinking in relative terms.

The surrounding seas are a major economic asset for Japan. They are the source of Japan's chief protein supply—fish—and also vitamin rich seaweeds, which the Japanese use extensively in their cuisine. Coastal waters have always provided vital food resources for the Japanese, and today there is considerable cultivation of fish, shellfish, and seaweed. Japanese fishing fleets also harvest the seven seas. In fact, Japan is the leading fishing nation in the world in terms of value and comes second in bulk only to Peru, which takes fabulous quantities of anchovies from its coastal waters.

The oceans also provide the Japanese with easy communication within their country and constitute their highways to the resources and markets of the world. With the exception of the old capital of Kyoto, all of Japan's six biggest cities and a majority of its middle-sized cities are located directly on the sea. In most cases, they have themselves been extended seaward by the construction of new docking facilities and factory sites through the filling in of large stretches of shallow water. The bulk of Japanese heavy industry thus can be located efficiently for transportation purposes, not on inland waterways and railroads, but directly on the sea.

In mineral resources Japan is poorly endowed. The volcanic origin of the islands has given them an abundance of sulphur, and they do have plenty of limestone, clays, sands, and the like, but otherwise Japan is short of almost every important mineral resource. A wide variety of minerals is to be found in the islands and these were adequate for Japanese needs in preindustrial times, but today they provide for the most part only marginal support to Japanese industry. There is, for example, sufficient coal to have been of critical importance in Japan's early industrialization, but the seams, being thin and broken, are not easily exploited, and today more than two thirds of the coal it uses must be imported. Once Japan was a copper exporter, but even in this commodity it is now five sixths dependent on the outside world, and some two thirds of its lead and zinc, two other minerals with which the islands are reasonably well supplied, must come from abroad. In most other important minerals, including iron ore, Japan is entirely or almost entirely dependent on imports. Worst of all, it is virtually lacking in the key energy resource of petroleum, which accounts for roughly three quarters of total Japanese energy consumption. Moreover, it has only very meager prospects for offshore oil and no appreciable fuels for nuclear power.

DESPITE the paucity of natural resources and the extremely limited agricultural base, Japan's population has more than doubled since the beginning of the twentieth century and its standard of living has increased many times over. Obviously, this sort of growth has only been possible because of rapid industrialization. But because of Japan's narrow and poorly endowed geographic base, this industrialization has brought with it a heavy dependence on foreign sources of energy and raw materials and therefore an equal dependence on foreign markets for industrial exports to pay for necessary imports. Japan is the world's largest importer of oil, coal, iron ore, a large number of other ores and metals, cotton, wool, lumber, and a great variety of other commodities. Although Japan once grew its own cotton, it has long since converted the land used for cotton to food crops and buys its cotton abroad. It has even become a net importer of silk, a labor-intensive semi-agricultural product (because of the mulberry leaves on which silk worms are fed), which was its greatest export item from the 1860s until the 1920s. Japan's dependence on global trade for its very survival is the most important single fact about its economic geography and the chief determinant of its relationship with the outside world.

Industrialization naturally means cities, and Japan is indeed a heavily urbanized land today. But in fact, even the pre-industrial, isolated Japan of the eighteenth century was economically and politically centralized enough to have had surprisingly large cities. Edo, as Tokyo was then called, had a population of about a million and may have been the largest city in the world around 1700. Osaka, the great trade center, and Kyoto, the ancient capital, both had several hundred thousands. The rest of Japan was dotted with castle towns which ranged up to 100,000 in population and were the seats of the roughly two hundred and sixty-five semi-autonomous feudal lords.

In the middle of the nineteenth century there was already a sizable urban population, and the growth since then has been prodigious. Tokyo

alone now has more than eight and a half million people in its main urban areas (the portion divided into wards) and over eleven million counting in the suburban cities of Tokyo Prefecture. Packed alongside it are Yokohama with more than two and a half million, Kawasaki with over a million squeezed between Yokohama and Tokyo, and heavy industrial and suburban populations in the adjacent portions of surrounding prefectures. The whole population node exceeds fifteen million, making it, next to the New York area, probably the largest concentration of people in the world.

The Kansai region around Osaka is another great metropolitan area of more than twelve million people. Meaning "west of the pass," the Kansai is the one great regional rival to the Kanto area ("east of the pass") around Tokyo. In addition to Osaka, which has close to three million people, the Kansai region includes the great port city of Kobe and the old capital of Kyoto a little way inland, each with close to a million and a half, and large numbers of smaller municipalities in between these big cities.

Nagoya, midway between the Kanto and the Kansai, is the center of another major node of well over two million people. Sapporo, the capital of Hokkaido, has a million and a quarter; Fukuoka, the old capital of northern Kyushu, and Kitakyushu, a large industrial center made up of a number of once separate municipalities and located as its name, North Kyushu, indicates, both exceed a million; and Hiroshima, the city of atomic-bomb fame on the Inland Sea, has more than 850,000. In addition there are more than one hundred and fifty other cities of between 100,000 and 750,000 population, and an industrial sprawl permeates most of the countryside wherever there is a relatively heavy rural population and adequate transportation facilities.

Japanese industry is located in the nonmountainous fifth of the country, but it is particularly thick along the old main line of Japanese history, which extends westward from the Tokyo area along the Pacific coast through Nagoya to the Kansai region and then on down the Inland Sea to northern Kyushu. Here lies an almost continuous band of factories and houses, interspersed at places with agriculture and broken only occasion-

Facing page: The streets outside Shinjuku station, one of the major commuting centers in Tokyo, where the national railways, private commuting lines, and subways all converge. The structures that look like ships' funnels are air intakes for a virtual underground city of walkways, stores, and restaurants—a common feature of commuting centers like Shinjuku. (*Consulate General of Japan,* N.Y.)

ally by mountain ridges. The eastern end of this line from the Kanto to the Kansai is a sort of great megalopolis, comparable to the strip city of the American east coast from Boston to Washington and containing about one third of Japan's total population.

As a result of political centralization and then industrialization during the past century, Japan now has excellent internal communications. The metropolitan areas are serviced by superb networks of commuting railway lines and the cities of Tokyo and Osaka by fine subway systems as well. Where commuting lines converge, large secondary "downtown" areas have developed, as is most notably the case at Shinjuku in Tokyo. A complex and efficient railway network ties the whole country together, and modern highspeed highways are beginning to spread to most areas. The water breaks between the main islands are being overcome by giant bridges and tunnels. These already connect Kyushu with Honshu, a tunnel to Hokkaido is being built, and bridges are being started across the Inland Sea to Shikoku. Planes, though essential for travel abroad, are only a minor aspect of transportation within Japan. Instead of depending on them almost exclusively for distant travel, as is the case in the United States, the Japanese have constructed a series of "new main line" (*Shinkansen*) railways, sometimes known in the West as "bullet trains." The first of these between Tokyo and Osaka runs the three hundred and forty-three miles in only a little over three hours at speeds averaging over a hundred miles an hour, with departures both ways every fifteen minutes, and with a punctuality that usually is phenomenal. Planes are much less reliable and, counting the travel time between city centers and airfields, not much faster.

Japan's cities and general industrial sprawl are scarcely its most attractive features. Part of the reason for this has been the speed with which industrialization has come to Japan and the adverse conditions under which it was achieved. At the end of World War II most of the cities had been in large part destroyed and had to be rebuilt in a period of great economic want. Many of their structures, as a consequence, were flimsy and even tawdry. Little effort was put into city planning; economic necessity seemed to override all other considerations.

Today the rate of growth is more leisurely, and attention can be given to matters other than economic production, but Japan still faces great problems. As the world's most crowded land in terms of habitable area, it suffers acutely from a general lack of space, and this situation is, of

High rise office buildings at Shinjuku, one of Tokyo's several "secondary downtowns." Shinjuku is located five miles west of the original downtown, and this view looks outward from the center toward the vast urban sprawl that continues for another ten to twenty miles. Shinjuku, like other commuting centers, has huge department stores and vast numbers of restaurants, bars, coffee shops and other places of entertainment. (*Japan Tourist Organization*)

course, worst in the cities. Land prices are extremely high, and crowding is inevitably severe in personal living accommodations and in public facilities. An apartment in the complexes of four to six story concrete apartments that ring the larger cities is likely to be no larger than a good sized room in a Western apartment, though it may be divided up into two small rooms and an even tinier kitchen and bathroom. A third of the housing facilities of Tokyo average only eleven by eleven feet in area, and over half the population of the city does not have access to flush toilets. Roads in Tokyo and Osaka occupy only 12 and 9 percent of the area, respectively, as compared to 35 percent in New York. Tokyo residents have less than a tenth as much park space per person as residents of New York and hardly more than a twentieth that of Londoners. In contrast to Japanese urban conditions, even the most crowded cities of the United States seem almost like the proverbial wide open spaces.

The net result is that Japanese cities and their surrounding areas of urban sprawl are not only terribly crowded but form a vast esthetic wasteland. Private homes often wall off quiet islands of beauty, and many small side streets are quite charming, but the outer face of most cities is almost unrelievedly ugly, contrasting sharply with the beauties of sea, mountain, and the rural countryside, where these remain undisturbed by industrialization. The great moats and castle walls of the imperial palace grounds have always given charm and dignity to the center of Tokyo, but otherwise Japanese cities are only slowly beginning to take on some shape and grandeur, as broad thoroughfares are cut through the jumble of houses and handsome new buildings rise, sometimes to the height of forty or fifty stories.

The scarcity of space in Japan, combined with a much smaller investment in the past in permanent, paved roadways and in longer lasting structures of brick and stone, mean that actual "living standards" in Japan may be quite a bit lower than per capita GNP figures would suggest. Space up to a certain point is a vital element in well being. Though it cannot be factored into our statistics, its scarcity justifies the Japanese in their argument that they are quite a bit poorer in "gross national living standards" than the GNP figures would indicate. In any case, in Japan's cities, with their vast industrial production, vibrant life, but deplorable overcrowding, one encounters as clearly as anywhere in the world the mixture of triumphs and mounting problems that characterize industrialized society today.

Facing page: The imperial palace grounds (below) in the heart of Tokyo consist of the core of the great castle area from which the Tokugawa family ruled Japan from 1600 to 1867. The western section, adjacent to the downtown banking district, is open to the public. The main palace was completed in 1968 to replace buildings destroyed in World War II. The great moats, stone walls, and exposed approach ways (above) reflect the state of gunnery at the time the castle was constructed around 1600. (*Sekai Bunka Photo* above, and *Embassy of Japan*)

Isolation

3

ONE FINAL, vital fact about the geographic setting of the Japanese is their relative isolation. Japan lies off the eastern end of the Old World, in much the same way the British Isles lie off its western end, but at considerably greater distance. The more than a hundred miles that separate the main Japanese islands from Korea is roughly five times the width of the Straits of Dover. In the time of primitive navigation it constituted a considerable barrier, and the roughly four hundred and fifty miles of open sea between Japan and China were even more formidable.

Throughout most of its history Japan has been perhaps the most isolated of all the major countries of the world. Until the dawn of oceanic commerce in the sixteenth century it was fitfully in contact with its two closest neighbors, Korea and China, but influences from further afield came to Japan only as filtered through these two lands. In more modern times, Japan's rulers took advantage of their natural geographic isolation to fix on the country a firm policy of seclusion from the outside world. For more than two centuries, from 1638 to 1853, the Japanese were almost completely sequestered from foreign contacts. It was a unique experience at a time of quickening international and interregional relations elsewhere in the world.

Thus natural geographic isolation at first, compounded later by human design, forced the Japanese to live more separately from the rest of the world than any other comparably large and advanced group of people. Or perhaps one should say that this combination of natural and artificial isolation enabled them more than most other peoples to develop on their own and in their own way. Certainly the Japanese throughout history have been culturally a very distinctive people, diverging sharply even from the patterns in nearby China and Korea, from which much of their higher civilization originally came. Even today, Japan occupies a unique spot in the world as the one major industrialized and fully modernized nation that has a non-Western cultural background.

Isolation has had a number of important by-products. It has made other people, even the nearby Koreans and Chinese, look on the Japanese as being somehow different and has produced in the Japanese a strong sense of self-identity. Such things are hard to measure, but the Japanese do seem to view the rest of the world, including even their close cultural and racial relatives in Korea and China, with an especially strong "we" and "they" dichotomy. Throughout history they have displayed almost a mania for distinguishing between "foreign" borrowings and elements regarded as natively "Japanese."

Isolation thus has ironically caused the Japanese to be acutely aware of anything that comes from outside and to draw special attention to its foreign provenance. The civilization of any country is much more the product of external influences than of native invention. If one subtracted everything from English culture that had foreign roots or antecedents, there would be little left. But borrowing from abroad has usually been a slow and unconscious process or at least went unrecorded. The Japanese, on the other hand, were always sharply conscious of the distinction between "foreign" and "native" and made the fact of cultural borrowing a major theme of their history. Thus they have given themselves and others the impression that they are somehow uniquely cultural borrowers. A myth has grown up that, unlike other peoples, the Japanese are mere mimics, incapable of invention themselves and unable to understand the inner essence of what they have borrowed. In actuality, their isolation has probably forced them to invent a greater part of their culture and develop a more distinctive set of characteristics than almost any comparable unit of people in the world. What distinguishes them is not their imitativeness but rather their distinctiveness and their skill at learning and adapting while not losing their own cultural identity. Others have tried to do the same but with less success.

Another by-product of isolation may be Japan's unusual degree of cultural homogeneity, which has already been remarked upon. Of course, isolation and homogeneity do not necessarily go together, as can be seen in the case of the British Isles. But prolonged separation from the outside world perhaps aided in the spread of uniform cultural patterns throughout the Japanese islands, despite their internal barriers of terrain.

THE THEME of homogeneousness will reappear frequently in our story, but let me illustrate it here by the racial composition of the Japanese people, which might be regarded as part of the natural setting for Japanese civilization. The Japanese, like all other peoples are the product of long and largely unrecorded mixtures. In fact, the diversity of facial types in Japan suggests considerable mixing in the past. But the important point is that, whatever their origins, the Japanese today are the most thoroughly unified and culturally homogeneous large bloc of people in the whole world, with the possible exception of the North Chinese. There are few important physical variations throughout the islands, and, while there are differences in folkways and accents, not unlike those among the English, French, Germans, and Italians, there are none of the sharp divisions as between Gaelic and English speakers and Protestants and Catholics in the British Isles, between speakers of French, Breton, German, and Basque in France, or the profound differences of all sorts between north and south Italians.

Actually the Japanese islands form a sort of cul-de-sac into which various peoples drifted over time and, finding no exit, were forced to mix with later comers. Among these were the Ainu, who may represent an early type of man dating from a period before the modern races became clearly differentiated. In any case, they combine some characteristics of the white race, notably their hairiness of face and body, with characteristics associated with other races. Thus the Ainu may account for the somewhat greater hairiness of some Japanese as compared to most other members of the Mogoloid race. At one time the Ainu, or people who at least were in part their ancestors, occupied either all or most of the Japanese islands, and until the eighth century they still controlled the northern third of the island of Honshu. But bit by bit they were conquered and absorbed by the main body of Japanese, until today fewer than 20,000 Ainu survive as a culturally identifiable group in the northern island of Hokkaido, and even these are on the brink of absorption.

Basically the Japanese are a Mongoloid people, much like their neighbors on the nearby Asian continent. Both archeology and historical records attest to a broad flow of peoples from northeastern Asia through the Korean Peninsula into Japan, especially during the first seven centuries of the Christian era. There may also have been an earlier flow of people or at least cultural traits from more southerly regions, which gave rise to certain "southern" characteristics that Japanese culture shares with the peoples of Southeast Asia and the South Pacific. An early diffusion of peoples and cultures may have occurred from South China southward but also eastward to Japan by way of Korea. These "southern" strains may account for some of the mythology of Japan, the flimsy, tropical nature of its early architecture, and the fact that Japanese in physical build are more like the South Chinese than their somewhat taller and sturdier neighbors in Korea and North China.

Scraps of the historical record suggest that there was some ethnic diversity in western Japan up until the eighth century, and at that time the whole north was still in the hands of the ancestors of the Ainu. But there has been no major infusion of new blood into Japan since that time. In fact, for over a thousand years immigration of any sort into Japan has been only infinitesimal. There has thus been a long time for racial mingling and the development of a high degree of cultural homogeneity. This process was no doubt aided by the artificial seclusion of Japan from the seventeenth to the nineteenth centuries and has been further fostered by strong centralized rule since then. But long before this the Japanese had developed a picture of themselves as a racially distinct and pure group, often portrayed in terms of a single great family. It is a concept more frequently encountered among primitive tribal peoples than among the citizens of a large modern nation.

Japan's imperial conquests in modern times and its present global trade have attracted some foreigners into the islands in recent decades. The only sizable group, however, is a Korean community of about 600,000 left over for the most part from the much larger numbers imported during World War II to replace Japanese workers gone off to war. There are also a few tens of thousands of Chinese, mostly merchants, from Japan's former colony in Taiwan or from the mainland, and a few thousand other outlanders from more distant parts of Asia and the West.

Altogether, these outsiders number much less than 1 percent of the population, and only the Koreans constitute any sort of a real ethnic problem. Since they are physically all but identical with the Japanese and are closely allied to them in language, they could be readily absorbed both culturally and racially, and Koreans born in Japan usually do lose the language of their parents in much the same way as people of non-English-speaking origin become linguistically absorbed in the United States. The Japanese, in their extreme ethnocentrism, however, tend to reject Koreans as full members of their society, while the Koreans, resentful of this attitude and of Japan's colonial domination of their homeland in the past, often cling to their ethnic identity. In fact, the Korean community injects a disruptive element into Japanese society and politics by its passionate adherence to one or the other of the two rival Korean regimes and the respective supporters of these regimes in Japanese politics. The Korean problem, however, is a tiny one compared to that of ethnic diversity in North America or even the problems caused by floods of recent immigrants and industrial workers into the countries of North Europe.

One extraordinary exception to Japanese homogeneity, however, deserves mention. This is the survival from feudal times of a sort of outcast group, known in the past by various names, including the term *eta*, but now usually called *burakumin*, or "hamlet people," a contraction from "people of special hamlets." This group, which may number about 2 percent of the population, probably originated from various sources, such as the vanquished in wars or those whose work was considered particularly demeaning. Clearly they included people engaged in leather work or butchery, since the Buddhist prejudice against the taking of all animal life made others look down on such persons, though, it should be noted, not on the butchers of human life in a feudal society dominated by a military elite.

The *burakumin* have enjoyed full legal equality for more than a century, but social prejudice against them is still extreme. While they are in no way distinguishable physically from the rest of the Japanese and are not culturally distinct except for their generally underprivileged status, most Japanese are loath to have contact with them and are careful to check family records to insure that they avoid intermarriage. In the highly urbanized Japan of today, the *burakumin* are becoming progressively less recognizable, but their survival as an identifiable group is a surprising contrast to the otherwise almost complete homogeneity of the Japanese people.

ONE FINAL point should be made about Japan's isolation. It is now entirely gone. Japan, in fact, is in a sense the least remote of all nations today. None is more clearly dependent on a massive worldwide flow of trade simply to exist. As a result, it has developed strong trade relations with almost all parts of the world. The seas that once cut it off now bind it effectively to all regions. The great distances that once lay between it and all other countries have now shrunk to insignificance. Military destruction can be projected across the oceans in a matter of minutes. Floods of words and visual images are transmitted instantaneously throughout the world. A person can be in both Tokyo and New York on the same calendar day. With the coming of giant tankers and container vessels, the costs of oceanic transportation have plummeted as compared to land transport. Mountain ranges, deserts, tropical jungles, and arctic tundra can still be serious barriers to commerce, and man-made barriers can be even greater, but oceans are now the cement that bind the world together economically. It is for these reasons that, in drawing my population and GNP maps, I largely eliminated the oceans and seas, leaving only enough of them to help demarcate the various countries and continental land masses, and I placed Japan, not on the periphery as it seemed to be in the past, but in the center, a spot to which it is as much entitled as any nation because of its massive involvement in worldwide trade.

The shift from almost complete isolation little more than a century ago to complete involvement today has, in historical terms, been sudden. The impact of outside economic and military power as well as of culture and ideas was once cushioned by what were then great intervening distances and also by firm man-made barriers. The psychological effects of isolation still linger on among the Japanese themselves and perhaps in the attitudes of other peoples toward them. Linguistically the Japanese remain quite separate, having a most unusual and difficult writing system and a very distinctive language. But the original geographic isolation and the self-imposed isolation of more recent times exist no more.

This has been a huge and upsetting change for the Japanese. Attitudes and skills once suitable to their position in the world do not serve them as well today. The adjustment to the new conditions has not been an easy one to make. There is a grave uncertainty in Japanese minds about their position in the world and even about their very identity. What does it mean to be Japanese today and what should Japan's role be in the contemporary world? These are questions the Japanese frequently ask themselves, and I shall return to them in the final section of this book.

HISTORICAL BACKGROUND

PART TWO

The thirteenth century Great Buddha (Dai-
butsu) at Kamakura, the military capital of
Japan from 1185 to 1333, is still one of the
largest and most beautiful bronze figures in
the world. The temple building that once
housed it was destroyed by a tidal wave. Students in some high schools still wear uniforms. (*Sekai Bunka Photo*)

Early
Japan

4 ⊥✓

JAPAN'S location and natural endowments helped determine the
path the Japanese took, but these physical features alone can
scarcely account for what they are today. Without some knowledge of
their past experience, the contemporary Japanese and their potentialities
cannot really be understood. And there is another reason for looking back
at Japanese history. Unlike Americans but like the other peoples of East
Asia, the Japanese have a strong consciousness of history. They see themselves in historical perspective. They will delve a thousand years and more
into their past in analyzing their contemporary traits. To understand
Japan and its problems as these appear to the Japanese themselves, one
must know something about their background. Thus, before concentrating on the present scene and attempting to peer from that vantage point
into the murky future, we would do well to take a quick look at the past.*

The islands of Japan were reached relatively late by the higher civilization of the Old World. Some of the oldest pottery in the world has been
found in Japan, but the islands were thousands of years behind Europe,
the Middle East, the Indian subcontinent, and China in the introduction
of agriculture and centuries behind in the use of bronze and iron. These
metals seem to have begun to enter the islands at the same time as agriculture in the third and second centuries B.C.

* For those who desire a more detailed consideration of Japanese history, I suggest my
book *Japan: The Story of a Nation* (New York, Knopf, 1974).

41

Our first clear view of the Japanese is afforded by Chinese records of the third century A.D. They are described as having sharp class divisions and living by agriculture and fishing. They were divided into a hundred or more tribal units under female or male chieftains of semi-religious status. What the records call the "queen's country" had a certain hegemony over the others. The presence of women rulers suggests an originally matriarchal system, which fits well with the mythological tradition of the descent of the historical imperial line from the sun goddess.

Starting around 200 A.D., Japan seems to have been overrun by waves of mounted invaders from the Korean Peninsula, or at least by cultural influences from Korea. During the next three centuries many large burial mounds were built throughout the western two thirds of the islands, suggesting considerable concentrations of wealth and power in the hands of a military aristocracy. By the sixth century a group centered in the small Yamato or Nara Plain, which lies across a range of hills a little to the east of Osaka, had established clear leadership over most if not all of western Japan. The political and economic organization of the country had become complex but was still relatively primitive. Most of the land remained under the control of semi-autonomous tribal units called *uji*, which were bound to the ruling family of the Yamato group by mythological ties and real or fictitious bonds of kinship. These *uji* had their own chiefs and their own *uji* shrines. Each also controlled a number of subordinate *uji* and pseudo-family groupings of farmers, fishermen, weavers, and other types of workers.

The religious practices of these early Japanese were later given the name of Shinto, "the way of the gods," to distinguish it from the imported religion of Buddhism. It centered around the worship of the gods, or *kami*, which were natural phenomena or mythological ancestors, the latter often nature gods as in the case of the sun goddess. The line between man and nature was not drawn sharply, and unusual or awesome men were easily made into deities. The leaders were both high priests and temporal rulers—in fact the same words were used for "religious worship" and "government" and for "shrine" and "palace." There were no ethical concepts associated with these religious ideas, except for a sense of awe and reverence before nature and a concept of ritual purity, which some believe may have contributed to the Japanese insistence on cleanliness and love of bathing.

The main gate and five-storied pagoda of the Horyuji monastery, founded by Prince Shotoku in the early seventh century. The existing buildings, which probably date from late in the century, are the oldest wooden buildings in the world. Their architectural style illustrates the classic simplicity and balance of the T'ang Dynasty of China. (*Sekai Bunka Photo*)

ALREADY by the sixth century there had been a heavy flow of cultural influences into Japan from the nearby continent. Agriculture as well as bronze and iron were examples of this. But in the middle of the sixth century the flow quickened, and the Japanese became conscious of it in a way they had not been before. It started with a fight at the Yamato court over the acceptance of Buddhist images and beliefs as a magical system of equal or possibly greater power than the native Shinto. The supporters of Buddhism won out, and a generation later Prince Shotoku, from 593 to 622 the regent for his reigning aunt, proved a great champion of the new religion and the continental civilization that accompanied it.

Shotoku himself wrote commentaries on Buddhist scriptures and erected Buddhist monasteries. One of them, the serenely beautiful Horyuji near Nara, is noted for having the oldest wooden buildings in the world and a wealth of beautiful Buddhist images dating from this period. Shotoku also dispatched embassies to the Chinese capital to learn directly from this source of high culture, and he began to copy Chinese political institutions and drafted a so-called "constitution," embodying Buddhist and Chinese precepts.

In the next generation a group of innovators, seizing power at the court in the so-called Taika Reform of 645, pushed forward the borrowing of Chinese technology and institutions with increased vigor. The effort continued at full flood for almost two centuries more, tapering off only in the ninth century. It transformed Japan from a backward, tribal area into a full participant in the higher civilization of the Old World, modeled, even if imperfectly, on China, which at that time was embarking on what was to prove to be almost a millennium of leadership as the economically and politically most advanced nation in the world.

Western history shows no parallel to the conscious Japanese effort at massive cultural borrowing, with the possible exception of the much later and far less difficult and less ambitious attempt of Peter the Great at the beginning of the eighteenth century. There were somewhat similar efforts, however, among other peoples in the penumbra of Chinese civilization, such as the Koreans and the tribal peoples of Manchuria. This difference with the West may have been more the result of the glory and appeal of Chinese civilization than some special characteristic of the Japanese or the other peripheral peoples. Rome at this time was by comparison a tragically decayed model. In any case, from the sixth to the ninth centuries the Japanese, who had in earlier times been decidedly behind the peoples of northern Europe, surged ahead of them in art, literature, technology, and political and social skills. They also developed a clear awareness of the distinction between borrowed and "native" elements in their culture, thus achieving an early realization of the value of learning from other countries but also laying the foundation for the myth that they were an uncreative race of borrowers.

The Chinese since antiquity had seen their civilization as centering around the political unit, and the Japanese and other peoples of East Asia accepted this concept of the primacy of a unified political system. This concept contrasted with the emphasis on religion as the unifying element in South and West Asia and the acceptance in the West, after the fading of Rome, of religious unity but political diversity. The East Asian emphasis on the political unit may help account for the fact that among the nations of the contemporary world those which first took shape as recognizably the same political units they are today are China in the third century B.C. and Korea and Japan in the seventh century A.D.

The Japanese also accepted the Chinese concept of an all powerful monarchy, attempting to transform their native, semi-sacred leader into a secular ruler of the Chinese type. Ever since, the Japanese emperor has in theory had the dual character and functions of a religious leader of the native Shinto cults and the secular monarch of a Chinese type state. In actuality, however, he rarely operated in the second capacity. The Japanese emperors had not in remembered times come to power as conquerors, and already by the seventh century they were largely symbols of authority, rather than wielders of personal power. As time went on, an occasional strong man on the throne might attempt to rule as well as reign, but for the most part emperors were manipulated by other members of the extensive imperial clan, by the broader court aristocracy, and in time by the feudal nobility of the provinces. Under these circumstances, the onerous ceremonial functions of the emperors overshadowed their satisfaction at exercising power, and it is therefore not surprising that early abdication had become almost the rule by the ninth century. The present status of the emperor as merely the "symbol of the State and the unity of the people" is no modern anomaly but has more than a millennium of history behind it.

Below the emperor, the Japanese borrowed the Chinese organs of a centralized state. The country was divided into provinces administered by officials dispatched from the capital. The Chinese law codes were taken over almost verbatim. At the capital, an elaborate bureaucratic form of government was created, though with innovations on the Chinese model to fit it better to Japanese conditions. For example, the traditional six ministries of Chinese government were increased to eight in order to accommodate an Imperial Household Ministry and a central secretariat, and a Council of Deities, representing the native religious side of the emperor's functions, was set up to balance the political Council of State.

An elaborate system of court ranks of the Chinese type was instituted to supercede the traditional ranking system of the court families and local *uji*, and innumerable bureaucratic posts were created. In the Chinese system, particularly as it developed after the late seventh century, the higher posts in government were filled in large part by bureaucrats who had displayed their qualifications through elaborate and highly scholastic, state-administered examinations. But this system had not developed fully at the time the Japanese started to borrow the Chinese model, and in any case it was probably too foreign to their highly aristocratic society to be really acceptable. Both rank and position in the Japanese bureaucracy quickly became determined by inherited family status rather than by individual merit.

One of the most amazing aspects of the Japanese borrowing from China was the adoption of the extremely complex landholding and tax system. According to this, all land in theory belonged to the central government and most of it was to be periodically assigned in equal proportions to all peasant families, so that each could bear a uniform tax burden, assigned largely by head and divided into the three categories of agricultural products, textile products, and labor. This cumbersome system worked only imperfectly in China and broke down periodically. In a still relatively backward Japan, it is surprising that it worked at all, but it clearly was applied to a large part of the land and operated after a fashion for several centuries, though reassignments of land probably never took place. One other feature of the system never was put into effect. This was the creation of a large draft army as part of the labor service due the government as taxes. In their island fastness, the Japanese had no need for large foot-soldier armies, and military service remained for the most part an aristocratic profession.

A centralized political system required a central capital city. Until this time the Japanese had not even had towns, but now they attempted to build capitals in the Chinese style, centered around extensive palace and government buildings. The first city to have much permanence was Heijo, or Nara, as it was later known. It was laid out in the Yamato Plain in the checkerboard pattern of the Chinese capital. Since it served as the seat of government from 710 to 784, the eighth century is commonly known as the Nara Period. A second permanent capital, Heian, was founded in 794 in a small plain north of Yamato, and the next few centuries are known as the Heian Period. Heian too had a Chinese checkerboard plan, which is still to be seen in the main streets of Kyoto, as this city later came to be called.

———————

WHILE political innovation lay at the heart of the borrowings from China, all of Japan's higher culture was affected. The scholarship, philosophy, and literature of China were much studied and deeply influenced styles of thought and even habits of life. There was a great surge forward in technology in such diverse fields as weaving, lacquer ware, and metallurgy. An orchestral court music and dance were learned from China and Korea and are still preserved in Japan as probably the world's oldest authentic music and dance traditions. The arts of Japan were completely transformed, and in architecture, sculpture, and painting Japanese created works of art in the Chinese style that were comparable to the best in China.

Most of the art centered around the new religion of Buddhism. Buddhism unlike Shinto was a highly sophisticated religion of universal appeal. It had started in India a millennium earlier and centered around the concepts that life, made perpetual by an endless cycle of reincarnations, was basically painful but could be escaped through careful self-cultivation and the achievement of enlightenment, leading to Nirvana, or the blissful merging of the individual identity with the cosmos. In its course through the centuries and spread throughout the eastern two thirds of Asia, Buddhism had acquired a huge literature, a rich art, a tremendous pantheon, and a wide variety of doctrines and beliefs. It was the magical aspects of some of these beliefs and the glory of Buddhist art, rather than the austere early doctrines, that first appealed to the Japanese court. The new religion was at first limited largely to court circles, and it was not until the eighth and ninth centuries that it began to spread widely throughout the country.

The Japanese were lucky to be able to learn from China, then the most advanced nation in the world, but it was most unfortunate for them that the Chinese had a writing system that was ill-adapted to Japanese needs. Any of the phonetic scripts, which by that time had spread over all regions west of China, could have been easily applied to the writing of Japanese. The Chinese writing system, however, consisted of unique symbols, or characters, for each of the thousands of Chinese words, and these could not easily be adapted to other languages, especially a highly inflected one like Japanese. As a consequence, the Japanese were forced to keep their records and conduct the written aspects of government in a foreign language. The great cultural advance in Japan during these centuries is all the more remarkable for having been achieved through the medium of an entirely different type of language and an extraordinarily difficult system of writing.

Despite these handicaps, the Japanese of this period did produce voluminous writings. The Chinese considered the compilation of an accurate historical record to be an important function of government, since past experience was seen as a valuable guide to the present. The Japanese dutifully recorded their own meager history, attempting to make it stretch back to a creditable age—in fact, all the way back to 660 B.C. From this effort emerged two early histories, the *Kojiki* of 712 and the *Nihon shoki* (or *Nihongi*) of 720, which recorded Japanese mythology in its relatively pristine, primitive form, as well as more sober recent history.

DESPITE the massive wave of influences that swept over the Japanese between the seventh and ninth centuries, they seem to have managed to retain a clear sense of their own identity. One is reminded of the survival of Japanese self-identity despite the waves of Western influence during the past century. In both cases, geographic location and language probably helped account for the outcome. Because of their island position, the Japanese were never subject to invasion from China, as the Koreans repeatedly were, and therefore they could maintain a sharper sense of separateness. There language also helped insulate them from absorption into the Chinese cultural unit. It is as radically different from Chinese as it is from English, and, even though the Japanese of the time were forced to write in Chinese, they spoke only Japanese. They also expressed their poetic emotions best through their own language. Although they did compose some poetry in Chinese, their greatest early poetic achievement was the *Manyoshu*, an anthology of some 4,516 native Japanese poems, collected shortly after 759 and laboriously written down syllable by syllable in Chinese characters used phonetically.

The Japanese not only survived the cultural flood from China but by the ninth century were beginning to blend it with their own culture to form a new synthesis. After several generations of acclimitization in the Japanese environment, borrowed Chinese institutions and culture had taken on a life of their own and, when further modified by native traits, produced an essentially new culture. Although it showed clearly the Chinese origin of many of its components, it was basically different both from what existed in China and from the earlier culture of Japan.

One of the clearest signs of the emergence of this new culture was the development in the course of the ninth century of an efficient system of writing Japanese. This was the *kana* syllabary, in which Chinese charac-

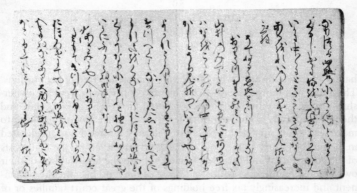

A page from the massive *Tale of Genji* (*Genji monogatari*), the world's first great novel, written around the year 1000 by Lady Murasaki. The development of *kana*, which are abbreviated Chinese characters used phonetically, made possible the composition of such great works in Japanese, but this thirteenth century manuscript has occasional Chinese characters mixed with the *kana*. (*Sekai Bunka Photo*)

ters were simplified and used phonetically to represent Japanese syllables. *Kana* permitted the Japanese to record with ease prodigious amounts of native poetry, almost exclusively in the form of brief 31 syllable *tanka*, or short poems. The best of these they collected in imperially commissioned anthologies. They also began to write extensively in prose. The ladies of the court often kept long diaries—the Japanese have ever since been the world's most enthusiastic diarists—and from these developed the world's first novels. The monumental *Tale of Genji* by Lady Murasaki, written around the year 1000, remains not only the world's first great novel but one of the literary masterpieces of all time. It portrays in brilliant detail and psychological subtlety a court life that could hardly have been more different from that of China—or for that matter from the roughness of life in Europe at that time. All that seemed to matter for these lady diarists and novelists was the sensitivity of esthetic feelings and the style in which the participants in this life conducted themselves, dressed, and wrote down their poems. The world of economic and political strife and its commonplace people did not seem to exist at all—and perhaps it really did not for these sheltered members of the high aristocracy.

Back of the refined and gentle court life portrayed in the literature of the tenth and eleventh centuries was a series of profound changes that had greatly altered the borrowed Chinese economic and political system. Much of the land had gradually gravitated from state control into the hands of private owners, who often were completely free of tax burdens. This trend had started already in the eighth century, when private ownership of new agricultural lands was permitted, first for a period of time and then in perpetuity, as an incentive for the large investments required to make wild lands suitable for paddy irrigation. The trend was accelerated in the ninth century by the hold of the court aristocrats on the high posts of the government and their willingness to bend the laws in favor of their own economic interests. More and more of the land became the permanent and increasingly tax-free holdings of the great court families or of influential Buddhist monasteries or Shinto shrines associated with the court. Sometimes small holders in the provinces would commend their lands to these families or institutions, in order to assure their fredom from the tax collector. By the twelfth century a great part of the agricultural land of the country had become divided up into tax-free private estates, usually made up of scattered agricultural fields, and even the remaining taxed lands were becoming a form of private property, since the right to appoint provincial governors and control the tax yield was becoming a hereditary privilege of certain families.

The resulting pattern of land ownership was a complex one. At the bottom was the actual cultivator, above him a local strong man who managed the estate for its absentee owner, above him a powerful court family or institution which had titular ownership, and above it possibly a still more powerful patron who could guarantee the estate's tax-free status. Each had a specific share in the income. As this system developed, the flow of goods in the country became less a product of the tax system and more a matter of the payment of agricultural dues from provincial estates to owners or patrons in the capital area.

These developments starved the central government of both revenues and functions. As a result, the elaborate Chinese structure of centralized government began to atrophy, and simpler organs of government developed to take its place. But that did not mean that the old system disappeared. All the ranks and bureaucratic positions continued in existence but tended to become symbols of prestige and factors in court ritual rather than the instruments of real power. It was this situation that permitted the great emphasis on outward show and style which *The Tale of Genji* portrays. Meanwhile the private administrations maintained by the great court families and religious institutions became more and more the real governors of the land.

Another change from the Chinese system was that during the ninth century one of the aristocratic court families established its dominance over the imperial family. This was the Fujiwara, descended from one of the leaders in the Taika Reform of 645. The basic reasons for Fujiwara dominance were their ownership of the greatest number of private estates and their growing monopoly of high government posts. Their technique of control was to have successive Fujiwara family heads named as regents for the emperors and to marry their daughters to the monarchs and put the resulting issue on the throne. Only retired emperors, freed of the ritual burdens of reigning, could challenge Fujiwara supremacy, as some who happened not to be the sons of Fujiwara mothers did with considerable success in the late eleventh and twelfth centuries.

The whole system that was evolving in Japan had indeed strayed far from the Chinese model. It was perhaps a system only possible in an isolated country like Japan. In China, a comparable decentralization of power would have invited conquest by nomadic neighbors or a usurpation of the throne by some vigorous new dynastic founder, better able than the old emperors to defend the country from invasion. In a Japan relatively free from outside pressures, there could be both a diffusion of control and a transfer of actual power at court without a change in the imperial line. Isolation permitted the Japanese to hold onto outmoded forms and institutions even when reality had passed them by. The result was a curious form of cultural conservation in Japan—in other words, the survival of institutions and cultural traits from one historical stage into periods with very different conditions.

The change in Japanese society during the ninth to twelfth centuries was not limited to economics, politics, and court life but affected all aspects of the culture. Japanese literature was creatively forging new paths quite distinct from Chinese prototypes. In the arts, the Japanese also displayed their own particular genius. For example, in painting, while still using the techniques learned from the Chinese, they developed what they themselves called *Yamato-e*, or Japanese painting, in which they experimented in a bold use of color and in a sense of design that still help differentiate Japanese artistic tastes from those of the Chinese. The Japanese thus demonstrated not only that they had maintained their cultural identity but that they were indeed an extraordinarily creative people.

Feudalism

5

BY THE twelfth century Japan was on the threshold of an even greater departure from East Asian norms. This was the development of a feudal system, which over the next seven centuries was to go through phases that had many striking parallels to the feudal experience of Western Europe between the ninth and fifteenth centuries. These similarities with Europe cannot be laid to mutual influences, since there was no contact between the two. The parallels are more likely to have been the result of similarities in the social and cultural ingredients that became mixed together in these two areas—namely, tribal societies and relatively advanced political and economic systems. In the West, tribal German groups fell heir to the wreckage of the administration and land system of the Roman Empire. In Japan, the tribal islanders had adopted the political institutions and land system of the Chinese Empire. In both cases, these two elements worked on each other over a long period of time in relative isolation, and out of the amalgam emerged a complex political system based on bonds of personal loyalty in a military aristocracy and the fusion of public authority and personal property rights to land.

As the authority and power of the central government declined in Japan, various groups of local leaders in the provinces banded together for mutual protection. These groups were made up of the officers of the old provincial administrations and the local managers or owners of estates. At first such groups consisted of relatives or neighbors, centered frequently around some charismatic figure who inspired loyalty. Because of the strong Japanese sense of hereditary authority, nothing was more prestigious than imperial descent. Thus, many of the groups came to be led by cadet branches of the imperial family which had received the family names of Taira or Minamoto and had moved out to the provinces to make their fortunes as the representatives of central authority.

Organized to protect their own interests, the local groups were in essence vigilante bands of warriors. Their members formed a petty local aristocracy, somewhat like the knights of early feudal Europe, for they too were mounted, armored warriors. Their chief weapons were the bow and arrow, skillfully used from horseback, and the curved steel sword, which came to be the finest blade in the world. Their armor was quite different from that of the West, being much lighter and more flexible and therefore probably more efficient. It consisted largely of small strips of steel, bound together by brightly colored thongs and fitted loosely over the body.

These warrior bands slowly grew in the province and in the twelfth century became involved in the affairs of the central government at Kyoto. Succession rivalries within the main Fujiwara family and the imperial line induced the two sides to call on the armed support of warrior bands associated with their provincial estates. These fought two brief wars between 1156 and 1160, from which a Taira leader emerged as clearly the dominant military power over the court. He settled down at the capital, took for himself high positions in the central government and, in the Fujiwara manner, married his daughter to the emperor and put the resulting grandson on the throne.

Meanwhile Yoritomo, the heir of the defeated Minamoto leader, raised the standard of revolt in the Kanto region in eastern Japan. By 1185 his forces had swept the Taira into oblivion, and he had become the undisputed military master of the land. Instead of establishing himself in Kyoto or taking high civil office there, he made his base at Kamakura in the Kanto, today a seaside suburb of Tokyo, and took only the title of shogun, meaning the generalissimo of the emperor's army. He rewarded his followers with the estates once managed or owned by the members of the defeated faction, creating for them the new managerial position of steward (*jito*) and grouping the stewards together for defense purposes by provinces under the leadership of a "protector" (*shugo*).

In theory Yoritomo left the old central government intact, with the court aristocrats still occupying the high civil posts and drawing income from the estates they owned, but within this somewhat hollow shell of the

Section from a thirteenth century scroll painting, illustrating the burning of the Sanjo Palace, an incident in the Heiji War of 1159–60, which brought the Taira family to power in Kyoto. The mounted knights, with their bows, quivers, curved swords, helmets, and loosely draped armor are typical of the medieval warriors of Japan. (*Museum of Fine Arts, Boston*)

old imperial system, he had established effective control over the whole land by spreading throughout its estates a thin layer of warrior families from the Kanto who were personally loyal to him. Simple organs of family government in Kamakura gave direction to the whole group and administered justice on the basis of local customary law, rather than the old Chinese-type law codes of the imperial court. Because so much of the old pre-feudal government and economy remained unchanged, the Kamakura system was only proto-feudal, but it was efficient and lasted almost a century and a half, surviving during this period two very serious challenges.

One challenge was the early disappearance of the main Minamoto family, the focus of personal loyalty on which the whole system theoretically depended. First Yoritomo's suspicions of his close relatives and then the machinations of his widow and her Hojo family, ironically of Taira descent itself, led to the extinction of the line by 1219. Thereafter Hojo shogunal "regents," utilizing figurehead shoguns of Fujiwara or imperial origin, demonstrated once again the Japanese tendency to allow supreme authority to become purely symbolic. They also demonstrated the persistent Japanese preference for group over individual leadership. Power was usually shared by paired officers or collegial groups.

The other great challenge to the Kamakura system was the one serious invasion Japan faced between unrecorded antiquity and World War II. The Mongols had overrun Korea, Central Asia, much of the Middle East, and the eastern part of Europe and then more slowly and with much greater difficulty the powerful Chinese Empire. They next attempted to invade Japan, sending against it in 1274 and again in 1281 the greatest overseas expeditions the world had as yet seen. These were turned back more by the weather than by the relatively small groups of Japanese knights who tried to beat them off. The fortuitous intervention in 1281 of a great typhoon—called the *kamikaze* or "divine wind"—strengthened the Japanese in their belief in the divine uniqueness of their land.

The Kamakura system, depending as it did on the personal loyalty of a single warrior band spread thinly throughout the nation, eventually succumbed to the ravages of time. Repeated divisions of patrimonies impoverished many of the descendants of the original stewards, and they became increasingly dependent on local strong men, often the descendants of the original provincial "protectors." Moreover, loyalty to the central symbol of authority in Kamakura wore thin over the generations and came to be replaced by loyalty to better known local leaders.

These trends resulted in a sudden breakdown of the whole system in the fourteenth century. The emperor Go-Daigo, who was an anomaly for his age, attempted in 1333 to take back political control, and the Kamakura general sent down to Kyoto to chastize him defected to his cause. The once unitary warrior clique immediately fell apart into a number of more localized bands of lords and vassals.

The turncoat Kamakura general, Ashikaga Takauji—Japanese family names precede personal names—soon broke with Go-Daigo, set up another member of the imperial family as emperor in Kyoto, and assumed the old Kamakura title of shogun. But there was no possibility of reestablishing the unity of the warrior class under a single lord. Instead Takauji and his descendants, who settled down in Kyoto and held on to the title of shogun until 1573, attempted to create a three-tiered feudal system. They asserted their supremacy over the various local warrior leaders and left it up to these supposedly vassal feudal lords to attempt to maintain control over the warriors of their respective regions as their own sub-vassals.

In practice, no such neat system ever emerged. Until 1392 Go-Daigo and his descendants maintained a rival imperial court in the mountains south of Kyoto, and the various local lord and vassal groups battled one another, ostensibly in behalf of the rival claimants to the throne but in reality over their own conflicting interests. After the reunification of the imperial court, the Ashikaga for several decades did exercise considerable authority in the central part of Japan around Kyoto, but leaders in more distant areas paid little or no attention to their claims of overlordship.

In 1467 a prolonged war broke out between the great lords active at the shogun's court in Kyoto, and the rest of Japan also disintegrated into chaotic fighting. In fact, warfare became endemic throughout Japan for the next century, and during this time an almost complete turnover in power took place. The authority of the Ashikaga shoguns faded entirely, and most of the great lords were destroyed by new military families. The lords of the early Ashikaga period, who were largely the descendants of provincial "protectors" of the Kamakura system, usually claimed authority over a wider area than they really controlled. During the prolonged fighting that started in 1467, these families were for the most part replaced by new leaders who had established complete control over the warriors of smaller but more tightly held domains. It was men of this type who became the daimyo, or feudal lords, of later Japanese feudalism. In absolute control of their own vassals and lands, they appeared to the Europeans who arrived in Japan in the sixteenth century to be petty kings.

During all the fighting that swept Japan from the fourteenth century on, the warrior holders of power in the provinces had ample opportunity to whittle away at the residue of tax payments and dues from estates that had formerly gone to the Kyoto government and its aristocratic families, and by the late fifteenth century these payments had disappeared entirely. As a result, the imperial court and its aristocracy, though maintaining as best they could the old court ranks, positions, and ceremonials, sank almost out of sight into relative poverty. The descendants of the once all-powerful Fujiwara subsisted mostly on dues paid them by Kyoto merchant guilds, and emperors were even known to discreetly sell samples of their calligraphy. With the virtual disappearance, except in vague theory, of the old imperial system, Japan had become a fully feudal land.

JAPAN'S feudal culture was in many basic ways more like that of feudal Europe than China. The warriors, who were known by the generic term of samurai, or "servitors," placed great emphasis on the military virtues of bravery, honor, self-discipline, and the stoical acceptance of death. Lacking any religious injunctions against suicide, they commonly took their own lives in defeat, rather than accept humiliation and possible torture in captivity. Suicide by the gruesome and extremely painful means of cutting open one's own abdomen became a sort of ritual used to demonstrate will power and maintain honor. Vulgarly called *harakiri*, or "belly slitting," but more properly known as *seppuku*, this form of honorable suicide has survived on occasion into modern times, and suicide by other less difficult means is still considered an acceptable and basically honorable way to escape an intolerable situation.

The prime virtue in the Japanese feudal system, as in that of Europe, was loyalty, because the whole system depended on bonds of personal loyalty. Of course, loyalty was in actuality the weakest link in both systems, and the medieval histories of both Japan and Europe are full of cases of turncoats and traitorous betrayals. In Europe, with its background of Roman law, the lord-vassal relationship was seen as mutual and contractual—in other words, as legalistic. In Japan, the Chinese system had placed less emphasis on law and more on morality—that is, on the subordination of law to the moral sense of the ruler, since his right to rule was theoretically based on his superior wisdom and morality. Hence, the lord-vassal relationship was seen as one of unlimited and absolute loyalty on the part of the vassal, not merely one of legal contract between the two. There was thus no room for the development of the concept of political rights, as happened in the West.

Loyalty to the ruler was important in the Chinese Confucian system, but it was usually overshadowed by loyalty to the family. In fact, three of the five basic Confucian ethical relationships had to do with filial piety and other family loyalties. In Japan, loyalty to the lord was more central to the whole system and, despite the importance of the family, took precedence over loyalty to it. Thus in Japan, the supra-family group early became established as more fundamental than the family itself, and this made easier the transition in modern times to loyalty to the nation and to other nonkinship groupings.

Still, family lineage and honor were of great importance in medieval Japanese society, because inheritance determined power and prestige as well as the ownership of property. Family continuity was naturally a matter of vital concern. The Japanese avoided many of the problems of

Western hereditary systems by permitting a man to select among his sons the one most suitable to inherit his position and also by using adoption when there was no male heir by birth. The husband of a daughter, a young relative, or even some entirely unrelated person could be adopted as a completely acceptable heir. While inheritance is no longer a keystone of Japanese society, these types of adoption are still common.

Japanese feudal society differed from that of Europe in two other revealing ways. In Japan there was no cult of chivalry which put women on a romantic pedestal, though as fragile, inferior beings. The Japanese warriors expected their women to be as tough as they were and accept self-destruction out of loyalty to lord or family. Also Japanese warriors, though men of the sword like their Western counterparts, had none of the contempt that the Western feudal aristocracy often showed for learning and the gentler arts. They prided themselves on their fine calligraphy or

Illustration from a fifteenth century scroll showing a warrior, with his bow and sword placed behind him, and a scholar engaged in the refined literary sport of composing alternate lines of a poem. Medieval Japanese warriors, unlike their feudal counterparts in Europe, prided themselves on their mastery of the literary arts. (*Sekai Bunka Photo*)

poetic skills. Perhaps the long coexistence of the culture of the imperial court with the rising warrior society of the provinces had permitted a fuller transfer of the arts and attitudes of the one to the other.

The political and social organization of medieval Japan is extremely remote from contemporary Japanese society, but many of the attitudes developed at this time, as preserved and reshaped in the later phases of Japanese feudalism, have continued into modern times. Thus the warrior spirit and its sense of values were easily revived by the modern Japanese army, and a strong spirit of loyalty, duty, self-discipline, and self-denial still linger on from feudal days as shapers of the contemporary Japanese personality.

THE LONG, slow decline of the Kyoto court has given rise to a picture of feudal times as the dark ages, but this is even less true of Japan than of Europe. Literature, art, and learning showed remarkable continuity, and the high culture that once was largely limited to the capital region spread widely throughout the nation. Naturally new themes and new styles also appeared in both literature and art. Stirring war tales recounted the military exploits of the twelfth century. These as well as the histories of Buddhist monasteries and the lives of Buddhist saints were graphically portrayed in marvelous scroll paintings. The thirteenth century witnessed a brilliant Renaissance of sculpture. The Great Buddha at Kamakura remains as a symbol of this age and is one of the largest bronze figures in the world. In the late fourteenth and fifteenth centuries a sophisticated dramatic form was developed at the court of the Ashikaga shoguns in Kyoto. This was Noh, in which a handful of masked and costumed actors presented, through sonorous chanting, measured movements, and stately dance, historical stories and early myths, usually centering around Buddhist concepts of the vanity of life or Shinto ideas of the permeation of nature and man by the spirit world of the gods. The use in Noh of a chorus accompanied by musical instruments to fill out the story is reminiscent of ancient Greek drama.

Under the rule of the provincial warriors, the peasants had sunk from taxpayers to the status of serfs but had probably gained in security in the process. In any case, the common man at this time began to make his appearance in both art and literature, and he seems to have found a new way of self-expression through the spread and spiritual resurgence of Buddhism. The court aristocrats had been most interested in a form of Buddhism that emphasized magic formulae and rituals, but during the eleventh and twelfth centuries a new emphasis developed, especially among more plebian Japanese. This was belief in salvation and entrance into paradise through simple faith—that is, through reliance on the grace of one of the many Buddhist deities. Such concepts were an almost complete reversal of the original Buddhist doctrine of the merging of the personal ego into the cosmos through austere self-cultivation leading to enlightenment. Popular preachers spread the idea that, in this supposedly corrupt "latter age" of Buddhism, people no longer had the strength to achieve enlightenment through their own abilities but must rely through faith on "the strength of another."

These concepts gave rise in the twelfth and thirteenth centuries to new sectarian movements that were in time to become the largest Buddhist sects of Japan. One of these, which emphasized the Pure Land, or Western Paradise, of the Buddha Amida, championed the congregational, instead of monastic, organization of the church and the marriage of the clergy, a custom that in time spread to most sects. Another sect, which emphasized the Lotus Sutra as the central object of faith, is popularly known by the name of its founder, Nichiren. His thinking also took a peculiarly nationalistic bent, emphasizing that Buddhism had declined in India and China in turn and that Japan was now the central land of the religion. These sects in the fifteenth and sixteenth centuries developed religious congregations which in some places contended with the feudal warriors for local political power.

Many of the warriors preferred a different sort of Buddhism. This was Zen, which was introduced from China in sectarian form in the early Kamakura period. Zen emphasized concepts of meditation, simplicity, and closeness to nature. The austere life of its monasteries appealed to the Spartan warriors, and they saw in the rigorous self-discipline of the practice of Zen meditation a way to develop the self-control and firmness of character their way of life demanded. Under the patronage of the feudal leaders, Zen monasteries around Kamakura and Kyoto became the great intellectual centers of medieval Japan. Zen monks were used by the Ashikaga shoguns as advisers, particularly in their contacts with China. Through these men there was a great resurgence of interest in Chinese scholarship and literature and a revival of skill in the writing of the Chinese language. Zen monks also imported the then relatively new Sung

The garden of the Sambo-in Temple in Kyoto. Landscape architecture, originally introduced from China, was among the artistic skills cultivated by Zen monks. This garden, dating from the late sixteenth century, represents a later, more grandiose approach to garden architecture than the smaller, more constrained efforts of medieval Japanese to catch in miniature the essence of the grandeurs of nature. (*Consulate General of Japan*, N.Y.)

style of monochrome landscape painting, which Japanese artists mastered as they had the earlier Chinese styles. Other Zen imports were tea drinking and landscape gardening.

Around late medieval Zen there grew up a whole esthetic system that became a lasting element in Japanese culture. The small, the simple, the natural, even the misshapen were valued over the large, the grandiose, the artificial, or the uniform. In architecture, natural wood textures and twisted trunks were esteemed more than precisely shaped and painted pieces of wood, and simple, irregular structures, fitted to the lay of the land, were preferred to the stately, balanced majesty of Chinese buildings. Small gardens were designed to represent in microcosm the wild grandeur of nature, contrasting sharply with the Western love of great geometric patterns. The epitome of the Japanese taste can be seen in the famous rock garden of the Ryoanji in Kyoto, dating from the fifteenth century, which in a tiny space evokes through sand and a few scattered rocks a majestic seascape. In painting, a few bold, expert strokes in black India ink caught more of the essence of nature than could be portrayed in realistic paintings replete with color and detail. The tea ceremony was developed as an esthetic cult, gracefully performed in simple surroundings and with simple utensils. This medieval Zen esthetic was well suited to the austere life of feudal Japan, but, curiously enough, it also has great appeal in the modern age, surfeited as it is with abundance, machined regularity, and unlimited technical skills.

The close contacts of the Zen monks with China were made possible by a great increase in trade with the continent, which in turn was the product of considerable development of Japanese technology and growth in its economy. The increasing export of manufactured goods, such as folding fans, screens, and the highly prized swords of Japan, shows that the islands were beginning to draw abreast of China in technology. The devel-

A sixteenth century ceramic bowl for use in the tea ceremony. In its simplicity, roughness, and purposeful imperfections, it demonstrates medieval Japanese tastes, which seem sophisticated and modern to contemporary Westerners. The tea ceremony itself illustrates a love of grace and serenity, which modern man finds harder to emulate. (*Sekai Bunka Photo*)

opment of guilds of merchants and artisans within the country was a sign of commercial growth. As in feudal Europe, such guilds were needed to give artisans and merchants some protection against the tax barriers and many other restrictions on trade in a divided, feudal land.

Since the ninth century, there had been relatively little contact with the continent, but overseas trade began to pick up in the thirteenth century. For a while in the fifteenth century, the Ashikaga shoguns attempted to monopolize it by allowing it to be fitted into the Chinese pattern of tributary relations, including even the "investiture" of the shoguns as the "kings" of Japan by the Chinese emperor—to the lasting shame of Japanese nationalists. A more significant feature of overseas commerce was the fact that Japanese traders commonly turned into pirates when frustrated in their commercial objectives, taking by the sword what they were not able to gain by trade. Japanese pirates started along the nearby shores of Korea, then became a serious scourge to the coasts of China, and by the sixteenth century were roaming the seas of all Southeast Asia.

Centralized
Feudalism

6

IN THE course of the sixteenth century, the more efficient of the new type of tightly organized feudal domains grew through the subjugation and incorporation of less successful ones, until by the end of the century Japan had again become politically unified. It had in fact achieved a type of centralized feudal system that seems almost the antithesis of the decentralized feudalism that had existed in Europe. The basic pattern was the one attempted but never attained by the Ashikaga. A supreme overlord kept close rule over a large number of vassal lords, who in turn controlled their respective vassals and samurai retainers.

The appearance of the Europeans at this time may have contributed to the process of reunification, because they brought with them new military technology. After rounding Africa and reaching India in 1498, the Portuguese pushed on rapidly eastward, and in 1542 or 1543 some reached an island off the southern tip of Kyushu. The Portuguese were seeking trade, but they were accompanied by Jesuit priests, who embarked on missionary activities, winning close to a half million converts by the early seventeenth century. This was a much larger percentage of the Japanese population of the time than are Christian today.

The Japanese, however, showed an even greater interest in the guns the Portuguese brought with them. Firearms spread rapidly throughout Japan, contributing to the success of the more efficient feudal realms. Castle building also increased, possibly under European influence. The white-walled wooden structures of the castles of this period were largely decorative, but they were surrounded by broad moats and huge earth-

CENTRALIZED FEUDALISM

backed stone walls that were quite impervious to the cannon fire of the time. These Japanese castles were more like sixteenth century European fortifications than like medieval castles. Many built around the turn of the sixteenth century still stand, including beautiful Himeji, a short distance west of Kobe, and the imperial palace grounds of downtown Tokyo constitute a good example of the central core of one of these great fortresses.

The political reunification of Japan was largely the work of three successive military leaders. The first, Oda Nobunaga, seized Kyoto in 1568, ostensibly in support of the last Ashikaga shogun, and then subjugated the lesser lords of central Japan and destroyed the power of the great Buddhist monasteries. After Nobunaga was assassinated in 1582, his mantle fell to the ablest of his generals. This was Hideyoshi, who once had been a common foot-soldier and was of such humble origin that he originally lacked a family name. By 1590 Hideyoshi had established his authority over the whole country, destroying all his rival lords or forcing them to become his vassals.

Hideyoshi never took the title of shogun, but he did assume high posts in the old imperial government and by his patronage brought it back into modest affluence. He monopolized foreign trade, which by this time had become very lucrative. He had the whole land surveyed and assigned fiefs on the basis of a clear knowledge of the areas and agricultural yields involved. He confiscated the arms of the peasantry, drawing a sharp line between them and the samurai, who were increasingly becoming a salaried, professional military, living not on the land but at the castle towns of their respective lords.

Hideyoshi also embarked in 1592 on the conquest of Korea, ostensibly as the first step in an effort to conquer the world, which to him meant largely China. The Japanese were stopped by Chinese armies in northern Korea and, after a long stalemate, withdrew upon Hideyoshi's death in 1598. This Japanese invasion has been emphasized in the historic memories of the Koreans and still contributes to the bitterness between them and the Japanese.

Since Hideyoshi did not leave an adult heir, a scramble for power followed his death. The victor at a great battle in 1600 was his foremost vassal, Tokugawa Ieyasu, who had been enfieffed by Hideyoshi at Edo, the present Tokyo. Ieyasu, instead of moving to Kyoto, retained his base of power in eastern Japan and devoted his energies to consolidating the supremacy of his family on the basis of the pattern already established by

CENTRALIZED FEUDALISM

Hideyoshi. He was successful in this, and his heirs remained the rulers of Japan until the middle of the nineteenth century.

Ieyasu assumed the old title of shogun and divided up the country between his own domain and those of his vassals. He saved for himself a fourth of the agricultural land and all the great cities, ports, and mines. The two hundred and forty-five to two hundred and ninety-five vassal lords, or daimyo—the number varied over time—had domains ranging in size from tiny areas that produced only 10,000 *koku* of rice (a *koku* being about five bushels of rice and the equivalent of what a person would eat in a year) to the largest, which in theory produced 1,022,700 *koku*. The domains were divided into three categories. Some went to Ieyasu's sons or relatives—the collateral daimyo. A large number of relatively small domains were assigned to men who had been Ieyasu's vassals already before 1600, and these were known as *fudai* or hereditary daimyo. His major allies and some of his enemies in the battle of 1600, who were called *tozama* or "outer" daimyo, were allowed to retain relatively large domains on the western and northern periphery of the nation. The shogun in addition maintained a large body of direct samurai retainers, as did each of the daimyo.

The central Tokugawa administration at Edo developed into a large bureaucracy, staffed by the hereditary daimyo and the shoguns' direct retainers. It showed the old propensity toward shared authority and group decisions. At the top were two councils, the "elders" and "junior elders," under which paired officers or groups of four officials administered the various branches of the shogun's government and supervised the whole country. The shoguns themselves in time became largely figureheads, thus serving basically as symbolic authority figures, like the emperors, in whose behalf the military government of Edo theoretically ruled.

The domains followed the same general pattern and trends of development, with daimyo often becoming no more than figureheads and sa-

Facing page: Himeji Castle, forty-five miles west of Osaka, is one of the best preserved castles of the late sixteenth and early seventeenth centuries. These castles were the headquarters of the daimyo, or feudal lords, and around them developed castle towns. Broad moats and earth-backed stone walls were their defenses against the cannon of the time, while the white-walled wooden buildings that crowned the walls were designed more for show. (*Consulate General of Japan*, N.Y.)

murai bureaucrats governing through councils and group decisions. The domains were in theory entirely autonomous and paid no taxes to the central government, but they were in actuality held on a tight string. They were assigned costly duties of castle or palace construction or coastal defense, and a system soon developed whereby all the daimyo spent alternate years in attendance on the shogun at Edo and left their families there as permanent hostages. The daimyo were also held strictly accountable for the peace and efficient administration of their domains and, particularly in the early years, might be expropriated for misdeeds or demoted to lesser domains.

In order to assure the stability of their regime, Ieyasu and his successors were eager to eliminate all sources of possible challenge. They viewed the activities of European Catholic missionaries and their converts as particularly dangerous, since they involved a foreign source of authority and object of loyalty. First Hideyoshi and then the Tokugawa persecuted the religion, until it was virtually stamped out by 1638. Foreign trade also fell victim to the anti-Christian mania. Overseas Japanese were prohibited in 1636 from returning to Japan for fear that they might reintroduce the virus of Christianity, and Japanese ships were limited to coastal vessels unsuitable for ocean voyages. Relations with the outside world were limited to a few contacts with Korea and through Okinawa with China and to a small Dutch trading post and a group of Chinese merchants, both confined to a strictly supervised trade in the Kyushu port of Nagasaki. Thus Japan embarked on its more than two centuries of self-imposed seclusion.

Since the two centuries that followed witnessed the rise of modern science in Europe, the commercial revolution in world trade, and the start of the industrial revolution in the West, a Japan that had been abreast of most developments in the world in the early seventeenth century had fallen technologically far behind by the nineteenth. But isolation did contribute to stability within Japan. For more than two centuries the country enjoyed absolute peace. The political history of the time is marked only by periodic reform efforts and occasional riots by oppressed peasants. The most exciting political event was the incident in 1703 of "the forty-seven *ronin*," or masterless samurai, in which the former retainers of an expropriated petty daimyo revenged themselves on the Edo official who they felt had caused their lord's downfall and then paid the price for this act by commiting suicide through *seppuku*. Despite its old-fashioned feudal pattern, Japan in the seventeenth and eighteenth centuries was

A sixteenth century folding screen, depicting Portuguese in the streets of Japan. Reaching Japan in 1542 or 1543, the Portuguese were the first Europeans the Japanese had ever seen, and the Japanese were fascinated by their strange costumes and curious physiognomy. In 1549 St. Francis Xavier inaugurated a missionary movement which proved very successful, converting a higher percentage of the Japanese population than is Christian today. Subsequently the Japanese, fearful that Christianity would prove politically subversive, drove out the missionaries and eventually all Europeans, except the Dutch. By 1638 Christianity had been virtually stamped out in Japan. (*Sekai Bunka Photo*)

certainly more orderly and in many ways more uniformly and efficiently ruled than any country in Europe at that time.

Peace and stability also permitted the Japanese to work over and perfect their own rich cultural heritage. During this period they became culturally more homogeneous and developed an extremely strong sense of national identity. At the same time, the continuation of a basically feudal system into the nineteenth century permitted the somewhat anachronistic survival into modern times of medieval feudal attitudes, such as respect for military leadership, unquestioning loyalty, and the emphasis on group organization. In fact, group identification was strengthened by the tight organization and long continuity of the various feudal domains.

THE POLITICAL pattern established in the early decades of the seventeenth century remained basically unaltered until the middle decades of the nineteenth. Although it was well suited to conditions as they had existed at the end of the sixteenth century, it became increasingly ill adapted to conditions as they developed in Japan after that. However, within this rigid political structure, great economic, social, and cultural changes did take place.

The most fundamental change was a huge growth of the economy. Peace and stability permitted a great initial leap in production during the seventeenth century. Another spur to economic development was the system of alternate residence of the lords in Edo, which forced each domain to maintain at least one large establishment at the Tokugawa capital and to spend a great part of its revenues to pay for this establishment and the travel of the lord and his retinue to and from it. This situation required the domains to produce excess rice or specialized local crops for sale to the cities and the nation at large, in order to acquire the liquid assets they needed for travel and in Edo. The result was considerable regional specialization in production and the development of a national, monetized economy of a more advanced type than existed in any other Asian land.

These conditions also led to the appearance of large cities. Edo, where half the feudal lords and a large percentage of the whole warrior class were congregated at any one time, grew to be a city of around a million, while Osaka, as the great commercial center for West Japan, and Kyoto, the imperial capital with its fine industries, each came to have populations numbering in the hundreds of thousands.

Economic growth in preindustrial societies has usually been accompanied by a corresponding growth in population. This did occur during the economic surge of the seventeenth century, when the Japanese population rose to the twenty-five or thirty million level, but subsequently population remained relatively steady, despite a slow continuing rise in technology and production. The result was that living standards for most Japanese rose above mere subsistence levels. The Japanese, like the early modern Europeans, in a sense had got a step ahead of Malthus. The reasons for this are not clear, but one factor may have been the combination of feudal patterns of inheritance, in which a man had only one heir, and Japanese practices of adoption, which made it unnecessary for this heir to be his natural child. As a result, a man did not need a large number of children for financial security and family continuity and, in fact, usually found a big family more of a liability than an asset. In any case, Tokugawa peasants are known to have practiced infanticide to keep down the number of mouths to be fed, and the population did remain quite static for a century and a half despite the growth of the economy. This rise beyond subsistence levels may help account for the relatively high levels of literacy and of economic, social, and political integration of the Japanese in the nineteenth century and the vigor and dynamism they were able to display at that time.

The natural agrarian bias of a feudal society produced a curious irony during the Tokugawa period. The political leadership esteemed agriculture and therefore taxed it heavily, while it despised trade and therefore taxed it only indirectly and lightly. This situation, together with the nationwide integration of the economy, permitted the growth of a prosperous urban merchant class, particularly in the large cities under the direct rule and protection of the shogun's government. During the seventeenth century, great merchant houses developed out of such economic activities as sake-brewing, the retailing of dry goods, and money lending. An example is the house of Mitsui, which was to become in modern times one of the greatest private business enterprises in the world.

The various domains as well as their samurai retainers, tied as they were to fixed incomes in rice from agricultural taxes, fell increasingly in debt to urban merchants. This situation was corrosive to the whole Tokugawa system, because in theory society was divided into four classes—the warrior rulers, the peasants who were the primary producers of wealth, the artisans who were the secondary producers, and at the bottom the merchants, who were deemed to perform a role in society that was more parasitic than productive. This concept of a four-way division of society was a borrowing from early Chinese thought, but it was quite natural to a feudal system. The shogun's government and the individual domains periodically attempted to reverse the growing indebtedness of the ruling class by cutting down on expenses, including salaries to their retainers, and placing sumptuary laws and other restrictions on the merchants. In desperation, they also created commercial monopolies but all to no avail. The indebtedness of the ruling class to the theoretically lowest class continued to grow.

The sharp line that had been drawn in Hideyoshi's time between peasants and warriors led to a freeing of rural Japan from close supervision by the feudal rulers. In effect, Hideyoshi had forced the warriors of rural Japan to decide whether they would follow their lords to their castle towns as salaried samurai or stay with their lands and become classified as peasants. Many who had the most land to lose took the second option, becoming village headmen and the leaders of rural society. The villages thus had a strong local leadership that had many of the attitudes and ethical values of the samurai class, and they were allowed a considerable degree of autonomy in running their own affairs and assigning and collecting taxes.

As the national economy developed during the Tokugawa period, villagers in the more advanced central parts of Japan increasingly shifted from subsistence farming to the growing of cash commercial crops, and the richer peasants often found it more advantageous to let out much of their land to tenant farmers and concentrate their own energies on the processing of foodstuffs, silk, and other agricultural products. In the late eighteenth century there was a veritable outburst of entrepreneurial activity of this sort in rural Japan, and poorer peasants increasingly became accustomed to supplementing their incomes by working for wages in the enterprises of their richer neighbors or in nearby towns. Thus rural as well as urban Japan was developing far beyond the normal limits of a feudal society.

During the long Tokugawa peace the warrior class too underwent great changes. It constituted about 6 percent of the total population, including as it did the common soldiery and the clerks and underlings of the feudal establishments. Although it was basically a fighting force at the outset of the Tokugawa period, it became in time more a hereditary civil bureaucracy than a standing army. The samurai wore their traditional two swords as their badges of rank, and they still attempted to maintain their martial prowess, but in actuality they had become men of the writing brush rather than the sword.

Virtually the whole of the samurai class became literate, and for that matter most merchants and the richer peasants also developed this skill. Chinese scholarship once again had a great appeal to a Japan at peace, and during the seventeenth century the Japanese for the first time delved deeply into Confucian doctrines as these had become standardized in twelfth century China. Confucian scholars flourished in Edo and in the domains of the great daimyo, and there was a great surge forward again in skills in the Chinese language. For the first time also there was a wide use of printing, which actually had been known to the Japanese ever since the eighth century.

The rapid growth of intellectual and scholarly activities in the seventeenth century was greatly furthered by the nationwide intellectual cross-fertilization made possible by the system of alternate residence of the lords and their retainers in Edo. Leaders from all over Japan came into constant contact with one another, and a large flow of students and teachers between Edo and the various domains developed. Just as Japan had become a single economic unit, it also became a single intellectual unit in a way no other Asian nation was.

Chinese Confucian philosophy and the historical scholarship it inspired, however, injected some intellectual elements that were subversive to the feudal system. The Chinese ideal was rule by men of superior education and morality, rather than by men merely of superior birth. In the Tokugawa system status was fundamentally determined by birth, and individual merit played only a subsidiary role. The two systems were obviously in sharp conflict with each other, and by the nineteenth century there were increasing demands by ambitious but low ranking samurai that greater responsibilities should be given to men of merit.

Confucian philosophy and historical studies also called attention to the fact that China was ruled by emperors, not by feudal lords, and that Japan too had once had this system. As a result, increasing attention was focused on the emperor, and doubts were raised regarding the shogun's relationship to him. Among the common people, too, a movement arose, called "national learning," which started in the eighteenth century with the study of early Japanese poetry, *The Tale of Genji*, and the *Kojiki*, the eighth century work of history, and increasingly came to emphasize the concept that the true glory of Japan was its divine origin and unbroken imperial line of divine descent. Such ideas were of course potentially subversive to Tokugawa rule.

Isolation is usually associated with cultural stagnation, but the long peace, stability, and economic growth of the Tokugawa period led instead to a veritable cultural explosion. There was a great diversity of Confucian and other philosophical schools of all sorts, and men in touch with the Dutch traders at Nagasaki in the eighteenth century developed an interest in Western science, particularly medicine, metallurgy, and gunnery. Since this knowledge was laboriously mined from books and encyclopedias in the Dutch language, it was called "Dutch learning." Thus the isolated Japanese remained intellectually very much alive.

THE EARLY Tokugawa period witnessed an architectural outburst of lavishly decorated buildings, best seen today in the mausoleums of the early Tokugawa shoguns at Nikko. Many schools of painting, derived from Chinese styles or from native concepts of design, flourished at the courts of the shogun and daimyo, and a school of painting that experimented with the use of Western oil paints and perspective emerged from the "Dutch learning" in the late eighteenth century. Porcelain making also became for the first time a great art in Japan, and artistic skills were lavished on lacquer ware, weaving, and brocades.

Perhaps the most interesting cultural development in the Tokugawa period, however, was the rise of an urban merchant culture quite distinct from that of the ruling samurai class. It centered around the amusement quarters of the cities, where the merchants, who were essentially hardworking, sober, moneymakers and family men, went to relax in the company of professional female entertainers, called geishas in modern times. Here they were free from family and business responsibilities and the oppressive regulations of the feudal rulers. In this demi-monde milieu grew

Facing page: Gateway of the mausoleum and shrine, erected at Nikko, 75 miles north of Edo (Tokyo), for the first Tokugawa shogun, Ieyasu, who died in 1616. Baroque in style, the structures are ornate and elaborately decorated with carvings, including the famous three monkeys who "see, hear, and speak no evil." The setting of towering cryptomeria trees (related to the redwoods) is majestic. (*Embassy of Japan*)

A scene from Kabuki, a dramatic form developed during the seventeenth century in urban merchant society. Kabuki utilizes elaborate scenery, and it early developed the revolving stage, rising and sinking platforms, and a runway through the middle of the audience. The men seated on a raised area at the right are musicians and a chorus, which helps recount the story. (*Consulate General of Japan*, N.Y.)

up a rich art, theater, and literature quite distinct from the arts cultivated by the samurai. This new merchant culture matured in Osaka and Kyoto in the late seventeenth century and subsequently came to center chiefly in Edo.

The art of this merchant culture was known as *ukiyo-e*, or "pictures of the fleeting world." The fleeting world was a Buddhist concept in origin, but it had come to connote "up-to-date." The *ukiyo-e* style was reminiscent of the emphasis on color and design in the *Yamato-e* painting of some seven centuries earlier, but the subject matter was quite different—largely stylish courtesans, popular actors, and familiar scenes of urban life. From it developed multicolored woodblock prints, also called *ukiyo-e*, which met the greatly increased demand of a prosperous urban society for works of art. These, too, featured beautiful courtesans and actors but in time also added famous scenes of nature, such as Mount Fuji, and spots of interest in the cities and along the highways of Japan. In a sense, these woodblock prints were the world's first true mass art and the forerunners of the picture postcard.

The theater of this merchant culture was at first limited largely to puppets, but in time kabuki dramas with human actors won out in popularity. Kabuki, while very stylized in its own way, was much more lively and realistic than the medieval noh and developed elaborate and extremely realistic stage settings and even the revolving stage for quick shifts of scene.

The literary activities of the samurai were largely scholarly and philosophical, but poetry was popular with them as well as with other groups, especially the witty, epigrammatic seventeen-syllable haiku. Most other new literary trends came entirely out of merchant society. Guidebooks to the amusement quarters developed into amusing descriptions of urban social types and these into spicy novels.

Thus Japan, though isolated from most foreign stimuli, was large and diverse enough to have a very lively society with a richly creative culture. The Japanese did not stagnate. Packed together in great numbers in big cities and a crowded countryside and bound down by a complex, oppressive feudal system of government, they developed great skills in social and political organization and group cooperation. While the general political pattern remained rigidly unchanging, beneath the surface there were great dynamic tensions between Confucian and feudal values and between economic growth and a frozen class society. Japan, far from becoming an immobile society in its isolation, remained capable of great change, as it was to demonstrate brilliantly in the second half of the nineteenth century.

The Meiji
Restoration

7

D ESPITE the many problems and tensions within the Tokugawa
system, it still showed no signs of collapse in the first half of the
nineteenth century, and it might have continued for much longer
if Japan could have maintained its isolation. But rapid technological advances in the West made this no longer possible. Industrialization and
steam power applied to ships were beginning to bring Western economic
and military power around the shores of Japan with a pressure incomparably greater than that exercised by the early seventeenth century Europeans, whom the Tokugawa had driven away.

By the middle of the nineteenth century the European maritime
powers had completed the subjugation of the Indian subcontinent, had
taken over much of Southeast Asia, and were beating down the doors of
China and foisting on it a semi-colonial system of unequal treaties. The
Russians had extended their hold over all of Siberia and were pushing
southward into the islands north of Japan. American ships sailed past the
shores of Japan on their way to the China trade or frequented Japanese
coastal waters in search of whales.

Repeated efforts had been made by various Western nations to persuade the Japanese to open their doors, before the United States in 1853
dispatched about a quarter of its navy, under the command of Commodore Perry, to force the Japanese to give American ships access to their
ports. The Japanese had to bow to *force majeure*. Perry's ships with their
more modern cannon could have destroyed Edo and could even more
easily have cut off its essential food supplies by blockading the entrance to

Edo Bay. The treaty signed in 1854 achieved only a limited success, but Townsend Harris, the American consul permitted by this agreement to reside in Japan, finally managed to negotiate a full trade treaty in 1858, using the threat of British naval power then engaged in war in China to persuade the shogun's government to comply. In each case, the principal European powers followed suit with similar treaties.

Through these treaties and subsequent agreements, the full unequal treaty system developed in China was applied to Japan. Foreign traders became ensconced at the new port of Yokohama near Edo and at other treaty ports, protected by European military forces and the extraterritorial privilege of trial by their own judges under their own laws, while treaty limitations on Japanese tariffs left the whole economy open to the machine production of the West. Japan, with its purely pre-industrial economy and its archaic feudal system of autonomous domains, seemed as defenseless before Western imperial expansion as the other countries of Asia that had already succumbed.

Trade developed more slowly than the Westerners had hoped for. The Tokugawa authorities threw up every possible obstacle, and the people were not very receptive to strange foreign goods. Moreover, a silk blight in Europe produced a strong demand for Japanese silk, which helped the Japanese with their trade balance. Nonetheless, the sudden opening of the country was disruptive to domestic markets and the monetary system, and the political repercussions were even worse. The shogun's military dictatorship was in theory justified by his role as military protector of the nation, but he had been proven incapable of fulfilling this role. The shogunate thus was laid open to attack by all those discontented with current conditions or resentful of Tokugawa overlordship, as some of the "outer" domains had been ever since 1600.

The Edo government, in the face of Perry's demands, had sought broad national support for its policies by taking the unprecedented step of consulting the daimyo. The response, though mixed, was generally negative, and this breach of precedent together with the national crisis opened the gates to a flood of criticism. When subsequently Edo felt constrained to sign the commercial treaty of 1858, it again consulted the lords, and it also asked for the emperor's approval, but without success.

Popular sentiment ran high against the opening of the country, and there was a growing feeling that, in order to meet the foreign menace, the nation would have to pull itself together more effectively around the emperor, as the legitimate symbol of unity. Moderates called for "a union of court and military," that is, of Edo and Kyoto, but some radicals advocated a refurbished imperial regime to replace the Tokugawa. The slogan of this policy was "honor the emperor," which was joined with the cry of "expel the barbarians" to form a pithy four-character motto, *sonno joi*, "honor the emperor and expel the barbarians." Young samurai hotheads, inspired by these only vaguely defined concepts, sometimes cut loose from their domains as *ronin*, or "masterless samurai," and assassinated shogunal officials or even an occasional Western diplomat or trader.

Some Japanese had realized from the start that the only defense against the West was to adopt its superior military and economic technology and thus to "expel the barbarians" in the modified sense of achieving security from the West and political equality with it. The leaders of two particularly large "outer" domains, Satsuma at the southern end of Kyushu and Choshu at the western tip of Honshu, were won over to this view by demonstrations of Western naval might. When Satsuma samurai killed an Englishman near Yokohama, a British fleet in 1863 destroyed Kagoshima, its capital city. Similarly, when Choshu fired on Western ships passing through the Straits of Shinonoseki, an allied fleet in 1864 leveled the Choshu forts. The new concept came to be expressed by another four-character slogan, "rich country; strong military" (*fukoku kyohei*). Men knowledgeable about Western technology through their study of "Dutch learning" were useful in this attempt, and, as the country opened up to Westerners, the "barbarians" themselves were used in growing numbers.

The Tokugawa system had been shaken to its foundations by the events since 1853, and the whole antiquated structure began to disintegrate. All policies had become subject to debate by samurai from all over Japan. Some of the great domains vied with one another and with Edo for influence over the Kyoto court, and Choshu openely defied Edo's authority. A military expedition sent in 1864 to chastise it produced only a compromise settlement, and a second expedition in 1866 ended in complete failure. Finally a coalition of Satsuma, Choshu, and some other "outer" and collateral domains seized control of the imperial court and in the name of the emperor announced the resumption of direct imperial rule on January 3, 1868. The shogun and a few loyal domains put up a half-hearted resistance, but a so-called "imperial" army seized Edo, putting an end to more than two and a half centuries of Tokugawa rule.

THE LEADERSHIP of the "imperial" forces was ostensibly provided by imperial princes, court nobles, and a few feudal lords, but actually the initiative for policies and their execution fell largely to a group of able, young reformers of largely middle or lower samurai rank and mostly from Satsuma and Choshu. These men realized that, although the cry of "expel the barbarians" had been useful in their seizure of power, it would be disastrous for Japan to attempt to carry out such an unrealistic policy. Instead they made clear at once their acceptance of the Western treaties negotiated by the Tokugawa. But they still faced the herculean task of replacing the old feudal system by a more effective centralized rule and starting Japan on technological modernization that would give it security from the powerful and predatory nations of the West. The new regime had fallen heir to no more than the broken down, bankrupt shogunal domain, in a country long divided into autonomous feudal units and still limited to a purely pre-industrial economy.

Although the theory of imperial unity had had little practical content for almost a thousand years, a major asset of the new government was its control over the fifteen year old emperor, and it utilized this to the full. He was moved in 1869 to the great shogunal castle in Edo, which was accordingly renamed Tokyo, or "Eastern Capital," and everything was done in his name. As a result, the whole great transformation came to be known as the Meiji Restoration, named after the Meiji "year period" inaugurated in 1868, which became also the posthumous name of the emperor when he finally died in 1912. (Incidentally, year periods, corresponding in length to reigns since 1868, are still used in Japan. For example, the year World War II ended is known in Japan both as 1945 and as the twentieth year of Showa, the year period of the still reigning emperor.)

Replacing the old feudal domains by more centralized rule proved relatively easy because of the largely symbolic role of the daimyo. Already in 1869 the new regime persuaded them to return their land registers to the emperor and receive appointment as governors of their domains, and two years later it simply replaced the old domains by new prefectures of roughly uniform size, administered by officials appointed by the central government. The feudal lords were recompensed generously with govern-

A portrait of the Meiji emperor in middle life. The seizure of power from the Tokugawa in 1868 and the subsequent modernization of the country were done in his name and so became known as the Meiji Restoration. Meiji originally was the name of the year period of his reign (1868–1912). The beard, military uniform, and medals are all innovations borrowed from nineteenth century European royalty. (*Sekai Bunka Photo*)

ment bonds, which insured their continuing prosperity but also their financial dependence on the success of the new order.

It was a more difficult task to wipe out the class divisions of the old system and the special privileges of the samurai. With the disappearance of the domains, the samurai lost their position as a hereditary bureaucratic class, and in 1873 universal military conscription was substituted for the old class basis for military service. In 1876 the samurai were even prohibited from wearing their swords, their badge of distinction. Samurai stipends were also drastically reduced and by 1876 were entirely commuted into relatively small lump-sum payments of cash or government bonds. Thus the samurai in a brief nine year period were deprived of all their special privileges, and Japan was started on a great change which was to transform its society in a mere generation or two from one in which status was primarily determined by heredity to one in which it depended largely on the education and achievements of the individual.

Meanwhile the government was being modernized, largely on the model of the nineteenth century West. Ministries like those of Western governments were formed. These included a Finance Ministry, which was the most powerful because of its control over the purse strings; Army and Navy Ministries, which in 1878 were paralleled by General Staffs on the German model; and an Education Ministry, which embarked on an ambitious program of universal education that took some three decades to put fully into effect. A modern court and legal system, based first on French and then on German models, was laboriously built up but, being closely tied to social realities, was not perfected until 1899. To stabilize revenues and clarify land ownership, fixed monetary taxes were substituted in 1873 for the traditional percentages of agriculture yield, and the payers of the tax, who were the peasants themselves, were confirmed as the outright owners of the land. Japan, unlike post-feudal Europe, had no continuing problem of land ownership by the old feudal classes.

At the same time, efforts were being made to modernize the economy. A modern banking system was created, and the monetary system was reformed with the yen as its unit, worth roughly half an American dollar. Lighthouses were built, and port facilities improved. The country was tied together by a telegraph network. Railroads were started, and a line between Tokyo and its port at Yokohama was completed in 1872. Silk production was improved by the mechanical reeling of silk, a simple innovation largely achieved through private capital. Other industries were more costly and took long years to become profitable. The government itself built up strategic industries in the production of weapons and ammunition, developed mining, and pioneered with pilot plants in a variety of other fields. In order to secure the northern island of Hokkaido from Russian penetration, the government also embarked on a costly program of building up the population and agriculture of the island, largely on an American model, complete with silos and herds of cattle.

To carry out all these innovations, the government needed a great deal of Western technical knowledge. It dispatched students abroad to acquire new skills and hired Western experts at great expense to come to Japan. In these efforts, the Japanese were carefully selective, utilizing the specific national model they felt was best in each field. Since they paid for foreign assistance themselves, they appreciated it more and used it better than have many countries which in more recent times have received aid gratis. But some assistance was free even then. Much of the teaching of English, the necessary language of contact with the West, was provided by Protestant missionaries, largely from the United States.

The restructuring of the government and economy was not accomplished without confusion, much trial and error, serious setbacks, and a great deal of opposition. The most spirited opposition came from elements of the large samurai class, which had the most to lose. There were several samurai uprisings, culminating in a great revolt in 1877 in Satsuma itself. This was put down only with great difficulty by the new conscript army, but Tokyo's victory in 1877 made it clear that the new government was now safe from military challenge at home.

Meanwhile, however, the new regime was drifting toward financial collapse. Its many costly undertakings, the commuting of samurai pensions, and finally the suppression of samurai resistance, had produced a serious inflation by the late 1870s. The government was forced in 1881 to start a program of stringent fiscal retrenchment, including the sale of the pilot industrial plants, mines, and the enterprises in Hokkaido, which were transferred at whatever prices they would bring to whoever gave promise of being capable of operating them successfully.

These drastic measures brought Japan financially back to an even keel, and at much the same time the new industries began to pay for themselves. The first success in the early 1880s was in cotton spinning, which within another decade had become competitive with the West and began to enter the export market. Success in other fields followed. Thus, within two decades of its shaky start, the new government had achieved military and financial security at home, and the country was well launched on its effort to win military and economic security from the West.

T O L D in this brief way, the so-called Meiji Restoration may seen to have been an almost inevitable development. In fact, many scholars make of it simply the expression of supposed laws of history, according to which "absolutist" trends or "bourgeois revolution" automatically followed in the same sequence as in modern Europe. But when the history of Japan between the 1850s and the 1880s is compared with that of other non-Western countries, it stands out as a truly extraordinary experience. No other country responded quickly and successfully to the challenge of superior Western economic and military technology. China, for example, starting a dynastic collapse in the 1840s, did not achieve a unified and stable new political system until a full century later, and it is still to a large extent a pre-industrial country. Most of the other lands of Asia succumbed to colonial rule, were not stirred by a national awakening until inspired by the Japanese defeat of the Russians in 1904–05, did not regain their independence until the middle of the twentieth century, again in large part thanks to the Japanese destruction of Western imperialism during World War II, and are still only partially industrialized in their economies or modernized in their institutions.

The relatively quick success of the Japanese is not to be attributed mainly to external factors, such as the nature of the impact of the West or the relative size of Japan, for other countries of comparable experience or size reacted quite differently. The reasons should rather be sought more in internal characteristics, such as the great homogeneity of the Japanese people and their strong self-identity. Their clear awareness of the possibilities of learning from abroad was also a distinct advantage. Even the social tensions of late Tokugawa times were an asset to a country facing great changes. And it should be remembered that, although pre-industrial in economy and feudal in political pattern, Japan's economic and political institutions were highly complex and sophisticated, and the country had standards of bureaucratic rule that did not suffer by comparison with the West in either honesty or efficiency. With perhaps 45 percent of its men literate and 15 percent of its women, Japan also had literacy levels not far behind the leading countries of the West. Another important factor was that the whole great change could be justified in Japanese minds, not through newly learned foreign concepts, such as democracy or later communism, but by Japan's own ancient system of imperial rule. The utilization of a native ideology undoubtedly smoothed the pains of an otherwise wrenching change and made it somewhat less traumatic.

No one can be sure just what combination of traits best explains the extraordinary contrast between Japan and all other non-Western lands in the nineteenth century, but there can be no question of the advantages Japan gained by its early start in modernization. For one thing, the technological gap with the West was not as great as it was to become in the twentieth century. More important, the lack of precedent and the general skepticism at the time about the possibility of any non-Western country achieving standards comparable to those of the West permitted the Japanese some freedom from unrealistic expectations of instant industrialization or overnight democracy, and more chance for pragmatic experimentation. The lead in modernization over other non-Western lands already achieved by the end of the nineteenth century allowed a further widening of the gap in succeeding decades, until Japan seemed to stand more with the world powers of the West than with the colonial or semi-colonial lands of Asia.

The Constitutional System

8

B Y T H E 1880s Japan had survived the birth pangs of its new order, and its leaders, now settling into middle age, were eager to consolidate the gains of two decades of rapid improvisation into a permanent system that would continue after they were gone. Born in the stable certainties of Tokugawa days, they longed to have once again an unchanging order that would be clearly known to all and accepted by everyone. Influenced by the experience of the leading countries of the West, they decided that such a system should be embodied in a constitution.

A more surprising decision was to include in the new constitutional system a popular assembly on the Western model. Popular political movements had always been regarded as subversive in Japan, but Western experience suggested that an elected assembly strengthened a government by giving it wide popular support or at least served as an ingenious safety valve for popular discontent. A parliament would also be useful in gaining the respect of the Western powers, which was needed if Japan were ever to get out from under the unequal treaties that had been imposed on it. Another factor was the need to broaden the base of government. Under the old system a large proportion of the whole samurai class had been involved in the administration of the shogunate or the domains, but in the new system many former leaders had been frozen out of the government and were demanding a chance to participate.

One of the original leaders of the Meiji Restoration, a man named Itagaki from the Tosa domain in Shikoku, fell out with his colleagues in 1873 and, returning to Tosa, formed his samurai supporters into a political party, which was soon joined by urban merchants and peasant taxpayers. Drawing its ideas from liberal French thought, this group came to be known as the "freedom and people's rights movement." A second popular party, which gained considerable support from the rising business community, was founded by Okuma, another government leader, who was ousted by his colleagues in 1881 because of his advocacy of the immediate adoption of the British parliamentary system. These two movements were the start of lasting streams in Japanese politics which can still be discerned today.

When Okuma was dropped in 1881, the government issued a promise in the emperor's name that a constitution would be in force by 1890. Ito, a former samurai from Choshu, took the lead in a detailed study of European systems, particularly the conservative German one. He also experimented carefully with elements in the proposed new system. After much meticulous preparation, the new constitution was finally issued in 1889.

The constitution naturally centered around the emperor and his authority, since a restoration of his supposedly direct rule had been the justification for the overthrow of the Tokugawa. In actuality, however, the emperor was not expected to rule but merely to validate the decisions made by his ministers. There was, of course, an ambiguity as to who appointed the ministers, but this was not perceived at first, because the surviving members of the group who had been in control since 1868 went on performing this task in the emperor's name, even though the constitution made no mention of them. Reduced in number through deaths and greatly enhanced in prestige by their long leadership, this select group was in effect a Satsuma and Choshu oligarchy, as its critics claimed, and it came in time to be known as the *genro*, or "elder statesmen."

Below the emperor and the oligarchy, the ministries of the government were grouped together in a Western-style cabinet under a prime minister. The early cabinets constituted little more than rotating rosters of the *genro* themselves. Under the cabinet a thoroughly modernized civil service was created on the then most progressive German model. At first graduates of Tokyo University, the government institution founded in 1877, automatically qualified for the higher civil service posts, but a system soon developed of qualification for these positions by examination, and under it Japan built up an elite, highly independent, and extremely efficient civil service bureaucracy.

The constitution had a number of articles granting broad rights to the people, but each clause was qualified with phrases such as "within the limits of the law," which greatly reduced the protection afforded. The judicial system, though highly centralized, was given an admirable degree of independence, and it administered justice with scrupulous adherence to the laws.

The most innovative aspect of the constitution was the creation of a bicameral national assembly, which was in part elective. The upper house, or House of Peers, modeled on the British House of Lords, was filled almost entirely by heredity or appointment. It required a peerage, which was created in 1884 out of former court nobles, feudal lords, and the members of the new leadership group. The House of Representatives was elected by male taxpayers who paid more than 15 yen in taxes—a very select group constituting not much more than 1 percent of the population. A majority vote of both houses was required for the budget and for any law to remain permanently on the books.

This was a very limited sort of popular government and has been frequently described as a great setback or "betrayal" of democracy, but the Japanese had no intention of creating a full democratic system and informed Westerners at the time felt that they were if anything rushing too fast on a path suitable only for Occidentals—trying to run, as one commentator put it, before they could walk. In view of the lack of popular experience with elections or understanding of parliamentary institutions, it is extremely doubtful that a more democratic system would have worked at all in 1890. In any case, limited though it was, the Japanese Diet, as it was called, turned out to be the first successful parliamentary experiment outside the West, and, despite a shaky start, the system survived and proved itself flexible enough for remarkable evolutionary growth.

I N 1894, not long after the introduction of the new constitutional system, the British, impressed by Japan's modernization, agreed to relinquish their extraterritorial privileges by 1899, and the other nations followed suit. Within a few years, the Japanese had also regained full control over their tariffs. They also fought in quick succession two successful wars which demonstrated that, on the basis of their new economic strength and institutional reforms, they were winning their effort to achieve military security from the West.

The first of these wars was in 1894–95 with China over the control of Korea. To the surprise of the world, Japan easily defeated its giant neighbor. Chinese influence was eliminated from Korea, and Japan annexed the Chinese island of Taiwan, thus starting to build its own empire in imitation of the Western powers. It also acquired the southern tip of Manchuria, but Russia, covetous of this strategic piece of terrain, persuaded Germany and France to join it in forcing Japan to disgorge the peninsula. This lesson in power politics was made all the more bitter for the Japanese when the Russians appropriated the area for themselves three years later.

In 1904–05 Japan fought Russia, again over the control of Korea. Three years earlier, Japan had signed a pact with Britain—the Anglo-Japanese Alliance—which was the first truly equal alliance between a Western nation and a non-Western one, and it insured that the European powers would not again gang up on Japan. To the world's amazement, Japan once again emerged victorious, acquiring the southern tip of Manchuria, the southern half of the Russian railways in Manchuria, the southern half of the island of Sakhalin in the north, and such complete control over Korea that it quietly annexed the country in 1910.

Japan thus was becoming a major colonial power, and it continued the process during World War I. The involvement of the European nations on the other side of the globe left Japan the paramount power in East Asia, and it took advantage of this position in 1915 to force new concessions from China through the so-called "twenty-one demands." It also seized the German holdings in Shantung province in China and acquired control over the German islands of the North Pacific in the form of a mandated territory. At the Versailles Peace Treaty, Japan sat as one of the five major victors—the first non-Western nation to have made it into the club of Western great powers.

MEANWHILE great changes had been taking place within Japan. Although the constitution of 1889 had been meant to embody a permanent, unalterable system, it proved but one step in the unending series of changes that seems to characterize modern life in Japan as elsewhere in the world. In 1889 industrialization had only just begun, and with each succeeding decade it moved at a faster pace. The shift from a class leadership to one determined by education and examinations was only just taking hold. Universal education for six years became a full reality only in 1907. University education was expanding rapidly. A white collar class of relatively well educated people was beginning to take shape between the rulers and the ruled. Newspapers were growing to great size and influence. Life in the cities was beginning to approximate that of the urban West.

The framers of the constitution had not counted on such basic changes, and they had even misread existing conditions. The small body of voters proved to be far more politically conscious and cantankerous than expected. In preparation for a national assembly, the government had experimented with various elected local assemblies, and through these anti-government politicians had gained experience in elections. As a consequence, they dominated the first national election in 1890 and every succeeding one—even the second election in 1892, when the government did all it could to win a majority through brutal police suppression and bribery. Far from proving a meek debating society and government claque, the Diet became something of a Frankenstein monster, attacking its makers on the grounds that they were nothing more than a "domain clique" made up of men from Satsuma and Choshu. And it proved to have more power than had been intended. On the advice of German scholars, Ito had put into the constitution a provision that, if the Diet failed to vote the budget, last year's budget continued in effect, but this supposed trump card proved almost useless. In a rapidly growing economy, last year's budget was never enough. Utilizing their control over the size of the budget, the politicians in the Diet did their best to wrest a share of real political power from the oligarchs, not accepting the original concept of the constitution makers that the cabinet should be "transcendental" and above politics.

The first four years of the Diet's existence was a period of open battle between it and the government, eased at the end by a patriotic outburst over the war against China. Then for a few years a sort of compromise was worked out, with either Itagaki or Okuma, the two former oligarchs now in leadership of the parties, admitted into the cabinet in return for the support of their following in the Diet. This compromise was further developed in 1900, when Ito and his bureaucratic supporters joined with the politicians of the Itagaki line to found a new party, called the Seiyukai. For the next twelve years the Seiyukai served as a sort of government party, securing a number of cabinet seats and other plums for the politicians and getting its views taken into account in the formulation of

policies, in return for the assurance that the cabinet would have majority support in the Diet.

By this time the original leadership was growing old and tired of the unexpected turmoil of parliamentary politics. Ito resigned the prime ministership for the fourth time in 1901, and thereafter none of the original
oligarchs, except for the ousted Okuma, ever took the top position again.
In their place, their bureaucratic followers took over as prime ministers
and cabinet members. Between 1901 and 1913 two men alternated as
prime minister. One was Saionji, a member of the old court aristocracy
who had developed a strong liberal tendency as a student in France, had
become Ito's protege in the bureaucracy, and succeeded him as leader of
the Seiyukai party. The other was General Katsura, a man of Choshu samurai background, who was the protege of Yamagata, a former Choshu
samurai who was the chief shaper of the army and the main rival of Ito
among the oligarchs.

The period between 1900 and 1912 was one of relative political tranquil-
ity, but this was destroyed by a political blowup in the winter of 1912–13.
It started with the army's removal of the army minister from a Saionji cabinet in pique over the cabinet's refusal to go along with the army's desires
for expansion. This situation revealed another ambiguity in the system.
Yamagata had seen to it that the army and navy in theory would be directly
under the emperor and free of civilian control, in order to be sure that
venal and disloyal politicians, as he saw them, would not emasculate the
armed forces. But as the oligarchs aged and shrank in number, their control in the name of the emperor over the military and civilian branches of
government began to wane, permitting this military challenge to cabinet
leadership.

General Katsura was brought back in as prime minister to work out a
compromise, but the Seiyukai men in the Diet refused to accept him,
even defying an "imperial" request to do so. Katsura desperately attempted to organize a new party to gain the needed Diet support but
failed. The press and the public clamored for "normal constitutional government," by which they meant, not the original "transcendental" concept, but cabinets responsive to Diet majorities. The upshot was the appointment of a neutral navy admiral as prime minister, with a substantial
increase of Seiyukai representation and power in the cabinet.

This political incident, named the "Taisho political change" for the new reign and year period that had just started, was a clear sign of the changes that were sweeping Japan. The cabinets that followed were usually more dominated by the parties than those before the incident had been. The party formed originally by Katsura gradually grew into a second contender for power in the Diet and served as the "government party" under the Okuma cabinet of 1914–16. In 1918, Yamagata, who after Ito's assassination by a Korean in 1909, had become the chief wielder of the emperor's prerogatives, accepted as prime minister the head of the Seiyukai party, who was a party politician by profession. This man was Hara, who, though of very high samurai origin, came from North Japan and thus was an outsider in the Satsuma–Choshu dominated central government and had had to fight his way to power through parliamentary politics.

Hara was assassinated by a deranged youth in 1921, and between 1922 and 1924 the cabinets were briefly headed by nonparty men. In 1924, however, Kato, a retired Foreign Ministry bureaucrat who was the head of the other major party, was appointed prime minister, and for the next eight years the respective presidents of the Seiyukai and of this newer party, renamed in 1927 the Minseito, alternated as prime ministers. The Diet thus had increased steadily in power since 1890, until it had come to assume leadership in the civil government and had replaced "transcendental" cabinets with openly party ones.

Meanwhile the electorate for the Diet had expanded along with its powers. The tax qualification for the franchise was reduced substantially in 1900 and again in 1919, greatly increasing the number of voters, and finally in 1925 the franchise was given to all adult males. Japan seemed well on its way to becoming a full democracy. In fact, the period between 1913 and 1932 is generally known as the time of "Taisho democracy."

Behind these political changes lay great economic growth and social and intellectual development. The European powers, by becoming involved in World War I, had left their Asian markets to Japan, which prospered greatly. The victory of the democracies in the war also brought a new wave of liberalizing ideas and ways from the West. This contributed to the victory of universal manhood suffrage in 1925 and produced in the cities a Japanese variant of the flapper and jazz age. As a result of the Russian Revolution, radical ideas won a small following among intellectuals, and a growing labor movement appeared and even stirrings among tenant

farmers. Business interests became more influential through their financial support of the parties, and an expanding middle class increasingly set
the tone for the new Japan.

In response to the leading role of the Diet and its business backers, Japanese foreign policy shifted from its earlier military orientation to policies
more in line with business interests. The imperial expansion of the Meiji
period had been basically for strategic reasons. The new foreign policy
was more concerned with the need of Japan's growing industries for
foreign raw materials and markets to pay for them. Hara's government in
1921 was responsive to an American invitation to a conference in Washington to limit naval expansion and stabilize the Far East. Japan accepted
a ratio in capital ships of three to five with the United States and Great
Britain, in return for American and British promises not to build bases
beyond Hawaii and Singapore, and it agreed to return to China the
German rights it had seized in Shantung. It also backed out of an expedition into Siberia, launched together with smaller American and British
forces, originally on the grounds of maintaining an eastern front against
the Germans, following the Communist Revolution. A cut in the standing
army in 1924 and drastic reductions in the military share of the budget
further showed the tendency of the party governments to rely for Japan's
economic security on trade with the outside world rather than on military
expansion.

The
Militaristic
Reaction

9

A LL IN ALL, Japan seemed to be approaching the norms of the democracies of the West, but beneath the surface lurked grave problems. For one thing, the Japanese version of the British parliamentary system had certain notable imperfections. Prime ministers were not produced by parliamentary majorities but were chosen by the few men who exercised the imperial prerogative, and only after appointment did they hold elections in which they usually won their parliamentary majorities. The "king makers" were the remnants of the old oligarchy—principally Yamagata until his death in 1922 and thereafter the court noble Saionji, who came to be classed with them as the "last *genro.*" In other words, Diet control over the prime ministership and cabinet was by no means part of the established constitutional system but merely a political convenience.

An even more serious imperfection was the division between the military and civil branches of government, which the "Taisho political change" had revealed. Army and navy ministers remained military men, outside party discipline. To be sure, control by the Diet over the military was gradually being established. The Diet after all had to vote the military as well as the civilian budgets. Ambitious military men, like civil bureaucrats, sometimes joined the parties after retirement in order to achieve ultimate political power, as happened in the case of General Tanaka, who as president of the Seiyukai party became prime minister in 1927. Still, the armed forces were in theory and in their actual internal operations completely free of civilian control.

Japan's economic underpinnings were also far from firm. World War I had permitted phenomenal industrial growth, but the adjustment after the war to resumed competition by European industry proved extremely painful. Japan grew economically more slowly during the 1920s than at any other time in its modern history, except for the period of World War II and its immediate aftermath. The whole world was in economic doldrums, and international trade stagnated. Rural Japan was particularly hard hit by a drastic fall in price of its two most important crops—rice because of competition from its own empire in Taiwan and Korea and silk because of the virtual disappearance of the American silk trade following the collapse of the American stock market in 1929. The plight of tenant farmers, who tilled some 45 percent of the soil, was especially serious. In many parts of Japan the poorer peasants fell into dire want and in some cases were forced to sell their daughters into prostitution to avoid starvation.

Even in urban Japan there were serious economic problems. A great gap in productivity had appeared between the new industries, with their modern technology, and the more traditional industries, including agriculture, which were still largely unmechanized. This "dual structure" in the economy is a common feature of countries during the early stages of industrialization but was particularly marked in Japan because of the speed with which industrialization had come. The leadership was not attuned to such problems of the industrial age and was slow to pass remedial social legislation.

Another weakness of Japan in the 1920s was the unevenness of the social and political terrain on which its parliamentary institutions stood. The dual structure of the economy was paralleled by a dual structure throughout society. Modernization had progressed much more rapidly in urban Japan than in rural areas, which lagged behind as a great reservoir of past attitudes and ways. The products of higher education had achieved ever broadening intellectual horizons and were abreast of the ideas of the whole world, but the much larger number of people who had gone no further than the six years of compulsory schooling had not been educated so much as indoctrinated in ideas of strict loyalty and conformity. Some Japanese looked eagerly forward to all that was new; others looked nostalgically back to the past.

People who were dissatisfied with the economic record or the other policies of the party governments and their businessmen supporters yearned for the more patrician and supposedly less self-serving leadership of the past. A great deal of corruption and self-seeking "pork barrel" politics did characterize the Japanese parliamentary system, and the whole contentious nature of electoral, democratic politics was distasteful to many Japanese, who had in mind the old ideal of harmonious decisions achieved through consensus and executed by dedicated, loyal, servants of the state. The influence of capitalistic businessmen in government seemed particularly corrupting, and there was increasing criticism of the great business magnates, who by this time were pejoratively known as the *zaibatsu*, or "financial clique." The peaceful, trade-oriented foreign policy of the party governments was seen by some as a betrayal of Japan's real strategic interests for the selfish benefit of the captains of industry.

Traditionally minded Japanese tended to lump parliamentary institutions, big business, individualism, and the liberal style of life emerging in the cities as related signs of the corrupting influence of the West. Oddly enough the new radical left shared these same prejudices, but this did not prevent conservatives from showing particular fear and hatred for it. In 1925, ironically the year that universal manhood suffrage was achieved, the Diet passed a repressive Peace Preservation Law, making it a crime to advocate a basic change in the political system or the abolition of private property. Thus, despite the seeming triumph of democracy in Japan, it did not have a firm institutional framework as in the West and lacked wide emotional and intellectual support.

IT IS impossible to say whether these conditions would have led to a breakdown of the system if Japan had not encountered what was perceived as a foreign policy crisis. As international trade shrank, following the outbreak of the world depression in 1929, and countries resorted to nationalistic economic policies of attempted self-sufficiency, the Japanese realized that their new industrial economy was dangerously extended beyond what their own small empire would support. Great Britain, France, and the Netherlands had huge overseas possessions and the Russians and Americans vast continent-wide territories, but Japan had only a relatively small geographic base. To many Japanese, it appeared that they had started their empire building too late and stopped too early, unwisely influenced by the attitudes of the already satiated Western nations.

The situation was commonly described as a population problem. The white race had appropriated for itself the lightly inhabited, desirable lands in the Western Hemisphere and Australia and was excluding the Japanese from them. By the early twentieth century Japanese had been effectively banned on openly racial grounds from the United States and the British Dominions, and the United States made this policy brutally clear again in 1924 in a new exclusion act based on race. As the Japanese saw the situation, they were not only being discriminated against in a humiliating way but were being economically bottled up. The only answer, some felt, was military expansion again on the nearby Asian continent.

China was the obvious target, but nationalism was at last on the rise there, and the days of easy colonial pickings were clearly over. In fact, the newly founded Nationalist government of Chiang Kai-shek was attempting to gain back some control over Manchuria, which the Japanese by now had firmly in their economic grip. Rising Chinese nationalism made it clear that time was fast running out for any further cutting up of the Chinese melon. It was, in a sense, now or never.

The relative independence of the Japanese armed forces made it possible for them to transform this sense of national crisis into an actual change in foreign policy and a shift in political structure. Already in 1928 certain elements of the Japanese army in Manchuria had engineered the assassination of the Chinese warlord of the area and, protected by the army as a whole, had escaped censure by the civil government. In 1930 the cabinet forced the navy to accept the London Naval Treaty, which extended to heavy cruisers the three to five ratio with the United States and Great Britain that was first established at the Washington Conference, but this was achieved only at the cost of almost open insubordination by the navy. Then on September 18, 1931, a group of army officers in Manchuria, with the tacit approval of their army superiors in Manchuria and Tokyo, staged an incident on the railway near Mukden, the Manchurian capital, which gave an excuse to the Japanese army to overrun the whole of Manchuria during the next few months and set up the puppet state of Manchukuo there the next February. The civil government, unable to control the situation for fear of provoking an army *coup d'état*, found itself forced to accept this abrupt return to empire building and to attempt to justify it before the rest of the world. It was also swept along by a huge outpouring of popular patriotic fervor. When the League of Nations condemned Japan's actions in Manchuria, the Japanese simply walked out, thus sealing the fate of the League.

The shift in foreign policy and the change of mood within Japan soon brought an end to party cabinets. Small bodies of ultra-rightists among military officers and civilians had for some time been agitating for a military coup. The prime minister who forced through the London Naval Treaty in 1930 was shot by a fanatic and subsequently died. Other leaders were assassinated early in 1932, and the prime minister was killed by a group of young navy officers in May of that year. Saionji selected in his place a moderate naval admiral, and he was followed by a similar figure in 1934. Party men continued in the cabinets, and the parties continued to win smashing victories in the elections in 1932, 1936, and 1937. In the 1936 election, the Minseito actually won a strong plurality under the slogan, "Will it be parliamentary government or fascism?" Even the new leftist vote was rising rapidly. But parliamentary control was waning. The military virtually dictated foreign policy, and the cabinets, now called "national unity" cabinets, had drifted back toward the "transcendental" concept of the early constitutinal system.

National euphoria over the seizure of Manchuria strengthened the hand of the military leaders immensely, and pressures by rightest zealots, particularly among the younger officers, gave them arguments for tilting national policies in the directions these groups advocated. The ultra-rightists tended to champion the impoverished peasantry, who provided the bulk of the fighting men, and to excoriate the privileged classes of rich businessmen and powerful politicians. They saw their own function to be the assassination of "evil leaders" around the throne, thus clearing the way for a military seizure of power and an undefined "Showa restoration," named for the year period of the new emperor, which had started in 1926. Young army officers almost brought off a *coup d'état* on February 26, 1936, when they killed a number of government leaders and seized part of downtown Tokyo, but, after some indecision, the army and navy commands suppressed the movement and executed its leaders. The more moderate element in the army then reimposed sterner control over its officers and put an end to the factionalism between the higher officers, which had become severe in recent years. At the same time, the 1936 incident resulted in another decline in the powers of the Diet, and in 1937 all party participation in the cabinet was eliminated under a prime minister who was an army general.

THE ARMY meanwhile had been extending its control over parts of Inner Mongolia and North China. On the night of July 7, 1937, fighting broke out accidentally between Japanese and Chinese forces near Peking. Chiang Kai-shek's government demanded an overall settlement of Japan's creeping aggression, and the Japanese military dug in its heels in response. World War II had started. The Japanese military machine won an almost uninterrupted series of victories, pushing deep into North and Central China and seizing the southern coast in an effort to knock out or strangle the Chinese government, but the Chinese kept fighting on as they withdrew inland, and guerrilla warfare and lengthening lines of communication began to take their toll on the Japanese. The Japanese army was sinking into what subsequently came to be known as the quagmire of Asian nationalism.

Full-scale war in China heightened patriotic fervor in Japan, and many trends that had been observable since 1931 became accentuated. The military increasingly came to dominate the government and pushed its men into various newly created civilian agencies. The government steadily extended its control over industry in an effort to strengthen the economic base for war. Parliamentary power continued to decline, and in 1940 the government forced all the parties to disband and enter the political wing of the Imperial Rule Assistance Association, a large, amorphous organization which was meant to be a nationwide popular movement, like the Nazi or Fascist parties. Indoctrination of the people through education and the mass media became increasingly narrow and virulent, and deviant ideas were suppressed with growing vigor, often more by neighborhood enthusiasts than by the government or police. A turning point in free thought had been the suppression in 1935 of the works of Professor Minobe of Tokyo University and his expulsion from the House of Peers on the grounds that his once accepted theory that the emperor was an "organ" of the constitution was now *lèse majesté*.

The Japanese experience is often compared to the fascism of interwar Europe, and certainly the resemblances are in some ways striking. But, unlike the Italian and German cases, there was no dictator and the system was not the product of a well-defined, popular movement, but more a vague change of mood, a shift in the balance of power betweeen the elite groups in Japanese society, and a consequent major shift in national policies, all occurring within the framework of the constitutional system established in 1889. There was no revolution, no successful *coup d'état*, no formal change of the political system. The military-dominated government of the late 1930s was fully as constitutional as the parliamentary-dominated government of the 1920s, though neither was at all what the designers of the constitution had intended. Not many people had stood out boldly in opposition to the trends of the time and gone to prison for their beliefs. Quite a few of those who did — and these were largely Communists — were persuaded to recant. For the rest, opponents had largely been cowed into silence and unhappy conformity to the new consensus.

The war in China stretched on, and the Japanese eventually found no escape from it, except by expanding it into a broader and ultimately disastrous conflict. The outbreak of the war in Europe in 1939 and the ultimate involvement of the Soviet Union in this war freed Japan from pressures from the European powers but increased American opposition to Japan's conduct in China. All along the United States had adopted the moralistic attitude of not recognizing the fruits of Japanese aggression but had been unwilling to take any but verbal measures. The growing threat that Hitler would establish his hegemony over Europe, however, put in a new light the threat of Japanese hegemony in East Asia, which the Japanese came to describe as the Greater East Asia Co-Prosperity Sphere. Pacts signed between Japan, Germany, and Italy heightened the association in American minds of these twin menaces to American hopes for a more open world order and raised the specter of a world dominated largely by Nazis and Japanese.

Following the fall of France, Japan seized North Vietnam in the summer of 1940, in order to strengthen its strangle hold on South China, and the United States reacted with economic sanctions. When Japan occupied South Vietnam the next summer in order to gain bases for a possible push southward, the United States took the further step of banning oil shipments. Faced with the prospect of a dwindling oil supply with which to prosecute its war in China and meet possible attack by the United States, the Japanese were forced to make a quick choice between three courses: backing down in China, negotiating a compromise settlement with the United States, or waging a war to seize the oil of Indonesia, then called the Dutch East Indies. The government was unwilling to do the first and unable to achieve the second and therefore settled on the third choice, striking brilliantly at Pearl Harbor on December 7, 1941, in order to neutralize the American navy while Japan pushed south. Before starting the war, the military consolidated its political position at home. General Tojo, the most influential man in the army, became both prime minister and army minister.

The Japanese knew that the United States had far greater economic and military capacities than Japan, but they thought that, if they struck rapidly and seized the whole of the Western Pacific, Americans would find the road back to victory too long and arduous to be worth pursuing, especially if the Nazis had in the meantime won in Europe. Within a few months the Japanese did successfully overrun all Southeast Asia and a vast region stretching from the borders of India to New Guinea and Guadalcanal. But the "sneak" attack on Pearl Harbor, timed to be simultaneous with the delivery of a declaration of war in Washington, helped drive the Americans to a frantic but sustained response. Building vastly greater naval and military power than the Japanese were capable of, they fought their way slowly and painfully across the Pacific. Meanwhile their submarines and aerial mines sank the greater part of the Japanese merchant marine, immobilizing the Japanese army in its far-flung military conquests and cutting off the necessary flow of raw materials to the factories of Japan. By November 1944 American air power was close enough in the islands south of Japan to start a systematic destruction by fire bomb raids of its highly inflammable cities, driving the working force away from the already faltering factories. It was a double kill of Japanese industry, and Japan's military strength began to falter.

The situation was hopeless, but the Japanese social order remained surprisingly strong, and the military continued in its proud tradition of no surrender. Only after the Americans dropped two atomic bombs, which all but wiped out the cities of Hiroshima and Nagasaki on August 6 and 9, 1945, and the Soviet Union came crashing into Manchuria on August 8 in an eager effort to get in on the kill and the disposition of the Japanese carcass, did an anguished Japanese government bow to the inevitable. On August 14 it accepted the "unconditional" surrender demanded, though on the basis of clear but stern conditions set forth by the United States on July 26, in the so-called Potsdam Proclamation. Japan had risked all and lost all. Eighty years of prodigious effort and extraordinary achievement lay in ruins. For the first time in history Japan felt the tread of a foreign conqueror.

The
Occupation
Reforms

10

D EFEAT in World War II brought great and sudden shifts to Japan, comparable only to the changes of the Meiji Restoration. The war itself had been a traumatic experience. At its end Japanese industry was at a virtual standstill, and even agricultural production had fallen off about one third, because of long years without new tools, adequate fertilizer, or sufficient labor. All of Japan's great cities, with the exception of Kyoto, and most of its lesser cities had been in large part destroyed and their populations scattered throughout the country. Around 668,000 civilians had been killed in aerial bombardments. The economy, critically maimed, cut off from its normal flows of trade, and disrupted by the uncertainties of foreign rule, recovered only very slowly—much more slowly than in war-devastated Europe. It took a full decade before per capita production had crept back to the levels of the mid-1930s.

The psychic damage to the Japanese was even more severe. They had been under mounting psychological pressure for fifteen years and had lived under full wartime conditions for eight. Life had become constantly more difficult. Ersatz materials first replaced normal fabrics; then all consumer goods slowly disappeared, food ran short, and finally urban housing vanished in flames. Forced to scrounge on the black market just to stay alive, city dwellers suffered a collapse of morale. A people punctilious in their observance of the law became accustomed to petty legal infractions. The leaders had expected to win through the superiority of Japanese will power, and the people had responded with every ounce of will they possessed, until they were spiritually drained. Not just the cities but the hearts of the people had been burned out.

There was a great popular revulsion against the war, against the leadership that had steered the nation into this disaster, and against the past in general. Instead of feeling guilt, the people felt that they had been betrayed. To their surprise, they discovered that their armies, far from being welcomed in Asia as liberators, were universally hated. The great respect for the military as selfless patriots and servants of the emperor turned to anger and contempt. In the early postwar months, most Japanese were absorbed in the struggle to keep body and soul together, but underneath these immediate concerns there was a great longing for peace and a determination to avoid any repetition of this great catastrophe. People wanted something new and better than the old Japan that had come to grief. They were confused but open to change in a way they had never been before.

It was these Japanese attitudes that made the American military occupation of Japan, which lasted until the spring of 1952, an effective shaper of change. The United States in its determination to stop the Japanese militarists had not overlooked planning for a postwar Japan, and the American forces thus entered the country on September 2, 1945, with broad policy directives for sweeping reforms. They were under the command of General MacArthur, who acted not just for the United States but for the coalition of victorious nations, under the title of Supreme Commander for the Allied Powers, or SCAP as both he and his headquarters came to be called.

The allied aspect of the occupation, however, was more theory than reality. The defeat of Japan had been almost completely the work of the United States, and while the British sent an Australian contingent to serve under MacArthur in Japan, the Chinese were too involved in their own civil war to do so, and the Soviet Union demanded a separate zone of occupation and, when this was refused, declined to put its troops under an American commander. A Far Eastern Commission of all the victorious nations was created in Washington early in 1946 to set the general policy of the occupation, and an Allied Council for Japan made up of the four chief powers was established in Tokyo to advise on its execution, but neither body was permitted by the United States to have any real influence. Thus, the occupation was almost entirely an American show and was regarded as such by the Japanese.

MacArthur was an extremely self-willed, dynamic, and charismatic leader, who brooked only general guidance from Washington and none at all from the allied nations. His messianic cast of mind and phrase appealed to the Japanese, who in their desperation looked for inspiring guidance. The Japanese, to their surprise, also found the American troops to be not vindictive but essentially well intentioned and benevolent. Since the United States had apparently proved its superority by defeating Japan, the disillusioned, demoralized Japanese, instead of reacting to the army of occupation and its leader with the normal sullen resentment of a defeated people, regarded the Americans as guides to a new and better day.

The Americans, for their part, found the Japanese people, not the die-hard fanatics they had expected from their experience with the Japanese army in the battlefields of the Pacific, but a well-educated, disciplined, docile people, eager to cooperate in reforming and rebuilding their nation. Even the more sophisticated leaders, realizing the completeness of Japan's defeat and the necessity of bending to the American will if Japan were to recover its independence, proved surprisingly cooperative. American tendencies toward didactic self-confidence and benevolent patronage and the old Japanese habits of effective cooperation and loyalty to leaders blended together well. The military occupation of one advanced, modernized nation by another, instead of proving the unmitigated disaster that most people might have expected, turned out on the whole to be a surprising success.

THE FIRST and most basic objective of the American occupation was the demilitarization of Japan, since Japanese military expansionism was viewed at the time as the one overriding problem in East Asia. The country was flooded with allied troops and was shorn of all its conquests. In fact, it was even deprived of territories to which no other country had a valid claim. The Kurile Islands north of Hokkaido were given to the Soviet Union, and the United States took Okinawa for itself. Japanese troops and civilians were rounded up from all over East Asia and the Pacific, and more than six and a half million were dumped back into Japan. Then, the army and navy were completely demobilized and their ships and weapons destroyed. Members of the military who were convicted of committing atrocities were punished, and seven men, including General Tojo and one civilian former prime minister, were executed on the dubious grounds that they had brought about the war through their personal plotting.

In the flush of the postwar mood of pacifism and MacArthur's enthusiasm for Japan as the Switzerland of Asia, as he described it, both the Japanese leaders and the American authorities happily agreed to an article in a new constitution that in very specific terms renounced war forever and the maintenance of any war potential. By the time a peace treaty was finally negotiated in 1951, however, it was deemed more realistic to make no mention in it of any military restrictions on Japan. On the economic side, all excess industrial capacity beyond the needs of a completely demilitarized country was declared available for reparations to the countries that Japan had despoiled. Little, however, came of this program for three reasons: no one could agree on how these industrial facilities should be divided; there was almost nothing in a war-destroyed Japan worth transporting and setting up elsewhere; and Japan had no remaining excess industrial power but rather a terrible industrial deficit for its own civilian needs. In fact, during these years Japan was kept alive only by injections of American aid.

If the occupation had stopped with this program of demilitarization, it would not have differed much from previous historical cases of punitive settlements of wars. But it went far beyond this. The American thinking was that demilitarization was only a temporary cure for Japan's militaristic ills but that a democratization of the government might produce a Japan which would be less likely to go to war in the future. To this end, ultra-nationalistic groups were banned, all repressive laws were rescinded, political prisoners, who were mostly Communists, were released, and all former army and navy officers and whole categories of the top leadership in government and even in business and education were banned from occupying any positions of significant responsibility. The most important aspect of the democratization policy, however, was the adoption of a new constitution and its supporting legislation.

When the Japanese government proved too confused or too reluctant to come up with a constitutional reform that satisfied MacArthur, he had his own staff draft a new constitution in February 1946. This, with only minor changes, was then adopted by the Japanese government in the form of an imperial amendment to the 1889 constitution and went into effect on May 3, 1947. The American origin of the new constitution naturally raises skepticism as to its suitability and durability. But the American drafters wisely made their work not a new creation based on the American political system but a perfection of the British parliamentary form of government that the Japanese had been moving toward in the 1920s. As such, it was compatible with Japanese political experience and was enthusiastically embraced by the bulk of the Japanese people.

The new constitution focused in on the ambiguities and weaknesses of the old one. The emperor was unequivocally defined as the powerless symbol of the unity of the nation—which is what he in fact had long been. Supreme political power was assigned to the Diet, and all competing sources of power were eliminated or clearly subordinated to it. Cabinets were made responsible to the Diet by having the prime minister elected by the lower house. The House of Peers was replaced by an elected House of Councillors. However, the operations of the Diet and the electoral system, except for the enfranchisement of women, remained largely unchanged from what had been the situation in the late 1920s.

The constitution also included a greatly expanded list of popular rights—all that exist in the American constitution and a good many more recently formulated ones, such as the equality of the sexes, the right of labor to bargain and act collectively, and the right of everyone to receive an equal education. The judicial system was made as independent of executive interference as possible, and a newly created supreme court was given the power to review the constitutionality of laws. Local governments were given greatly increased powers, and the governors of prefectures were made elective officials, as mayors of municipalities had long been.

THE OCCUPATION did not stop at political reform but went on to a bold attempt to reform Japanese society and the economy in order to create conditions which were thought to be more conducive to the successful functioning of democratic institutions than the old social and economic order had been. Curiously, the American authorities held to the Marxist interpretation that the real villain behind Japan's imperialism had been the excessive concentration of industrial wealth and power in the hands of the *zaibatsu*, which was thought to have necessitated an aggressive foreign policy. Although Japan's prewar history scarcely bears out this theory, it led to a remarkable display of socialistic zeal on the part of MacArthur and his staff. Revolutionary reforms are easier and more fun in someone else's country.

The destruction of war had been a great economic leveler, since it had impoverished almost everyone, and the occupation confiscated much of the remaining personal wealth through a capital levy. It also disbanded the great *zaibatsu* firms, dispossessed the owning families, and started to break up the industrial and commercial units of which these great combines were made. By that time, however, it had become clear that further surgery to improve the Japanese economy for social and political reasons might kill it instead. The program therefore was terminated, and the emphasis shifted to attempts to revive Japanese industry.

Japan was plagued by high rates of tenancy, which had stood at around 45 percent of the land since the end of the nineteenth century. Much thought in Japan had gone into plans to reduce tenancy, and the injection of the American external *force majeure* now made possible an extraordinarily radical and effective land reform. Absentee ownership of agricultural land was banned completely, and a village landowner was limited to only a small area beyond what he himself farmed. The transfer of land to former tenants was effected on extremely easy terms—actually, at prewar prices, which meant virtual confiscation—and tenancy was reduced to only about 10 percent of the land.

The occupation also put into effect enlightened laws in behalf of urban labor and encouraged union organization as a balance to the power of management. The labor leaders surviving from the 1920s quickly built up a tremendous new labor movement, which ultimately grew to more than twelve million members. To the surprise of the American authorities, however, this movement took a decidedly more radical turn than in the United States. In the desperate economic conditions of early postwar Japan, there was little room for successful bargaining over wages, and many labor unions instead made a bid to take over industry and operate it in their own behalf. Moreover large numbers of workers in Japan were government employees, such as railroad workers and teachers, whose wages were set not by management but by the government. Direct political action therefore seemed more meaningful to these people than wage bargaining.

The occupation reforms spread to many other fields. Women were enfranchised and given full legal equality. The authority of a main family over branch families and of the family head over adult children was ended. Compulsory education was extended to nine years, efforts were made to make education more a training in thinking than in rote memory, and the school system above the six elementary grades was revised to conform to the American pattern. This last mechanical change produced great confusion and dissatisfaction but became so entrenched that it could not be revised even after the Americans departed.

Some of the occupation reforms thus were not very successful or much appreciated, but on the whole they were welcomed, and they undoubtedly brought huge changes. The transformation of postwar Japan, however, should not be viewed as largely the work of foreign intervention. The whole war experience—the failure of the bid for empire and the national collapse that had resulted—would in any case have forced Japan to move in the directions it took under the occupation. It had no way to survive economically except through reliance on peaceful international trade. Parliamentary democracy, whatever its faults, seemed the obvious alternative to the disasters of authoritarian rule. And the social changes that the militarists and ultranationalists had dammed up or diverted for a decade and a half would inevitably have swept across Japan once these barriers had collapsed. The occupation reforms succeeded in large part because they were headed in the same direction forces within Japan were pushing. The dynamic leadership of external military authority perhaps channeled these forces more narrowly and thus made them flow more swiftly than might otherwise have been the case, but basically the occupation facilitated rather than determined the postwar development of Japan.

Postwar Japan

11

THE REMAINDER of the history of postwar Japan can be presented more briefly, for the rest of this book deals mainly with this period. The Japanese people went through the traumatic experiences of war and occupation with the same great social discipline that they had evinced during the even more basic shift from feudalism and isolation to centralized rule and international contacts almost a century earlier. The Americans, lacking adequate language skills and trained personnel to run Japan directly, exercised their authority through the Japanese government. They had at first left the way open for a revolution in Japan and had half expected one, but nothing of the sort occurred. There was confusion but no breakdown of law and order. Most Japanese shied away from violence whenever it was attempted by the more radically inclined. Government servants continued to perform their specific duties as best they could, teachers kept teaching, students kept studying, and everyone tried to adjust to the new conditions. Despite the whirlwind of change, Japanese society continued in its orderly ways, as it had for the past several centuries.

The major streams of change, as these had shown themselves in the early decades of the twentieth century, reemerged after the war almost as if the experiences of military dictatorship, war, defeat, and occupation had never occurred. In no field was this clearer than in politics. All the old parties were quickly reconstituted in the autumn of 1945, and the voting trends of the 1920s and 1930s picked up almost where straight line projections would have placed them. The two traditional prewar parties were revived and, faced by a rising leftist vote, merged in 1955 to form the Liberal Democratic party, a name which reveals its dual origin. The members of this party had been the liberals of prewar days, but in the postwar situation they were considered the conservatives. The parties of the left, which were from left to right the Communists, the Socialists, and the Democratic Socialists, all had prewar antecedents. The only postwar party that did not have prewar roots was a small one called the Komeito, sometimes translated the Clean Government party, which started as the political wing of a new religious movement, the Soka Gakkai. It and the three parties of the left, by splitting the opposition vote, contributed to keeping the Liberal Democratic party in power ever since its founding.

The early postwar years were a time of great political as well as social and economic uncertainty and turmoil. Organized labor made a bid for the control of industry and direct political power. Socialists and Communists, under the tolerance of MacArthur, agitated for the early establishment of a fully socialist or communist society. Leftists, intellectuals, and the urban white collar classes, who had suffered most from repression by the militarists, were extremely suspicious of the intentions of the conservatives in power. Political rhetoric tended to suggest all-out confrontation, not reasoned debate, and this spirit of confrontation was not confined to elections and Diet politics but overran into the streets. People rallying in huge numbers and marching under inflammatory banners, usually proclaiming absolute opposition to something or other, became a highly visible part of the whole process. While everyone acclaimed democracy, *demo*, the most ubiquitous postwar political terms, was an abbreviation not of democracy but of demonstration.

The early honeymoon of the occupation with the Japanese people gradually turned sour. Conservatives became progressively more irked with American meddling, which in its details often seemed uninformed and needlessly damaging to the economy, while leftists became entirely disenchanted when the emphasis in occupation policies shifted between 1947 and 1949 from further reform to economic recovery. This shift was natural, for the original American reform program was nearing completion and the continued economic weakness of Japan was coming to be seen as the chief threat to its success. But a shift in American perceptions of the world outside Japan was also involved. The cold war was developing, China was being "lost" to communism, and Japan no longer appeared the unique threat to peace in East Asia but rather as a hopeful base for democracy and American military power in that part of the world.

There were several turning points in the attitude of the left toward the occupation. One was when the labor unions, in a bid for political power, planned a nationwide general strike for February 1, 1947, and Mac-Arthur, fearing the resulting damage to the economy and his own re-form program, banned the strike. Another was when the occupation early in 1949 insisted on a stringent financial retrenchment in government and business, which gave an excuse to the conservatives for a wholesale firing of troublesome leftists—the so-called Red Purge. And finally there was the sudden invasion of South Korea by Communist North Korea on June 25, 1950, and the American military response from bases in Japan. Japanese leftists came to the conclusion that the occupation had made, as they put it, a one hundred and eighty degree shift in policy and had changed from patron to enemy.

Ever since, the political fight between left and right in Japan has focused to a large extent on the relationship with the United States. This situation, in a sense, has merely been a reflection of the fact that the fate of a Japan vitally dependent on foreign resources and markets was likely to be determined more by its foreign relations than by what happened within the country. The predominant role of the United States in these relations was magnified in Japanese eyes by the whole occupation experience as well as by continuing dependence on the United States for Japan's military security and roughly 30 percent of its foreign trade. The leftists argued that heavy dependence on the United States tied Japan to capitalism and therefore prevented the achievement of socialism. They saw American bases in Japan as dangerously involving Japan in the cold war and involving it still in militarism. The presence of American bases and troops also led to endless friction that could be exploited by the opposition parties to their political advantage.

The termination of the occupation through a peace treaty was delayed longer than the United States had planned, because of the obvious unwillingness of the Soviet Union to accept the sort of treaty the Americans believed to be necessary. Eventually, however, the United States went ahead with a "separate peace treaty," without Soviet endorsement or Chinese participation, and concluded at the same time a bilateral Security Treaty providing for American bases in Japan and a commitment to defend the islands. The two treaties were signed in September 1951 and went into effect the next March.

During the early post-occupation period, a major source of political controversy was the desire of the conservatives to revise the constitution in order to make clear the sovereignty of the emperor—a largely theoretical point—and to get rid of the limitations on military defense, which was a much more practical issue. Lacking a two thirds majority in both houses of the Diet, they failed in the face of determined opposition by the left, but a tacit reinterpretation of the no-war clause did occur. A modest military establishment was built up and was named in 1954 the Self-Defense Forces. Some modifications of the occupation reforms were also made during the early post-occupation years. The purge of the wartime leaders was ended, and the police and educational systems were reconsolidated under central government leadership. The opposition parties put up a tremendous fight against this return toward centralized controls, fearing that these moves would start a general erosion of the liberties guaranteed in the new constitution. A running battle between left and right has continued ever since over controls the ruling party felt were necessary for administrative efficiency and the left feared might open the way to a return to the prewar system.

During these years, the Japanese government also reestablished its relations with the outside world and won a place for itself again in the community of nations. Starting in 1954 it began to make reparation settlements with most of the countries it had despoiled. In 1956 a termination of hostilities, though not a full peace treaty, was negotiated with the Soviet Union, which then dropped its veto of Japan in the United Nations, permitting it to gain membership. Contact with Japan's closest neighbors, Korea and China, remained less satisfactory. It was not until 1965 that relations with South Korea were normalized on the basis of large financial payments by Japan, and not until 1972, following the Sino-American rapprochement, that Japan established full diplomatic relations with Peking.

The biggest political crisis in the postwar period came in 1960 over a revision of the Security Treaty with the United States, necessitated by Japan's growing self-confidence and status in the world. This produced a violent political explosion and massive demonstrations in the streets, but once the revision had been ratified, excitement subsided, and the next few years proved to be the calmest politically in the whole postwar period. Ikeda, the new prime minister, adopted a "low posture" of not forcing political decisions against determined opposition and instead drew popu-

Protesting against the new Security Treaty with the United States, rioting students meet policemen at the gate of the prime minister's official residence in Tokyo on May 20, 1960. Hundreds of thousands of citizens demonstrated day after day during this greatest political crisis in postwar Japanese history. As a consequence, President Eisenhower cancelled his planned visit to Japan, and Prime Minister Kishi was forced to resign. (*Associated Press*)

lar attention to Japan's economic success, promising a doubling of incomes within ten years. President Kennedy also had a charismatic appeal for many Japanese, particularly the young, thus reducing some of the political heat over relations with the United States.

Tensions over these relations, however, mounted once again as the Americans became deeply involved after 1965 in the war in Vietnam. Most Japanese were opposed to the American position in Vietnam and saw it as threatening to involve Japan in American military adventures. Such attitudes merged in the late 1960s with growing excitement once again over the Security Treaty, since its initial ten year term was coming to an end in June 1970 and either side would then be able to demand its revision or termination. Student unrest, which was at its height around 1968 in Japan as elsewhere in the world, contributed to the political turmoil, and by then demands for the return of Okinawa to Japan had become strong, injecting a very pronounced nationalistic overtone to the attack on the relationship with the United States.

The mounting foreign policy crisis, however, just as in 1960, dissolved once more, and Japan continued on its remarkably steady course. The United States pulled slowly out of Vietnam; the security treaty problem never came to a head, since neither government proposed termination or revision and the treaty simply continued in effect; and in November 1969 the reversion of Okinawa to Japan was announced and went into effect in May 1972. Japan steamed into the 1970s on a more even keel than ever before.

BEHIND Japan's relatively stable political course in the years following the occupation lay the so-called "economic miracle" that had made Japan by the end of the 1960s the third largest economic unit in the world and had brought the Japanese people a personal affluence that they had never even dreamed of before. Economic recovery had at first been very slow but began to be evident in the early 1950s. The severe retrenchment policies of the occupation in 1949 had created a sound financial foundation, and American offshore procurement for the war in Korea provided a strong stimulant. Once revived, the Japanese economy began to move at an accelerating pace, and by the mid-1950s the Japanese had regained their per capita production levels of the prewar years and were humorously talking about the "Jimmu boom," meaning the greatest economic boom in Japanese history since the mythical founding of the nation by the Emperor Jimmu in 660 B.C.

By the late 1950s the Japanese economy was racing ahead and for more than a decade thereafter averaged annual growth rates around 10 percent in real terms—a record no other major nation has ever equaled. Ikeda's talk in 1960 of the doubling of incomes in ten years proved a gross underestimation, because the Japanese economy actually was doubling every seven years. By the 1960s the Japanese were feeling downright prosperous, and the country was swept by a mood of consumerism. Fine cameras, stereos, refrigerators, washing machines, air conditioners, even cars became possessions almost anyone could aspire to, in rural areas as well as the cities. Japanese basked in a sense of pride in their country, which they had not felt for some years, and enjoyed the wonderment if not the admiration of the rest of the world. They showed off their country to foreigners with self-satisfaction at the Olympic Games in Tokyo in 1964 and the Osaka International Exposition of 1970. They talked of a leisure boom, going in enthusiastically for golf, skiing, and bowling, and, when exchange controls were eased, they stampeded abroad as tourists. Per capita GNP passed southern Europe and came to be close to two thirds that of the United States.

Growth in per capita GNP was aided by a decided slowdown in population growth, after an initial postwar baby boom occasioned in Japan, as in the West, by the reuniting of husbands and wives after years of wartime separation. In the course of the 1950s and 1960s, the rate of births slowed down rapidly, until it produced only a little over 1 percent population growth per annum and gave promise of stabilizing around 135 million in the year 2000. Public and private advocacy of birth control—there were no religious scruples about it—and lax abortion laws, which were not enforced in any case, contributed to this decline, but the basic reason, as elsewhere in the world, was probably the rapid urbanization of Japanese society. The typical city family became limited to two children, which is usually all there is room for in a small urban apartment and all the family can afford to see through the long years of education at a university. The rural birth rate, however, actually slowed down even more, because most people of child-bearing age had deserted the countryside for the city. But, whatever the reasons, the Japanese who saw themselves as facing a population crisis in the 1930s now saw no population problem at all, for the small annual increase in population took only an insignificant bite out of the much more rapid growth of the economy.

Meanwhile Japan's industrial success was flooding the world with Japanese cameras, radios, television sets, cars, ships, steel, and all sort of other industrial goods. By the late 1960s, Japan had become the first or at least the second largest trading partner of almost every country, Communist or capitalist, in East and Southeast Asia and the Western Pacific. It was beginning to invest heavily in neighboring lands and even in the countries of the West. Its aid was becoming important to less developed countries and its participation in international bodies a matter of importance to all.

As economic anxieties waned, some of the fire went out of political controversy in Japan, even though the rhetoric and style of bitter confrontation remained. Rural Japanese were clearly well satisfied, and blue collar workers in private industry shifted gradually to the pattern of collective bargaining for economic interests, leaving direct political action more to white collar employees and government workers. The great annual May Day demonstration of the left became a sort of good-natured folk festival. While some of the discrepancies in the "dual economy" remained, general prosperity and a growing tightness of the labor market made them less marked. Moreover, rural affluence together with an explosion of communications, particularly through television, wiped out much of the social and intellectual differences that had existed before the war between modernized urban areas and a stagnant, old-fashioned countryside. Without this brilliant economic advance, postwar Japan would probably not have proved politically so stable nor its democratic institutions so successful.

Economic vigor was paralleled by comparable but less measurable achievements in the social and cultural fields. Despite the bitterness of political debate, a general feeling developed that Japan had a happy society—"bright" (akarui) was the word Japanese liked to use. The rights guaranteed by the constitution were well observed. Despite vast increases in urban population, crime rates remained low—actually less than half those of any major industrialized country in the West—and Japan experienced virtually no drug problem. Education levels soared, giving perhaps the best statistical evidence of social health. School dropouts were practically unknown, and the percentage of the age group that completed the twelve rigorous years of education leading to graduation from senior high school grew to about 90 percent—very possibly a world record. More than 30 percent of the age group continued on to some form of higher education—a percentage well above that of most countries of Western Europe.

Culturally Japan was also in boom conditions. It was vibrantly alive. There was great creativity and tremendous vitality in literature, art, and music. Traditional cultural currents ran strong in all these fields, but at the same time Japan participated fully in worldwide cultural trends. For example, while traditional Japanese music showed more vigor than for many decades, Japanese musicians and conductors of Western-type music won worldwide acclaim, and Tokyo supported five full professional symphony orchestras. Japanese films achieved international renown, and Kawabata, one of the more traditional writers, won the Nobel Prize for Literature in 1968.

The international milieu in which Japan found itself also began to mellow, as the cold war faded and a spirit of detente grew in the early 1970s between the United States and the Communist powers. Under these circumstances, it is not surprising that old political tensions within Japan relaxed and some of the old anxieties about Japan's position in the world began to fade.

J A P A N' S very success, however, contributed to the rise of a whole new set of problems. In their headlong industrialization after the war, the Japanese had despoiled their natural environment and created conditions of terrible crowding and pollution in the urbanized areas. In all industrialized countries people were becoming conscious of these problems, but the Japanese suddenly realized that they faced perhaps the most serious conditions of pollution and overcrowding in the whole world. It was no easy matter to shift gears from the long accepted policy of all-out industrial growth and find a new consensus on the alleviation of these newly perceived ills of industrialization and urbanization.

As Japan became an industrial superpower, it also discovered that others expected more of it. The less developed countries, particularly those in East and Southeast Asia, demanded more generous treatment in trade and aid than the Japanese, intent on their own economic growth, had given them in the past. The other industrialized countries, particularly the United States, also demanded economic reciprocity from Japan in place of the strongly protectionist policies under which the Japanese economy had grown so fast and had come to build up large trade surpluses. In short, Japan was being forced to make more of a contribution to the open international trade system on which its well-being depended.

The whole relationship with the United States seemed to be changing. A strong, self-confident United States in the past had taken a weak, dependent Japan for granted as a safe even if somewhat reluctant ally, and Japan had in turn taken for granted the protection and benevolent support of the United States, but now the reliability of the United States as a partner for Japan was coming into question. How far would the United States, shaken by its failure in Vietnam, withdraw from Asia and the Western Pacific? Confidence in the United States was particularly damaged when President Nixon suddenly announced on July 15, 1971, a new policy on China, without consulting or even informing the Japanese government, despite numerous promises in the past to do so. This "Nixon shock" raised the possibility in Japanese minds of a basic rivalry in the future with the United States, rather than the close cooperation that had existed ever since the end of the war. In any case, the time had clearly come for a careful rethinking of Japan's position in the world.

Overshadowing these various concerns was the new realization of the limitedness of the natural resources of the world that came with the Arab oil embargo of October 1973. Japan is about three quarters dependent for energy on imported oil. The quadrupling of oil prices was a body blow to the Japanese economy, which helped account for an inflation rate that was higher for a while than in any other major industrialized land. Even more threatening was the obvious implication that Japan could be denied by others commodities essential to its very life. For some time specialists had been pointing out the ultimate limitations of natural resources and the environment, but the Arab oil crisis made the whole world suddenly feel a new vulnerability, and no country was more vulnerable than Japan. A dark shadow seemed to fall across Japan's future, calling for sober stock taking.

The old political balance within Japan also seemed to be on the point of disappearing. The Liberal Democratic vote had shrunk slowly but steadily over the years, and there were signs that soon no party would have a parliamentary majority. These were conditions that the Japanese had not faced since they had regained their independence after the war, and no one was sure what would result. But by this stage in our historical account, we have come too close to the present day for clear perspective. It is time to shift to a broader, more analytic consideration of what the Japanese are like today and where they may be heading, leaving a more detailed consideration of the problems touched upon here until we have established this wider base.

SOCIETY

PART THREE

Rooters at a baseball game between Waseda
and Keio, arch rivals in the "Big Six" University League in Tokyo. Waseda and Keio,
though Japan's most prestigious private universities, are outclassed by Tokyo University
and some of the other national universities.
(*Sekai Bunka Photo*)

Diversity and Change

12

T HE BRIEF account above of Japan's historical heritage reveals a story of considerable diversity and constant change. It should suffice to correct some of the facile stereotypes with which the outside world tends to explain the Japanese and write them off. Perhaps their isolation and extreme sense of distinctiveness have left the Japanese particularly open to such stereotyping. They are all too often seen as human leopards who never change their spots—though there may be some dispute as to just what these spots are, depending on the time and angle of vision.

Some have seen the Japanese as complete esthetes—the descendants of the delicate and sensitive courtiers and ladies of *The Tale of Genji*, or of medieval Zen artists, or of the gentle folk who so attracted Lafcadio Hearn in the late nineteenth century. Others have seen them as merely the modern version of the arrogant, punctilious, rule-bound samurai of Tokugawa times. A common view among Japan's East Asian neighbors is that they are basically militarists, as was illustrated by the long dominance of feudal military leadership and the conquests of the brutal Japanese army in modern times. A more recent stereotype, contrasting with militarism in content but paralleling it in the emphasis on single-minded fanaticism, is of the Japanese as "economic animals," incomparably efficient in their organization and absolutely ruthless in their willingness to sacrifice all else to their own economic gain.

Our brief run-through of Japanese history should show that the Japanese have changed over time as much as any people, and considerably

123

more than many. They have been extremely responsive to changing external conditions. Of course, there are cultural continuities and the persistence of some traits more than others, but no more so than elsewhere in the world. Contemporary Japanese are no more bound by the patterns of feudal warriors, Tokugawa samurai bureaucrats, or prewar militarists than Swedes are bound by Viking traditions or early modern military conquests, Germans by their premodern political disunion or their more recent Nazi experience, or Americans by their Puritan heritage or traditions of isolationism. Japan since the war differs in many fundamental ways from what the country was in the 1930s, just as it differed greatly in that period from what it had been a half century earlier, and the late nineteenth century from the early, and so on back through history.

Our historical account, highly simplified though it is, should also have revealed that Japan does not have a simple, uniform society, but an extremely complex one. Though a homogeneous people culturally, the roughly 115 million Japanese display great variations of attitudes and ways of life by age group and according to their diverse roles in society. A teenager and an octogenarian, a day laborer and a corporation executive, a bank clerk and an artist show about as much diversity in attitudes as their counterparts would in any Western country. Almost anything that might be said about Japanese in general would not be true of many and might be flatly contradicted by some.

But despite this complexity and the rapid changes that have swept Japan, foreign observers have commonly sought to find in some one trait or tightly knit group of traits an open sesame that would explain everything in Japan as it is today and was in the past. Japanese too in their self-consciousness have endlessly sought to do the same. Perhaps it is the feeling both share that Japan is somehow unique that encourages this search for some one simple explanation for this uniqueness.

In the past, Japanese frequently cited the unbroken line of emperors since antiquity as explaining everything else about Japan, though our historical sketch has shown how little that had to do with most developments. Ruth Benedict in *The Chrysanthemum and the Sword*, a remarkable pioneer effort published in 1946, used a combination of the samurai ethics of the Tokugawa period and the attitudes that came to the fore in the 1930s to paint a coherent picture of the Japanese, which, though insightful on certain aspects of Japanese psychology, scarcely portrays the Japanese as they are today. More recently, Chie Nakane has attempted to explain Japanese society through the key role of hierarchical groupings in what she calls a vertical, as opposed to a horizontal, society, and Takeo Doi has made the crucial ingredient a sense of "dependence" in human relationships.* For Japanese these penetrating looks into their society from a single point of view can be stimulating and are not seriously misleading, for they know that these are but glimpses into a far more complex reality. For foreigners, however, such one dimensional interpretations may prove somewhat distorting. Japan's complex society is made up of a great variety of elements, some of which do not fit well together and all of which are subject to change.

The speed of change makes sharp analysis particularly difficult. I personally have been observing Japan and writing about it long enough to be acutely aware of this problem. The firm generalization of one decade may start to break down in the next and be almost gone by the one after. The salient features of Japanese life seemed quite different in the 1930s from the 1920s and even more different again in the 1950s and 1970s. Younger Japanese who have received their total education since the end of World War II appear to be almost a new breed when compared with their prewar elders. What Japanese will be like in the future no one can tell. If one thinks about how much has changed in American life and attitudes decade by decade since Civil War days, one can realize how much Japanese have changed during this same period, for they have lived through greater and more sudden shifts in the external environment and far more traumatic transitions at home.

A final problem in analyzing Japanese society is the uncertain ground from which we view it. Any study like this one is inescapably comparative, for one can make no statement about things in Japan being either great or small without having in mind some standard by which they are being judged. But what is that measuring stick? No two Americans have exactly the same attitudes or standards, and, if we include other Westerners, the diversity becomes still greater. And norms keep changing in America as elsewhere in the world. Where Westerners were scandalized by Japanese openness about exposing the human body in the nineteenth century,

---

* Chie Nakane, *Japanese Society* (Berkeley, University of California Press, 1970), and Takeo Doi, *The Anatomy of Dependence* (Tokyo, Kodansha International, 1973). In these two cases, as in most Western literature on modern Japan, the surname is given last in the Western manner.

today they might consider the Japanese in some ways slightly prudish in such matters. The picture of war-mongering Japanese and peace-loving Americans of the 1930s in time was transferred into almost a mirror image. It is as if we were trying to get our bearings on one fast moving, ever changing cloud in its relationships with another that is equally subject to movement and change. The best we can hope for is some rather vague approximations.

Still, when all is said and done, the Japanese do remain a very distinctive people. This is true even though modern technologies which Japan shares with the West tend to produce a certain convergence of traits. Without doubt, basic trends in Japan are flowing for the most part in the same directions as in the United States and Europe. And within these trends the spread in individual variation in any particular trait is about as wide and covers much the same range as in the West—for example, from very bold to very timid or from wildly ambitious to extremely passive. Still, in some traits the Japanese turn out on average to have quite different norms from those common in Western countries. And significantly, some of these differing norms have behind them long historical antecedents and therefore may be all the more likely to persist to some extent into the future. Toqueville a century and a half ago, in attempting to explain to Europeans the Americans of that time, made certain generalizations that have some applicability even today. One cannot hope to do the same for this faster moving country in this more volatile age, but, in attempting to describe Japanese society as it now exists, we may lay bare some characteristics of continuing relevance.

One thing, however, is certain. Japanese society is too complex and too rapidly changing to fit into any tight, neat model. Obviously certain traits do mesh smoothly, but others do not. I shall therefore make part of my study of Japanese society an analysis of characteristics that do fit together, looking outward as it were from these core elements to their external manifestations. For the remainder, however, I shall look from the outside at certain salient aspects of Japanese society, such as education, business, and religion, to see what these may reveal about the complexity and diversity of Japan's culture as well as about the structures that may lie beneath the surface. Such a double approach, while leaving a litter of contrasting or even conflicting elements, may give us a better feel for the complex realities of contemporary Japan.

The Group

13

A GOOD place to start the analysis is the balance between the individual and the group. The human race is made up of individuals, but each is born and for the most part lives his life in a group context. Between various societies there can be great differences in the relative emphasis placed on the individual and the group. Certainly no difference is more significant between Japanese and Americans, or Westerners in general, than the greater Japanese tendency to emphasize the group, somewhat at the expense of the individual.

The Japanese are much more likely than Westerners to operate in groups or at least to see themselves as operating in this way. Where Westerners may at least put on a show of independence and individuality, most Japanese will be quite content to conform in dress, conduct, style of life, and even thought to the norms of their group. Maintaining "face," originally a Chinese term but one of universal applicability, is much on Japanese minds, but it is "face" before the other members of the group that most concerns them.

Part of this difference between Japan and the West is myth rather than reality. We have so idealized the concept of the independent individual, alone before God, the law, and society, that we see ourselves as free and isolated individuals far more than the facts warrant. Prevailing Japanese attitudes have tended to make the Japanese do the reverse. Group affiliations in Japan are very important, but the Japanese tend to emphasize these even beyond reality, attempting to interpret everything in terms of such things as personal factional alignments (*habatsu*) in politics, family interrelationships, university provenance (the "academic clique," or *gaku-batsu*), and personal patronage and recommendations. They like to insist that what counts is not one's abilities but one's *kone*, an abbreviation of the English word "connections." The actual situations in Japan and the West, however, are much less widely different than the American Lone Ranger myth, for example, or the traditional Japanese ideal of selfless merging with the group would lead one to believe.

The balance between group and individual is also in flux in Japan as elsewhere, and there are signs of convergence in this regard between Japan and the West. Modern technology in the Occident clearly produced conditions in which more individuals could win economic and other forms of independence from their families or other groupings than in earlier ages. In fact, the trend in this direction has become so extreme that the isolation and anomie of contemporary urban life are giving Westerners pause and are causing a sort of groping once again for closer group relationships. In Japan the effects of modern technology have by no means gone so far, but they have had the same general effect as in the West, deemphasizing the group somewhat in favor of the individual.

When the Japanese first confronted the superior technology of the Occident, they comforted themselves with the idea that they would adopt "Western science" but stick to "Eastern ethics." The Chinese and other Asian peoples had much the same concept. But the Japanese soon learned that there was no clear dividing line between techniques, institutions, and values. They tended to be all of a piece. Fukuzawa Yukichi, who took a leading role in the 1860s and 1870s in popularizing knowledge about the West, stressed the importance of individual self-reliance as the secret of Western success, and two very influential translations of the time were Samuel Smiles' *Self-Help* and John Stuart Mill's *On Liberty*.

The Meiji leaders recognized the necessity of putting more emphasis on the individual and rapidly got rid of strict class barriers and the whole feudal system, making of the citizenry individual taxpayers and candidates for universal education and military service. Individual rights were written into the 1889 constitution, even though they were strictly limited by the provisions of law; industrialization bit by bit produced greater individual economic freedom as in the West; and the 1947 constitution brought a great number of clearly defined and unrestricted individual rights, which the courts have rigorously enforced since then. Thus the balance between the group and the individual has shifted greatly in Japan during the past century, but, nonetheless, great differences from the West still persist both in attitudes and in realities.

O N C E these differences were clearly embodied in the family, though this is no longer the case. The premodern Japanese family, known as the *ie*, might include subordinate branch families under the authority of the main family and other members who were distant kin or not related at all. It also gave absolute authority over the individual members to the father or else the family council. This sort of family was to be found particularly among the more prominent members of the feudal warrior class, rich merchants, and certain peasant groups.

The traces of this system lingered on in modern times but have largely disappeared since the war and the adoption of the new constitution. In any case, the bulk of the population even in premodern times held to a simpler family pattern. This was the nuclear family of parents and children, or more properly the stem family variant in which one child, usually the eldest son, and his spouse remained with the parents to inherit the farm or business and then gradually took over from the old folks, who went into retirement while still living in the old home.

The modern Japanese family is in structure not very different from the American nuclear family, though with a strong survival of the stem family system. The Japanese have never gone in for ancestor worship—the term applies better to Chinese society than Japanese—but the tablets of a few recent ancestors may be kept in a Buddhist shrine on a shelf and be passed on to one of the children, usually the eldest son, thus symbolizing continuity of the family through him, while the other children are considered to have entered or established separate families. The retired parents are likely to live with the child who receives the ancestral tablets whether or not there has been a farm or business to pass on. Those families who can afford it may have a separate but adjoining house or wing of the family residence for them. This situation is not only a reflection of old customs but is also necessitated in part by inadequate retirement pay and social security benefits, which make retired persons more dependent on their children for support than in the West. Tiny urban apartments, however, may preclude live-in grandparents, often to the open relief of the daughter-in-law, and there is growing resistance to accommodating the old people in this way. Nevertheless, some three quarters of retired persons still live with their children, though with urban crowding growing worse and old people becoming a larger proportion of the population—some 8 percent in 1975—isolated living for the aged and old peoples' homes are beginning to be serious problems for Japan too.

The nuclear family in contemporary Japan is somewhat less eroded than its American counterpart. Parental authority is stronger, and family ties on the whole are closer. But these are not structural differences. Beyond the nuclear family, ties of kinship, as with uncles, aunts, and cousins, are as varied and vague as in the United States. Basically the Japanese nuclear family is reminiscent of the American nuclear family as it existed a half century or so ago. The differences are more of degree than of kind, and the trends in both countries are in the same direction, toward smaller units and less binding ties.

A typical middle-class family at dinner. Seated on the floor, they are eating some specialty dish, cooked on a gas burner. They hold their bowls of rice in their left hands. A family with two rather than three children and a mother who dresses in Western style would perhaps be more common. (*Sekai Bunka Photo*)

The differences with the West come out more clearly in extra-family groupings. Even in premodern times these often took precedence over the family, though familial terms were sometimes used to describe these relations. For example, the ruler or lord was the "father" of his people. Even today in gang parlance a boss is known as the *oyabun*, or "parent status," and his followers as *kobun*, or "child status." In everyday speech the term *uchi*, meaning "within" and by extension one's home or family, is also commonly used for the business firm to which one belongs. But the important point is that the key groupings even in premodern times were not essentially kinship units. They were instead such groups as the agricultural village, which shared water resources for the rice fields and co-operated in handling its taxes and other administrative problems, or at a higher level the tight lord and vassal units of feudal society. The groups that play such a large role in Japanese society today are more the echo of units of this sort than of the family.

The original village group, organized on a basis of households rather than individuals, is still strong, though it is a much smaller part of society as a whole than it once was and even in rural Japan has become overshad-owed by other larger units, such as the powerful agricultural cooperative or, in politics, the administrative village, which is a grouping together for efficiency of a number of natural villages. The term "village" (*mura*) is now used for these artificial larger units, while the original village has slipped to the status of *buraku*, or "hamlet."

For the great majority of Japanese who are not village dwellers, the neighborhood associations of towns and cities do not have much signifi-cance and only loomed large when fostered by the government in the 1930s and the war years as a means of political and economic control from above. There is, however, a great variety of other groupings that are important in their lives. Of these, the firm where one works is probably the most important.

A job in Japan is not merely a contractual arrangement for pay but means identification with a larger entity—in other words, a satisfying sense of being part of something big and significant. Employment for both management and labor is likely to be until the normal age of retire-ment. For both, this brings a sense of security and also a sense of pride in and loyalty to the firm. There is little of the feeling, so common in the West, of being an insignificant and replaceable cog in a great machine. In other words, there is no loss of identity but rather a gaining of pride for both workers and executives through their company, particularly if it is large and famous. Company songs are sung with enthusiasm, and company pins are proudly displayed in buttonholes.

Where the American tends to see himself as an individual possessing a specific skill—a salesman, accountant, truck driver, or steamfitter—and is ready to sell this skill to the highest bidder, the Japanese is much more likely to see himself as a permanent member of a business establishment—a Mitsui Trading or Mitsubishi Heavy Industry man—whatever his specific function may be. The same spirit applies to other work groups, as in the various ministries of the government. As we shall see later, this identification of the worker with his work group has had a profound influence on how Japanese business and the economy operates.

Japanese business is also pervaded by other sorts of groupings. Associations of business enterprises, from groups of petty retailers by street or ward to nationwide associations of the great banks or steel producers, are more widespread and more important a feature of the Japanese scene than the American. Such associations are pyramided together into comprehensive and effective national organizations, culminating in the Japan Chamber of Commerce for smaller businesses and the Federation of Economic Organizations, the famous Keidanren, for big business. Doctors, dentists, and other professional groups are closely organized in a similar way, and agricultural cooperatives and the federations of labor unions fit into this pattern. The Japanese, in short, are almost the perfect "organization men."

Schools, particularly at the college level, are another important area in which individuals find group identification. Americans too talk nostalgically about alma mater, but links established in school days are likely to be far more important in Japanese life, and university provenance often affects hiring patterns in business. Major universities have the ideal of staffing themselves exclusively from their own graduates and achieve this goal to a surprising degree. Very few students attend more than a single university, and throughout life individuals identify themselves and are identified by others on the basis of the university they attended in a way that finds only a pale reflection even among Ivy League schools in the United States.

Groups of every other sort abound throughout Japanese society and usually play a larger role and offer more of a sense of individual self-identification than do corresponding groups in the United States. There are great congeries of women's associations, pyramided into prefectural and national associations. Youth groupings are important. The Parent Teachers Association, known in Japan as in the United States as the PTA, is a far more influential and well organized body, particularly in rural Japan, than is its American prototype. There are numberless hobby groups for everything from judo and the other martial sports to the gentler arts of flower arrangement and tea ceremony, all tightly organized and occupying a larger role in the lives of their members than would usually be the case in the United States. Rotary is organized on a huge scale, larger than anywhere else in the world except for the United States and the United Kingdom, and instead of being mostly a small town movement goes right up to the captains of industry in the metropolitan centers.

Naturally, large groups are often subdivided into smaller ones. The work team or office is an important social as well as operational subunit within a factory or business. There is a particular solidarity between persons of the same age in villages, business firms, and the bureaucracy. Political parties and ministerial bureaucracies often are divided into sharply contending factions. Student life in universities centers around "circles" or interest groups, whether these be for various organized sports, hobbies like photography, more academic concerns, such as the English Speaking Society, or political action groups. Students for the most part develop the bulk of their social contacts within the one such group they choose to join. In society as a whole, artistic and intellectual life tends to break up into small, exclusive, club-like groupings, which support their own publications and do not mingle much with one another.

Some people on the periphery of society do not qualify for any of the various types of groups described above, but for them the so-called "new religions" often fill the void. As we shall examine more closely later, religion as a whole plays less of a role in group life in Japan than an American might expect from his own experience with church congregations or parishes, but during the past century and a half a number of tightly organized new religions have arisen, perhaps in response to the uncertainties of an age of rapid change and unquestionably serving to give a sense of group identity to those who otherwise lack it. The most outstanding example of such new religions in postwar Japan is the Soka Gakkai, which may have around six million members, many of whom are casual workers in small enterprises or other persons without any strong identification with work groups or with other well-organized bodies.

A group of girls singing together at a Soka Gakkai rally. Such group activities lie at the heart of the appeal of Soka Gakkai and other so-called "new religions," which minister as much to the social as to the spiritual needs of Japanese who feel themselves to be left out or on the fringes of society. (*Associated Press*)

THE EMPHASIS on the group has had a pervasive influence on Japanese life styles. The Japanese love group activities of all sorts, such as the school or company field day or the association outing. College boys and girls tend to go hiking, skiing, or on other expeditions as groups, and there is correspondingly less getting together on a one-to-one basis. Male groups from work habitually stop at a bar on the way home for a bit of relaxation, and parties are characterized by group drinking and group games, rather than by tête-à-tête conversations with shifting partners, as at Western dinners and cocktail parties. Nowhere is group activity clearer than in sightseeing, to which the Japanese have always been addicted. Groups predominate over individuals or families—groups made up of school classes, associates at work, village organizations, women's societies, and the like, each herded along by a tour guide or bus girl carrying a little flag. With the growth of world tourism, the Japanese tourist group has become a common sight abroad. In fact, in Southeast Asia, where many groups from agricultural cooperatives have gone in recent years for sightseeing, local merchants have been known to call out to any passing Japanese tourist *Nokyo-san*, or "Mr. Agricultural Cooperative."

Some people feel that the Japanese are especially prone to the herd instinct. This is a common enough phenomena everywhere, particularly noticeable when a society is viewed from the outside, but it does seem stronger in Japan than in many other places. The Japanese have always been very susceptible to fads and styles. The postwar Japanese are continuously describing themselves in terms of prevailing "booms" or "moods," using the English terms. An unkind commentator has likened the Japanese to a school of small fish, progressing in orderly fashion in one direction until a pebble dropped into the water breaks this up and sets them off suddenly in the opposite direction, but again in orderly rows.

The group emphasis has affected the whole style of interpersonal relations in Japan. A group player is obviously appreciated more than a solo star and team spirit more than individual ambition. Where the American may seek to emphasize his independence and originality, the Japanese will do the reverse. As the old Japanese saying goes, the nail that sticks out gets banged down. A personality type which in the United States might seem merely bluff and forceful but still normal is defined in Japan as a neurotic state. Cooperativeness, reasonableness, and understanding of others are the virtues most admired, not personal drive, forcefulness and individual self-assertion.

The key Japanese value is harmony, which they seek to achieve by a subtle process of mutual understanding, almost by intuition, rather than by a sharp analysis of conflicting views or by clear-cut decisions, whether made by one-man dictates or majority votes. Decisions, they feel, should not be left up to any one man but should be arrived at by consultations and committee work. Consensus is the goal—a general agreement as to the sense of the meeting, to which no one continues to hold strong objections. One-man decrees, regardless of that man's authority, are resented, and even close majority decisions by vote leave the Japanese unsatisfied.

To operate their group system successfully, the Japanese have found it advisable to avoid open confrontations. Varying positions are not sharply outlined and their differences analyzed and clarified. Instead each participant in a discussion feels his way cautiously, only unfolding his own views as he sees how others react to them. Much is suggested by indirection or vague implication. Thus any sharp conflict of views is avoided before it

A sight-seeing group has its picture taken at a favorite spot—in front of the two bridges that must be crossed in succession to pass from the public part of the imperial palace grounds to the restricted area where the palace itself is located. (*Wide World Photo*)

comes into the open. The Japanese even have a word, *haragei*, "the art of the belly," for this meeting of minds, or at least the viscera, without clear verbal interaction. They have a positive mistrust of verbal skills, thinking that these tend to show superficiality in contrast to inner, less articulate feelings that are communicated by innuendo or by nonverbal means.

In a highly homogeneous society like Japan's, such nonverbal forms of communication may have been easier to develop than in the countries of South and West Asia and the Occident, where greater cultural diversity made verbal skills more necessary and therefore more highly prized. To Americans the Japanese style of negotiation can be confusing and even maddening, just as our style can seem blunt and threatening to them. An American businessman may state his case clearly from the start and in maximal terms for bargaining purposes. The Japanese may be appalled at this as an opening gambit, wondering what more the American may really have in mind. And the American in turn may feel that the cautious indirection of the Japanese is not only unrevealing but smacks of deceit.

To avoid confrontations and maintain group solidarity, the Japanese make wide use of go-betweens. In delicate transactions a neutral person scouts out the views of the two sides and finds ways around obstacles or else terminates the negotiations without the danger of an open confrontation or loss of face on either side. The go-between is particularly employed in arranging marriages, thus obviating the hurt to pride and feelings that so commonly occur in mating procedures elsewhere.

The group skills and virtues that the Japanese have developed contribute to a personality type that is at least superficially smooth, affable, and mild. Westerners seem to them by contrast a little rough, unpredictable, and immature in their ready display of emotions. In the West unpredictability in a person may be seen as amusing or spirited, but to the Japanese it is a particularly reprehensible trait. Their society does indeed run in more clearly fixed channels and is relatively placid and tranquil, at least on the surface. Outside labor and political demonstrations, voices are rarely raised, except in convivial group activities. There is little of the scolding mother, loud-mouthed youth, or cursing fishwife that one finds elsewhere in the world. In fact, the Japanese have a strong aversion to most open displays of feelings, whether of anger or of love, though like most rules this has its exceptions in their toleration of maudlin drunkenness and their unabashed sentimentality. The desire to hide their emotions may be the origin of the ubiquitous Japanese smile, in sorrow and embarrassment as well as in pleasure, and the reluctance ever to say a flat no. In public, physical demonstrations of affection, except toward small children, are avoided, and kissing, which traditionally is associated with the sexual act, is little seen or even practiced except in this restricted context. In a country in which a mother would not even kiss her grown daughter, the ritualized and sometimes indiscriminate embracing and kissing of the West and the Middle East seem strange indeed.

Whether all these characteristics are really the result of their group orientation is hard to say. Perhaps they, as well as the emphasis on the group itself, may more basically be the product of a dense population living in little space over a long period of time. In particular, it may be the outgrowth of cramped and relatively flimsy living quarters which require great personal restraint and consideration for others if living conditions are to remain tolerable. Under these conditions, the development of skills in cooperation and in avoiding confrontations was virtually necessary, as was also the toning down of individual whims and idiosyncrasies. But whatever the origins, there can be no doubt that Japanese are more group oriented than are most Westerners and have developed great skills in cooperative group living.

Relativism

14

I N A SOCIETY that sees itself as made up of independent and equal individuals, any organizing principles must almost perforce be universalistic, applying to all individuals equally. Right and wrong, whether in ethics or law, must be clear and invariable, regardless of one's personal status. This is indeed the way the West sees itself, harking back for justification to the Christian emphasis on the individual soul, though for long periods, as under feudalism, universalism was honored more in the breech. In a society in which people see themselves primarily as members of groups, specific intragroup and also intergroup relationships may reasonably take precedence over universal principles. In other words, ethics may be more relativistic or situational than universal.

The dichotomy on this score between Japan and the West, however, cannot be sharply drawn. In Japan, Buddhism, the most important religion historically, like Christianity in the West, emphasized the salvation of the individual soul. In modern times, moreover, there has been growing emphasis on the individual and his rights and an increasing tendency to see things in universalistic terms, as in the West. Still, there undoubtedly remains a deep underlying difference with the West in the greater emphasis on particularistic relations and relativistic judgments. Not only did the whole social organization of feudal times lean heavily in that direction right up into the nineteenth century, but so also did the influence of Chinese thought.

The Chinese clearly recognized universal principles, but tempered them by strong particularistic considerations. The five basic Chinese rela-

138

tionships were all specific ones and not applicable universally. They were those between ruler and subject, father and son, husband and wife, elder brother and younger brother, and friend and friend. Among the virtues most emphasized were filial piety, loyalty, and love, or human-heartedness, but to the Chinese this love was not to be applied uniformly to strangers as well as relatives but was carefully graded according to the nature of the specific relationship. There was no thought of loving one's neighbor as oneself. It would be grossly immoral to treat a stranger as one would a relative. Ethics was a harmonious part of the cosmos, but the centerpiece of that cosmos was human society itself, with all its many specific relationships. There was no sharply drawn line between individual men and a wholly different, all-powerful God, applying clear and inflexible laws to all men alike.

It is interesting that both the East Asians and Westerners saw the world in terms of a basic duality, but there was a significant difference. In the West the division was between good and evil, always in mortal combat with each other. In East Asia the division of *yang* and *yin* was between day and night, male and female, lightness and darkness, that is, between complementary forces which alternate with and balance each other. There was no strict good-bad dichotomy but rather a sense of harmony and a balance of forces.

Much of the flavor of these Chinese attitudes as well as of the particularism of Japanese feudalism lingers on in contemporary Japan, though it is important to remember that it is just a lingering flavor rather than a well-organized system of ideas contrasting to Western norms of rigid law codes and universalistic ethical principles. Most Japanese have pretty clear concepts of right and wrong basically defined in universal terms. Their law codes are as universalistic as our own. In 1973 the courts overturned the concept of heavier punishments for patricide than for other forms of murder—an old concept in keeping with ideas of the importance of filial piety—as being discriminatory between individuals. The Japanese revere the individual rights defined in their present constitution as if they were the Ten Commandments. But still, the whole tone and feel of the way society operates in Japan is often quite different from ours.

Some observers have characterized Japan as having a shame culture rather than a guilt culture like that of the West, that is, shame before the judgment of society is a stronger conditioning force than guilt over sin in the eyes of God. There is considerable validity to this concept, though it should not be pushed too far. Shame and guilt easily blend in the feelings of the average person. For example, all too many Westerners are worried more about being found out by neighbors or the law rather than by a sinful act itself. Or again, a Japanese, fearing shame in the judgment of his family or society, may develop a guilt complex over his failure to live up to expectations. The end effect of shame and guilt may not be very different. Still, there can be no doubt that the Japanese on the whole do think less in terms of abstract ethical principles than do Westerners and more in terms of concrete situations and complex human feelings. To the Westerner the Japanese may seem weak or even lacking in principles; to the Japanese the Westerner may seem harsh and self-righteous in his judgments and lacking in human feelings.

THIS difference between Japanese and Westerners is probably not the result of formal education, which in Japan is about as didactic about good and bad or right and wrong as in the West. It probably stems more from child rearing techniques. We have seen that structurally the Japanese family is much like the American, but the inner relationships are often quite different. During World War II there was a rash of speculation by Western psychologists that harsh toilet training practices produced the Japanese personality as it was perceived at that time. Unfortunately for these theories, they contradicted the facts of toilet training and had only an extremely biased view of Japanese personality. But other aspects of child rearing do seem to be significant.

The Japanese infant and small child is treated quite permissively, is in almost constant contact with his mother, and is practically never left alone. This contrasts sharply with the American tendency to put children on strict sleeping and eating regimes, to have them sleep alone from the start, to separate them in their own rooms, to hand them over on occasion to the care of unknown baby sitters, and to have more verbal interplay with them than body contact. The Japanese child is nursed for a relatively long period, is fed more at will, is constantly fondled by its mother, in more traditional society is carried around on her back when she goes out, and sleeps with its parents until quite large. Even after that, Japanese tend to sleep in groups rather than singly in individual rooms. Instruction is not by generalized verbal rules reenforced by punishment so much as by intimate contact and patient example. In short, the Japanese child is babied rather than treated as a small, incipient adult. The result, not surprisingly, is a degree of dependence, especially on the mother, that would be unusual in the West.

Out of this situation emerges a child and then an adult who is accustomed to bask in the affections of others. This attitude is defined in Japanese as *amae*, the noun form of the verb *amaeru*, which is cognate with the word for "sweet" and means "to look to others for affection." It is an attitude that begins with physical and psychic dependence for gratification on the mother and grows into psychic dependence for gratification by being enveloped in the warmth of the group and receiving its approval. The child develops an expectation of understanding indulgence from the mother but also an acceptance of her authority, and in time this attitude becomes expanded into an acceptance of the authority of the surrounding social milieu and a need for and dependence on this broader social approval. In this way, the Japanese child moves with surprising ease from the permissiveness of his earlier years to the acceptance of strict parental and school authority in later years and then to acquiescence to the judgments of the groups to which he belongs or of society as a whole. Parental disapproval, backed up by admonitions that "people will laugh at you," comes to have devastating force with the child, and later the sanction of the group has the same effect. In the traditional village, ostracism (*mura hachibu*) was the extreme punishment, and in ancient times exile from the court to a distant island or province was the most feared penalty.

Amae blends easily with the concept of *on* derived from Chinese philosophy and Japanese feudal society. *On* actually means the benevolence or favor of the ruler, feudal lord, or parent but has been turned around in most usage to signify the unlimited debt of gratitude or obligation of the recipient to the bestower of this grace. As such it has been much emphasized in formal expositions of traditional Japanese ethics. Both *on* in premodern times and *amae* today underlie the Japanese emphasis on the group over the individual as well as the acceptance of constituted authority and the stress on particularistic rather than universal relationships.

THE GENERAL relativism of Japanese attitudes shows up in a number of ways in modern Japanese society. Despite the didacticism of their education, the Japanese certainly have less of a sense of sin than Westerners or of a clear and inflexible line of demarcation between right and wrong.

There are no obviously sinful areas of life. Most things seem permissible in themselves, so long as they do not do some damage in other ways. Moderation is the key concept, not prohibition. There is no list of "Thou shall nots." Homosexuality has always been accepted and was quite openly acknowledged among feudal warriors and Buddhist monks in medieval times. The Japanese, despite their tendency to be hypochondriac and much interested in psychological and psychiatric problems, have not found Freudian psychoanalysis, with its strong orientation to sex and sin, of much relevance.

Except for a small number of Christians, whose attitudes derive from late nineteenth century Protestant missionaries, there is no objection to drinking or even drunkenness, so long as they do not get out of hand. With such relaxed attitudes, Japanese easily and happily get drunk on very small quantities of liquor. Liquor shows almost at once in their flushed faces for physical reasons—reportedly the lack of an enzyme and possibly also the low fat content of their diet—but more important is the fact that they readily accept inebriation. Drunks are forgiven almost anything, except drunken driving, and significantly alcoholism has never been a serious problem in Japan.

Contemporary politics in Japan may be couched in harsh, absolute terms, but people on the whole remain both relativistic and lenient in their judgments. Where Westerners may feel unmitigated indignation, contempt, or condemnation, Japanese are more likely to emphasize extenuating circumstances and the pitifulness of the miscreant. Young officers who murdered political leaders in the early 1930s and student radicals who wrecked their universities in the 1960s were both forgiven by much of the public because of their youth and the "purity" of their motives. Laws in Japan have always been relatively lenient for the time and the social system. For a long period before the coming of feudalism, there was no capital punishment—a truly remarkable situation for that day and age. Today great efforts are made to solve disagreements by compromise or conciliation in terms that have something for both sides, rather than by a black and white legal decision in favor of one party. In legal sentencings, the post-crime attitude of the culprit, that is, his degree of penitence, is considered as important as his pre-crime motives and, if felt to be sincere, will lead to judicial leniency.

The emphasis on particularistic relations rather than universal principles naturally leads to a great number of specific rules of conduct rather than a few clear ethical signposts. Ethics blends off into politeness and good manners. There is little esteem for "diamonds in the rough." Instead the good man shows his worth by the shine of each facet of his many relationships, each specific to the situation. There are thousands of rules, all to be meticulously observed. Japanese are the most punctilious people in the world, even if not necessarily the most polite.

The multiplicity and complexity of the rules of conduct were much greater in premodern times. Relations between the various classes and their subgroups were carefully prescribed and scrupulously observed. In today's mass society, the rules have been considerably simplified and generalized. Still, to the Westerner, the Japanese seem extraordinarily formal in all but their most intimate relations. A decorum is observed even between members of the same family that would seem stiff to Americans. The lengthy bowing, all carefully graded as to depth of bows and duration of the exchange according to the relative status and the relationship of the participants, is the most obvious and, to Westerners, the most amusing outward expression of this Japanese politesse. Gift giving on a great variety of occasions, such as formal calls, major events in one's life, New Year's, and midsummer, has been elaborated into a very complex and extremely onerous art of reciprocity. The Japanese language has endless gradations of politeness, and these are carefully used to fit each occasion. Humble forms are reserved for oneself and what belongs to one and increasingly polite forms are used for persons of higher status and of greater remoteness from oneself. Older Japanese, however, continually complain that young persons are losing these skills.

One result of the emphasis on detailed codes of conduct is a tendency toward self-consciousness on the part of the Japanese—a worry that they may not be doing the right thing and thus are opening themselves to criticism or ridicule by others. This is particularly marked in their relations with foreigners, whose mores are not fully known, but it also exists in dealings between Japanese. Each Japanese seems to be constantly worrying about what the other person thinks of him. He tends to be painfully shy in many of his personal relations and bound down by what the Japanese call *enryo*, which means "reserve" or "constraint." One of the commonest polite phrases is "please do not have *enryo*," but it seems to have little effect. This self-consciousness, of course, makes Japanese often ill at ease with others and may help account for the tendency of young girls to giggle and simper and men to suck in air while speaking, producing a sound foreigners sometimes describe as hissing. Many Japanese—at least those of the older generation—seem to be at ease only in their most habitual contacts. This makes the familiar group all the more dear to them.

For these various reasons, Japanese do not develop new associations lightly. It may be easier for two people to continue to pass as strangers than to take on the burdens of a recognized relationship. Japanese on the whole are less inclined than Westerners to enter into casual contacts and are likely to seem forbiddingly formal in any new encounter. Pauses in conversation can be agonizingly long, at least to the Western participant. The Japanese, with their low estimate of the value of verbal communication, seem almost oblivious to them. Friends are less easily made, but once made may be held on to with a strength that the more socially casual Westerner finds puzzling. Japanese are inclined to stick to already established group contacts and to put all other persons into a well-defined category of "others." This clearly reduces both public-spiritedness and casual involvement in the problems of other people. These are tendencies that are growing in the urban West as well, but they seem much stronger in Japan.

One result of an ethical system oriented more to specific relationships than to abstract principles is that in an unfamiliar situation it gives less clear guidance. When confronted by the unfamiliar, a Japanese is more likely to feel unsure of himself than a person who is smugly confident of the universality of his own principles. This is particularly true of a Japanese abroad, but even within Japan itself there are areas where the traditional relativistic ethics do not seem to have been successfully applied to modern conditions. For example, the commuting stampede on and off trains turns the mild, polite Japanese into wild scramblers and shovers.

In wartime the soldiers of any nation may find difficulty in applying their peacetime ethics to the new situation and are likely to act abroad in ways that would not be condoned at home, but the problem seems to be especially difficult for the Japanese with their particularistic emphasis. Certainly there seems to have been an especially wide gap between the brutalities of the Japanese army in World War II and the gentleness and orderliness of life in Japan. Of course, in the treatment of prisoners another factor entered in. The Japanese soldiers had been deeply indoctrinated to believe that surrender was the ultimate disgrace which they must never suffer, and their contempt for prisoners and harsh treatment of them was no worse than what they would have expected themselves. A better example of loss of ethical bearings under strange circumstances may be the massacring of many Koreans by rampaging crowds at the time of the great Tokyo earthquake of 1923, merely on the basis of wild rumors. A loss of ethical bearings of this sort may be a more likely possibility among Japanese than among some Western peoples. On the other hand, carefully reasoned atrocities, like the extermination of millions of Jews by the more principle-oriented Germans, would seem less of a possibility than in the West. But this dichotomy should not be too sharply drawn. Seventeenth century Japanese coldly exterminated the Christians of Japan, and Americans have had their My Lai massacres.

Individuality

15

ONE SHOULD not overstress the group orientation and relativistic ethics of the Japanese. To do so would be to suggest that they are a nation of pliant, apathetic robots, meekly conforming to one another and endlessly repeating the approved patterns of society. All Japanese history contradicts this picture. The Japanese have shown themselves to be extremely dynamic and capable of rapid and purposeful change. Their art reveals them to be both very sensitive and creative. Their literature shows them as painfully self-conscious individuals. There clearly is another side to the picture. Although the Japanese subordinates his individualism to the group more than the Westerner does, or at least thinks he does, he retains at the same time a very strong self-identity in other ways. He is insistent on emotional self-expression, even if he limits this to more channeled ways than does the Westerner. Most important, he appears to develop at least as much drive and ambition.

The clash between individual self-expression and social conformity naturally exists in Japan as elsewhere in the world. In fact, the stronger demands in Japan for conformity make the social patterns weigh all the more heavily, producing greater extremes of social revolt when it does erupt. It takes more daring and determination to be a social rebel in Japan than in a society of looser weave, and the result thus is likely to be more violent, as in the political assassinations of the 1930s, the explosiveness of the student movement in the late 1960s, and the atrocities of the Red Army (*Sekigun*) and other small terrorist bands of young people since then—though it should be noted that even the rebel against society is usually a member of his own closely knit, little group and not a lone operator or individual eccentric.

Below the level of open revolt, there is a general restiveness, especially among youth—a search to break out of the rigid molds and escape the smothering presence of social constraints. Young Japanese often feel they must get out of Japan at least once in their lives to savor the supposed fresher atmosphere of the outside world. They freely express resentment at the limitations on their lives imposed by a tightly organized educational and employment system. If fact, they rank highest among young people in the industrialized nations in their avowed dissatisfaction with the way society works. They passionately desire to own their own homes, which is by no means easy because of high land values, and many seek a meaningful private life, free of group pressures. All this has been dubbed "my-home-ism" (*mai-homu-shugi*) and is sometimes criticized by older Japanese as a neglect of higher responsibilities.

Such signs of restiveness are not new. They go back at least to the early 1920s, and over time this constant straining at the established order has indeed brought much change. Younger people, generation after generation, but especially after World War II, often seem to their elders to have lost all moral fiber and become ethically loose and wildly eccentric. One cannot tell how far this drift from older Japanese norms toward individual self-expression will go.

Still, to the outside observer, older attitudes and ways appear to remain strong. The American picture of the college radical becoming in time the grey-flanneled corporation executive is even truer of Japan, though there the costume might more properly be described as the dark blue suit. Even the word "individualism" (*kojin-shugi*) is still an ambivalent word in Japan, as it has been ever since the first contacts with the West, suggesting as it does to the Japanese selfishness rather than personal responsibility. Recent college students, in groping for the concept of individual self-expression, often bypassed "individualism" in favor of the word "subjectivity" (*shutaisei*), in the sense of one being the active subject rather than the passive object in one's life.

DESPITE much restiveness and some open rebellion, the traditional stress on conformity does retain much of its validity in Japan. Within this cake of custom, however, the Japanese is no human ant. He has learned to cultivate his own individuality, but in ways that are socially acceptable. One such way is through a personal approach to nature, which affords many Japanese a sort of refuge from the omnipresence of a restrictive society and a sense of personal fulfillment through identification with the beauties and processes of nature. Nature plays the same role for many people in the West, but the great Japanese love of nature and sense of closeness to it makes this all the more important to them.

The press of population and rampant economic growth in recent years have made the Japanese among the worst despoilers of nature, but at the same time they retain a passion for it, even though often this can be expressed only through miniaturized versions of nature. They love outings and hiking in nature, but few can have extensive gardens or wild acres of their own. Instead they cultivate tiny landscape gardens, designed to represent in miniature the grandeur of nature as a whole. They love to paint vignettes of nature and dote on dwarf potted trees (*bonsai*). Some women cultivate the minor arts of tray landscapes made of colored clay (*bonkei*) or sand (*bonseki*), and many more are devoted to the art of flower arranging (*ikebana*), in which a few carefully shaped and placed flowers and sprigs are used, instead of the massed bunches of flowers popular in the West. Some aspects of this cult of the little, such as landscape gardening and flower arrangement, have had a great impact on the West in recent years.

The whole field of literature also provides a broad area for self-expression, or at least for vicarious participation in the individualistic self-expression of others. From the time of its strong resurgence around the turn of the century, Japanese literature has been characterized by the search for self-identity. Much of this has been with regard to the survival of a Japanese identity in the tidal wave of Western cultural influences, but another aspect of this search has been for a personal identity within a cloyingly compact society. The Japanese writer has particularly favored what the Japanese call the "I novel"—the introspective, almost embarrassingly frank examination of the writer's personal feelings in a basically hostile environment. Such works usually look at Japanese society from so restricted and individualized an angle as to give only a very incomplete and distorted view of society itself, but they are revealing about the subtleties and vagaries of the individual human spirit, and that is what the Japanese reader is interested in. It is this same interest that probably accounts for the great popularity of pre-revolutionary Russian literature in

Japan. Japanese and Russian personalities and societies are very far apart, but the Russian portrayal of the clash of the individual spirit with an oppressive society and the search for self-expression obviously struck a deep chord in the Japanese soul.

Not many people can be successful authors, but millions of Japanese find self-expression in writing in one form or another. The penchant for keeping diaries is part of this, as well as the widespread efforts at poetry composition. Both the classical thirty-one-syllable *tanka* and the more modern seventeen-syllable haiku are very restricted poetic forms, even further limited by countless traditional poetic restraints, but nonetheless huge numbers of Japanese find satisfying self-expression through them. Poetry magazines and study groups abound, and there is an annual national *tanka* contest on a set theme, with the winning poems read in the presence of the emperor, who himself contributes a poem.

Millions of Japanese also find self-expression through the various art forms and music and dancing. The various types of dance associated with the premodern theater and with geisha, the traditional female entertainers, are the focus for numerous well-organized schools of instruction, each with its ardent group of devotees. The same is true of all types of traditional music, and the numbers of people who acquire skills in the various instruments and forms of Western music are far greater. The Suzuki technique of starting young violinists at the age of two or three, often in large groups, is world famous. All the traditional forms of painting and pottery making have their proliferating schools, as do also the various Western art forms and the traditional arts of tea ceremony, flower arrangement, and the like. Judo, karate, and the other martial arts fit in as part of this tradition of the cultivation of individual skills.

Each of these schools of instruction, in the Japanese style, forms a sort of in-group for those who participate in it, but the important point in the present context is that most Japanese do have their own personal literary, artistic, or performing skill, and this is not only a means of emotional self-expression but a treasured element of self-identity. Only in recent years has the United States begun to see anything like this sort of huge popular artistic endeavor that Japan has had for long, and here too it may in part be the product of the need for self-expression and self-identification in a crowded, constraining social environment.

We tend to dismiss such activities rather lightly as hobbies, but the Japanese value them as *shumi*, or "tastes," which help establish their identity

and commonly become of increasing importance to them as they grow
old. The individual Japanese takes pleasure in displaying at parties his particular skill—say chanting in the Noh manner. In fact at such parties,
each Japanese may perform in turn, while the foreign participant, in embarrassment over the lack of any appropriate ability, settles for trying to
sing his half-forgotten college song. The ardent pursuit of a hobby is almost necessary for self-respect in Japan. I know that on many occasions
when I have lamely had to explain to interviewers that I lacked hobbies,
since my work was also my hobby, I felt that I was making a damaging admission of spiritual incompleteness.

The Japanese cherishes and flaunts his hobby, even if it may be only
the traditional one a person in his position is expected to have. The big
businessman feels that, as a big businessman, he must make a fetish of his
interest in golf and prattle endlessly about handicaps. A more sporting
type may perform feats of incredible endurance to cram eight hours on a
distant ski slope into a day and a half weekend. All this is somewhat familiar in American life too, and possibly for some of the same reasons, but
still, personal skills and hobbies are probably a bigger aspect of self-
identity in Japan than in the United States.

A LOOK at the ways Japanese develop personal skills also reveals how the
Japanese nurture their individuality. The traditional skills in particular are
learned not so much by analysis and verbal explanation as by personal
transmission from master to disciple through example and imitation. The
teacher-disciple bond is a very important one, and this fits in with the
whole group orientation of the Japanese, but of equal importance is the
fact that learning is more an intuitive than a rational process. The individual is supposed to learn to merge with the skill until his mastery of it has
become effortless. He does not establish intellectual control over it so
much as spiritual oneness with it. We are reminded of the original Buddhist concept of losing one's identity by merging with the cosmos through·

enlightenment. But the significant point is that acquiring a skill is essentially an act of will—of self-control and self-discipline. The teacher of archery emphasizes control over one's stomach—that is, the emotions—rather than sharpness of eye or deftness of hand. Mastery of a skill is seen as more a matter of developing one's inner self rather than one's outer muscle. Here is an important area of individual self-development that is not only socially approved but is very much encouraged.

When we look beyond these traditional arts to the art of living, we see that the same approach applies. The cooperative, relativistic, group-oriented Japanese is not thought of as just the bland product of a social conditioning that has worn off all individualistic corners, but rather as the product of firm inner self-control that has made him master of his less rational and more antisocial instincts. He is not a weak-willed yes-man but the possessor of great self-discipline. In contrast to normal Western perceptions, social conformity to the Japanese is no sign of weakness but rather the proud, tempered product of inner strength.

No people has been more concerned than the Japanese with self-discipline. Austere practices of mortification of the flesh, such as frigid baths in winter, were and sometimes still are performed not for the reasons of the Western or Indian mystic but to develop will power. Since medieval times Zen meditation has been popular but often less for the original reason of achieving transcendental enlightenment than for the cultivation of self-discipline. It may well be that it is for this same reason that such practices have appealed to some Western youths, who are unconsciously groping for a new form of self-control.

The Japanese commonly make a fetish of self-discipline and the cultivation of will power. They regard these as essential for the proper performance of one's duties in life. They strive for inner calm and the selfless blending of right thought and right action into instantaneous and forceful performance. Their constant preachments shows clearly that they do not regard social conformity or the fulfillment of one's role in the world as coming naturally, but as being hard learned skills. In earlier days they talked about the heavy burdens incurred from the benevolence (on) of parents, rulers, and lords. Even today they are sharply aware of the need for great effort to live up to the rigid demands of society.

Many Japanese seem overburdened by the demands of duty—to family, to associates, and to society at large. This sense of duty, usually called gimu, is so onerous as to have produced the underlying restiveness among the young, but it is a clear continuity from premodern times, when the word used was *giri*. *Giri* incurred in a thousand ways could not be allowed to be submerged by the personal human feelings, known as *ninjo*, that come spontaneously and can lead to social turmoil and disaster. A favorite theme in traditional literature was of the conflict of *ninjo*, in the form of some illicit love, with the *giri* of family responsibilities and broader social duties—a conflict that was commonly resolved, at least in literature, by the suicide of the ill-starred lovers.

S O M E T H I N G should be said in passing about the role of suicide in Japan, simply because it looms large in the minds of Japanese and others as a very special characteristic of Japanese society. In its traditional form of *seppuku* it was very much part of the cult of self-discipline, and even today suicide is looked on as an acceptable or even honorable way out of a hopeless dilemma, though in actual society, as opposed to popular imagination, suicide is statistically no more prevalent than in the Occident. *Seppuku* remains a favorite theme in dramas and movies but has virtually disappeared from real life. Except for a rash of such suicides by prominent personages, mostly military, at the end of World War II—and these were perfectly understandable even from a Western point of view—the last notable case of genuine *seppuku* was that of the Russo-Japanese War hero, General Nogi, and his wife in 1912 to follow the Meiji Emperor in death. The spectacular *seppuku* of the great novelist Mishima in 1970 was more a matter of dramatic posturing than an act of duty or valid political protest, and it left the Japanese public, though thrilled by the drama, somewhat puzzled and contemptuous. Incidentally, the large number of prominent literary figures who have taken their own lives, though in more prosaic ways, is more a commentary on the introspective nature of modern Japanese literature than a sign of the prevalence of suicide in Japanese society.

Most suicides in contemporary Japan occur for reasons much like those in other countries and by similar means. As in some other East Asian countries, the rate for women is closer to that for men than it is in the West, perhaps reflecting greater social pressures on women in East Asia, and rates for youths from around 15 to 25 are much higher, probably reflecting the greater pressures of the educational system. What is more significant is that suicide rates in modern times have fluctuated widely with

political tensions and economic conditions and have of late tended downward, particularly for young people, until Japan's overall suicide rate is
now only a little above that of the United States and well below those of
several European countries. The Japanese, however, continue to be fascinated by suicides and to make a great deal of them in their news and literature, just as Americans are fascinated by murders.

TO RETURN to the theme of self-discipline and will power, it must be
admitted that insistent preaching does not necessarily produce prevailing
characteristics in a society. In fact, they sometimes seem almost like
mirror contrasts. But in the Japanese case there appears to be considerable correlation between the two. The Japanese on the whole do have a
pronounced toughness of character. An extreme example of this is the
persistence for a quarter of a century of a Lieutenant Onoda in his solitary
war with the United States on a jungle island in the Philippines. The Japanese high command in World War II assumed that greater will power on
the part of their people, which they took for granted, would provide the
margin of victory over a United States that all knew was vastly superior in
natural resources. The Japanese often seem convinced that any obstacle
can be overcome so long as one has enough will power and tries hard
enough. Older Japanese often feel that all these gutty characteristics are
breaking down in this more affluent and relaxed age, and this may be true
to some extent, but beneath their surface shyness and cooperativeness
the Japanese on the whole do continue to have a relatively high quotient
of firmness of character.

Many observers have noted that the emphasis on hard work, individual
drive, and economic achievement, pridefully described as the "Protestant
ethic" in the West, is even more characteristic of the Japanese, who have
no Christianity, let alone Protestantism, in their background. The work
ethic, as I have suggested, may be basically associated with climate, but it
has probably been strengthened rather than weakened by the group orientation of the Japanese. A good group cooperator is also a good worker,
and the camaraderie of group work can be a positive pleasure, even when
the artisan's pride in individual work has been replaced by more routine
machine production in modern times. Diligence (*kimbensei*) is generally
recognized by the Japanese themselves as one of their most outstanding
characteristics. Certainly the primary identification of the individual Jap-

anese with his work group and his enthusiastic, even joyous, participation in its activities are reasons why the Japanese work ethic even today seems little eroded, as compared to the situation in countries of the vaunted Protestant heritage.

A group society made up of self-disciplined, strong-willed individuals can produce sufficient tensions to explain all the drive and ambition the Japanese show. Beneath the surface of harmonious conformism have always seethed great pressures. The premodern Japanese was deeply concerned with honor and face—attitudes that still linger on in the Japanese consciousness. The watchword of the Meiji period, that age of transition between feudalism and modern times, was "success in life" (*shusse*), by which was meant ambitious personal success. William S. Clark, a president of the Massachusetts Agricultural College (later the University of Massachusetts), who was in Japan briefly in 1876 to set up an agricultural school (the future Hokkaido University), is still widely remembered for his parting injunction to his students: "Boys, be ambitious." The dependent child may be compulsively driven by his mother's expectations of him. One hears overtones of the traditional "Jewish mother" in her Japanese counterpart.

All in all, the modern Japanese seems as much motivated by personal ambition and drive as any Westerner. It may puzzle Westerners to find these characteristics in such a group-oriented people, but the Japanese in fact are often quite unrealistically ambitious. It is difficult to measure such traits, but the record of Japanese-Americans does afford some comparative data. Although handicapped by a very different cultural and linguistic background and subjected for long to severe prejudice and discrimination, Americans of Japanese ancestry have within two or three generations risen to levels of education, income, and status that are at or near the top of all ethnic groups, including WASPs and Jews. Surviving Japanese traits are all that can account for this record.

If there are parallels between Japanese characteristics and the Protestant ethic of the West, they may lie in the fact that the latter appeared in a West still divided from feudal times into classes or estates, in which merchants and peasants, denied the possibility of feudal political power, made economic achievement a goal in itself. This certainly happened in Tokugawa Japan, where merchants, completely barred from participation in politics, developed a philosophy justifying economic success as a service to society comparable to the political service of the samurai class.

Such attitudes probably help explain why former samurai in the Meiji period could easily shift to business enterprise as a legitimate and worthy field of endeavor. In countries like China and Korea, the lesser barriers between functional classes meant that economic success commonly led to an attempt to gain political status and was therefore never justified as an end in itself. If this analysis is correct, it would mean that the class divisions surviving from feudalism, rather than Protestantism itself, may be the determining factor behind this aspect of the Protestant ethic. But the main point I am trying to make is that the individual ambition and drive of the Japanese people, instead of being an anomaly in this group society, is an old and basic part of it.

Hierarchy

16

ONE OBVIOUS contrast between Japanese and American society, though by no means all of the West, is the much greater Japanese emphasis on hierarchy. Despite clear allocations of authority to individuals in the United States, often to a degree that seems almost dictatorial to Japanese, Americans have a strong sense of equality or at least a compulsion to feign equality—"Just call me Joe." Japanese consider differing ranks and status natural and inevitable. In fact, their interpersonal relations and the groups into which they divide are usually structured on the assumption that there will be hierarchical differences.

Some groups do consist of equals, as, for instance, men of the same age who form groups within a business or government bureau, or former school classmates among women. Most groups, however, are clearly made up of leaders and followers in the pattern of the traditional family, or *ie*. Even where there is no obvious ranking order, as there is between teacher and students or company president and common workers, a hierarchical structure is often achieved through the election of officers and the recognition of status by age and length of membership.

This emphasis on hierarchy undoubtedly derives in part from the long history of hereditary power and aristocratic rule in Japan. Class divisions, hereditary authority, and aristocratic privileges characterized all of Japan's premodern history. The imperial line is a good case in point. Clearly traceable back to the fifth century, it has always been the symbol of the unity of the nation and until quite recently the unique source, at least in theory, of all legitimate authority. When in the seventh and eighth centuries the Japanese borrowed the Chinese system of bureaucratic administration, they could not accept the Chinese method of choosing bureaucrats on the basis of their merit as determined by education but slipped back to the native concept that all ranks and positions should be determined by birth. Subsequently, the whole feudal system depended from start to finish on inherited authority. By Tokugawa times, a very sharp line had developed between the samurai class and all others, and the samurai were divided into dozens of hereditary ranks, which largely determined the level of the jobs for which each person qualified. A small degree of flexibility remained among the samurai, because an excess of candidates for all the higher posts allowed some choice according to merit among those who were eligible for a post by heredity, and in time a system developed permitting supplementary salaries and even permanent promotions for particularly talented individuals who were needed for more important jobs than they qualified for by birth. But by and large the two and a half centuries of Tokugawa rule witnessed one of the most restrictive and carefully enforced hereditary systems that the world has ever seen.

Even the arts during feudal times fell into the hereditary pattern. All artistic skills came to be regarded as secret family possessions to be passed down from father to son. Schools of painting and of theatrical performance were organized on this hereditary principle, though the almost filial teacher-disciple relationship and the lenient system of adoption actually meant that artistic skills were more often passed on through talented adopted disciples. Curiously it is this aspect of traditional hereditary authority that persists perhaps most strongly in contemporary Japan. Schools of tea ceremony or flower arrangement, for instance, may be tightly organized on a family pattern, and the supreme authority in them may still be transmitted by inheritance.

With this strong and recent background of class distinctions and hereditary authority, one might suppose that Japan still has sharp class divisions. The continuing emphasis on hierarchy, in fact, is often interpreted by foreigners as part of a class system. But this notion is quite wrong. Hierarchy is taken for granted. Status is vastly important. But a sense of class and actual class difference are both extremely weak. In most essential ways, Japan today has a very egalitarian society—as egalitarian in many respects as that of the United States and considerably more so than the societies of most Western European countries.

By the late Tokugawa period considerable restiveness against the rigidities of the hereditary system had developed, but nonetheless the sharp break with this pattern in the Meiji period was an amazing achievement. Legal distinctions within the samurai class and between it and the other classes were wiped out within a few years, and the category of samurai in census records became a grouping of only historical significance. The samurai who lived through the great change of the nineteenth century often remained distinct from other Japanese in their attitudes and pride, and the elite in Japanese society continued to be drawn heavily from the 6 percent of the population that had constituted the samurai class. It has been estimated that half the elite were of samurai origin as late as the 1930s and around a fifth even at the end of the 1960s. But the great majority of the samurai in the Meiji period were unable to make a successful economic transition and sank into the commonality. The greater rapidity with which they disappeared than did the feudal classes in the West may have been because the samurai had already lost their direct hold on agricultural land in the late sixteenth and early seventeenth centuries. Unlike the West, there was no survival of feudal estates into modern times, and the peasantry from the early 1870s on became the complete and undisputed owners of the soil.

With each succeeding generation the distinction between samurai and commoners became less meaningful. Eventually the samurai category was dropped entirely, and the difference between samurai and nonsamurai origins became largely irrelevant to the average Japanese. Some families may on occasion make reference to their distinguished antecedents but much less than do the supposed descendants of Mayflower passengers or plantation owners in the antebellum South. Young Japanese seem no more interested in such matters than young Englishmen in the proportions of Celtic, Saxon, Danish, or Norman blood in their veins.

The one class distinction that was maintained in the modern period was that between the nobility and commoners. The old Kyoto court aristocracy, the feudal lords of Tokugawa times, and some of the new leaders were constituted into a modernized nobility in 1884 in order to staff the House of Peers of the new Diet. For sixty years a great deal was made of this nobility, but the all-out war effort forced it to adopt more egalitarian ways, and at the end of the war, when the American authorities decreed its abolition, it disappeared almost without a ripple. Even the various branches of the imperial family became commoners. Older people, especially those with a historical cast of mind, may still pay attention to aristocratic pedigrees, and there have been cases of a descendent of a feudal lord finding his name an important electoral asset in the home prefecture where his ancestors once ruled. But today all the old nobility, unlike that of France and other European countries, is known simply as Mr. and Mrs.—except among some of the foreign embassies, including for a while even the American. The bulk of the Japanese could not be less interested in the former nobility and simply ignore it in a completely un-self-conscious way.

Class distinctions can exist even in the absence of a nobility and legal class lines. But consciousness of any sort of class distinction is relatively weak in Japan. Actually the type of group identification the Japanese emphasize works against class feeling. The Japanese group, unlike the Indian caste, is normally not made up of people of the same status and function, but of people of different function and status. The two major exceptions to this rule, as noted earlier, are the *eta* or *burakumin* and possibly the recent Korean immigrants, but these account for only a tiny part of the population. Otherwise, group associations, by emphasizing discrete hierarchical relationships and reducing lateral contacts with groups of similar function and status, play down class feelings as these are known in the West.

The Japanese do not tend to identify themselves in class terms, and when asked to do so, some 90 percent opt vaguely for the middle class. One effort to divide the Japanese by class suggests 3 percent as upper class, 69 percent as middle class, and only 28 percent as unskilled or semi-skilled lower class workers. The lack of class feeling in a sense mirrors reality. The spread of incomes in Japan is roughly similar to that of the United States in the middle brackets but differs markedly from it at the two ends, since there is much less great wealth at the upper end of the scale and much less of a clearly "underprivileged" group at the other. A recent study ranks Japan with Sweden and Australia as the three industrialized democracies with the least spread in income between the rich and the poor.

The war and the American reforms wiped out most wealth, and the top management of Japanese big business is on the whole more moderately paid and participates less in the ownership of the company's stock than is the case with comparable groups in the United States. Windfall profits, particularly those resulting from a fabulous rise in real estate values, have created some new fortunes, but progressive income taxes and extremely stiff inheritance taxes make the accumulation and transmission of wealth far more limited than in the past. At the other end of the scale, great cultural homogeneity and a relatively small and uniform geographic environment have meant that there are no large ethnic or regional groups of "underprivileged" persons, as in the United States. The *burakumin* and the Koreans offer some problems, and there are a few other people who do not make the grade and become skid-row derelicts or drift into crime. The relative smallness of these problems, however, is revealed by the statistic that in 1968 only 1.43 percent of the population was classified as needy and a large proportion of these needy persons were widows and their children who had lost their chief economic support but were by no means destined to remain underprivileged.

Another sign of the relative classlessness of the Japanese is the lack of class differences in speech. Regional differences can be detected, particularly among the less educated, and there are obvious differences in the quality of a person's vocabulary depending on his degree of education, but there are no class accents, such as are so pronounced in the United Kingdom and are discernible even in parts of the United States.

Starting in 1868 far behind the British in terms of strong class lines and hereditary authority, the Japanese have swept well past them within a century. It is indeed an amazing achievement. While part of it may be attributed to the special characteristics of group affiliation in Japanese society, the greater part can only be explained as a conscious product of education. The Japanese adopted the Western concept of universal education, open at least in theory to everyone on an equal basis and used this system to sort people out for their respective roles in society. The result has been steadily growing social mobility ever since the Meiji Restoration, until Japan today has at least as high a degree of social mobility as the United States or any country of Western Europe. We shall look at the role of education in more detail in a later section, but here we need only note that the shift from a hereditary to an educational system for determining hierarchical status is now virtually complete. The Japanese achieve their various functions in society and find their respective status levels, not chiefly through inheritance or class and family considerations, but through formal educational achievements, followed by rigorously equal qualifying examinations for most of the positions of greatest prestige. There are some survivals of the older system in Japan, as there are almost anywhere in the world, even in most socialist countries. Children of well-educated parents, because of environment and family tradition, usually have advantages in the whole educational and examination process. Small family businesses as well as the family farm are commonly passed on by inheritance. Even a big business, if it was recently founded by some successful entrepreneur, may be handed on to a son. The great Matsushita firm, which produces under the Panasonic trade name for the American market (its regular "national" trade name would not be very appropriate) is a good case in point. The presidency of the firm was passed on to an adopted son-in-law, but judging from the experience of similar companies in the past, transmission by inheritance is not likely to go on for more than a single generation. Doctors' sons commonly take over their father's practice. Certain artistic activities still recognize hereditary principles, as do an occasional private school or "new religion." But that is about it. There being much less inherited wealth than in the United States, inheritance probably figures quite a bit less in Japanese society than in American and distinctly less than in some countries of Western Europe.

HIERARCHY, however, remains fundamental and all-pervasive throughout Japanese society, giving it its shape and character. Japan is divided up into numberless groups, each organized into multiple layers of status. This is what Miss Nakane means by a "vertical society," as opposed to the more horizontal structure of American society. This vertical, hierarchical arrangement is quite natural to many institutions, such as government bureaucracies and business firms, but it shows up in other groupings as well. Even the village (now "hamlet") organization, though a somewhat egalitarian grouping by households, had in earlier days a clear pecking order, from households which traditionally provided the head men down to tenant farmers. Many modern groupings, such as agricultural cooperatives or women's associations, which have, beneath the hierarchy of officers, an egalitarian mass membership, achieve a sort of hierarchical pattern through a strong sense of age distinctions.

In government bureaucracies as well as in big business firms, age groups reenforce the hierarchy of rank, since those who have entered together in any given year form a "class" that will stay in step with one another in both salary and rank through most of their careers. One may enter a business firm or government service at different levels leading to different careers, but each career consists of a sort of age escalator of pay and status on which everyone advances together. The factory worker, for example, is on a lower escalator of pay and status, while the executive has qualified by higher education and a competitive entrance examination for a higher escalator that may lead all the way to the boss's job, but within each category, status as well as pay is determined primarily by age and length of service.

It is as natural for a Japanese to shape his interpersonal relations in accordance with the various levels of hierarchy as for an American to attempt to equalize his interpersonal relations despite differences of age and status—in fact the Japanese approach may be considerably more natural. Older people or persons otherwise recognized as having higher status walk first. People are seated in clear order of precedence on any formal occasion. In a Japanese-type room the seat of honor is at the opposite end from the entrance and in front of the *tokonoma*, or alcove for art objects. As a result, entrance ways not infrequently get seriously jammed by people who, either in doubt or humility, insist on sitting in the place of least honor. One addresses a person who is recognized as being of higher status with regard to wisdom by the title *sensei*, a general term for "teacher." Among men, intimates of the same or younger age will be addressed as *kun*, instead of *san* or very formally *sama*, which are used for everyone else, male or female, single or married, and are thus equivalent to Mr., Mrs., and Miss. (Incidentally, persons are almost never addressed by their first names, except for children, younger members of the family, and persons who have known each other intimately since childhood.)

Actually one of the commonest forms of interpersonal address is by specific status appelations. Within the family, these go beyond such terms as "daddy" and "grandma," familiar to Americans, to include such categories as "elder sister" or "younger brother." In addition, any intimate older person may be addressed as "uncle" or "auntie," or if the age is appropriate, "grandpa" or "grandma." But what is much more significant is the prevailing use in direct address of such terms as *okusan* or *okusama* (lady of the household), *kocho-sensei* (teacher-principal), *Kyokucho-san* (Mr. Bureau Chief), and *Shacho-san* (Mr. Company President). The only equivalent American usages, aside from military ranks, are a few rarified terms such as "Mr. President" or "Mr. Ambassador," which most people never have the occasion to use.

Unlike the American propensity for the elderly person to try to act young or the company president to be one of the boys, the Japanese try to live up to their status. In earlier times, the concept of taking one's proper station in life had to do with unchanging hereditary status, but now it means to act one's age and one's position as one moves up in life. A good part of one's personal self-identification is by one's status role. Others will treat one according to one's status, and there is nothing less becoming than for the person himself not to act accordingly. The ignoring or breaking of the order of status on either side is felt to be extremely awkward. A foreigner's attempt to show equality across status lines, though forgiven as an outsider's ignorance, is embarrassing to Japanese.

The importance of hierarchy and status is one of the reasons for the constant exchanging between Japanese of *meishi*, which we call by the antiquated term of "calling cards." It is true that some Japanese names are extremely difficult to read in the Chinese characters with which they are always written, and a card with the name clearly printed, and possibly with a phonetic gloss to help the reading, can be of help. Addresses and phone numbers, which are usually included on the card, may also be useful for later reference. But the main significance of the exchange of *meishi* is that they make clear a man's specific position and group affiliation—Managing Director of the Fuji Bank, Director of the Treaty Bureau of the Foreign Ministry, Professor of Economics at Tokyo University —and this then helps establish the nature of the relationship with the other person and the degree of politeness and deference to be shown.

The hierarchical arrangement of society has some of the lingering flavor of earlier days. Those in the top ranks of any hierarchy are expected to show a sort of benign paternalism to those further down on the scale, including a personal concern for their private lives that might in the West be considered an infringement of privacy. For example, bosses in government or business are commonly asked to serve as go-betweens in marriage arrangements. In return for this benevolence, those in inferior positions are expected to demonstrate respect and loyalty. There is an overtone here of the old concepts of *on* and *giri*.

The pattern of hierarchy within groups is paralleled by a hierarchy between groups. Japanese are prone to think in terms of rank order. Almost anyone has a pretty clear idea of the informal order of universities, with Tokyo University unquestionably at the top, Kyoto University next, and so on down to a broad base of undistinguished private universities and below them the junior colleges. Business firms are patterned the same way in peoples' minds, with great, prestigious firms at the top and small, weak ones at the bottom. To speak of a country as number one or as a third or fifth rate power is not just vaguely figurative, as in the American mind, but is a much more precise and meaningful statement to the Japanese.

STRONG hierarchy to a Westerner suggests firm, almost autocratic, authority, but this is not the situation in Japan. In fact, some of the emphasis on hierarchy is purely symbolic, as is most strikingly shown by the role of the emperor in the greatest Japanese hierarchy, the state. Another example is that, in organizing almost any activity, the Japanese put great store on honorary committees of big names that are used for prestige purposes. Below these top committees will be the real operating committees of junior and more active persons. This is a common enough pattern in the United States too, but it is even more pervasive in Japan. Another sign of the symbolism of hierarchies is that the person at the top of any organization, regardless of his actual function and authority, may feel such a sense of responsibility for all that transpires under his supposed jurisdiction that, in the event of any major untoward occurrence, he is likely to "accept responsibility" formally and resign from his post, even though in Western eyes there may have been not the slightest suggestion of his legal or moral culpability. In an earlier age, suicide might have been the expected act.

Even in the case of actual, not symbolic, leadership roles, the Japanese approach is quite different from the American. Leaders are not expected to be forceful and domineering, but sensitive to the feelings of others. Their qualities of leadership should be shown by the warmth of their personalities and the admiration and confidence they inspire, rather than by the sharpness of their views or the vigor of their decisions. What the American might consider as desirably strong leadership causes suspicion and resentment in Japan. Consensus through prolonged consultation is the norm. The purported boss more often seems to be just the chairman of the committee. Subordinates, who are lifetime members of the group and who in time will be carried to higher posts and status by the escalator of age, expect to be in on decisions and not just receive them as dictates from above. They expect to be treated as junior associates or even disciples rather than as mere underlings. I shall explore such matters further in connection with a consideration of Japanese business and the government bureaucracy, but here I need only emphasize what seems to Westerners to be the surprising contrast between the great emphasis on hierarchy in Japan and the relatively wide sharing of authority and decision-making powers.

One final point about Japanese hierarchy is that it breeds less of the tensions and resentments that are caused in the West by differences in status. This is not surprising for a number of reasons. Those higher on the career escalator are seen as merely older persons who got on the escalator earlier, not as persons who have scrambled unfairly to the top. One's own time will come in due course. Or if they are on a superior career escalator than one's own, this is because of their superior achievements in education and examinations. In a homogeneous society, differences in educational performance are more likely to be seen as the result of differences in personal ability, not of an unfair society. The lack of dictatorial authority on the part of the leaders and the wide consultations and sharing of decision-making powers tend to make a subordinate's position in Japan less irksome than in the West. The close solidarity of the group, the lingering sense of paternalistic concern on the part of those on top, and the personal loyalty on the part of those below give a feeling of warmth and intimacy across status lines. And finally the sense of belonging—of achieving a self-identity through membership in the group—makes the individual more willing to accept his status, whatever it may be. Not that restiveness against superiors does not exist. The young officer problem of the 1930s almost led to open revolt, and today there is much grumbling about old men blocking the way to promotions for their juniors. Still, the traditional sense of hierarchy of the Japanese has been fitted very smoothly into what is now a basically egalitarian society, and thus it remains a major and efficiently functioning feature of contemporary Japanese society.

Education

17

F ORMAL education and examinations have taken the place of class
and birth in determining which organizations and career patterns
one qualifies for—in other words, one's function and status in
Japan's modern meritocracy. High literacy rates and excellent educational standards are also major reasons for Japan's success in meeting the
challenge of a technologically more advanced West in the nineteenth
century and for its subsequent achievement of a position of economic
leadership. Nothing, in fact, is more central in Japanese society or more
basic to Japan's success than is its educational system.

The emphasis on education in Japan is natural, stemming from the
very sources of East Asian civilization. From the start the Chinese
stressed the importance of literacy and book learning, attributing the
authority of the rulers to their greater knowledge and consequent superior
moral insights. In time these concepts became institutionalized into an
elaborate system of selecting high government officials through a ponder-
ous process of scholastic examinations. The Koreans took over this
system whole, and the Japanese, though failing to fit it into their society,
imbibed the spirit of these Chinese ideas and by the late Tokugawa period
had actually developed literacy and educational institutions far beyond
the Chinese or Koreans. Much of Tokugawa education was conducted
through private tutoring, but by the middle of the nineteenth century
most of the feudal domains had official schools for their samurai youth;
there were well over a thousand private academies enrolling commonors
as well as samurai; and there were tens of thousands of village institutions,

known as *terakoya*, or "temple schools," because of their usual location in the local Buddhist temple, where the children of commoners, including some girls, could acquire the three Rs. As mentioned previously, about 45 percent of the male population was literate by the middle of the nineteenth century and perhaps 15 percent of the female—figures not far below those of the most advanced Western countries at that time.

Because of the traditional emphasis on formal learning, the leaders of the new Meiji government had no difficulty in comprehending the key role of education in acquiring the technology of the West and the necessity of a modern school system if Japan were to catch up to the leading Western powers. In 1871, only the fourth year of the new government's existence, it created an Education Ministry, which the next year adopted an ambitious plan for a highly centralized and uniform school system, based on the French model and leading to universal literacy. Making this plan a reality was no easy task, for the Japanese lacked sufficient teachers, school buildings, or funds. The plans changed repeatedly, and the realities developed slowly. But the important point is that this was an entirely fresh start in education. None of the domain schools and *terakoya* and hardly any of the private academies survived for long into the new age. Thus Meiji Japan, unlike the nineteenth century West, was not encumbered with the aristocratic or religious overtones of earlier education but was in a sense already out ahead of most of the West in the wholly secular and egalitarian nature of its educational system.

It was not until about 1907 that the Japanese managed to get virtually all their children into schools, which that same year were made mandatory and entirely free up through the six grades of coeducational primary education. Above the elementary schools a more elite system was forming: a five year middle school, separate for boys and girls and paralleled by lower technical schools, then a three year higher school for boys only, comparable to the German *Gymnasium* or the French *lycée* and again paralleled by higher technical schools, and finally on top of the higher schools a university of three or four year's duration, depending on the subject studied. The higher schools were purely preparatory to the universities, and it was in them, more than the universities, that the future leadership elite came to know one another and form bonds of close association.

The whole system was rigorously egalitarian, at least for men, opening up the track to the top to any young man who could complete the necessary preliminary schooling and pass the necessary entrance examinations. Thus it could serve as the chief selector of national leadership, as it already was doing by the early twentieth century. The system was also closely tailored to national needs as the leaders saw them. It created a literate mass of soldiers, workers, and housewives, ample middle-level technical skills—an aspect of education that many of today's modernizing countries have failed adequately to appreciate—and a thin stream of highly talented young men emerging from the universities to occupy the positions of leadership in government and society. The great bulk of education, including its whole central core, was in the hands of the government. Christian missionary schools and a few Buddhist or other private institutions did exist, especially at the middle school and upper technical school levels, and the Christian schools were important in women's education, but these other schools were merely peripheral to the government system.

At the top of the educational pyramid stood Tokyo University. It grew out of an amalgam of three shogunal schools inherited from the Tokugawa period—a Confucian academy (later dropped), a school of medicine, and a school of foreign learning—which after several reorganizations was named Tokyo University in 1877 and finally Tokyo Imperial University in 1886. Its graduates at first qualified without examination for high civil service posts, but in time the supply exceeded the demand, and graduates of Tokyo University, together with those of other universities, as these were founded, became subject to a uniform examination system for entrance into the high civil bureaucracy.

The government created new Imperial Universities one after the other—Kyoto in 1897, Tohoku (in Sendai) in 1907, Kyushu (in Fukuoka) in 1910, Hokkaido (in Sapporo) in 1918, and so on. In 1918 a number of private schools were also accorded university status, thus greatly expanding the number of university graduates. The oldest and most prestigious of the private schools were Keio and Waseda. Keio had grown out of an academy founded before the Meiji Restoration by Fukuzawa, the great popularizer of knowledge about the West, and Waseda was founded in 1882 by Okuma, who had been ousted from the ruling oligarchy the year before. There were also other large private universities, such as Meiji, Nihon, and Chuo, which had grown up around the turn of the century, primarily to teach modern law. All five of these private institutions and many others were located in Tokyo.

Following the war the Japanese educational system was restructured by the American occupation to conform to American concepts and to be less elitist and more fitted to the type of mass society Japan was developing. The structural changes may have been largely unnecessary and at first were very confusing, but they have stuck. In place of the prewar six-five-three-three system, as it is called—the numbers corresponding to the respective years of elementary, middle, and higher schools and then university—the American six-three-three-four system was adopted: six years of elementary, three of junior high school, three of senior high school, and four of university. Above the universities are graduate schools, while paralleling the universities are two- or three-year junior colleges. All institutions of higher learning are called universities (*daigaku*), not colleges. This is true even of junior colleges, which in Japanese are called short term universities (*tanki daigaku*).

Education was made compulsory and entirely free through the nine years leading to graduation from junior high school. It was also made co-educational throughout, and, instead of the sidetracks of the prewar system that led off into terminal technical schools, most education was placed on a single track, with each level leading to the next. The only exceptions, besides the junior colleges, are a few relatively small five-year technical schools started in 1962 at the senior high school and junior college level, and various types of peripheral specialty schools.

Within this structure, the Japanese have become one of the most highly educated nations in the world. All children go through junior high school, and the number of senior high school students has mounted rapidly until it is now around the 90 percent mark. More than a third of the age group continues on to higher education, which is somewhat less than the American rate of close to a half but appreciably ahead of the countries of Western Europe.

Education is not to be measured merely in terms of years. The intensity of the educational experience counts too, and here Japanese education on average rates well above the American, except at the university level. The school day is longer, the school week is five and a half days, and the school year is broken only by a short summer vacation of a little over a month in late July and August, a New Year's holiday, and a break before the start of the school year at the beginning of April. Discipline within schools is firm, and the children devote prodigious efforts to their studies. In addition, they are assigned daily homework from the first grade on. About a third of the age group is sent by its parents to kindergarten to get a running start at the educational process, and huge numbers of children at every level receive outside tutoring or attend private after-class academies for further drill and instruction. Japanese, in their keen desire to get the best possible education, classify schools in their own minds in accordance with the record of their graduates at subsequent levels of education, but Japanese schools actually achieve remarkably uniform levels of excellence, with few of the great discrepancies in quality that are common in the United States between city, rural, and suburban schools.

The net result of all this is that the Japanese are indeed a highly educated people. Despite lesser numbers and somewhat poorer quality at the university level than in the United States, the Japanese probably absorb more formal learning on average than the people of any other nation. General levels of educational achievement are usually not susceptible to measurement across language barriers, but where they are, as in the field of mathematics, the Japanese have tended to rank first in the world.

THERE is no mystery about the vast educational effort in Japan. It not only fits in with traditional concepts about the importance of formal education but is a natural product of the key role of education in determining function and status in society. In the looser American system, the self-educated man can more easily make his mark or the late bloomer can make a brilliant finish after a slow start. There is less room for such types in Japan's tighter society. There are, of course, many men who have made great careers in business on the basis of little or inferior educations, and Tanaka Kakuei, who was Prime Minister from 1972 to 1974, lacked any university education. But the great bulk of Japan's top leadership in every field consists of graduates of the most prestigious universities who qualified for these universities by high scores in their entrance examinations, which were in turn the result of academic excellence throughout their schooling.

The close link between academic achievement and success in life is taken for granted by everyone in Japan. Families undergo economic privations in order to have their children receive the advantage of kindergarten training or later tutoring. Despite household crowding, children are given adequate space for their school homework, and the mother rides herd on them to see that they perform it and live up to their other scholastic tasks. This special role of the mother is recognized by the common term *kyoiku mama*, or "education mom." It is sometimes thought that the drive for education has been a contributing factor to birth control in Japan, since people, especially in the cities, believe they should have few enough children to be able to afford higher educations for all of them.

The importance of preparing for entrance examinations helps account for the seriousness with which education is taken in Japan and for its high levels of excellence, but it is also responsible for some of its chief flaws. As the child approaches his crucial entrance examinations, the whole life of the family centers around facilitating his studies. These examinations are not only for entrance into university but before that often for entrance into a particularly distinguished high school, which is known for the good record of its graduates in university entrance examinations. The pressures on the examination taker are tremendous, and the whole process is commonly referred to as the "examination hell."

Once students have been accepted into a school, the Japanese are very skillful at avoiding overt competition between them and in downplaying differences in ability. In fact, almost no one is ever failed. But the ruthless, one-shot entrance examinations are competition at its worst and cast a shadow far in advance, subjecting the student to severe pressures through most of his schooling and even distorting the content of his education. Much of the training in senior high schools is devoted, not to learning as such, but to preparing students to pass university entrance examinations. In a field like the English language, for example, this means there is careful preparation for the sort of complex grammar questions that are asked on examinations, but less attention is paid to actually learning to read English and virtually none to speaking it or understanding it by ear. High school entrance examinations cast a similar though lighter shadow on instruction in junior high schools. The relatively high suicide rates for youth may be in part attributable to the "examination hell," and there can be no doubt that the restlessness and rebellion of university students, once they have achieved the safe haven of the university, come in part as a reaction to the pressures they have been under before then.

There are other problem areas in elementary and secondary education. The American occupation authorities felt that the prewar system had been too much one of rote memory work, producing indoctrinated followers rather than thinking citizens. It is hard to say how far their efforts at reform succeeded. Japanese education is a great deal more lively than it was before the war and calls for much more student initiative, but on the whole it would seem somewhat old-fashioned by most American standards—a statement which could be interpreted as either criticism or praise, depending on one's point of view. The extreme difficulty of the Japanese writing system and the vast amount of rote memory work it requires may inevitably tip Japanese education somewhat in that direction.

The control of public education has been a matter of hot political contention ever since the war. Mindful of the role of the prewar educational system in militaristic indoctrination, the American occupation insisted on the dispersal of educational controls to elected prefectural and municipal boards of education, somewhat in the American manner, but subsequently the Japanese in part recentralized the system under the Ministry of Education. Prefectural and municipal education boards remain, but they are appointed by governors and mayors, not elected, and, though they have the right to select the textbooks used and these are produced privately, all textbooks must first receive Ministry approval.

Most elementary and secondary teachers are members of the Japan Teachers Union (*Nikkyoso*), which ever since the war has been dominated either by Communists or other leftists, who have pitted the union in open battle against the Ministry of Education on the question of the control of education and on a number of other issues. This situation has dangerously politicized the school system, but it fortunately has had little effect on the quality of the teaching. While a hot debate rages within the union as to whether it is, as its leaders claim, just an ordinary labor union or its members are part of a "sacred profession," the truth of the matter is that the traditional special aura about learning and the teacher's role lingers on in Japan, and teachers remain for the most part proud and dedicated participants in this heritage. For all its problems, including even the baneful influence of the examination system, elementary and secondary education in Japan has high standards of morale and efficiency, which merit the envy of most other advanced nations.

HIGHER education is in greater trouble and probably fills less of a role in society than the turmoil over the entrance examinations would suggest. Actually the entrance examinations perform one of the university's most significant functions, for they, almost as much as a student's work while at the university, help sort Japanese out for their lifetime careers. The university years are usually not as important as they are for many American students. Because of the excellence of education up through senior high school, there is no need for the remedial work that occupies much of college education in the United States. Passing the entrance examinations usually means acceptance to a specific faculty—that is, branch of the university, such as law, economics, humanities, science, medicine, engineering, or agriculture. There is therefore no need or opportunity to experiment and shop around while at the university for a field of specialization. That has already been determined by the faculty into which the student has won admittance. Both big business and government recruit directly from among university graduates, giving the men they accept further in-service training, which takes the place of much of graduate study as it exists in the United States, or else they subsequently send selected persons in their employ abroad for further study or to graduate schools in Japan to acquire the master's or doctoral degree. For other students, graduate schools are largely limited to preparation for an academic career. The role of the university in research activities, once very important, is also shrinking in comparison with research conducted directly by business or government.

Recruitment into big business and government is normally by examination. What is learned in university is of course vital for the examinations, but at the same time it is clear that those persons who were best at taking the examinations for entrance into university at age eighteen, and thereby got into the most prestigious universities, again prove to be the best at age twenty-two or twenty-three when they take the examinations for business or government. The fact that the pyramid of relative university prestige is almost perfectly mirrored in the results of these professional examinations is probably to be attributed more to the native talent of the students of the prestigious universities than to the excellence of their instruction. A further factor is that many businesses only invite candidates from the more prestigious universities to take their examinations.

This situation makes the pressure to enter the best universities all the greater. Rejection or acceptance by a prestigious university is seen as determining one's whole life. Students who fail will commonly get off the educational track for a year to attend one of the many cram schools and try again the next year and possibly the next and the next. Such persons are facetiously called *ronin*, the term for a masterless samurai in feudal times. Some private universities have a system of accepting without examination students from their own affiliated private secondary schools, and there are cases of students buying their way into some private universities, but these routes available to wealth lead at best only to second or third rate institutions.

The pecking order of universities remains essentially what it was before the war. Tokyo University still ranks far at the top and after it the other former Imperial Universities (the term "Imperial" was dropped after the war) and a few specialized prewar national universities, such as Hitotsubashi for economics. Next come the two most prestigious private universities, Keio and Waseda, and the national universities that were founded in each prefecture after the war by combining former higher schools and higher technical schools and upgrading them. Next come the great mass of private universities, divided into several prestige levels, and at the bottom the junior colleges. The strict correlation between university affiliation and jobs and status in later life is gradually breaking down, but even today the great bulk of the higher bureaucracy comes from the most prestigious national universities, particularly Tokyo, while Keio is noted as a source of business executives, Waseda as a producer of politicians and journalists, and the less distinguished private universities pour out the masses of also-rans, who become the lesser businessmen and white collar workers.

Private universities, being supported mainly by tuition, must charge relatively high fees, while the national universities and the few prefectural and municipal ones, operating as they do on public funds, charge only nominal fees. This means that the best and most prestigious universities cost the least, while the poorest cost the most—a reversal of the traditional American pattern. The prestigious national universities as a result of this situation not only draw the best students but recruit them from all economic strata of society. The percentage from the top fifth economically is a surprisingly small 37 percent and that from the lowest fifth an amazingly high 10 percent, with an almost uniform 17 percent for the three middle fifths. Affluence is more highly represented in the less prestigious private schools.

Students who have won admittance to the prestige universities as well as those who have had to settle for lesser institutions often find university life disappointing, and many react to it with apathy or unrest. This is in part a psychological letdown after the years of preparation for the entrance examinations, but it is also a natural response to insufficient intellectual stimulation. One reason for this, particularly in national universities, is the rigidity of the Japanese university system and its strong resistance to changing needs. Another reason is the serious underfinancing of universities, particularly private ones, which results in very large classes, a poor student-faculty ratio, and little personal contact with professors.

While Japan devotes about the same percentage of its national income to elementary and secondary education as do the other advanced countries, it provides notably less for higher education, despite the fact that a considerably higher proportion of young people attend university than in the countries of Western Europe. This underinvestment in higher education is seen particularly in the heavy burden the Japanese place on private universities and the near bankruptcy of these institutions. In other advanced countries, all or most students are in government or government-financed institutions—even in the United States the figure has risen to 75 percent—but in Japan, since the government simply has not met the expanding demand for higher education, some 80 percent of the students are in private universities. None of these have any appreciable endowment or can count on substantial outside giving. Until recently no tax credit was given for this or other charitable giving, and in any case the Japanese do not have much of a tradition of eleemosynary largess. Though tuition fees are much higher than in government universities, they average only a quarter or a third of comparable fees in the United States. All that has kept some of the private universities financially afloat has been the high entrance examination fees, which they milk from masses of unsuccessful applicants, and borrowing from banks, which apparently count on the government eventually to pick up the bill. Actually no solution to the problem is possible other than a system of national financing.

The problem of the government universities is not so much finances as rigidity of organization. This may be in part the product of the German pattern copied in the late nineteenth century and in part the result of a fierce fight for academic freedom waged against the oppressive prewar government, which has left a jealously guarded tradition of autonomy in universities and in their various subdivisions. Universities even at the undergraduate level break up into sharply divided faculties, which have only minimal contact with one another. These faculties in turn are usually divided into chairs (*koza*), each made up of a professor, an assistant professor, and one or a few lecturers and assistants. Both the faculties and the chairs have almost complete autonomy and tenaciously protect their respective academic domains and budgets. Courses of study for students are rigidly prescribed, new fields of study are hard to start, and the mixing of fields of study is almost impossible. Presidents and deans, being elected by their peers, have extremely little power. On one side the Ministry of Education provides the money but through a rather mechanical budgetary process, and on the other side faculties and chairs have virtual veto power over any change in the use of these funds. Little room remains for innovation, and as a result universities today still operate in the patterns established under very different conditions three quarters of a century ago.

Another problem is that the reshuffling of the levels of education decreed by the American occupation meant that the postwar Japanese university is a rather unnatural joining of the last two years of general education of the old higher schools with the first two years of specialization of the old universities. At Tokyo University these two elements still exist in almost total segregation from each other on two far separated campuses.

It is not surprising that students in both private and government schools evince considerable disenchantment, which mounts at times to open rebellion. Some students show little interest in their studies, devoting themselves instead to outside activities, such as sports, hobbies, and radical politics. This is particularly true during the first two years, before students settle down in their final years to completing their studies in preparation for the next round of examinations for business or the bureaucracy.

Student government organizations, supported automatically by fees assigned from tuition payments, have for the most part been dominated ever since the war by leftist extremists and have spawned a wide variety of explosively revolutionary splinter groups. These student organizations are usually known by the name of their national federation, the Zengakuren. Student unrest often focuses on intramural issues, such as raises in tuition or the costs of student facilities, rather than genuine academic problems, but the peaks in student unrest have usually coincided with times of political tension in society at large over domestic and, still more, international issues, as at the time of the Security Treaty riots of 1960 and the great upheavals of the late 1960s. At such times, all university life may be paralyzed. Tokyo University simply did not function for a whole year in 1968–69, and many other universities were thrown into prolonged turmoil.

The Japanese are well aware of the problems of higher education, and, since the student troubles of the late 1960s, they have been making efforts to overcome them though, so far, without great success. A start has been made in providing government financial aid to the private universities. The goal is 50 percent of their instructional expenses, but the actual figure at present is closer to 20 percent. In 1975 brakes were placed on the further proliferation of private universities. There have been experiments aimed at reducing the psychological pressures of entrance examinations, though without much effect as yet. The government has even experimented with a new structure of internal university organization, closer to the departmental divisions and strong administrative leadership of American universities. Tsukuba University, near Tokyo, was founded in 1973 on the new model, but against determined opposition from much of the academic community, and there is little assurance that the pattern will actually spread.

Higher education remains one of the major problem areas in contemporary Japanese society. The number of students in institutions of higher learning is coming close to the two million mark—roughly half of them in the Tokyo area and another large body in the Kansai metropolitan region around Kyoto, Osaka, and Kobe. That Japan continues to operate as well as it does despite the problems of higher education seems at first surprising but probably is to be explained by the excellence of pre-university education and the system of advanced in-service training for new employees in business and government. Efficiently functioning universities may be less vital to the Japanese system than they are to the American. In any case, despite the troubles of the universities, education as a whole is one of Japan's strongest points and an absolutely pivotal feature of the social system.

Business

18

T HOUGH education may lie behind Japan's phenomenal success in modern times, it is in business and industry that that success has been most clearly manifested. The story of Japan's rapid rise over the past century to become the third largest economic unit in the world today, however, is a subject that is too large to be encompassed in a volume of this size. Nor is there much need to attempt to treat it in detail here, for there already exist many good analyses of the Japanese economy. In this chapter I shall limit myself instead to a brief consideration of how business fits into Japanese society as a whole—a subject already touched on elsewhere in this book but deserving more systematic attention.

The postwar economic "miracle" in Japan caused the rest of the world to look with wonderment at it and to note certain distinctive features in its business and industry, such as lifetime employment patterns, wages determined by seniority, warm bonds of personal loyalty between bosses and workers, and close cooperation between government and business. These were usually attributed to a feudal heritage, and sometimes they were described as direct survivals from Tokugawa practices. In the early postwar years, when Japan did not appear to be a serious economic competitor, such idiosyncrasies were thought of as signs of social immaturity, which Japan would outgrow as it "modernized." More recently they have been regarded as sinister attributes giving Japan an unfair competitive advantage. In actuality, this combination of characteristics is largely new, having been developed by the Japanese in modern times though in keeping with earlier traditions; some of these characteristics are eroding a little as group spirit weakens in Japan and the individual is emphasized more; and insofar as they represent a departure from business practices elsewhere in the industrialized world, they may be more suggestive of the wave of the future than of a dying wave from Japan's distinctive past.

Japan entered its modern period with a complex, even if pre-industrial, economy. There was a unified nationwide market, banking institutions were well developed, large family enterprises like Mitsui operated in several regions and diverse fields, such as banking and dry goods, and retailing was done not by haggling but at fixed prices. Only Mitsui among the largest firms of the Tokugawa period successfully made the transition to the new age, but agriculture, most retailing, and the traditional forms of manufacturing continued on little changed and became the lower level of the so-called "dual structure" of the economy, as large-scale modern industry developed to form the upper level. This more traditional side of the economy, which came to include much of the machine production that could be performed in small units, remained tiny in scale and family centered, with extra-family workers accepted as apprentices and treated as lesser members of the family. Although it has been a steadily shrinking proportion of the economy, it still lingers on with many of its inherited premodern characteristics. This, however, is not the aspect of the Japanese economy that inspires in others either wonder or fear, but rather its newer elements.

The distinctive new Japanese economic institution that first caught the attention of the outside world was the *zaibatsu* system, as this had developed by the 1920s. The zaibatsu were the great commercial and industrial combines, which embraced a remarkably large proportion of the upper level of the economy. The concentration of wealth and economic power that they represented had been aided by the sale at reduced prices of government enterprises and properties in the early 1880s to those individuals who appeared to the government leaders to be capable of managing them well. This sale was not motivated by a desire to create a strong capitalist class, as is generally charged by Marxist historians, but by the government's desperate financial situation and its desire to have Japanese industry succeed. The zaibatsu were widely condemned in the 1920s and 1930s as being elements of Western decadence in Japanese society, a corrupting influence on the parliamentary system, and money-grubbing betrayers of Japan's imperialistic destiny. Then after the war they were ironically attacked by the American occupation for being the root cause of Japan's military expansionism. Their owning families were expropriated, and the combines themselves were broken up into their component corporate units.

The four greatest zaibatsu combines were Mitsui, Mitsubishi, Sumitomo, and Yasuda, but there were other lesser ones and some later comers known as the "new zaibatsu," associated in particular with military-related industry and the exploitation of Manchuria. The zaibatsu combines, and particularly the big four, spread widely across the fields of banking, manufacturing, mining, shipping, and foreign marketing. Each centered around its own bank, which financed the other component parts. Another key institution was the general trading company (*sogo shosha*), which started in foreign trade and then began to move into domestic trade as well.

The trading companies were a distinctive Japanese invention which probably developed because of the dependence of the modern Japanese economy on foreign raw materials and foreign markets and the difficulty for each individual company to develop for itself the necessary language skills and an adequate worldwide purchasing and selling network. This factor together with the scarcity of commercial capital made it reasonable to pool both capital and skills for this side of the activities of the zaibatsu group as a whole. Even today the trading company, now freed from its limitation to a single zaibatsu group, performs this role for much of Japanese industry and increasingly for businesses around the world. The "big ten" among the general trading companies had in 1974 a total sales volume of an amazing 37 percent of the Japanese GNP, though they retained for themselves only very slim margins of profit on this huge turnover.

Zaibatsu combines were made up of a central holding company, owned by the controlling family, which held the stocks of major affiliates, which in turn held the stocks of scores of lesser affiliates. This sort of pyramid of control is common enough in the West, but what made the Japanese case unique was the fact that often the zaibatsu held only a minority interest in affiliated members but still controlled them completely through other techniques. Dependence on the banking, shipping, and trading facilities of the combine was one of these techniques, but more important was the personal loyalty of the executives in all the firms to the group. Interlocking directors were common, and executives were switched around among the component firms as though they constituted a single organization. Young executives joined the group for a lifetime career and developed correspondingly strong loyalties. The lifetime commitment of executives and employees is the feature of the system that is most reminiscent of Japanese feudal practices and survives most strongly in the postwar system.

No zaibatsu combine had a monopoly in any field, and in fact they developed parallel sets of companies which were often intensely competitive with their counterparts in other zaibatsu groupings. In many fields, however, a few zaibatsu concerns formed a virtual oligopoly that in times of stress could easily be transformed into a cartel. The concentration of wealth through the zaibatsu system undoubtedly had unhealthy social and political consequences, but economically it allowed for great capital concentrations that could be used to pioneer new fields, and the narrowness of the owning group, together with traditional frugal Japanese ways, permitted a high rate of reinvestment and growth.

It is frequently asserted that, despite the efforts of the American occupation after the war to break up the zaibatsu system, it has been restored since then, but this is not correct. It is true that the former component corporations of the zaibatsu combines have drawn together again in informal ways, but ownership has passed entirely from the original zaibatsu families to scattered shareholders; there is no longer any centralized control of any sort or even the control of any large corporation by any other; and former members of the combines, though perhaps looking first to the old zaibatsu bank for financing, are free to look elsewhere as well, and do so. The presidents of former combine affiliates meet together periodically in a sort of informal social club; the group may cooperate in new industrial undertakings; it controls the use of the old group name by new firms; it may give collectively to charity under the old name—in other words, there is a degree of mutual back scratching among the members of the group. But such relations are by no means exclusive and are much less significant than relations with other firms in the same economic field. In fact, a new system of cartelization by fields under government sponsorship has completely superseded the old zaibatsu integration.

THE ZAIBATSU system has not survived the war and occupation, but many of the features of Japanese business and industry that first appeared under this system are still characteristic of contemporary Japanese big business. I have already noted the lifetime careers of executives in prewar zaibatsu firms, and a system of lifetime employment for labor also began to develop following World War I. This was not, as is frequently assumed, a survival from premodern customs. Early Japan machine production, as in the West, was mostly in textiles and was staffed largely by women, who proved to be extremely transitory workers, as in the early industrial West. Even when they were herded into dormitories and kept under close control and chaperonage—again in ways similar to those in the West— women tended to stay only for a few years after ending their schooling, while they built up dowries for marriage.

It was only at a subsequent stage in the development of Japanese industry that lifetime employment grew up as a rational response to the scarcity of well-trained labor for technically more demanding jobs. Skilled labor was worth holding on to through a system of special privileges, the chief of which was job security. The hold on this labor could be made more secure by a wage system in which monetary rewards were in large part deferred by basing wages fundamentally on length of service. Promising young men were recruited at low wages determined by the overabundance of unskilled labor, were trained for specialized jobs at company expense, and were retained by a promise of job security and a wage system which rewarded seniority. The system was basically the same for company executives, though they were on a higher wage track than workers, determined by greater educational qualifications. This system, which first appeared in prewar zaibatsu firms, was continued and developed in postwar Japan.

The assumption in large companies that employment for both management and labor will be for life breeds a strong sense of loyalty in both groups, which the company assiduously cultivates. Initial in-service training includes a great deal of company indoctrination, and the company takes a paternalistic interest in both workers and young executives. Warm relations of intimacy and trust are encouraged between superiors and subordinates, and the former often function as personal counsellors to those below them. Often cheap company housing is provided for workers and executives, and most big firms have vacation resorts which can be used in turn by groups from the company. Sports teams and other activities are sponsored by the company in order to make the lives of the young workers center around the company as much as possible.

Although the whole system of lifetime employment and compensation by seniority grew out of labor needs, it fit well into basic Japanese group attitudes. It also produced a number of significant side benefits. The rise of wages with seniority fits sociological needs, because the worker does require a steady increase in pay as he progresses through the various stages of life—marriage, having children, paying for their higher educations, and finally saving for his own retirement. Wage scales determined in other industrialized countries more by skills and levels of energy leave many, as they age, with static or even declining incomes.

The permanent work force of a factory or office becomes for the individual workers a lasting group to which they are proud to belong. Their loyalty to the company assures it of an enthusiastic labor force which takes pride and satisfaction in its work. Both blue and white collar workers are happy to work overtime, and many, especially among junior executives and white collar workers, do not even take full advantage of the vacation time allotted them. They are all diligent workers and can be counted on to police the quality of their own work. The lack of the need for outside inspectors stands in sharp contrast to the situation in Western factories.

The identification of workers with the company as a whole, and not with a specific craft, also meant that, as labor unions developed, these were not organized by crafts but by companies, and the workers saw no need to oppose technological progress in behalf of their specific skills by demanding feather-bedding or the like, for they knew that the company would train them in new skills if their old company-acquired skills were no longer needed. Labor in Japan, thus, has not opposed technological advances, as it often has in the West.

A final side benefit of the system has been the avoidance of periodic rises in unemployment, since companies do their best to continue all their permanent workers even during an economic turndown. For the past two decades unemployment in Japan has usually been kept below 2 percent (though it should be pointed out that Japanese unemployment figures are deceptively low, since many persons who would be reported as unemployed in the United States are not classified as such in Japan). For the economy as a whole and even for individual taxpaying companies, it actually is no more burdensome in the long run to retain employees during slack periods of work than to pay for their sustenance through unemployment benefits financed largely through taxes on the companies.

For the individual workers the resulting job security is infinitely more self-respecting.

As described above, the Japanese employment system sounds somewhat idyllic, but it has its limitations. It has never applied to the bulk of Japanese workers in the lower level of the dual economy. Most women have always been considered temporary employees, and workers in petty retailing and small industrial plants have no assurance of lifetime employment or steadily rising wages geared to seniority. Around each of the great manufacturing corporations are gathered scores of small subcontracting firms, which serve as feeder plants, supplying simple elements in the manufacturing process but affording their workers none of the privileges of the system. Even within the big corporations are whole categories of workers who are considered temporary workers outside the system, however permanent their employment may actually be. These various peripheral workers receive lesser financial benefits and suffer the risk of unemployment, while only the elite workers of the big companies enjoy the full privileges of the system.

Even among these there is some erosion in the system now going on. Sophisticated young workers today are less enchanted by distant economic rewards, and, finding the paternalism of Japanese companies somewhat stifling, they demand more freedom in their personal lives. They give their loyalty less fully to the company and are more inclined to shift jobs. And the wage system, in its highly complex computations, is moving toward a little more emphasis on skills and production results and less on seniority. Still, the system seems firmly established, and, as the Japanese economy moves ahead and overall labor shortages begin to appear, the lower levels of the economy show signs of becoming absorbed into the pattern of the upper level, rather than the other way around. Even during the oil crisis depression of 1973–1976, though there were some cases of dismissals of supposedly permanent workers, industry did its best to avoid this by resorting to such stratagems as early retirements. Unemployment even during the height of this crisis did not much exceed 2 percent.

It seems probably that the system of lifetime job security and wage levels geared to lifetime needs will increase rather than shrink in Japan. In fact, it may represent the wave of the future elsewhere in the world too. The English sociologist Ronald Dore has pointed out in his book *British Factory–Japanese Factory* (Berkeley, University of California

Press, 1973) that these patterns correspond to other modern employment systems, as in the army or civil service, and seem to represent a twentieth century approach to employment problems, in contrast to the classical British nineteenth century concept of supply and demand bargaining between management and workers possessing individual skills.

Japanese employment practices have helped shape Japan's labor union movement. The basic unit is the enterprise-wide union made up of all the workers—blue collar, white collar, and junior executives—employed by a single company. These unions might best be called "company unions," except for the fact that this term has been preempted in the United States for unions controlled by the company, which is not the situation in Japan. An enterprise union is naturally sympathetic to the enterprise on which the livelihood of its members depends, but it is independent of management and bargains hard over wages and work conditions, particularly in the annual nationwide "spring offensive" for higher wages and better working conditions.

The rapid growth of the economy in recent decades usually permitted annual wage increases averaging around 15 percent and well ahead of the rate of inflation. This situation alone tended to dampen labor unrest, but more important was the fact that labor union members naturally identified their own economic interests with those of the company that permanently employed them, and therefore they did not want to hurt it economically in any way. They had no desire to slow its technological advance or engage in damaging work stoppages. Management for its part wanted good will and harmony with its permanent work force. The result has been that strikes are likely to be symbolic displays of bargaining muscle, rather than crippling, all-out fights. Unions representing government workers, such as national railway and postal workers, teachers, and national and local government employees, may be more militant, particularly on political issues, because they do not see their economic well-being as tied to an employer engaged in economic competition with other companies. Nonetheless, man-days lost in strikes in Japan have averaged less than a quarter of the rate in the United Kingdom and less than a third that of the United States.

The individual enterprise unions are usually organized into national federations embracing all unions in the same general field, and these then into overarching, nationwide federations, which tend to be very active politically. The twelve million union members represent 34 percent of the labor force, about the same percentage as in West Germany and decid-edly higher than in the United States. Of these, some four and a half million are affiliated with Sohyo, a federation which is strongest among white collar workers and government employees and is closely associated with the Socialist party. Close to two and a half million are in Domei, which is largely made up of blue collar workers in private industry and is affiliated with the much more moderate Democratic Socialist party.

THE JAPANESE employment system contributes to a spirit and style of operation in business management and the government bureaucracy that differ greatly from what one finds in the United States. Junior execu-tives and bureaucrats, entering through examinations directly from univer-sity undergraduate programs, are grouped as members of annual classes which will keep in step with one another most of their careers in both pay and rank, though the more able will be selected for the more interesting and significant assignments. No one is normally asked to serve under a person of the same class or younger, and only as the group approaches the top are the less able retired in order to avoid such a situation. In a ministry, when one of the members of a class reaches the top bureau-cratic post of vice-minister, probably in his early fifties, all the others must be retired. In big business only a small number in each class con-tinue on as top executives, often to a very advanced age, while the rest are retired around fifty-five. Early retirement enforces a pattern of post-retirement employment for bureaucrats in businesses or government councils and for businessmen in subordinate firms affiliated with their original company.

This system eliminates any sense of competition across age or status lines. The subordinate cannot leapfrog an incompetent superior, and the superior therefore has nothing to fear from an able or ambitious subordi-nate. All see themselves as members of a team. No one tries to demon-strate individual brilliance or dynamic leadership. The leader consults fully with his subordinates and tries to bring out their initiative and abili-ties. The subordinate speaks up without fear but gives his full support to his superior, regardless of the latter's ability or lack of it. The result is a system of easy consultation and cooperation between the various levels of management or the bureaucracy and the expectation that initiatives might emerge from any level.

This system is so perplexing to Americans accustomed to a more dictatorial style of leadership from the top down that it has given rise to the myth that the Japanese have a mysterious bottom to top form of leadership called the *ringi* system. The *ringi* system is the wide circulation of documents to which large numbers of persons affix their seals as a sign that they have seen the document and do not actively oppose what it says. It is analogous to the clearance system in American bureaucracies and to the distribution of memorandums for information. Some relatively routine matters can be settled in this way on the basis of documents originating at a relatively low level. But it is not a peculiar Japanese system for making important or difficult decisions.

If the Japanese have a special decision-making process, it is the system of careful and extensive consultations before a decision is arrived at by general consensus. Instead of an individual decision by the man at the top, the Japanese conduct wide informal discussions, involving subordinates. From this may emerge a consensus, which might be embodied in a *ringi* document drafted by some subordinate. Or the final decision may have to be made by a small group at the top. But in any case all members of the staff are made fully familiar with the problem and are in a position to carry out the decision much better than if they had been suddenly handed a surprise decision by their superiors.

On the other hand, the corporative nature of the Japanese decision-making process makes it difficult for Japanese companies to utilize foreign executives even in their foreign branches and affiliates. The system calls for a familiarity with the whole company, with Japanese patterns of interpersonal relations, and with the subtleties of the Japanese language that no foreigner is likely to possess.

THE NATURE of the Japanese business system has contributed to the rapid growth of industry since the war, but certain external factors have probably been even more important. There was an open world trading system which Japan could join and a worldwide abundance of raw materials. New technologies had been developed in the West during Japan's period of relative isolation in the war and prewar years and were now made available to the Japanese at modest costs, largely by American companies. Finally, the lack of heavy defense burdens in Japan and the low levels of social security benefits allowed a relatively low tax rate—actually 23 percent in 1975 compared to 30 percent in the United States and up to 50 percent in some countries of Western Europe. The importance of these factors cannot be overemphasized, but at the same time certain features of the Japanese system did gear it to rapid growth and contributed greatly to the resulting "miracle."

One of these factors is that the Japanese people have shown a remarkable and steadily rising propensity to save, even under the adverse economic conditions of the early postwar years and during the subsequent period of a huge increase in consumer spending. Saving rates were some two or three times higher than in the West and during the 1960s came close to 40 percent of GNP. Corporations reinvested the vast bulk of their profits, and even urban workers saved about 20 percent of their disposable income, which is a far higher rate than in any Western country. In part this may be attributed to traditional frugality and the lack of much buying on credit, but it is also linked with the system. Low retirement pay and social security benefits necessitate lifelong saving in preparation for retirement, and wages are paid in a way that makes saving particularly easy. Around 20 to 30 percent of total wages and salaries comes in the form of special bonus payments at New Year's and midsummer. Since these are additional to the regular monthly or weekly payments, on which the family is accustomed to live, they can easily be squirreled away in savings, usually in the very conservative form of savings accounts in banks or post offices, which pay interest at rates near or below the rate of inflation.

The seniority system in wages also is a built-in spur to economic expansion. A rapidly growing company will have a disproportionately large number of newly hired young workers who are underpaid in terms of their productivity, while a more stagnant company will have on average an older and more costly work force. There are thus strong economic incentives and high rewards for rapid expansion. Growth in Japanese business breeds more growth. And the fact that wages are a fixed cost that cannot be reduced much even in adverse times militates strongly against any reduction of production, regardless of demand or prices.

Another factor is the way in which Japanese big business is financed. It runs largely on bank loans, tending to have an eighty to twenty ratio of borrowing to equity capital in stocks, to the wonder and consternation of American businessmen, who consider such ratios hazardous. In part, this situation may be an outgrowth of the confiscation of most personal wealth at the time of the occupation, in part the continuation of the central role of banking institutions, which already was a feature of the prewar zaibatsu system. In any case, this has become the established postwar method of financing big business, and it really is not hazardous, because the Bank of Japan, representing the whole national economy, stands behind the commercial banks and their loans. This system of financing industry makes the Japanese businessman more conscious of a good growth record, which would entitle him to more bank loans, than of a high profit record (above the need to meet bank interest rates), which would enable him to sell more equity capital. The result is a greater drive in Japanese business for growth rather than simply for profits.

Another factor that leads to an emphasis on growth over profits is the ethos of Japanese big businessmen. Commonly called today the *zaikai* or "financial world," they are the successors to the samurai businessmen of Meiji days, who saw themselves as saviors of Japan on the industrial front from the menace of the West. The managerial revolution was already well advanced in the zaibatsu firms before the war and is now virtually complete. The postwar economic collapse unstuck the system momentarily, allowing a sudden rush of innovations and successful individual entrepreneurship, but the system has now reasserted itself, and most big businessmen are essentially "business bureaucrats."

Japanese businessmen receive relatively modest salaries by American standards, and they do not have the stock options of American business that would make them part owners as well as managers. Their positions give them great power, prestige, and privilege. The perquisites of their posts, in the form of company residences, cars, chauffers, luxurious offices, and liberal expense accounts, are considerable. In fact, liberal tax provisions allow a lavish expense account life for many businessmen, providing the monetary backbone for expensive restaurants and fancy night life in Japan. But their salaries which could be salted away as permanent wealth are relatively small and are not closely tied to profits. Japanese businessmen derive satisfaction, not so much from high profits, as from the size of their economic empires, the importance of their companies in the life of the nation, and their rate of growth. Profits and growth are closely linked, and motivation for the one cannot be clearly distinguished from motivation for the other. Still, there does seem a basic difference in emphasis on growth and profits between Japanese and Western businessmen.

ONE OF THE most important factors in Japan's rapid economic growth is the special relationship between government and business. In fact, this is one of the chief differences between Japanese and American business, though it affords less of a contrast with some Western countries, such as France or West Germany. The relationship in Japan between government and business is not that of mutually suspicious adversaries, as in the United States, but of close collaborators. The contrast is so great that Americans have frequently exaggerated it, mistakenly claiming that government and business in Japan form a single entity—"Japan, Inc."—in which either the government is said to control business completely or conversely a mysteriously unified big business world is said to control the government.

While in premodern Japan business was felt to be an irritating reality disrupting the feudal system, in modern times the Japanese have seen no basic divergence in interests between government and business and have never believed, like Americans, that the less government the better for business. The Meiji government was deeply concerned with the development of industry as one side of its defense against the West. It started pilot plants, sold these off to competent managers when the government finances made this necessary, but continued to aid and shape Japanese industry through subsidies and special privileges. The new businessmen for their part saw themselves as engaged in a national endeavor and welcomed government aid and guidance. By the 1920s some Japanese felt that the zaibatsu combines had grown so large that the tail was wagging the dog, but subsequently, under militaristic leadership, big business was forced to mold itself again to objectives defined by the government.

In the postwar occupation the Americans imported their concepts of free and untrammeled competition in business and the adversary relationship between government and business. This resulted in the dissolution of the zaibatsu and an Anti-Monopoly Law and a Fair Trade Commission that remain part of the current system. But the dictatorial power of the occupation and the dire economic conditions of the time produced, in fact, a more comprehensive and delicate system of cooperation between government and business than had ever existed before. Measures thought of by the American authorities as temporary emergency expedients became the permanent tools through which the government directed business activities into preferred channels.

Much of this new control system has been epitomized by the powerful Ministry of International Trade and Industry—usually called MITI in English—which replaced the prewar Commerce Ministry. While the Economic Planning Agency formulated broad economic objectives and forecasts, MITI set goals for specific industries and gave direction to much of Japan's industrial growth. Through the control of foreign exchange and the licensing of foreign technology, it carefully supervised the acquisition of foreign technology with a view to insuring that the best of it was acquired on the best possible terms by those best able to make effective use of it and in such ways that it did not lead to monopolistic conditions in Japan but engendered fruitful competition between rival companies. MITI also helped in the formation of depression cartels, foreign export cartels when so-called "voluntary" controls on exports were demanded by foreign countries, especially the United States, or cartels for other purposes, and it also encouraged mergers of weak smaller firms into larger and stronger ones.

The Japanese tax system is also designed to encourage rapid industrial growth, particularly in certain key fields. The Bank of Japan, the central government bank on which the great private banks are ultimately dependent, helps shape lending policies that favor growth industries and work against declining ones. Both MITI and other ministries give "administrative guidance" on many matters, which Japanese businessmen accept. In particular, at times when the economic machine races too fast, inflation creeps up, and balances of payments deteriorate, the government has been able to persuade business through "administrative guidance" to slow down on its investments and thus cool the economy.

Through these means, the government after the war helped concentrate Japanese capital and business skills particularly on the rebuilding of the steel, shipbuilding, coal, electric power, and fertilizer industries, and subsequently it aided in the phenomenal growth of the chemical industries, electronics, automobiles, and other heavy industries. At present it is responding to the problem of high energy costs, raw material shortages, and pollution by attempting to damp down industries that pollute or consume much energy and raw materials in favor of "knowledge intensive" industries, such as computers, that require a high quotient of technical skills but less energy and raw materials. At the same time it has facilitated the reduction in relative importance of labor-intensive industries like textiles, which cannot in the long run compete with lower wage scales in such modernizing economies as those of Korea, Taiwan, and Hong Kong. Aiding in the transfer of labor and capital from dying to growing industries through retraining programs and financial controls is an important part of the effort to steer the economy in the most fruitful directions. By way of contrast, the American government for the most part tends to intervene in the economy in the opposite direction, by protecting naturally fading industries like textiles and thus slowing their decline at the expense of the more successful and therefore more taxable industries.

All this fine synchronization of the economic effort depends on two basic factors. One is public confidence in the honesty and excellence of the government bureaucracy, which does exist and seems well justified. The other is a capacity for big businessmen to cooperate with one another as well as with the government. Here the groupiness of Japanese society as a whole helps out. The various sectors of big business are organized into associations and these are brought together under the Keidanren (the Federation of Economic Organizations). During the crucial period of the 1950s and early 1960s in particular, the Keidanren provided big business with a unified voice that was helpful to the government in designing its grand business strategy. In addition the Keizai Doyukai (called in English the Committee for Economic Development), made up when it was first founded of slightly younger and more dynamic business executives than those at the head of Keidanren, serves to inject business thinking into considerations of high economic strategy, while the Japan Chamber of Commerce (Nissho) acts as a coordinator of slightly smaller businesses, and Nikkeiren (the Federation of Employers Associations) acts as a coordinator of business strategy in labor-management relations.

Some people feel that the partnership between government and business is fading and that government controls over business are eroding. Certainly MITI's control over the importation of technology will probably prove of declining efficacy in shaping Japanese business, though the increased need for pollution controls and the whole growing complexity of economic controls in general may still give the bureaucracy all the tools it needs. The chief thing that has changed is that the national consensus that gave priority to industrial growth over almost everything else and made business and government such congenial teammates in the past is in the process of disintegrating. Pollution and crowding have made mere economic growth a more dubious goal, and there are loud demands for better quality in life rather than mere quantity and for more attention to social welfare and consumer interests. Businessmen have plummeted in popular esteem from folk heroes to a more mundame role and to some people have become the villains in the piece. Efforts are being made through the government budget to shift more assets to the neglected social services and to miserably inadequate urban housing. Under these circumstances government and business are more likely in the future to see their interests as being in conflict than they have in the recent past.

The basic partnership between government and a dynamic, internally competitive business world, however, is likely to continue as a distinctive Japanese feature and a major reason for Japan's extraordinary economic success. In fact, this pattern may become more widely recognized as a successful middle path between the extremes of pure socialism and classic capitalism. The Japanese system might be called post-capitalistic in its leadership by salaried "business bureaucrats" and its orientation to national service and growth rather than merely to profits. It does not submit itself entirely to the unseen hand of the market, but accepts government guidance. At the same time, the government does not stifle economic growth, as it does in some socialist states, by insisting on planning everything and controlling the whole economy. There is ample room for free enterprise, though there is purposeful direction by the government at the same time. As the most successful economic model in the world in recent years, it is certainly worthy of study by others and, where possible, emulation, though it must be admitted that part of its success lies in certain basic Japanese characteristics that other peoples may not be able or wish to imitate.

Japanese business undoubtedly has been very successful, but it would be wrong to leave the impression that it is without problems and will continue to run as smoothly in the future as it has in the past. The vast increase since 1973 in the price of Japan's major imports—energy resources, food, and other raw materials—and the possibility of global shortages have made Japan's international economic climate less favorable than it seemed only a few years ago. Resulting problems of inflation could play havoc with the economy. During 1974 and 1975 inflation rose to two digit figures—as high as 26 percent for a while. Labor costs will inevitably increase because of the rising age of the labor force, and eventually there will be shortages in the labor supply. The Japanese are determined not to accept foreign workers in the North European manner, but it should also be pointed out that early retirement and considerable underemployment—as in the case of many young women workers who spend much of their time bowing to customers or pouring tea for fellow employees—still leave some leeway in the labor market. Greater labor unrest in the future seems probable, as well as a declining enthusiasm for work, as prolonged affluence takes its toll. Thus Japan in the future may seem less of an economic miracle than it does today. Still, on the whole, Japanese economic worries lie more in relations with the outside world than in the organization of the domestic economy.

Mass Culture

19

W E H A V E seen that the Japanese tendency to divide up into vertical, hierarchic groups naturally weakens horizontal bonds of class or calling. One might conclude from this that the Japanese are a sharply divided people, but nothing could be further from the truth. The uniform patterns of education and business and the close integration of all the people in a tight nationwide system belie any such idea. In fact, the mass society that is often hailed or deplored as the worldwide wave of the future and is thought to be best typified by the United States is even more pronounced in contemporary Japan.

In part, this may be attributable to the extraordinary cultural homogeneity with which Japan entered the nineteenth century, but it is even more the product of the complete political centralization of modern times and a conscious effort on the part of the government to develop a uniform, unified citizenry. Japan has none of the great regional and ethnic diversity of the United States and considerably less even than the larger countries of Western Europe, despite the fact that it has close to twice the population of any of them and is spread out geographically much more widely. Japan, even excluding Okinawa, extends along its longest axis from northeastern Hokkaido to southern Kyushu almost twice the distance of Italy, France, or the United Kingdom as measured along their longest axes. But only Okinawa, which is as far from Tokyo as Iceland is from London, differs significantly in local dialect, folk culture, historical traditions, and contemporary attitudes.

Education has been the chief tool in shaping national uniformity. In prewar Japan one could know that on a certain day every sixth grade child throughout the whole land would be learning the same Chinese characters, the same historical facts, and the same arithmetical rules. Education is no longer quite this uniform, since local boards of education make selections from among a variety of textbooks, though all must have Ministry of Education approval. However, curriculums at the lower levels are closely prescribed, and even in senior high school preparation for the same university entrance examinations produces a great deal of uniformity. Even higher education, swamped as it is by masses of students and inadequate finances, achieves little variation except for its division into a series of disciplinary faculties. All Japanese have had twelve years or at a minimum nine years of virtually identical education, which is not greatly diversified by the higher education a third of them receive, and they emerge into society with a uniformity of information and attitudes that is only matched in a small close-knit primitive society or a modern totalitarian state.

The mass media join education as major shapers of mass society. The role of television in Japan is similar to that in the United States. Nationwide networks, by providing almost identical fare, breed a great deal of uniformity. It is Japanese television more than anything else that has smoothed out the contrasts in values and attitudes between rural and urban dwellers, which were so divisive in the prewar situation. Television is present in virtually every home in rural as well as urban areas, and there are in fact slightly more color television sets in Japan than households. Incidentally, the Japanese, though calling television by its English name, have derived from it a different contraction—*terebi*, in contrast to the TV of the United States and the telly of England.

Japanese television is organized more like British than American television, but the programs on the whole are more like those of the United States. There are two national networks, known as NHK (Nippon Hoso Kyoku), which are supported by public funds derived from a special tax on television sets. One government network is highly educational, carrying much foreign language instruction, mathematics courses of amazing complexity, and the like. The other competes with the private networks in general interest, having much the same sort of news, drama, comedy, and quiz shows. There are five private networks that cover most or large parts of the country and are dependent for support on advertising, which is much like that on American television. The blend between private and government television works well on the whole. The financial resources and high quality of the general network of NHK force the commercial stations to strive for quality to compete, while the challenge of the private channels forces NHK to be lively in a way not characteristic of television that is a government monopoly.

While Japanese television is much like that of the United States, the newspapers are very different. Geographic size has forced American newspapers to remain local and therefore relatively small, and European newspapers tend to divide sharply along political lines, but Japanese newspapers are mostly national and politically neutral, thus fitting the term "mass media" even better than do the newspapers of North America or Europe.

With less than a tenth of the number of American newspapers, the Japanese have the largest newspaper circulation per capita among the larger countries of the world—close to twice that of the United States. The three greatest national newspapers are the *Asahi*, *Yomiuri*, and *Mainichi*, which have morning editions, distributed almost entirely to individual homes, of close to six million, around four and a half million, and around three and a half million respectively. In addition, each distributes more than half as many copies of an entirely different evening edition. Each is printed at some four different locations and distributed with slight local variations from a hundred or more. Two other national papers, *Sankei* and *Nihon Keizai* (comparable to the Wall Street Journal), have circulations in the millions, while four regional papers, known collectively as the "bloc"—the *Hokkaido Shinbun* in Sapporo, the *Tokyo Shinbun*, *Chunichi* in Nagoya, and *Nishi Nippon* in Fukuoka in Kyushu—have a combined circulation of around three and a half million.

Japanese newspapers are surprisingly uniform in format and content. They tend to be smaller than American papers in number of pages—only about 24 pages for the morning editions and less for the evening. Advertising forms a much smaller proportion of their financial support and, except for classified and book and magazine advertisements, takes up relatively little space. The main news appears on page one, and more detailed political, foreign, and economic news, editorials, letters, special features, art and theater sections, home news, and the like are to be found on almost the same pages in every paper. The next to the last page—known as "the third page news" (*sanmen kiji*) from an original four page format—is always reserved for crime, accidents, and other human interest stories, which are called "social news" but never contain the "society news" of American papers.

The material for the papers is collected by armies of newsmen stationed all over Japan and the world. The Japanese, for example, constitute the largest foreign corps of newsmen in both Washington and New York. The news is then concisely compiled, carefully edited, and meticulously proof-read by more such armies of newspapermen in the home office. By-lines are rare, illustrating once again the Japanese propensity to group action. The net result is a high quality product. One can safely say that the Japanese on average are provided with fuller and more accurate newspaper coverage of both national and international news than any other people in the world, and only an occasional newspaper elsewhere surpasses their great national dailies in either quantity or quality of news.

The great weakness of Japanese newspapers is their amazing uniformity in coverage and treatment. They have few individualized interpretive articles or analyses, and they commonly come out with headlines and editorials that seem to be almost paraphrases of one another. As a result, tens of millions of Japanese, intellectually armed with the same television and newspaper news and opinions, sally forth to work each day with the same facts, interests, and attitudes in their heads.

All the major newspapers profess to strict political neutrality, but in reality most of them tend to lean slightly to the left of center and to be critical of the government. This situation is in part the result of their history. Newspapers first grew up in Japan in the Meiji period as organs of protest for men of samurai origin who had failed to become members of the ruling group. From this beginning they developed the attitude that their role in society was to be helpful critics of what, at least before the war, was an all powerful government. Only during the period of military leadership during the 1930s and World War II were they forced to become the dutiful mouthpieces of the government, and in the postwar period they happily reverted to the role of critics, even though now the government was democratically controlled and very dependent on public opinion, which the newspapers did much to shape. Another reason for their prevailing leftist slant is that newspapers are produced by "intellectuals" (as the term is used in Japan) living in the great metropolitan centers, where opposition to the conservative government in power runs highest, especially among "intellectuals," or *interi* as the Japanese call them for short.

Still, the great Japanese papers see themselves and consciously strive to be politically neutral. They are less so than television, which tends to be politically bland, but, in any case, the major newspapers are definitely not voice pieces of governmental indoctrination, as they would be in a totalitarian society, nor are they the tools of owners or of some controlling political party, as might be the case in the United States or Western Europe. Ownership has little influence on editiorial policy, which is produced instead by factional struggles among the professional staff and secondarily by pressures from the unionized labor force.

Weekly and monthly publications play less of a national role than newspapers and add more of a note of diversity. There are a handful of monthly magazines—the so-called "general magazines" (*sogo zasshi*)—which have serious articles on a variety of subjects, but their circulations run at most only in the hundreds of thousands. The size and excellence of the daily press precludes the need for news weeklies like *Time* or *Newsweek*,but there are a huge number and variety of other types of weeklies. At least three claim circulations above a half million, and the top fifty have a combined circulation of about eight million. The weeklies tend to be more sensational and sometimes salacious than the monthlies or the newspapers, and they certainly are far more varied. They include large numbers of specialty magazines on a vast variety of subjects from sports to knitting. Most weekly and monthly magazines make no claim to neutrality and cater quite frankly to particular political biases or other specialized interest.

A WELL-ORDERED, smoothly functioning society reemphasizes the uniformity already instilled in the Japanese by their similar educations and their shared sources of information in the mass media. Japanese society runs in well-established channels. Individual careers are more predictable and follow more unvarying courses than in most other countries. Fads, enthusiasms, or new ideas sweep the whole land uniformly, inspiring mass reactions, though by the 1970s a growing sophistication may have begun to make their responses more diverse. The Japanese, however, still seem to be subject to nationwide "moods" (the English word is used). They also turn out by the millions for public events, such as the 1964 Olympics or the 1970 Osaka Exposition. Even political protest, as in the 1960 Security Treaty demonstrations, brings them out by the hundreds of thousands.

Mass-produced goods pass uniformly into the hands of mass consumers. Name brands in electric goods, cameras, or what not are advertised nationally through television and magazines and are retailed through

A shop specializing in audio equipment in the Akihabara district of Tokyo, where there are some 250 stores dealing exclusively in electrical appliances and electronic equipment. The trade names, which may be as familiar to Westerners as to Japanese, are written in Latin letters as well as in Japanese. (*Embassy of Japan*)

thousands of outlets. Over 95 percent of households have washing machines and refrigerators, and over half have cars—more in rural areas than in cities. Since the war a succession of the three sacred objects of family life—a joke on the "Three Imperial Regalia" of the imperial family—has gravitated upward in value until in the late 1960s they had become the "three C's," meaning color television, a car, and a "cooler," the term for an air conditioner.

Huge department stores, known as *depato*, cater to a mass clientele with a bewildering profusion of standardized goods and a series of peripheral services not found in their Western counterparts. They often have, for example, a children's zoo and playground on the roof, a large restaurant on an upper floor, a theater, and a hall for changing art exhibits, usually of high quality. Museums incidentally are not very common in Japan, and the average person is likely to see famous works of art either *in situ* in Buddhist temples or else at such department store exhibits.

Japan is a land of mass spectator sports and mass activities. Professional baseball, horse racing, and college baseball as well as the national high school championships regularly draw tens of thousands of spectators. The professional baseball teams are sponsored by business firms, often commuter railway lines along which their fields are located, and have names, always in English, which are sometimes familiar to Americans—the Yomiuri Giants—and sometimes strange—the Hiroshima Carps. *Sumo*, which is the traditional form of wrestling between "man mountains" and is vaguely associated with Shinto, has proved to make a fine television spectacular and as a result has gained new popularity. Ski slopes are hazardously crowded in winter. The Shonan beaches near Tokyo will attract over a million persons on a hot summer weekend. An endless antlike chain of people on the slopes on Mount Fjui turn mountain climbing in summer into a mass sport. Sightseeing crowds, mostly organized groups of schoolchildren and village and small town associations, inundate famous beauty spots in the spring and autumn sightseeing seasons and all but obliterate them from view or even from existence. Shopping streets and popular amusement areas, with their thousands of bars, cafes, and restaurants, are always filled with swarms of people. The usual first reaction of any Japanese visitor to an American small town or medium-sized city is wonderment at the relative paucity of people walking in the streets—as if they had been wiped out by some great catastrophe.

Japan's mass society spills over to some degree into a mass culture. Japanese girls learn the tea ceremony, flower arrangement, and traditional dancing in large groups and as part of a standardized training for young women. We have already encountered hundreds of small children sawing away together on their violins according to the Suzuki method. Occidental music, whether classical or popular, draws mass audiences, which are always overwhelmingly young.

These mass characteristics, however, are hardly all or even the most important aspects of modern Japanese culture. Much more significant is its tremendous vitality, creativity, and variety. In the field of Western music, Japan's many symphony orchestras rank with the best in the world, as do individual Japanese musicians and conductors. Japanese architects are world famous. Modern painters and woodblock artists are tremendously prolific. All the more traditional arts are more alive today than for many decades. Japanese traditional potters have set the styles that are copied worldwide. Literature is bounding with energy. People of all sorts

A summer Sunday on the Shonan beaches. These extensive beaches, which lie thirty to forty miles south of the center of Tokyo, attract more than a million people on a hot summer weekend. (*Associated Press*)

are sparkling with artistic creativity, and young people are bubbling with new life styles. No, Japan is by no means limited to a mass culture—but, nonetheless, mass culture is definitely an important part of modern Japan.

Much of Japan's mass culture is familiar enough to Americans, who perhaps run neck and neck with the Japanese in producing the modern mass society. But in some ways Japan is ahead. No sight in the world seems more characteristic of modern mass society than the hordes of commuters—actually in the millions—who each day surge like the tide through the great commuting terminals of Tokyo and Osaka. To the foreigner especially, these vast throngs, clad alike and looking very similar to the outsider, all moving determinedly but in orderly fashion to their destinations, and existing apart behind their invisible walls of a distinctive language, seem to be a vision of the robot-like future that may await us all.

Women

20

T HE POSITION of women and the relationship between the sexes are aspects of Japanese society that often stir indignation among Western women, particularly Americans. While women in Japan enjoy a position more comparable to that of women in the West than to the severely restricted position of women in most Islamic countries, still, attitudes of male chauvinism are blatantly evident in Japan. There is severe job discrimination against women. The old Confucian adage that a woman should in youth obey her father, in maturity her husband, and in old age her son still has some validity. In Western eyes, husbands frequently treat their wives coldly and even with disdain. Women are usually meek and long-suffering in their dealings with their menfolk, and girls hide shyly behind a screen of simpering. Social life, insofar as it exists, has little place for the married woman. A double sexual standard, which leaves the man free and the woman restricted, is still common. Thus sexual mores and attitudes toward love, marriage, and the place of women in society are areas of sharp differences between Japan and the United States, though it must be admitted that in both countries these are undergoing rapid change, and in Japan many of the changes are headed in the same direction as in the West.

The Japanese do not have the Western attitudes about the sinfulness of sexual relations. To them this has always seemed a natural phenomenon, like eating, which is to be enjoyed in its proper place. Promiscuity is in itself no more of a problem than homosexuality. Their attitudes have thus been in a sense permissive. But at the same time, they have a stronger awareness than contemporary Westerners of the necessity for bending the desires of the individual to the surrounding social environment. They abide by social rules that seem to Westerners extremely confining to the individual's emotional life. Thus Japanese may seem to Westerners to be at the same time both licentious and puritanical, with the license applying for the most part to males and the purity to females.

The primitive Japanese revered fertility not just in agriculture but among humans as well, and phallic symbols were common objects of worship in rural Japan until recent times. In the classical period, love became the main literary theme in a court life of astonishingly free sexual ways. Some of this sexual freedom survived into modern times in parts of rural Japan, where premarital sexual relations were condoned and marriages were frequently not registered, and therefore not made permanent, until the bride had proven her ability to bear children. Even today in Japanese society in general there is little condemnation of sexual acts but only anxiety over their social consequences.

Another characteristic of early Japan was a definitely matriarchal substratum in society. The mythical ancestor of the imperial line was a sun goddess; Chinese texts tell us that feminine leadership was common in the third century; and there were ruling empresses as late as the eighth. Women had great freedom in Heian court life and dominated much of its literature. Even in early feudal days women could inherit property and have a role in the feudal system.

Subsequently, however, Confucian philosophy and the long feudal experience combined to restrict the freedom of women and force them into complete subordination to men. Women, who in the age of swordsmanship were obviously less capable of fighting than men, were gradually pushed out of the feudal structure and into a peripheral and supplementary role to men. Confucianism, which was the product of a patriarchal and strongly male-dominated society in China, saw women as important for bearing children and perpetuating the family more than as helpmates or objects of love. Confucianism tended to be puritanical, considering romantic love to be a weakness and sex as merely a mechanism for maintaining family continuity.

Among the peasantry women always retained their importance as coworkers with men in the fields and consequently retained a more earthy independence as individuals, but in polite society women by the Tokugawa period had become the entirely subservient handmaidens and playthings of men. A daughter could, through her marriage, strengthen the family's relations with another family and was therefore raised carefully to be a decorous and unsullied item of value in the marriage mart. A wife was expected to devote herself selflessly to the well-being of her husband's family, under the usually strict or even harsh supervision of her mother-in-law. No extra-familial social life was considered necessary for her, and in fact any contact with men outside the family was seen as potentially dangerous. Since marriage was determined by family needs and was not the result of attraction between the young couple, who very likely had never seen each other before marriage, conjugal love seemed a secondary matter which might, or might not, develop between the pair.

In this system, sexual looseness or infidelity on the part of the women was considered socially very disruptive and was therefore carefully guarded against. Men, however in their greater freedom, could develop a broader social and sexual life, so long as they did not let it impinge on family duties. A rich man could maintain secondary wives or mistresses. All those who could afford it could frequent the amusement quarters of the larger towns and cities, where, in a setting of theaters and restaurants, men could be entertained by the sprightly conversation, artistic talents in dance and song, and sexual attractions of professionally trained women. These women themselves ranged from simple prostitutes to famous courtesans who required careful courting before they were likely to enter into a sexual relationship. It is women of this latter type who came to be known in the nineteenth century as geisha and still exist in contemporary Japan, though in very small numbers. To this demimonde of the amusement quarters were relegated the flirtation and courting that was a part of normal social life in the West but was entirely missing from polite society in Japan.

Most of the features of this social system of late feudal Japan existed at one time or another in the West, but in Japan they constitute a more recent tradition, having existed full blown past the middle of the nineteenth century, and it is therefore not surprising that more of the attitudes and customs derived from this system still persist even in a fast changing Japan. Arranged marriages, for example, remain part of the system, though ever since the 1920s increasing numbers of young people have insisted on finding their mates through love marriages in the Western manner.

At present the marriage situation is quite mixed. The continuing strictness with which most girls are raised and the tendency of Japanese to do things by groups means that there is much less pairing off of courting couples than in the West, and boys and girls as a result are much shyer in their one-to-one relations. While many do establish bonds that lead to marriage, others feel that family aid in identifying a suitable mate can be helpful. Young people never feel obliged to bow to family wishes against their own preferences, but a first meeting between a young man and woman is still commonly arranged by the respective families, and, if the principals are pleased, this will lead to marriage. Moreover an official "go-between" couple is likely to play a central role in the marriage ceremony itself, whether or not it has been a partially arranged marriage. One happy result of this system is that almost everyone who would like to get married and is free from serious disabilities can count on finding a spouse.

Conjugal love in such a marriage system is still likely to be something that develops more after marriage than before, and several external circumstances militate against its becoming as central to family life as it is in the West. The long hours devoted to commuting in urban Japan, the relative paucity of vacations, the five and a half day work week which is still common, the willingness of Japanese to devote long hours to overtime work, and the limitation of social life largely to men, all combine to make the amount of time a Japanese couple spends together much less than would be customary in the West. The confined living conditions of most homes and the custom of sleeping with the children also cut down on conjugal intimacies. Finally, premodern attitudes of disregard for conjugal love and harsh subordination of women still persist to some extent, especially among the more old-fashioned, and diminish the warmth of the conjugal bond.

The double moral standard also remains stronger in Japan than is some Western countries. Many young women, like their contempories in the West, now have premarital sexual freedom, but Japanese girls on the whole are still raised much more strictly in such matters than Japanese boys or than most girls in the West. Married women, moreover, are expected to be far more faithful than men. They have virtually no extra-family social life. Except for a very few at the top of society, who may participate stiffly and unhappily in formal banquets, usually those that include foreigners, married women do not go out with their husbands to dinners and parties or entertain outsiders in their homes, which are usually so small as to preclude this sort of entertainment. Their life is likely to be limited to husband, children, a few close relatives, some old schoolday girl friends, and possibly the activities of the P.T.A.

Meanwhile their husbands develop a fuller social life with their work group, which may include a few young unmarried women. Very commonly a group of men from work will stop on their way home at one or more of the myriad bars that are a feature of all cities. Here the bar hostesses, the successors to the geisha tradition, engage them in amusing conversation, skillfully tickle their male egos, and afford an atmosphere of sexual titillation, which can lead to more serious involvements and for some bar girls to a more prosperous and stable life as a mistress or even a wife. The milieu may be very different, but the spirit of the modern Japanese bar is close to that of the amusement quarters of feudal times.

ALL THIS IS, of course, changing, and the contemporary woman is by no means as browbeaten an individual as she was only a few decades ago or as she sometimes appears to be to Westerners today. Surface appearances can be misleading. Husbands and wives tend not to show overt signs of affection for each other in public, and the curtness and derogation some men show their wives—until recently an old-fashioned man might routinely refer to his spouse as "my stupid wife"—is at least partly a convention in speaking to or about a member of one's own family. Most wives for their part would never dream of praising their husbands before somebody else. These are for the most part superficial characteristics inherited from an earlier system. Underneath, great changes are going on, as women win a position of greater equality with men and the assumption grows that there should be a strong bond of love between husband and wife.

Perhaps these tendencies can be best seen through some small but significant examples. I can remember very well that in the 1920s a wife was likely to follow deferentially a pace behind her husband on the street, encumbered with whatever babies or bundles needed to be carried, while he strode ahead in lordly grandeur. Over the years I have seen the wife catch up with her husband, until they now walk side by side, and the babies and bundles are often in his arms. Where there is a family car, a wife is likely to drive it almost as much as the husband. Whereas once no husband would stoop to doing any housework, increasing numbers now help out with the evening dishes. And many a wife has made it clear that she will not tolerate bar hopping or other dalliances on the part of her husband. No one can say how far or how fast these trends will develop, but their direction is unmistakably toward a single standard either of mutual permissiveness at the one end of the spectrum or mutual respect and fidelity at the other.

There is another way in which the position of Japanese women is something more than it has often seemed to be. As we have seen, Japan may originally have had a matriarchal society, and elements of this matriarchy seem to have persisted all the way through, despite the heavy overlay of male supremacy resulting from feudalism and Confucianism. There is a hint of this in the expectation in medieval times that women would have every bit as much strength of will and bravery as men. In modern times, it is generally accepted that women have more will power and psychological strength then men, and there can be no doubt that the modern Japanese family centers around and is dominated by the mother, not the father. In fact, the father, though the financial support, is otherwise likely to be pretty much of a cypher in family affairs. Family finances are run almost exclusively by the mother, with the father often on a sort of allowance provided by her. He is likely to be away from home almost all of the waking hours of his smaller children. Their life is basically with the mother, and she becomes the "education mom" who sees to their good performance in school. American comic strips like "Blondie" and family situation comedies on TV and in the movies, which commonly depict a bumbling, henpecked father, have for long been popular in Japan as being entirely understandable despite their unfamiliar social setting.

The domineering father of Freudian psychiatry hardly exists in the Japanese psychological makeup, though another Freudian concern, the excessive attachment to and dependence of the male child on the mother, is a major psychological problem. This is the *amae* syndrome we have already encountered. A husband sometimes seems to be the wife's big grown-up child, requiring tender care and pampering like the other children, or else he shows a need for special feminine attention and flattery from other women—as from geisha in earlier times or bar girls today. Husbands are likely to demonstrate weaknesses of personality and cause family problems. On the other hand, wives are expected to have a strong character, to always be "lady-like," and to hold the family together—and for the most part they live up to these expectations.

THE WIFE may be the dominant member of the family, but women still have an overwhelmingly subservient position in the broader society. With education compulsory through the ninth grade and 90 percent of the age group going through twelve years, girls receive as much education as boys through secondary school, but they fall off badly at higher levels. Though the majority of junior college students are women, these colleges are looked upon, in a sense, as finishing schools, preparing women with polite accomplishments for marriage. At the four-year university level, women decline sharply in numbers. As recently as 1950 they accounted for only 2 percent of university students. There are a few women's universities, largely of Christian background, but in the other universities, all of which are now coeducational, women constitute only about a fifth of the student population and a mere 10 percent in the best institutions. An expensive four year university education seems less worthwhile for girls, who are expected to end up as no more than housewives.

Japanese tend to marry at a later age than Americans, averaging around twenty-four for women and twenty-eight for men, which is about three years later than in the United States. Most women thus have from four to eight years between the completion of their schooling and their marriages, and during this time they enter the labor market. Those with lesser educations commonly become the labor force in light industries, such as textiles and electronics, or perform menial jobs, such as waitresses, sales girls, or elevator attendants. Those with more education are likely to become secretaries and office girls, but these also perform menial jobs, such as serving tea to the men in the office. Both groups of workers, being temporary, are not on the employment escalator that leads to lifetime employment at constantly rising wages. Marrying later and being confined longer to motherly supervision of the children than in the United States, the Japanese wife returns later to the job market than her American counterpart and in smaller numbers, and once again she is excluded from the privileged lifetime employment and seniority system. Despite these conditions more than half of Japanese women are counted as members of the work force, and they constitute over 40 percent of its total, though they are overwhelmingly in its lower brackets.

In agriculture, where women have always had a large role, postwar conditions have made them even more important than before. Since the war, both farm boys and girls have for the most part streamed off after their schooling to more lucrative employment in the cities. Those young men who remained to inherit the family farm have found it very difficult to find brides, and these conditions of scarcity have resulted in a sharp rise in the relative status of farm wives. In many farm households, moreover, the husband has himself abandoned agriculture, commuting to work in a nearby factory or moving to the city permanently or seasonally. This splitting of families and the denuding of the countryside of able-bodied males has raised some difficult social problems, and it has also produced a common pattern of the housewife as the main farm worker, supported by aid from the husband's elderly parents.

The educated career woman does exist in Japan, but in lesser numbers than in most industrialized Western countries. There are many women executives in small businesses, but they are all but unknown in big business. Only a tiny number have recently crept into the higher bureaucracy. Women are relatively common in education, constituting about half the teaching force in elementary education and sizable numbers in secondary schools, junior colleges, and women's universities. There are many women doctors and occasional women judges, especially in the juvenile courts. There are about as many in the Diet as in the parliaments of the West—six in the lower house in 1977 and somewhat more in the upper house. Women are prominent in literature and the arts and even have a small role in journalism. More than half of the women belong to organizations, such as the ubiquitous Women's Associations (*Fujinkai*), and the P.T.A., which is actually run almost exclusively by mothers, has served as a medium through which many women have become actively involved in various citizens' and local residents' movements. However, most fields of higher endeavor still remain exclusively or predominantly the preserves of men.

Nonetheless, the position of women in Japan has changed greatly over the past century, especially since World War II, and it will obviously continue to change. The provisions of the 1947 constitution, which is quite explicit about the equality of the sexes, tip the scales quite definitively toward increased equality and greater prestige for them. The constitution is worth quoting in full on this subject:

There shall be no discrimination in political, economic or social relations, because of . . . sex. . . . Marriage shall be based only on the mutual consent of both sexes and it shall be maintained through mutual cooperation with the equal rights of husband and wife as a basis. With regard to choice of spouse, property rights, inheritance, choice of domicile, divorce and other matters pertaining to marriage and the family, laws shall be enacted from the standpoint of individual dignity and the essential equality of the sexes.

The laws now give women full legal equality. For example, whereas prewar laws made divorce easy for men and all but impossible for women, women now constitute the majority of applicants for divorce, though divorce rates remain far below those current in the United States and much lower even than in Japan a half century ago. The divorce rate is only one eighteenth that of the United States, though one reason for this is that the greater wage discrimination particularly against older women in the Japanese labor market makes it more difficult for a divorced wife in Japan to make a decent living, and another reason may be the greater difficulty for her to remarry.

Despite the great gains made by women in recent decades, social limitations on them and discrimination in employment remain severe. The average wage for women workers was still less than half that for men as late as 1971. Women still have a long way to go to achieve social and economic equality. Under these circumstances, Westerners are sometimes surprised that the organized "women's lib" movement has not become more prominent in Japan than it has. One reason may be that women in recent decades have made such huge advances that they are still busy digesting them. Labor shortages in the years leading up to and through World War II and then again in the postwar economic surge have given them a much larger economic role and therefore a greater chance for economic independence. The mechanization of kitchen and house work since the war, through washing machines, vacuum cleaners, electric cooking utensils, especially the electric rice cooker, and the like, have freed them from much of the drudgery of domestic labor, opening time for outside work or other activities. These factors combined with the postwar legal gains and sweeping social changes have given women ever wider opportunities that are still expanding rapidly.

There may, however, be another more important reason why Japanese women have not responded more to the "women's lib" movement, and this is simply that it does not fit their style. In part this may be because they are trapped by their own "lady-like" qualities, but a more fundamental point may be that, whereas a bitter underdog reaction may fit the traditional position of Western women as the "weaker sex," it is less to the taste of Japanese women, who are proud of their dominant family role and are so definitely the "stronger sex."

Religion

21

IF THIS BOOK dealt with a South Asian or Middle Eastern people, it might well have started with a consideration of religion. Even for most Western nations, religion would have required earlier and fuller treatment. But religion occupies a more peripheral position in Japan. Before the seventeenth century it did play much the same role in Japan as in the West, but the trend toward secularism that has recently become marked in the West dates back at least three centuries in Japan.

The secularism of Japanese society is the product of a Confucian philosophical background, which even earlier had this same effect on China and Korea—China after the ninth century and Korea from the fifteenth century on. Confucianism originally stemmed from the ancient Chinese philosopher for whom Westerners, though not East Asians, have named this philosophy. (East Asians call it "the teaching of the scholars.") Confucius lived from approximately 551 to 479 B.C., but Confucianism did not take final shape in China until the twelfth century A.D. It stressed a rational natural order, of which man was a harmonious element, and a social order based on strict ethical rules and headed up in a unified state, governed by men of education and superior ethical wisdom. It had revered texts but no concept of deity, no priesthood, and very little religious ritual. There was no worship, only right thinking and right living, as shown particularly through loyalty to the ruler, filial piety to one's father, and strict observation of proper social ritual and etiquette.

The Confucian classics, the five basic relationships, the emphasis on history, and many other features of the Confucian system entered Japan

213

with the first great wave of Chinese influence between the sixth and ninth centuries, but Confucianism tended to be overshadowed by Buddhism, until the emergence of the centralized Tokugawa system in the seventeenth century made it seem more relevant than it had before. From then on, Confucian schools of philosophy dominated thought and Confucian attitudes pervaded society, until the Japanese in the early nineteenth century had become almost as thoroughly Confucian as the Chinese or Koreans, despite their very non-Confucian feudal political system.

Confucianism, however, did not survive the great transition of the late nineteenth century as an organized philosophy. Its concepts of the cosmos were seen to be highly inaccurate when compared with the results of modern Western science, and its moral values appeared to be tied to a type of society and government that had to be abandoned in the face of the Western menace. In reorganizing inherited Tokugawa educational institutions into Tokyo University, the government finally dropped the old Confucian academy entirely and concentrated only on the Western scientific and medical aspects of these schools. A few old Confucian scholars fought a rearguard action, forcing Confucian terminology and concepts into the new system, wherever they could. The outstanding example of this was the Imperial Rescript on Education, issued in 1890 at the time of the adoption of the constitution. It has very little to say about education but was a purely Confucian statement of the Confucian relationships and the duties of citizens to the throne. Thus some Confucian attitudes survived, though Confucianism as an accepted body of thought died out completely with the passing of the older generation.

Contemporary Japanese obviously are not Confucianists in the sense that their Tokugawa ancestors were, but they are still permeated with Confucian ethical values. Confucianism probably has more influence on them than does any other of the traditional religions or philosophies. Any discussion of Japanese religions that overlooks this point would be seriously misleading. Behind the wholehearted Japanese acceptance of modern science, modern concepts of progress and growth, universalistic principles of ethics, and democratic ideals and values, strong Confucian traits still lurk beneath the surface, such as the belief in the moral basis of government, the emphasis on interpersonal relations and loyalties, and the faith in education and hard work. Almost no one considers himself a Confucianist today, but in a sense almost all Japanese are.

BUDDHISM is the Japanese religion that comes closest to paralleling Christianity, for it too is concerned with the after life and salvation of the individual. In this it shows its non-East Asian origin in India, a region that in religious and philosophical terms is more like the West than like East Asia. The historical Buddha, who was roughly contemporary with Confucius, started with the basic Indian idea of a never-ending cycle of lives, each determining the next, and added to this the concepts that life is painful, that its suffering derives from human attachment or desires, but that these desires can be ovecome by the Buddha's teaching, thus freeing the individual for painless merging with the cosmos in Nirvana, or "nothingness." As the teaching grew, it came to stress reverence for the "Three Treasures," which were the Buddha, the "law" or teachings embodied in an extensive literature, and the religious community, or the monastic organization.

The branch of Buddhism that spread throughout East Asia is called Mahayana, or the "greater vehicle," in contrast to Theravada, or the "doctrine of the elders," which survives in Ceylon and much of Southeast Asia. Mahayana taught salvation into a Paradise that seems closer to the Western concept of Heaven than to the original Buddhist Nirvana. It also emphasized the worship, not just of the historical Buddha, but of myriad Buddha-like figures, including Bodhisattvas, who had stayed back one step short of Nirvana and Buddhahood in order to aid in the salvation of others.

In Japan, Mahayana Buddhism developed three major emphases. One appearing in the ninth century was "esoteric" Buddhism, which stressed ritual and art as well as doctrines. The second emphasis starting a century later was on salvation through faith, particularly in Amida, the Buddha of the "pure land" of the Western Paradise, or in the Lotus Sutra, a scripture in which the Buddha promised the salvation of "all sentient beings," that is, of all animal life. This emphasis gave rise to the founding in the twelfth and thirteenth centuries of new sects—the Pure Land Sect (Jodoshu), the True (Pure Land) Sect (Shinshu), and Nichiren—which are today the largest Buddhist sects in Japan. The third emphasis was on self-reliance in seeking salvation through self-discipline and meditation. This became embodied in the two Zen, or "meditation," sects, introduced from China in 1191 and 1227. These developed regimens of "sitting in meditation" (*zazen*) and of intellectual self-discipline through nonsense conundrums (*koan*), which were supposed to lead to salvation through sudden enlightenment (*satori*) and also, incidentally, to character building.

As we have seen, Buddhism first came to Japan in the sixth century and played much the same role as Christianity in North Europe, as the vehicle for the transmission of a whole higher culture. A great part of subsequent esthetic expression in architecture, sculpture, and painting was associated with Buddhism, as it was with Christianity in the West. The monastic establishments became rich landowners, as in the West, and at times exercised considerable military and political power. Even congregations of lay believers were politically active in the fifteenth and sixteenth centuries. Indeed the whole intellectual, artistic, social, and political life of Japan was permeated with Buddhism from the ninth through the sixteenth centuries.

Not much of this survives in contemporary Japan after three centuries of the secularization of society. Buddhist concepts about such things as Paradise and the transmigration of the soul linger on in folklore but do not serve as guiding principles for many people. Monasteries and temples, both great and small, dot the Japanese landscape but usually play only a subdued background role in the life of the community, and the postwar land reform proved a financially crippling blow to many rural temples because it deprived them of the lands that had helped support them. A few people come to worship and find solace in the Buddhist message of salvation. Temple grounds are often the neighborhood playground for children. Most funerals are conducted by Buddhist priests, and burial grounds attached to temples are the place of interment for most people after cremation, a custom learned from India. Some families have ancestral tablets, which they place in small Buddhist altars on a shelf in the home. The Tokugawa system of requiring the registry of all persons as parishioners of some Buddhist temple—the purpose of this was to ferret out secret Christians—has given all Japanese families a Buddhist sectarian affiliation, though usually this only indicates the sect of the temple where the family burial plot is located.

Most temples and monasteries today maintain their rituals, though often with pathetically small numbers of monks or priests. Some sects took on new intellectual and religious vigor in modern times, in part in response to the Christian missionary movement. They developed publishing ventures, schools, and even a Buddhist missionary movement in East Asia and America. A few modern Japanese, such as some prewar military men and postwar business executives, have practiced Zen, but their numbers are small and their concern is usually less with Buddhist enlightenment than with the development of their own personalities. Contemporary Japanese life thus is full of traces of Buddhism as a sort of background melody, but it is not for many a leitmotif in either their intellectual or emotional lives.

SHINTO, the most distinctive of the Japanese religions, has also slipped into a background role in modern urbanized Japan. Early Shinto centered around the animistic worship of natural phenomenon—the sun, mountains, trees, water, rocks, and the whole process of fertility. Totemistic ancestors were included among the *kami*, or deities, worshiped, and no line was drawn between man and nature. Deities were worshiped through offerings, prayers, and light-hearted festivals at the many shrines, all marked by *torii* gateways. The shrines were dedicated to imperial ancestors, the ancestors of the local *uji*, the deity of rice, or the spirit of some outstanding natural phenomena, such as a great mountain, a beautiful waterfall, or simply an unusual tree or rock. There was no theology or even a concept of ethics, beyond an abhorrence of death and defilement and an emphasis on ritual purity.

Since Shinto was unconcerned with the problem of the afterlife that dominated Buddhist thought, and Mahayana was no exclusive, jealous religion but throughout its spread easily accommodated itself to local faiths, Buddhism and Shinto settled into a comfortable coexistence, with Shinto shrines often becoming administratively linked with Buddhist monasteries. The Japanese never developed the idea, so prevalent in South and West Asia as well as the West, that a person had to adhere exclusively to one religion or another. Premodern Japanese were usually both Buddhists and Shintoists at the same time and often enough Confucianists as well.

For most of the premodern period, Shinto was definitely subordinate to Buddhism, being thought of as representing the locally valid Japanese variants of universal Buddhist truths and deities. But Buddhist fervor waned after the sixteenth century, while the native origins of Shinto and its association with the foundation myths of Japan and with the cult of the

The *torii* gateway marking the entrance to a Shinto shrine in Kyoto. The precincts of shrines and Buddhist temples commonly serve as the playground for the neighborhood children. Snow falls occasionally in all of Japan except Okinawa, but it is heavy only in the higher mountains, the extreme north, and the northwest coast, known as "the snow country." (*Maryknoll*)

imperial ancestors focused new attention on it in a Japan that was becoming more nationalistic and eventually came to seek a new unity under symbolic imperial rule. A sort of Shinto revival, centering around reverence for the emperor, became part of the movement that led to the overthrow of the Tokugawa and the founding of the new regime in 1868.

The leaders of the Meiji Restoration were thoroughly anti-Buddhist, brutally cutting it off from Shinto, and they attempted at first to create a Shinto-centered system of government. Although they soon discovered that this concept could not be mixed successfully with their basically Western political patterns, they did create a system of state support for the great historic Shinto shrines and developed new national ones, such as the very grand and beautiful Meiji Shrine in Tokyo dedicated to the first modern emperor and the Yasukuni Shrine, also in Tokyo, for the souls of military men who had died in defense of the country. In order to maintain the claim that Japanese enjoyed complete religious freedom, this nationalistic "state Shinto" was officially defined by the government as being not a religion but a manifestation of patriotism. In a sense this was correct, because, even though it did impinge, at least in form, on the field of religion in its enforced worship at Shinto shrines and the reverential treatment of the pictures of the emperor and empress and copies of the Imperial Rescript on Education that was required of all schools throughout the country, it was essentially an artificial creation, far removed from the basic attitudes of Shinto and deriving more from modern nationalism, and it reached its peak in the frenzy of nationalism preceding World War II.

The American occupation attacked "state Shinto" with vigor as a dangerous manifestation of hypernationalism, and in the general postwar reaction against militarism and patriotism it disappeared almost completely. The occupation also demanded that a sharp line be drawn between government and religion. The great historical shrines were thrown back on their own individual sources of income, and as a result all but the most popular ones fell into dire financial straits. Although a few had wide support, which has enabled them to generate new sources of income, the ban on public funds for institutions connected with religion hit most of them hard and also, incidentally, contributed to the slowness with which the government came to the aid of private universities, many of which have Christian, Buddhist, or even Shinto affiliations.

With "state Shinto" gone, Shintoism has reverted to a more peripheral role in Japanese life. Shrines of all types are scattered everywhere, often in places of great beauty and charm, though usually with signs of quiet decay. They are visited by a few believers in the efficacy of their rituals and prayers to their dieties or, if they are historically famous or are known for their natural beauties, by throngs of eager sightseers. In a manner reminiscent of prewar days, even top government leaders will on occasion visit some great shrine, such as the one at Ise, dedicated to the sun goddess ancestress of the imperial line, while the Meiji Shrine continues as a sort of national monument analogous to the Lincoln Memorial in Washington, and the Yasukuni Shrine has a role like that of the Tomb of the Unknown Soldier. Children are often taken to shrines at certain prescribed points in their lives—shortly after birth, at special festivals in their third, fifth, and seventh years, and at annual boys' and girls' festivals. Shrines are also the setting for many marriages, and homes frequently have "god shelves" where offerings can be made to Shinto deities.

Traditional Shinto seems most alive today in the gay shrine festivals held annually on specific dates by all shrines of any importance. At these

During shrine festivals, local youths often carry around a miniature shrine temporarily housing the local deity. Here we see younger boys with their own still smaller portable shrines (*o-mikoshi*). Such festivals are gay occasions and give participants one of their few chances to dress up in traditional garb. (*Japan National Tourist Organization*)

times, scores of booths ply a brisk trade on the shrine grounds, and the shrine deity is boisterously carried about in a portable shrine by somewhat inebriated local youths. These shrine festivals remain a prominent feature of local life, particularly in rural Japan, though some of them are taking on the character of self-conscious, historical pageants, or else are losing out in urbanized areas to more secular community festivals, which feature marching bands and drum majorettes.

In these various ways, Shinto continues to be a part of Japanese life, and folklore remains full of Shinto elements. The Japanese love of nature and sense of closeness to it also derive strongly from Shinto concepts. But very few modern Japanese find in traditional Shinto any real focus for their lives or even for their social activities or diversions.

CHRISTIANITY is usually linked with Shinto and Buddhism as one of the three traditional religions of Japan, though it is considered a foreign religion in a way Buddhism is not. First introduced by the famous Jesuit missionary, Saint Francis Xavier, in 1549, it spread more rapidly in Japan during the next several decades than in any other non-Western country, and Christians came to number close to half a million, a much larger percentage of the population of that time than they are today. But Hideyoshi and the early Tokugawa shoguns came to view Christianity as a threat to political unity and suppressed it ruthlessly, creating in the process a large number of Japanese martyrs but virtually stamping the religion out by 1638.

The nineteenth century Japanese remained deeply hostile to Christianity, but they soon learned the strength of Western feelings about the religion and therefore tacitly dropped their prohibition of it in 1873 and subsequently made explicit a policy of complete religious toleration. But Christianity this time spread much more slowly. Even today its adherents number only around three quarters of a million—less than 1 percent of the population—divided fairly evenly between Protestants and Catholics.

After the Meiji Restoration, Protestant Christianity, largely brought by American missionaries, was taken up by a number of able young samurai, particularly those from the losing side in the civil war, who sought in Christianity a new ethics and philosophy of life to take the place of discredited Confucianism. These men injected a strong sense of independence into the native church. In fact, under the leadership of Uchimura Kanzo, a leading intellectual of the time, a "No Church" movement was founded in reaction against the sectarian divisions of Protestantism in the West. During World War II the government, for control purposes, forced the various Protestant sects into a United Church, and today some 40 percent of the Protestant movement remains in the United Church of Christ in Japan (*Nihon Kirisuto Kyodan*).

The influence of Christianity on modern Japanese society is far greater than its numbers of adherents would suggest. Christians, though few in numbers, are strongly represented among the best educated, leading elements in society and have therefore exerted a quite disproportionate influence. Another factor is that Christianity, as an important element of Western civilization, has attracted general interest and curiosity. Most educated Japanese probably have a clearer concept of the history and basic tenets of Christianity than they do of Buddhism. A superficial example of the general Japanese familiarity with Christianity is the enthusiasm with which Christmas decorations are displayed by department stores and Christmas carols are blared out along the shopping streets at Christmas time.

During the Meiji period, Christians played a major role in education, particularly at the secondary level and in schools for girls. Even today a large percentage of the private secondary schools and women's universities and some of the other private universities are of Christian origin, though in relative terms the role of Christianity in education is much less important now than it once was. In the early twentieth century Christians also led in the development of social work for underprivileged and handicapped persons, and Protestant Christians were also prominent in the founding of the Socialist movement. In fact, they remained an important element in the movement throughout the prewar period, and they continued even into postwar days as a significant, moderate branch of the Socialist party. But perhaps the largest area of Christian influence is in ethics. As modern Japanese turned increasingly to universalistic values, they adopted many ethical attitudes which both historically in the West and in the Japanese mind today are associated with Christinaity. The Christian influence on contemporary Japanese ethical values thus is at least more recognizable if not actually greater than the influence of either Buddhism or Shinto. Moreover, many Japanese look upon Christians as people of high moral principles, and they often envy the apparent firmness of Christian beliefs, though they find themselves unable to accept the accompanying theology.

CHRISTIANITY, though intellectually influential, is numerically only a tiny religion in Japan, and Shinto and Buddhism are for most people more a matter of custom and convention than of meaningful beliefs. Many if not most Japanese who feel strong religious needs today, instead of looking to these three traditional religions, turn instead to superstitious folk beliefs, prevalent especially in rural Japan and among the less educated, or to a great variety of popular religious movements, which are normally lumped together under the name of "new religions." The popular superstitious beliefs are usually an amalgam of concepts derived from

Shinto, Buddhism, and Chinese folk superstitions. There are numerous local cults of all sorts, and many people pay serious attention to lucky and unlucky days, astrology, and fortune tellers.

The "new religions" have grown in part out of an old Japanese tendency to form special groups for pilgrimages or other religious activities, outside the formal organization of the established religions, but a more important reason for their growth is that they have been responsive to the social needs of Japanese, as the movement to the cities broke their ties with rural religious bodies or left them isolated without a suitable social group to which to belong. The new religions, thus, do not cater to the typical Western religious need for individual strength through the establishment of a personal bond with God, but rather to the typical Japanese need for a supportive social environment.

The "new religions" tend to be highly syncretic, combining Shinto, Buddhist, and sometimes even Christian or Western philosophic influences. Most, however, are basically Shinto in their leanings, though the largest, Soka Gakkai (the "Value Creating Association"), purports to be a lay association supporting a branch of the Nichiren sect of Buddhism. The new religions usually stress this-worldly values, rather than the after-life, emphasizing the achievement of health, prosperity, self-improvement, and happiness through faith or through magical practices. Some were founded by individuals, particularly women, who felt themselves to be possessed by the deities in a shamanistic way. Other founders merely claimed to have discovered the true way. Leadership in these religions frequently becomes hereditary, and their organization tends to be hierarchical, made up of typically Japanese groups of leaders and followers. This makes them highly susceptible to fissions, and there is also a relatively rapid turnover of members in many of them.

The officially recognized new religions number in the hundreds, and there are many more small groups lacking official recognition. The total membership claimed is in the tens of millions. Soka Gakkai alone claims sixteen million, though six would probably be a better estimate of its actual membership at any one time. Some of these new religions are by now quite old. Tenrikyo ("Teaching of the Heavenly Truth"), with a present claimed membership of almost two million, was founded by a peasant woman in 1838. Others, like Soka Gakkai, were either founded or had their major development after World War II. The large new religions tend to have grandiose headquarters and to hold numerous elaborate mass festivals and rallies. Only Soka Gakkai has attempted to play a direct role in politics by founding a party, the Komeito, which later officially separated from Soka Gakkai. All the new religions, however, provide their participants with a tightly organized, protective community, with study groups and social activities that minister perhaps more to their social than their spiritual needs.

All in all, religion in Japan provides a confused and indistinct picture. Shinto shrines and Buddhist temples are found everywhere. The lives of most Japanese are intertwined with religious observances—shrine festivals, "god shelves" and Buddhist altars in the homes, and Shinto marriages, Buddhist funerals, and other religious rites of passage. But the majority of Japanese—some 70 to 80 percent—even though carried on the rolls of one or more religious bodies, do not consider themselves believers in any religion. The ethics of the Japanese for the most part are derived from Confucianism, to which none now "belongs," and from Christianity, which is the faith of less than 1 percent. Popular religious customs are derived mostly from traditional Shinto and Buddhism, in which few really believe. And most religious life among the minority that is religiously active is devoted to folk religious beliefs or new religions that have little prestige or general influence.

Psychological Traits

22

THE PRECEDING has been only a very partial account of certain aspects of Japanese society. It stresses the norms of behavior and does not attempt to look into the many aberrations and rich variations, which are only to be expected in so large and complex a grouping of people. Some features can be seen to fit well together. Others seem to clash. Still others that are worth noting have eluded our loose-flung net entirely.

Among these is the popular generalization that the Japanese are intellectually not very creative. No one can have any doubts about their great artistic creativeness, but their achievements in the realm of ideas and philosophy do seem less impressive. No modern Japanese thinker has appeared noteworthy to the rest of the world—though we should remember that the language barrier is probably in part responsible for this. Japanese have made relatively few contributions to basic science, and only three or four so far have been singled out for Nobel Prizes. The Japanese industrial triumphs have been based largely on efficient borrowing or ingenious adaptation of foreign techniques rather than on independent scientific discoveries. Political thought, philosophy, and scholarship in the social sciences in Japan are to a large extent the manipulation or synthesizing of ideas derived from abroad, rather than original creative work. When thinkers have drawn more heavily from native Japanese inspiration, as in the case of the philosopher Nishida in the early twentieth century, who was strongly influenced by Zen concepts, the rest of the world has not been much impressed.

This situation is natural in a country which has only recently come into close contact with the rest of the world and has been engrossed in the task of catching up in technology and ideas. Whereas premodern education in Japan had been heavily moral and theoretical, modern Japanese education has been overwhelmingly practical in its aims. It has concentrated on learning about the rest of the world and its technology. Scholarly activity has been largely devoted to absorbing large chunks of information from abroad and synthesizing it with what is already known. Industry has quite wisely stressed the learning and adaptation of already known technologies, rather than the creation of new ones, though many Japanese adaptations have been so imaginative as to border on real creativity.

These traits of relative weakness in theoretical innovation but great strength in practical application were characteristic of the United States too during its period of catching up with Europe. Americans have taken a leading place in science, scholarship, and thought only in recent decades. As Japan draws abreast of the West, the same change may occur there. A sign of this may be the sudden surge of research and development activities during the past few years, as Japan began to catch up with the West in technology and felt the need of forging ahead in its own technology in order to maintain its forward push. While quite negligible a few years ago, Japan's efforts in research and development are now the third largest in the world, trailing only the United States and Soviet Union, and its devotion of over 2 percent of its GNP to such purposes—mostly through private corporations or research institutes and less through government agencies or universities than in most other countries—does not fall proportionately far behind American efforts, especially if one takes into consideration the very large military component of research in the United States, which is almost completely lacking in Japan.

Still, there is reason to wonder if intellectual creativeness will ever be a special forte of the Japanese. Their past history is studded with prominent religious leaders, great poets and writers, outstanding organizers, and even distinguished synthesizers of thought, but not with great creative intellectual figures. Japanese have always seemed to lean more toward subtlety and sensitivity than to clarity of analysis, to intuition rather than reason, to pragmatism rather than theory, to organizational skills rather than great intellectual concepts. They have never set much store by clarity of verbal analysis and originality of thought. They put great trust in nonverbal understanding and look on oral or written skills in handling language and on sharp and clever reasoning as essentially shallow and possibly deceitful. Aside from the flat factual statements of newspaper reporting, they value in their literature, not clear analysis, but artistic suggestiveness and inference. The French ideal of simplicity and absolute clarity in writing leaves them unsatisfied. They prefer complexity and indirection as coming closer to the truth than apparently simple verities as defined by fallible men.

All this may seem to stand at variance with the strength of theories and ideologies in contemporary Japan. Japanese intellectuals tend to be very theoretical. More of them are distinguished by the ardor of their adherence to their theories than by their ability to derive their theories from the facts or to apply them to reality. Vague, sweeping generalizations have a wide appeal in philosophy and politics. But it may be that some Japanese are so doctrinaire in their political and intellectual beliefs just because they accept them more on faith than on reason. Certainly Japanese Marxists adhere with stubborn blindness to the perceptions and terminology that grew out of a nineteenth century Europe that differed markedly from contemporary Japan. Scholars hold faithfully to their respective schools of thought and indulge in little cross-fertilization across these lines. Intellectuals as a whole tend to be isolated by their hotly defended "isms" from both the unresponsive masses and the pragmatic controllers of government and business. Perhaps forced by their relative weakness as theoreticians into a rigid adherence to whatever theory they have espoused, they may have created, as it were, a reverse mirror image of the pragmatism and relativism of the society in which they live.

Westerners tend to look on the relative lack of intellectual creativity of Japanese as a sign of inferiority, but this may be only a Western cultural bias. Who is to say that truths reached by reason are superior to those attained by intuition or that disputes settled by verbal skills are preferable to a consensus reached through feeling. Hair-splitting analysis and great conceptual schemes, so typical of India and the West, are not obviously better than smooth cooperation and harmony through nonverbal understanding. It is possible that a Japan standing near the forefront of knowledge in the world may come to show more intellectual creativeness than it has in the past, but on the other hand these other traits may remain more characteristic of the Japanese and may continue to contribute more to their success.

A SECOND common generalization about Japan is clearly less true. Westerners, seeing in Japan much that is strange but even more that is familiar, since it is shared with the contemporary West, often come to the conclusion that the Japanese must be a schizophrenic people, split between Western characteristics and Japanese, or Eastern as they might define them. The same theme has sometimes been taken up by Japanese authors. But at least for contemporary Japanese, this dichotomy exists largely in the eyes of the beholder, and not in their own minds. In any fast changing society there are curious and sometimes uncomfortable contrasts between traditions inherited from the past and new characteristics produced by new technologies and institutions. Japan having moved faster and farther than any other country during the past century may be subject to particularly severe strains of this sort, but they are not different in kind—only in degree—from what the West itself experiences.

Japan has not been Westernized, as is commonly asserted. Nothing is more central to traditional Western culture than Christianity, but less than 1 percent of the Japanese population has embraced this religion. What the Japanese have taken over are the modern aspects of Western culture, which for the most part the West too has only recently developed in response to modern technology—things like railroads, factories, mass education, great newspapers, television, and mass democracy. In this sense Japan has more significantly become modernized, not Westernized, and the process of modernization has taken place on the basis of Japan's own traditional culture, just as happened in the West, with the same sort of resulting contrasts and strains.

A head start in the West of four decades in railroading and of a few years in television did not make these features of modern life distinctively Western as opposed to Japanese. Japanese are every bit as much at home with them as are Americans. Tea, an East Asian drink, coffee from the Middle East, kimono-like dressing gowns, or African rhythms in music have not produced traumas or schizophrenia in the West. Why should Western foods, dress, or music have this effect on Japanese? Brahms and Beethoven now belong as much to Japanese as to Americans or even Germans. "Happy Birthday," sung always in English, and "Auld Lang Syne," sung always in Japanese, are as solid and natural parts of Japanese folk culture today as of American. Only older ladies and some very

At weddings, grooms almost always wear cutaways, called *moningu* (from "morning coat"), and brides usually kimonos with a special head covering. This mixture of dress the Japanese accept as simply traditional. Her marriage may well be the first time the bride has worn a formal kimono. (*Consulate General of Japan, N.Y.*)

wealthy women commonly wear Japanese kimonos, while most other women reserve them only for very festive occasions, such as university graduation ceremonies, if they can afford them at all. The Japanese find nothing incongruous in the contrast between the traditional Japanese garb of brides at Shinto wedding ceremonies and the traditional Western white they usually wear at civil ceremonies or Christian weddings, which are popular even for nonbelievers. Grooms are almost always dressed in Western style, specifically in cutaways in more affluent circles, a costume that is much used for formal occasions in Japan and is called *moningu* from "morning coat." Hardly any men ever wear traditional garb of any sort. Neither did their fathers or many of their grandfathers, and they would feel almost as self-conscious in a traditional Japanese costume as an American in Indian dress. Cultural schizophrenia, which may seem obvious to the untutored Western eye, simply does not exist for the Japanese, except possibly for some self-conscious intellectuals. The Japanese live in a society, which despite its rapid changes, is to them a well-ordered, coherent whole.

Japanese society is remarkable, if anything, for its homogeneity, order-liness, and adherence to strict patterns. Though constantly changing, it remains thoroughly and distinctively Japanese. As compared to other industrialized societies, Japan seems relatively stable. There is much talk of crime and the rebelliousness and lack of moral fiber of youth, but, at least in comparison with the United States, crime rates are low and have been tending to drop. Despite the wild violence of a few, young people on the whole seem remarkably cheerful, well mannered, and conformist. Dropouts are rare, and almost all young people strive hard to get the best possible schooling and then settle fairly smoothly into the careers it has led them to.

Society is not rent by sharp cleavages, but is almost monotonously uni-form. There is almost no great inherited wealth and relatively little de-grading poverty. The social center of gravity is the huge stratum known by the Japanese-English term of the "salary-man" (*sarariman*)—a more accurate description than our own "white collar worker." Above these are only a handful of top executives and below them farmers and manual wage laborers, who aspire to and often approach *sarariman* norms of life.

On the surface Japan gives all the appearances of a happy society and probably deserves this evaluation as much as any country. Children always seem to be bubbling with good spirits. People everywhere seem cheerful and purposeful. The early retirement age for men and the greater confinement of married women to the home may account for the youthfulness of city crowds, as compared to those in the United States, and the consequent impression of greater energy and vitality. The problems of age may be kept more out of sight. Still, in terms of health and longevity, Japan measures high for old people too. Life expectancy at birth is over 76 for women and around 71 for men, which is appreciably higher than in the United States, especially for men. All in all, the Japa-nese show no signs of schizophrenic instability but instead seem to have a remarkably stable and smoothly functioning society, which could well serve as a model for others, including the Western democracies.

IF THERE is an underlying psychological malaise in Japan, it does not come from the mixed origins of contemporary Japanese culture but from the uniformity and strictness of the patterns society fixes on the individ-ual. A tightly knit social system leaves many tied down by heavy burdens of duty and obligation, or uncomfortably constrained by rules of social conformity. Young people, as we have seen, are particularly restive, chafing at the reins and occasionally breaking out in wild rebellion. A rapid rate of change has produced a wide generation gap, which probably makes true communication between the generations even more difficult than in the West, though this is masked on the surface by the typical Japanese desire to maintain a show of harmony and to avoid confrontation by a discrete silence between parent and child on matters of consequence.

In a fast changing Japan, no one can say that present conditions of stability and apparent contentedness will continue indefinitely. All industrialized societies are encountering difficulties in accommodating themselves to the rapid rate of change, and the problems Japan faces on this score may be particularly severe. The speed of change is greater than in most other industrialized societies, and the physical base is definitely worse. No country faces graver problems of crowding and pollution, and, although statistics show the Japanese well on their way to achieving a monetary standard of living close to the highest, the "standard of well-being," if one can draw this distinction, is relatively low. The Japanese lack adequate space for living and for their business activities. The resulting high cost of land inflates all prices; crowding produces great economic waste through traffic congestion, pollution, and long hours of painful commuting; and lack of adequate space for living and diversion cuts down on the enjoyment of life. Space is a very important component of wealth, but this the Japanese lack and always will. They are correct in their common complaint that they are in reality a lot poorer than statistics would indicate.

Some observers believe that Japan's present happy condition of relative stability, efficiency, and contentedness is merely a transitory phase, resulting from a fortuitous but temporary blend of inherited virtues and newly acquired skills, which will probably change over time into a less desirable mix. As they point out, Japan's resounding economic success and relative freedom from some of the ills that beset other industrialized lands may be merely a sign of cultural lag. There are many signs of the erosion or unraveling of the Japanese system as it exists today. The present may be but a fleeting "golden age" for Japan, which will be followed by a time of even greater ills than those which plague the other industrialized lands. On the other hand, it could be argued that Japan has brought into the modern age certain distinctive features that may permanently make for a

Japan's commuting trains are a miracle of efficiency and a catastrophe of overcrowding. Trains of six to ten cars run as close as two minutes apart and are crammed with passengers. Station attendants often have to shove the last few in, to close the doors. The greater bulk of overcoats requires more shovers in winter. (*Associated Press*)

good blend of characteristics and help the Japanese deal successfully with the problems of modern urban, industrial society. Only time will tell, but for the present Japan deserves to be considered one of the most successful of modern industrial societies.

Two aspects of contemporary Japanese life, however, are areas of particular concern. One is foreign relations. Japan can only live through trading with others. If it is to survive, it, more than most other countries, requires a world that is both peaceful and relatively open to trade. But it has little power to assure such worldwide conditions, nor has it shown much ability in exerting its influence toward achieving them. The very homogeneity and tight, efficient organization of the Japanese within their own national unit has tended to cut them off in feeling and understanding from others. Their great skills in interpersonal relations within their own country turn almost into handicaps in their dealings with others. The greatest need of the Japanese is to find ways to utilize their great capacities more effectively for the creation of the sort of world environment they must have for their very survival. This is a subject we shall look at more closely in the final section of this book.

The other chief problem area is politics. Modern mass democracies, as they have grown considerably in size and horrendously in complexity, have run into such serious difficulties that some people have raised questions regarding their ultimate "governability" under conditions as they seem to be developing. Among the great industrialized democracies, Japan has the shortest history of democratic rule and is the only one that lacks any trace of democratic concepts in its premodern history. Politics moreover is the area of sharpest and most open discord in contemporary Japanese society. The political decision-making process is so slow and cumbersome that many observers fear that Japan may become completely immobilized in political decisions, especially if the conservative majority that has predominated since the war wears away and is replaced by multi-party confusion. Politics is not only a key aspect of the highly centralized Japanese system but perhaps the most threatened. It is to this subject that we turn next.

朝日新聞衆院総選挙特

党　　派	改選前	候補者数	新議席数
自 民 党	265	320	242
社 会 党	112	162	116
共 産 党	39	128	16
公 明 党	30	84	5
民 社 党	19	51	26
新 自 ク 派	5	25	17
諸 派	0	17	
無 所 属	4	112	20
合　　計	474	899	488
欠　　員			

POLITICS

PART FOUR

Tabulation of the December 5, 1976, election results by the Asahi (Morning Sun) newspaper. The three columns of figures are "previous seats," "number of candidates," and "members elected." The party names are on the left, starting with the Liberal Democrats and ending with "totals." The full lower house of 511 has not yet been decided. (*AP Wirephoto*)

The Political
Heritage

23

HE JAPANESE do not have in their political heritage any experience with the concepts and practices of democracy. There is
much loose talk about a basic Asian village democracy but little
reality to this idea. At the village level almost anywhere there is likely to
be a certain degree of egalitarianism among persons in daily contact with
one another and frequently engaged in communal tasks. Group decisions
may be the rule, as they were in the traditional Japanese village. But the
member families of these villages had sharp differences in status and
authority. In any case, village communalism is a far cry from political
democracy, which depends on individual rights and representative institutions among large groups of people not in daily face-to-face contact.

In the West, both the concept of individual rights and the practices of
representation grew in part out of the feudal experience, which had
stressed the legal nature and the mutuality of feudal rights and obliga-
tions. In Japan, feudal bonds were seen as basically moral. At the height
of feudalism in the fifteenth and sixteenth centuries there was a degree of
mutuality and bargaining in feudal relations, and in the late feudalism of
the Tokugawa period there was a well-established and highly complex
system of interrelationships between lord and follower, but throughout
the Japanese ideally saw the feudal bond as committing the inferior to
absolute obedience and loyalty and granting the superior unlimited authority. There were no inalienable rights, no concepts that might have
underlain a Magna Carta, and no experience of any sort with representative bodies. In these terms, one could scarcely imagine a system less

congenial to democratic ideas and institutions than the Japanese polity on the eve of the opening to the West.

The Japanese of the mid-nineteenth century did not even have any desire to create a democratic system. Unlike so-called "modernizing" nations in the twentieth century, they did not find democracy an appealing concept, nor did they see any need to attempt to create a democratic system. What seemed imperative was to build as rapidly as possible a strong, centralized Japan capable of meeting the military and economic menace of the West. As they experimented with ways to do this, they came to realize that elements of the Western democratic system might be of use to them. But these were merely means to an end and in no sense primary objectives.

Despite the lack of democratic experience or leanings, the nineteenth century Japanese did, however, derive from their heritage many great assets for building a strong, centralized nation, and some of these qualities also underlay later democratic developments. One prime asset was a strong sense of the ethical basis for government, drawn from their Confucian heritage. Closely associated with this were their relatively high standards of honesty and efficiency in political administration. There were some cruel, inefficient, and even dishonest government officials. Gift giving to superiors was rampant but, though this would be viewed today as corruption, it was regarded at the time as part of the system and was usually limited by fixed custom. Within the limits of the system, almost all administrators were absolutely loyal to their superiors, scrupulously honest, meticulous in the performance of their duties, and efficient, at least by premodern standards. For example, the maintenance of order and the collection of agricultural taxes in the shogun's vast domain was performed by a handful of relatively low ranking intendants with a thoroughness and at a cost that would have been the envy of any regime in the world in the eighteenth century.

These high standards of administrative efficiency continued without break into the modern period, accounting for the relative smoothness of the transfer of power and the change of systems following the Meiji Restoration. Despite the tremendous confusion at the time, there was no general breakdown of law and order or any prolonged slump in the collection of agricultural taxes, which by the early 1870s had been successfully transferred from more than two hundred and sixty autonomous feudal domains into the hands of the new central government.

The new government also had surprisingly little difficulty in reorganizing the bureaucratized samurai officials of the old system into a new prefectural and central government bureaucracy and into a modernized police force and the officers of a modern army and navy. The division of the central civil bureaucracy into ministries like those of the Western political pattern was for them a relatively simple change, which was perfectly understandable because of the ministerial divisions of the system borrowed in ancient times from China and the incipient ministries of the Tokugawa period. There was not even any difficulty in making the shift at the end of the nineteenth century in the method of selecting the bureaucracy from the hereditary system of Tokugawa times or the reliance on personal contacts in the early Meiji period to a mechanical use of the new educational system and formal examinations. This was because the new system was consonant with late Tokugawa demands for more emphasis on individual merit and was reminiscent of the old Chinese concept of choosing the top administrators through examinations. Thus, most of the political changes were not very difficult for them, and there was throughout a great continuity in the spirit of bureaucratic loyalty, efficiency, and honesty, which had been inherited from the immediate past and which, even today, is largely responsible for the continuing high standards of government service in Japan.

Another important political heritage was the long tradition of group rather than personalized leadership. This, although contrasting sharply with the personalized nature of any feudal system, actually goes far back in Japanese history. As early as the Kamakura period in the thirteenth century, there was a tendency to share power, as through the various councils in Kamakura, paired deputies in Kyoto, and the system of having a "co-signer" who paralleled the shogunal Hojo "regent" in Kamakura. In Tokugawa times this sharing of power was even more marked. The councils of "elders" and of "junior elders" were the two highest decision making bodies, and most of the chief administrative positions below them were either paired or held by groups of four men, who like the members of the top councils rotated as officers in charge.

The Meiji leaders continued the same general pattern of group leadership. Unlike the situation in most countries undergoing rapid change, there was never any one dictatorial leader, not did any person ever attempt to gain such powers. The leaders, who, as we have seen, came to be known informally as the *genro*, or "elder statesmen," always formed a group, taking turns at the various administrative tasks and in the position of prime minister after this post was created in 1885 but yielding willingly to others when they ran into difficulty or tired of the responsibility. One of the early leaders, Okubo, before his assassination in 1878 and Ito while shaping the constitution in the 1880s enjoyed a certain predominance, but even they never fully dominated the political scene and operated basically as team players.

In time power became even more widely shared, not just between individuals but between the various institutions of the new system. Under the 1889 constitution there was a shifting balance of power among a large number of groups: the *genro* at first and later their successors as high officials surrounding the throne, the various ministerial branches of the civil bureaucracy, the military, the Diet and its contending parties, big business, and the general public. At first, the *genro* were in ultimate control, though not as fully as they had expected to be. By the 1920s the Diet and the parties were at the center of the balance, and both big business and the general public had increased in power through their influence over the parties. In the 1930s the military, particularly the army, achieved the leading role in the balance and on the eve of the attack on the United States in 1941 concentrated greater power in the hands of General Tojo than any individual had enjoyed for a half century or more. But even Tojo's authority was that of a group leader, not a dictator, and, when in 1944 the war was seen to be going badly, he meekly left office. Thus an aversion to dictatorial power or even to charismatic leadership and a strong tendency toward group cooperation were pronounced features of Japan's political heritage, and in my view they still constitute great political assets for the Japanese today.

Another heritage from the past was the strong orientation of society to formal education and the relatively high levels of literacy in the middle of the nineteenth century. The achievement of universal literacy was a practical immediate goal for a society of this sort, and it in turn made possible much of the technological and economic success of the new Japan. It also underlay the development of a successful mass democracy. The contrast is marked with many modernizing countries today, in which literacy is low to begin with and education must battle countercurrents of apathy or even hostility.

Still another important heritage of the nineteenth century Japanese was the strong entrepreneurial spirit which, though basically associated with economic development, also had political implications. Entrepreneurship is not characteristic of feudal societies or most premodern social systems, but it was marked in Japan by late Tokugawa times. The concentration of the samurai in the capital of the shogun and the castle towns of the lords had freed the countryside from close feudal control and had made the village a largely autonomous entity. The unification of the country into a single economic unit had also given wide scope for commercial activities. The big city merchants, who took advantage of this situation in the seventeenth century, had reached a sort of plateau by the eighteenth, but subsequently rural entrepreneurs developed the main push, processing local agricultural products and then marketing these in other areas. When Japan was opened to foreign trade and the new political system removed most social and economic barriers, great numbers of peasant entrepreneurs were prepared to seize hold of the new opportunities. It was this responsiveness of the Japanese people as much as the efforts of the government that accounted for the economic modernization of Japan.

Successful peasant entrepreneurs as well as affluent peasant landholders also had a large part in the development of demands for popular participation in government. It was quite natural that many members of the extensive samurai class who had been frozen out of power in the new system should agitate for a share in political influence, but it is more noteworthy that the samurai were joined already in the 1870s by peasants who, accustomed to running their own local affairs and to a wide area for economic entrepreneurship, were prepared to go beyond this and demand a voice in politics too.

One of the most important aspects of the Japanese heritage was the strong sense of political unity. This contrasted greatly with the situation today in many developing countries, which commonly have had to build their political unity after undergoing colonial subjugation. In Japan, feudal divisions might have obscured this unity, but it derived from Japan's relative isolation, from an ancient tradition of political centralization, and from the whole Chinese, or East Asian, emphasis on the centralized state as the highest embodiment of civilization. The contrast was sharp with most other lands of the non-Western world, which traditionally were either religiously oriented or tribally or linguistically divided.

The Japanese shared this tradition of political unity with the other countries of East Asia, but three factors distinguished them from their

The emperor (Hirohito), empress, their two sons and their wives, and the three imperial grandchildren. The crown prince (left) met his wife, Princess Michiko, (right) on the tennis courts. Of commoner descent, she is a graduate of Sacred Heart (Seishin) University. (*Consulate General of Japan*, N.Y.)

near neighbors. One was that the Japanese political unit had always been seen as contrasting with a Chinese political unit. The Chinese themselves saw all other lands as subordinate to theirs, and the Koreans accepted this idea. The Japanese view better fitted the Western international concept. The second difference was that in Japan the ideal of centralized political unity conflicted sharply with the feudal realities of local autonomy and class divisions. These contrasts created internal tensions in nineteenth century Japan which, by opening cracks in society, made change easier than in the more monolithic and long established political systems of China and Korea.

The third distinguishing feature from the rest of East Asia was that the nineteenth century Japanese could find adequate native justification for the great political, economic, and social changes being forced on them by the menace of the West. They found this justification in the "restoration" of imperial rule, which could satisfactorily explain the necessity of wiping away feudal political and social divisions and modernizing the economy. The Chinese, in contrast, had no native justification for major change, except for a dynastic transfer which would have brought no change in the

system. They therefore had to look to foreign ideologies, such as republi-
canism, democracy and eventually communism, to explain basic
changes, but to do this was a much more traumatic and time-consuming
process. Though challenged by the West earlier than the Japanese, the
Chinese found it difficult to carry through basic reforms, and, when a republican revolution did finally come in 1912, it only succeeded in destroying the old political order but not in creating a functioning republic to
take its place. Democracy, though honored in theory, was never established in practice. China instead degenerated first into warlordism and
then into the one-party dictatorship of Chiang Kai-shek's Nationalist government. It was not until 1949, over a century after its first war with the
West, that China at last was fully and efficiently reunited through a
foreign ideology—this time communism.

The Japanese went through no such traumatic spiritual shifts. The
great transformation of the nineteenth century was seen as a "restoration" of an old native institution, to which the other great changes were
subordinate. Thus they too seemed justified, even though in fact they led
to sweeping modifications of Japanese society. Among these were social
freedom and universal education, which made representative institutions
and democratic concepts both comprehensible and attractive. Democracy grew naturally in Japan, and, though it faltered in the 1930s, its
strong postwar revival has been basically a continuity from prewar days,
particularly the 1920s, and not an incomprehensible or uncongenial borrowing from abroad.

Japan's modern political development, thus, has not been marked by
the spiritual discontinuities that have characterized the development of
most of the non-Western world in recent times. Despite some periods of
very rapid change, its development has been basically evolutionary rather
than revolutionary, giving it a certain degree of stability and suggesting
that further changes, whatever they may be, are likely to grow naturally
out of conditions within Japan. In any case, there can be no doubt that
the Japanese of the nineteenth century, though lacking any background
in democracy, did derive from their heritage many other great political
assets and even certain characteristics that were to contribute to the subsequent development of democracy in Japan.

The
Emperor

24

JAPANESE have often claimed that the distinctiveness of their nation derives from its unique history in having had only a single reigning family ever since its shadowy protohistoric beginnings. To be sure, the emperors had lost actual control of the country around the ninth century, and, after the failure of Go-Daigo to reestablish imperial leadership in 1333, no effort was ever again made to restore actual rule to the emperors. Still, reverence for the imperial line always remained high, and no one before contemporary times ever challenged the concept that all legitimate political authority derived ultimately from the imperial line.

The first great step in the modernization of Japan in the nineteenth century, as we have seen, was justified as being the "restoration" of imperial rule. For a century and a half there had been growing interest in and respect for the imperial institution, and the groups that overthrew the Tokugawa found the slogan "honor the emperor and expel the barbarians" a powerful battle cry. Subsequently their control of the emperor proved their strongest weapon. The "restoration" thus brought the emperor back to the center of the political stage, and everything was done in his name, but it never occurred to the new leaders that the emperor should actually rule. A thousand years of reigning but not ruling emperors made this concept all but unthinkable. And in any case, the emperor was only a boy of fifteen in 1868. In time, as he matured, his views and preferences did come to have some weight, but his ministers simply took for granted that they would make the basic decisions and carry out the "imperial will" in his behalf. Following Meiji came Taisho (1912–26), whose mental incapacities made any participation in decision making quite out of the question. All the way up to the end of World War II the Japanese leadership was able to combine an extreme reverence for the emperor with a complete willingness to force decisions on him regardless of his own wishes. The one great concern of the Japanese leaders at the time of surrender in 1945 was the future status of the emperor. This combination of awesome respect for the emperor and callous manipulation of his person is hard for contemporary people, or at least for non-Japanese, to comprehend.

This curious dual attitude toward the emperor was embodied in the 1889 constitution. In drawing up this document, Ito quite frankly sought in the imperial institution the underlying spiritual force which he believed Christianity provided for constitutional government in the West. Lacking Christianity or any other suitable religion, Ito felt that Japan would have to find its spiritual unity through reverence for the throne. The constitution thus called the emperor "sacred and inviolable" and emphasized the continuity of the imperial line, "unbroken for ages eternal." Sovereignty and all powers of government were assigned to the emperor, but under conditions that assured that others would make the actual decisions. His powers seem unlimited when we read that "the Emperor determines the organization of the different branches of the administration . . . has the supreme command of the Army and Navy . . . [and] declares war, makes peace, and concludes treaties." But then we also learn that he "exercises the legislative power with the consent of the Imperial Diet," and he only "gives sanction to laws and orders them to be promulgated and executed." "All Laws, Imperial Ordinances, and Imperial Rescripts . . . require the counter signature of a Minister of State," and judicial powers are to "be exercised by the Courts of Law, according to law" and only "in the name of the Emperor."

The ambiguity regarding the powers of the emperor led to no misunderstandings. None of the three modern emperors made any real effort to assert his own will against the decisions of his ministers. The present emperor is known to have chafed at the actions of the military in his early years and to have attempted to get reconsideration of the steps leading to war, but the only political decision he himself made, though at the urging of his closest advisers, was when his ministers in August 1945 pointedly presented him with a tied vote on surrender and he opted for accepting the allied ultimatum.

The framers of the Meiji system were entirely successful in making the imperial institution into an effective symbol of national unity. The whole nation was inculcated with a fervent reverence for the emperor. This attitude, backed up by the whole cult of "state Shinto," reemphasized the aura of divinity, as divinity is understood in Shinto, which had always surrounded the throne. Common people were not supposed to look at the emperor directly. His pictures in all the schools of the nation were treated as holy icons and were housed if possible in separate little shrines, constructed in later years of concrete in order to avoid the catastrophe of their being burned. All Japanese in theory lived merely to repay the emperor's "benevolence," and millions of soldiers were willing to die abroad in his name. One is reminded of the cult of the national flag that is to be found in other modern countries, but the devotion of the prewar Japanese to the emperor as their symbol of national unity was probably the most extreme example of this modern nationalistic phenomenon.

The shapers of the Meiji system were less successful in achieving through the imperial cult the spiritual unity Ito had sought. Except for a few radicals in the twentieth century, no one, not even the party men in the Diet, disputed the duty of the government to put into effect the "imperial will," but there was little agreement over what the "imperial will" actually was. High officials around the throne felt that they were best able to interpret it, and at first they were able to override opposition by claiming imperial support for their views, but as early as 1913, in the so-called "Taisho political change," they discovered that the Diet would no longer knuckle under to this sort of pressure. The politicians felt that the "imperial will" was to be discovered through the voice of the people as shown in elections. Militarists and extreme nationalists believed that only they understood the "imperial will." No one thought of asking the emperor himself. Professor Minobe's liberal interpretation that the emperor was an "organ" of the constitution, which was accepted by most well-educated people in the 1920s, was declared *lèse majesté* in 1935. The military, by then in the saddle, repeatedly tried to clarify the *kokutai*, or "national polity," by which was meant the emperor-centered Japanese system, but the results were always mystical and vague.

The basic ambiguity of the constitution on the role of the emperor also left a dangerous hollow at the center of the system. All power stemmed from the emperor, but he exercised no power. It was not clear how the chief ministers who acted in place of the emperor were to be selected. The system for their selection, in fact, varied over time and was never

clearly defined. At first, the selection was largely the decision of the remaining "elder statesmen"; then it became a consensual decision among
leadership elites, in which party power in the Diet was the biggest factor;
and finally the consensual decision came to be swayed basically by the
military. The emperor's "supreme command of the Army and Navy" was
in time reversed to signify the independence of the military from the civil
government and ultimately their control over the emperor. The disastrous consequence of this particular ambiguity we have already seen.

THE POSTWAR constitution of 1947 has cleared up all these problems.
The emperor is defined as "the symbol of the State and of the unity of the
people, deriving his position from the will of the people with whom resides
sovereign power." The emperor's functions are described as purely symbolic, and it is expressly stated that the emperor "shall not have powers related to government." To make the point still clearer the constitution
adds that "the advice and approval of the Cabinet shall be required for all
acts of the Emperor in matters of state, and the Cabinet shall be responsible therefore." "State Shinto" was abolished, and the emperor, on January
1, 1946, issued a statement denying his own divinity—largely to please the
American occupation authorities, to whom "divinity" meant a great deal
more than it did to most Japanese. The emperor continues to perform
certain traditional Shinto ceremonies but these are officially defined as
having no religious significance. The Imperial Household Ministry,
which handled the affairs of the imperial family, was reduced to the rank
of an agency in the prime minister's office, imperial finances were drastically cut and put with the rest of the budget under the control of the Diet,
imperial properties were transferred to the state, and the imperial family
was limited to the emperor's immediate family and those of his three
brothers. Even the emperor's married daughters are now classed as commoners.

The emperor who personally underwent this great change in roles is
Hirohito, which is the personal name he uses to sign documents but is
never used for him by the Japanese. They refer to him by such terms as
"His Majesty" or "the present emperor." Hirohito, who has occupied the
throne for a longer period than any of his forbears in historical times—
his reign period of Showa passed the half century mark in 1976—has
fitted into his newly defined role with an apparent sense of relief. He is

obviously more at ease in his civilian clothes, playing a symbolic role for his civil government and his people, than he ever was before the war, dressed in military uniform astride a white charger and reviewing his conquering armies. The new role better fits his personality as a shy but friendly individual, a model family man, and an enthusiastic marine biologist.

Much more important than the emperor's personal reaction is the response of the Japanese people to this great theoretical change in the imperial institution. They appear to have accepted it with ease and even with enthusiasm, for it finally brought theory in line with reality. A tiny fringe of old-fashioned nationalists still call for a restoration of the old *kokutai*, whatever that was, and for a couple of decades after the war the more conservative politicians advocated the restoration of theoretical "sovereignty" to the emperor, but neither issue has any meaning for the great bulk of Japanese. Older Japanese continue to have a sense of reverence for the emperor, and large numbers of rural folk show their devotion by contributing their services to the upkeep of the extensive imperial palace grounds in Tokyo. Most people, however, have only rather vague feelings of respect or affection for the emperor, and many, particularly young people, are quite indifferent or even slightly hostile. But there is no substantial anti-emperor movement either. At present not even the Communist party calls for the abolition of the throne, and the marriage of the crown prince in 1959 to a charming daughter of a businessman, who was a commoner even by prewar standards, served to revive interest in the imperial family even among younger Japanese.

All in all, the postwar imperial institution has come to parallel closely the pattern for modern kingship already established by the mature democracies of northern Europe. Entirely divorced from politics, the imperial family serves as a symbol of national unity, a token of stability, and a comforting emotional link with the past. Any use of the throne that could in any way be interpreted as bearing on politics meets with vigorous protest, but otherwise the imperial institution seems to be generally accepted as a permanent, noncontroversial embellishment of the national scene. This form of monarchy appears to be a congenial pattern for countries like Japan and those of northern Europe, which are monarchies that have achieved their democratic systems largely through evolutionary rather than revolutionary means.

The Diet

25

THE 1947 constitution not only stripped the emperor of all claim to political power but also made clear where actual power did lie—in the hands of the Diet, or parliament. The Diet had already evolved a long way before World War II. In the 1889 constitution, the Meiji leaders had set it up to be a partially elected national assembly that was expected to win the respect of the Western nations, solidify the support of the common people, and serve as a harmless safety valve for discontent. They had preceded this daring innovation with various local experiments in elected bodies, starting with prefectural assemblies in 1878 and following these with village, town, and city ward assemblies in 1880 and then city-wide assemblies in 1888. These local assemblies as well as the new national Diet had only very limited powers and were elected by an extremely restricted electorate. Only adult males over twenty-five years of age and paying fifteen yen or more in taxes had the franchise in Diet elections. This amounted in 1890 to merely 1.26 percent of the population. Counting family members, this would give only about 6 percent of the population as belonging to enfranchised families, which curiously was about the same percentage as the old samurai class, though now the voting groups were largely peasant landowners and businessmen and therefore were mostly not of samurai origin.

While imperial ordinances could be issued between sessions of the Diet, the "consent" of the Diet was necessary for a law to remain permanently on the books, and the budget and all taxes specifically required action by the Diet. Many acts of the government, as in foreign affairs, were

249

not felt to require laws and therefore Diet approval, but financial matters were considered the Diet's special prerogative, because the money, after all, came as taxes from the people. But even here, the government sought to protect itself from popular control by the constitutional provision that, if the Diet fails to act on the new budget, "the government shall carry out the Budget of the preceding year." This trump card to prevent Diet control over the purse strings was borrowed from the Germans and was one of the first provisions agreed upon for the new constitution—already in 1881 in fact.

The powers of the popularly elected House of Representatives in the Diet were also restricted by a House of Peers, modeled on the British House of Lords and given a coequal status with the lower house. To man this House of Peers, as we have seen, the government in 1884 created a new peerage, made up of the old court nobility, the former feudal lords, and some of the new leaders. The upper ranks of this nobility were all members of the House of Peers, but the lower three ranks elected a limited number of members from among their ranks, and there were in addition imperial appointees, mostly of a scholarly nature, and one member elected from each prefecture by the highest tax payers. A body so constituted was obviously an extremely conservative check on any action by the lower house.

Despite all these precautions, the Diet proved extremely unruly and succeeded in rapidly expanding its powers and broadening the electorate. Starting with the experience gained in local elections after 1878, the popular parties swept every national election from the inception of the Diet in 1890 up until World War II. Even in the infamous second election of 1892, when the government leaders freely resorted to bribery and police suppression, their parliamentary supporters fell far short of winning a majority. And the prized budgetary trump card proved almost valueless. In a rapidly rising economy, last year's budget was never enough. The annual battle to get the budget through the Diet became so disagreeable and difficult that some of the government leaders even suggested that the Diet should be abolished, but they were overruled by the others, who feared that such an admission of defeat in attempted modernization would humiliate Japan before the West and endanger the prospects for getting rid of the unequal treaties.

A compromise was worked out, at first tentatively in the latter half of the 1890s and then more permanently after 1900 between the government leaders and the Seiyukai, the party Ito himself founded in 1900 by bringing together his own bureaucratic following with the political stream deriving from Itagaki. In return for support in the Diet, the Seiyukai would get some say on national policies and a few cabinet posts and other plums. The balance shifted over time. The Seiyukai, and after 1913 a second rival party as well, gained steadily in power, until finally in 1918 Hara, a pure party leader, was selected as prime minister basically because of the plurality position of his Seiyukai party in the House of Representatives. For the next fourteen years, except for a brief period between 1922 and 1924, all the prime ministers were party leaders, selected on the basis of their party support in the Diet, and the cabinets, except for the army and navy ministers, consisted mostly of party men.

Meanwhile, as education spread and Japan modernized itself in other ways, the franchise too had been steadily broadened. In 1900 the ballot was made secret and the tax qualification was dropped to ten yen, almost doubling the electorate. In 1919 the qualification was reduced to three yen, this time more than doubling the electorate. About a quarter of the families of Japan now had a member who had the vote. Finally in 1925 tax qualifications were eliminated entirely, and all adult males were enfranchised.

Thus the Japanese political system in a mere three and a half decades had evolved from almost complete authoritarianism to a fair approximation of British parliamentary democracy as that institution existed after the achievement of universal manhood suffrage in 1867. Of course, in Japan the system was much less securely established than in Britain, as the reversion to military domination was to show in the 1930s. The prime minister might be the president of the majority party in the lower house, but his selection as prime minister was not automatic nor was it made by the Diet itself but by persons acting in the name of the emperor. Moreover he and the Diet did not have firm control over the army and navy nor even over certain elements in the high bureaucracy. Still, it should be noted that the growth of this parliamentary system, imperfect though it was, had resulted largely from internal evolutionary developments, albeit with a knowledge of the British system in mind. It had taken only a small fraction of the time that the growth of British parliamentarianism had required, and the system was to prove strong enough to serve as the basis for a vigorous revival of parliamentary rule after the war.

THE PARLIAMENTARY system as established under the 1947 constitution was essentially a clarification and improvement of the system that had spontaneously evolved in Japan by the 1920s. As such it has been easily comprehended by all Japanese and has worked with reasonable efficiency. The chief innovations have been to make the Diet clearly "the highest organ of state power" and "the sole law-making organ" and to give it the power to select the prime minister. He is elected from among the members of the Diet, specifically by the lower house of that body in the event of disagreement with the upper house, and he in turn then selects the ministers of his cabinet and the other appointed officials. The lower house of the Diet always has the right to a vote of nonconfidence in the cabinet, in which case the prime minister must resign or else dissolve the lower house and hold new elections in an effort to gain majority support. This is not the American form of democracy but the straight British parliamentary system, toward which the Japanese had been clearly gravitating already in the 1920s.

Two other important postwar changes in the parliamentary system were the extension of the suffrage of all women as well as men above the age of twenty and the transformation of the nature of the upper house. An entirely elective House of Councillors was substituted for the House of Peers. It is chosen in a different way from the House of Representatives, in the hope of giving it a less narrowly partisan membership. One hundred of the councillors are elected from the nation at large, and originally 150 others, increased to 152 in 1972 when Okinawa reverted to Japan, are elected from prefectural constituencies. Half of each group is chosen every three years for a six year term. Each prefecture has at a minimum two seats in its prefectural constituency in order to have at least one seat in each election, and the more populous prefectures have more—eight in the case of Tokyo.

As a popularly elected body the House of Councillors does not form the conservative check its predecessor did, and its powers are, in any case, clearly subordinated to those of the lower house. The selection of the prime minister is made by the House of Representatives; the budget must be presented first to it, and its action on the budget becomes final in thirty days even if the upper house does not concur but remains in session. This same provision applies also to the ratification of treaties. On all other leg

The members of the House of Representatives shouting "banzai" ("ten thousand years"—the Japanese "viva") as it dissolves preceding a general election. The lower house, which is the more powerful of the two, as in most parliamentary democracies of the British type, has grown since World War II from 466 members to 511 in the 1976 election. Each member has a marker with his name on the desk in front of him, which he raises vertically when present. (*Associated Press*)

islation, a two thirds majority in the lower house is required to override a negative vote by the House of Councillors. Amendments to the constitution, however, require a two thirds vote in both houses, but so far none has been made, just as none was ever made to the 1889 constitution, until a so-called amendment changed it into an entirely new constitution in 1947.

In most other ways, the Diet functions very much as it did in the 1920s and builds its practices on prewar as well as postwar precedents. As before, the lower house is elected for a four year term, though commonly it is dissolved by the prime minister before the four years are up at a time politically advantageous to him or his party. The system of elections (see chapter 27) is also the same unusual one established in the 1925 Diet reform. Even the size of the lower house in the early years after the war was the same four hundred and sixty-six members established in 1925. As before the war, the Diet is annually convened in formal ceremonies in December but almost immediately adjourns for the New Year holidays and starts serious work only later in January. It normally completes action on the budget before the start of the fiscal year in April—a practice that contrasts sharply with the usual failure of the American Congress to vote the budget until the fiscal year is almost half over. The "ordinary" session of the Diet must be for a minimum of one hundred and fifty days, which takes it into June, but usually it is extended into the early summer. "Extraordinary" sessions are commonly called in early autumn to pass a supplementary budget and consider other emergency legislation. Moreover, when the lower house is dissolved by the prime minister, an election must be held within forty days and the new Diet convened in a "special" session within thirty days after that in order to elect a prime minister.

Each house elects its own presiding officers, who have very broad powers, including the right to put limits on debate in order to avoid filibusters. Such rulings can be challenged but can be upheld by a simple majority vote, which is no problem, since the presiding officer has been elected in the first place by the same majority vote that will naturally support his rulings. The presiding officer also has the right to make committee assignments—each member in both houses can expect at least one such appointment—though in reality these assignments are made by the respective parties, which traditionally have the right to a number of members on each committee corresponding to its strength in that house. In the House of Councillors, committee chairmanships are also assigned to the various parties in proportion to their strength in that house, but in the lower house all regular committee chairmanships were held by the majority party, until the thinness of the Liberal Democratic party's majority in 1977 forced it to share some of the chairmanships with the opposition. At the same time the position of vice speaker of the lower house also was given for the first time to a member of the largest opposition party, the Socialists.

Each house has the same sixteen permanent committees and creates special committees as needed for what are regarded as special issues. Most of the permanent committees correspond to major ministerial divisions of the cabinet and bureaucracy—such as foreign affairs, education, construction, or international trade and industry—but the two committees of greatest significance are of a different type. One is the Audit Committee in which wrangles over past government actions draw the close attention of the mass media. The other is the Budget Committee, which has become the traditional milieu for interpellations—that is, the questioning of cabinet members on almost any problem of government.

The whole committee set-up is a clear departure from the British parliamentary system and from Japan's own prewar Diet, which had only three regular committees. It is an effort, inspired by the occupation, to bring Japanese parliamentary procedures more in line with American congressional practices, but as such it has not succeeded, and the committee system has been diverted to other uses. The two systems of democracy, presidential and parliamentary, simply do not mix. Since the prime minister and his cabinet, as in the British system, are the creatures of the parliamentary majority and serve therefore as a sort of executive committee for the Diet, the legislature and the executive are not balanced as conflicting political forces, as they are in the American system. The result is that the great bulk of legislation, including all important bills, is produced, not by the Diet, but by the bureaucracy in behalf of the cabinet. It is presented by the cabinet to the Diet and is then passed by the same Diet majority that has chosen the prime minister in the first place. Legislation is dutifully cleared through the Diet committees before being presented to the full house, but committee sessions are not hearings designed to gather information for proposed laws or to hammer out and refine legislation and win votes for it, as they are in the United States. They are more perfunctory performances in which the results, as in the plenary sessions of the house itself, are largely determined by a disciplined party vote and are therefore known in advance of any debate.

While the Diet committees have not operated in the way envisioned by the American occupation reformers, they do perform other functions. The opposition parties can use any of the committees, as well as plenary sessions of the house, to slow down and attempt to block legislation, thus putting pressure on the majority party to compromise with them. The interpellations in the Budget Committee, or in any other committee forums, also have a major role in politics. Interpellations had developed before the war as a feature of Diet activity and correspond to the famous "Question Time" of the British House of Commons. Members of the opposition pose questions which are meant to embarrass the government and which the cabinet ministers or their bureaucratic representatives do their best to sidestep, and members of the party in power may ask questions designed to allow the cabinet ministers to bring out points they wish to emphasize. Neither sort of question and answer is expected to change a single vote either in the committee or later in the house itself. Instead they are all aimed at the mass media and the general public in an effort to build up mass support and a record for use in the next election. Thus the committee system, designed by Americans for one purpose, has been turned to a very different use that better fits the parliamentary system.

Other Organs
of Government

26

T HE PRIME minister, as we have seen, is elected by the House of Representatives from among the members of the Diet, though always actually from the lower house itself. Chosen by his peers and always replaceable by them, he has incomparably less personal power than an American president and in fact acts more like a chairman of a committee, which in a sense he is for his party. The only postwar prime minister who could be considered autocratic or even strong was so-called "one-man" Yoshida, a prewar diplomat, who held the post for two terms totaling seven years between 1946 and 1954. The secret of his power, however, was the absolute authority of the occupation under which he operated for five of his seven years.

The prime minister chooses the members of his cabinet, at present twenty in all, a majority of whom must be members of the Diet. In practice virtually all are, as in the British system. The only notable exceptions have been Fujiyama, a prominent businessman who was appointed Foreign Minister in 1957 before being elected a year later to the Diet, and Nagai, a university professor turned newspaperman, who was appointed Minister of Education in 1974. Twelve of the cabinet members serve as heads of the twelve ministries, of which Finance, International Trade and Industry (MITI), and Foreign Affairs are considered the most important. The others, who are ministers without portfolio, normally are the directors of some of the more important sub-ministry organs of government. One is the chief cabinet secretary (*kambo chokan*), who serves as a sort of chief of staff for the prime minister. Another is the director of the

The Diet Building, housing Japan's parliament, was ironically completed in 1936, just when Japan's democracy was being smothered by militaristic reactionaries, but since World War II it has been the focus of all political activity. Immediately behind it are three parallel office buildings for the members of the Diet. The government ministries are located nearby, largely out of sight to the left. As the streets pictured show, traffic in Japan, as in England, keeps to the left. (*Consulate General of Japan*, N.Y.)

Prime Minister's Office (*Sorifu*), which corresponds to the White House Executive Office. The directors of the Economic Planning Agency, the Defense Agency, and the Science and Technology Agency also are usually members of the cabinet.

While prime ministers usually stay in office for a number of years—the longest single stretch in Japanese history was the incumbency of Sato from 1964 to 1972—most other members of the cabinet are in office for much shorter periods of time, averaging around two years but often only a year. Coming to a ministry or agency from the world of politics and for only a brief time, ministers or agency chiefs establish at most only a very general policy control over their ministries or agencies. The only other outsiders, also chosen from among Diet members, are one or two parliamentary vice-ministers or vice-directors per ministry or agency, but these posts are of little real importance and have only vague liaison duties with the Diet.

For the rest, a ministry or agency is made up basically of a very solidly organized, elite corps of career bureaucrats, heading up in an administrative vice-minister or vice-chief (*jimu jikan*), who actually runs it. The situation is much like that to be found in the various parliamentary systems of Western Europe and contrasts sharply with the American departments, in which secretaries, under secretaries, and many assistant secretaries and lesser officials are presidential appointees who attempt to exercise a strict control in his behalf. The Japanese ministries and agencies thus have a much greater self-identity and political voice of their own than do most American departments or agencies. The chief exceptions to this general rule are the armed services in the United States, which have more self-identity and influence than do other administrative branches of government, and the Defense Agency in Japan, which has notably less than other comparable government organs. Since the ministry bureaucrats serve their whole careers in a single ministry, or else occasionally on loan from it to another ministry or agency or to local governments, each ministry constitutes a sharply defined, permanent group of officials, who fiercely defend their own prerogatives and powers. While there may be policy conflicts between subdivisions or factional groups within a ministry, each ministry develops its own stands and policies on controversial issues and fights for these in competition with other ministries and even with the party in power.

The contemporary bureaucracy is clearly the inheritor of the high levels of honesty, efficiency, and prestige established by the prewar bureaucracy. At that time the bureaucracy was divided into four ranks: a small group of top officials, who were in theory "personally appointed" by the emperor; the bulk of the high civil servants, who were selected by examinations and were divided into two ranks, the higher of which was considered to be "imperially appointed" and the other "imperially approved"; and the great mass of specialists and lower functionaries who qualified for their posts by educational attainments and sometimes by examination.

These categories do not survive in name, but the distinction in ways of selection remains. A very small group, including ministers and parliamentary vice-ministers, come out of the parliamentary political process. Below it, the higher civil service is a truly elite corps, which is the cream of the Japanese educational system, drawn from the most prestigious universities, especially Tokyo University, by a selection process of rigorous examinations. Professionally very competent and enjoying security in their positions, these higher civil servants are very self-confident in their dealings with politicians, in a way that would rarely be found in the United States. They are also very dynamic, because the system of early retirement around the age of fifty-five means that the holders of the top positions in all ministries are vigorous men in their early fifties who have had at least two decades of experience in the ministry. Despite their prestige and political power, however, the higher civil servants receive only quite modest salaries.

At the bottom of the bureaucratic pyramid come the great mass of lesser functionaries in the central administration as well as local governments and the various categories of specialists, such as professors and teachers in government schools, the police, and workers in the national railways and a few government monopolies, like tobacco. Some of these categories are selected through examinations, but for the most part they achieve their positions on the basis of educational records and past achievements, as is the case in most other modern countries.

The prewar bureaucracy tended to be haughty and to treat the common people not just officiously but with condescension or even contempt. This was particularly true of the police, who were greatly feared as well as respected, but even railway officials tended to strut around in their uniforms. These attitudes were probably survivals of feudal times when the ruling samurai class monopolized all political power and fuctions and the phrase *kanson minpi*—"the officials honored, the people despised"— characterized the basic attitudes.

The breakdown in respect for all authority that came with defeat and the postwar collapse, however, seems to have swept such attitudes away. The higher bureaucracy does continue to enjoy considerable prestige, but this is because of its high standards and its very obvious political power. The lower bureaucracy certainly evokes no particular respect and is actually looked upon with the same mixture of exasperation and contempt that Americans and Western Europeans show for the seeming pettifogging "bureaucraticness" of their own lesser officals. In reality, the minor functionaries of Japan are usually polite and businesslike, drawing on the same fine traditions as the higher bureaucracy, and both groups see themselves and are seen by others not as "officials" in the old sense but as modern public servants.

The standards of the bureaucracy, which numbers in the millions, and its smooth operation are overseen by the National Personnel Authority, which has a semi-independent status within the Japanese government. Among the welter of other government agencies, authorities, councils, and commissions, mention should also be made of the Board of Audit, which also enjoys a semi-independent status and performs an important budgetary watchdog role similar to that of the American General Accounting Office.

JAPAN is divided for purposes of local government into prefectures and these into cities, towns, and villages, with the largest cities being further subdivided into wards. The prefectures, which continue from the prewar system unchanged in size, are actually of four theoretically distinct categories. There is one metropolis (*to*), Tokyo; one circuit (*do*), Hokkaido; two municipal prefectures (*fu*), Osaka and Kyoto; and forty-three regular prefectures (*ken*). To speak of them all together, the Japanese have to refer rather clumsily to the forty-seven *to-do-fu-ken*. Below the prefectural level, local jurisdictions are the product of a long process of amalgamation forced by the central government. Villages are those areas with populations of less than 30,000, towns are areas with populations of less than 50,000, while cities have more than 50,000. In 1973 there were 808 villages, 2,007 towns, and 561 cities. All villages are made up of a large number of small natural villages, now known as hamlets (*buraku*), and so-called towns and smaller cities usually contain large stretches of countryside and hamlets as well as one or more urban center.

Before the war the powerful Home Ministry appointed the prefectural governors, controlled the police, and exercised close supervision over all local government, in a manner common among the countries of Western Europe. During the occupation, the American authorities were determined to break up this extreme centralization of power and foster greater local autonomy in the American manner. Even before the war, prefectures, cities, city wards, towns, and villages all had elected assemblies, and mayors of cities, towns, and villages were elected officials. After the war these assemblies were all continued and their powers were considerably expanded, while governors as well as mayors are now elected. (Incidentally postwar Tokyo has no mayor, only a governor.) The Home

Ministry was abolished, and its remaining functions were assigned to an Autonomy Agency (later made a ministry), which was by comparison small and weak. Control over the police was assigned to local jurisdictions, and much of the control over education was also transferred from the central Education Ministry to locally elected boards of education.

This effort to develop broad local autonomy, however, proved on the whole a failure. The old system of centralized national control was too deeply entrenched and probably fitted better the small size and intense crowding of Japan. Even greater centralization of power, after all, is the pattern in democracies like the United Kingdom or France. While elected governors, mayors, and assemblies breathe life into local Japanese politics, it remains strictly subordinate to national politics. Municipally divided police forces proved impractical in so compact a land, and therefore, after the occupation ended, powers of coordination were restored to the central Police Agency. Fearing that unqualified persons might gain control of elected boards of education, the Japanese also made these bodies appointive and restored much of the supervisory control to the Education Ministry.

One fatal flaw in the effort to foster greater local autonomy was the fact that the local powers of taxation proved inadequate to provide the financial base for the exercise of the wide powers permitted local governments. They collect only 30 percent of taxes, and much of their activities is financed by the 70 percent collected by the central government. With these funds, of course, comes control. It has been estimated that four fifths of the work of local government is actually performed in behalf of ministries of the central government, and key figures among the local officials are in fact members of the central ministries on temporary loan. There are a number of signs indicating how completely the central government dominates the local ones: much local legislation is based on model legislation suggested by the central government; each prefectural government maintains a large liaison office in Tokyo; and governors and mayors spend a considerable part of their time at the capital, negotiating with the central government. As political interest has shifted somewhat in recent years from international relations and national economic growth policies to the environment and the quality of life, local issues have gained in relative weight and have enhanced the importance of local government, but even on these issues national policies take precedence over local ones.

THE CONTEMPORARY Japanese judicial system also derives in large part from the prewar judiciary, which despite the authoritarian trends of the time maintained high standards of efficiency, honesty, and independence. The chief innovation of the new constitution in the judicial field was the creation of a Supreme Court in which all judicial power was vested and which nominates the judges for lesser courts and has the right to determine the constitutionality of all laws, in the American manner. The justices of the Supreme Court are appointed by the prime minister, but once appointed they and the judges of lower courts cannot be removed except by formal impeachment procedures or, in the case of Supreme Court justices, by popular vote, since their names appear on the ballot at the first general election following their appointment and then every ten years thereafter. This last provision, however, has proven a dead letter, because Supreme Court justices are not well enough known to stir up more than a trifling opposition vote.

Judicial review by the courts of the constitutionality of legislation is an American innovation which has been inserted into an otherwise pure parliamentary system with somewhat uncertain results. In the British system, nothing can override Parliament, and the Japanese Supreme Court for its part has tended to show a reluctance to go against political decisions of the Diet. In has not sought the vigorous role played by the American Supreme Court in shaping social and political developments but has tended instead to stick to narrow legal decisions and to defer to what the Diet majority has voted.

Though inferior courts, staffed by younger, more liberal judges, sometimes declare laws unconstitutional, the Supreme Court usually overrides them. In 1952 it established that it would not rule on abstract constitutional issues but only on specific problems, and in the next twenty years it declared only two laws unconstitutional. The grounds for avoiding such judgments has often been that important political considerations or public welfare interests were paramount. The first of these arguments has been used when the constitutionality of the Self-Defense Forces or the Security Treaty with the United States has been questioned by the lower courts, in view of article 9 of the constitution, in which "the Japanese people forever renounce war as a sovereign right" and the maintenance of "land, sea, and air forces." One of the most famous of these cases involving article 9 was the Sunakawa case finally settled in 1959. The effect of such rulings has been to accept the Diet's right to reinterpret the seemingly uncompromising language of the constitution to permit self-defense and the military forces and alliances needed for it. The general public, as seen through popular polls, seems largely to have gone along with this reinterpretation.

The Supreme Court and the lesser courts, however, have proved wide awake watch dogs guarding individual rights as defined in the constitution. No fewer than thirty articles in the constitution list these "fundamental human rights," which are not restricted by phrases such as "within the limit of the law," as was the case in the 1889 constitution, though the people are enjoined to use these rights for the "public welfare." The courts have been zealous in seeing that laws and regulations do not infringe upon the rights promised in the constitution. When in the early 1970s pollution, or rather the broader Japanese concept of public injury (*kogai*), became a popular issue and doubts grew concerning the validity of the policy of economic growth at any price, it was the courts which, through a number of landmark decision, established the principle that the polluter must pay the individuals who are damaged. The most famous of the cases was that of mercury poisoning through marine products at the Kyushu coastal town of Minamata, where the source of the pollution was identified as early as 1959 but a final Supreme Court decision was not handed down until 1973.

Another Supreme Court ruling made in the spring of 1976 might also have profound effects in the political field. This was the decision that the existing electoral system is unconstitutional, since it permits serious discrepancies between the numbers of votes needed to elect a person to the Diet in urban and rural constituencies, thus transgressing the constitutional guarantee of political equality among individuals.

Japanese law since the 1890s has been based on the codified law system of continental Europe, rather than the Anglo-American common law system, but it has been greatly liberalized since the war and most the constitutional safeguards familiar in American law have been introduced. The American adversary system of trial, however, is not followed in the courts. Instead, judges attempt to seek out the facts, and lawyers merely serve as council to the parties involved. The use of juries was optional for a period before the war, but, because their verdicts were unpredictable, choosing a jury trial was usually considered tantamount to admitting that one had a poor case. The jury system, therefore, was dropped without regret after the war.

In criminal cases, public prosecutors (the term is also translated as procurators), who correspond to American district attorneys as the representatives of the state's interest, will not bring charges unless they have strong evidence and, since the reactions of the judge can be predicted with fair accuracy, they have a stunning record of over 99 percent convictions. Plea bargaining is not part of the system, and knowledgable Japanese in fact are appalled by the American judicial system, which seems to them more a matter of plea bargaining than justice. Punishments imposed by Japanese courts are on the whole lenient, and judges take into consideration the attitude of repentance on the part of the criminal following his crime. A sincere expression of remorse is considered an important first step toward rehabilitation.

Special family courts handle most domestic and juvenile matters, and great efforts are made to settle civil cases through conciliation rather than formal court procedures. The Japanese, in fact, are not very litigious and prefer arbitration and compromise, turning to the courts only as a last resort. Thus their system does include a large measure of bargaining, but between individuals, not with the court. This situation fits well with Japanese concepts of interpersonal and group relations. Only in cases of traffic accidents, which bring entirely unrelated persons into conflict, has there been a sharp increase in litigation in recent years.

Politically sensitive cases, such as those based on charges of the unconstitutionality of the Self-Defense Forces, complex issues of damage from pollution, and cases involving the delicate line between rightful political action by demonstrators or strikers and the maintenance of law and order, may drag out for years of complicated trials and appeals, but on the whole the Japanese feel that their courts operate adequately, and there is little of the complaint, so common in the United States, that justice is inordinately slow and uncertain. Judges are felt to be honest and fair. The police are well respected, and the special riot police in particular turn in a magnificent performance in their skillful containment of violence. Most people are law abiding, and they approve of stringent and strictly enforced regulations which keep both guns and drugs out of the hands of the populace. There is virtually no drug problem, and crimes of violence are markedly lower than in the United States. Outside totalitarian countries, nowhere in the world is one safer from crime than on the streets of Japan, regardless of the time of day or night. All in all, the Japanese legal and judicial system would rate near the top in any listing .

With litigation relatively infrequent, the role of the lawyer in Japan is much smaller than in the United States. There are fewer than one fifteenth as many lawyers in Japan per capita as in the United States. Lawyers are produced by the same state operated system that turns out judges and public prosecutors. Graduates of university law faculties are eligible for the government legal examinations that select some hundreds each year for further training for about two years by the Japanese Legal Training and Research Institute, which operates under the direction of the Supreme Court. Successful graduates of this program are then free to

Members of the special riot police (the Kidotai, or "Mobile Unit"), protectively garbed, but with their helmet visors up, remove demonstrating students from outside an American military base. Some of the students are wearing working men's helmets, one emblazoned with "Zengakuren," the name of the federation of student organizations. (*Associated Press*)

choose careers as judges, public prosecutors, or lawyers. In the first two categories they receive prestige as distinguished government officials. As lawyers they may achieve greater financial rewards but, unlike lawyers in the United States, no great social recognition. Lawyers are not only relatively few in number but are largely concentrated in Tokyo and other large cities, where a surprisingly high proportion of their work concerns economic relations with more litigious foreign societies. Whereas some two thirds of the members of the American Congress have backgrounds as lawyers, there are few lawyers among the members of the Diet—actually no more than doctors.

Although Japanese are not very litigious, it should be pointed out that they are extremely legalistic. They are accustomed to a highly centralized system, overseen by a powerful bureaucracy and carefully regulated according to detailed law codes and myriad bureaucratic rulings. Much of their leadership in the bureaucracy, in business, and in politics is the product of the law faculties of the universities. Japanese tend to be meticulous in observing the letter of the law. But the central figures in this Japanese legalism are not the lawyers or even the judges, but the higher bureaucrats, who are largely the product of legal training, and the masses of petty functionaries who must live by the law codes and regulations.

Electoral
Politics

27

SINCE national political power is in the hands of an elected Diet, and elected governors, mayors, and local assemblies are locally important, elections are at the heart of politics in Japan. The most important elections, which are those for the lower house of the Diet, are conducted in a very distinctive way that gives a special flavor to electoral politics in Japan. Unlike the Anglo-American system, they are not held in one-seat constituencies, in which a single winner takes all. Nor are they conducted in the manner of any of the various systems of proportional representation practiced in continental Europe. Instead they follow a unique multi-seat system that produces a loose approximation of proportional representation but at the same time leaves the candidate, not as a mere name on a party list and almost entirely dependent on the party's political appeal, but as an individual who depends more on his own personal appeal to voters, as in the United States. This electoral system is one of the chief distinguishing features of the prewar Japanese political system that has been carried over into the postwar period.

The prewar Japanese engaged in a long debate over the respective merits of what they called the large and small electoral district systems. The small was the one-seat district of the Anglo-American type, and the large tended to be a whole prefecture or large city, electing at a single time a number of persons for the House of Representatives—as many as sixteen in the extreme case of Tokyo before 1919. Since each voter usually had only one vote, a relatively small minority party could win some representation, and the larger parties had the problem of dividing the votes of their supporters as evenly as possible between a number of nominees of usually differing popular appeal. The justification made for the large district system was that the broader the district, the broader in vision and more statesmanlike would be the men elected. There was never any empirical evidence to support this proposition, but it was firmly believed or at least asserted. The real reason for the strong advocacy of the large district system, however, was probably the government's realization that it prevented the large parties from sweeping the elections completely and, while complicating the electoral process for them, gave more chance for the election of some backers of the government, who never could count on more than minority electoral support.

In the first five elections for the lower house of the Diet between 1890 and 1898, the small district system was used except for a number of two-seat districts, but in 1900 the large district system was adopted as part of a deal between the government and the party politicians that saw the politicians benefit from the secret ballot and an extension of the electorate. This system lasted until 1919, when the party-dominated Hara government restored the small district system, though with sixty-eight two-seat, and eleven three-seat districts. Finally in 1925 a compromise middle-sized district system was adopted at the same time as universal manhood suffrage, and it is this system that continues almost unchanged today. Curiously the first postwar election under the occupation in 1946 reverted to the large district system, but since 1947 the 1925 system has been in force, with the country divided into districts (at present one hundred and thirty) with from three to five seats each. The only exception is the Amami Islands at the northern end of the Ryukyu chain, which were returned to Japan separately by the United States in 1954 and were made into a one-seat district.

The multi-seat electoral system permits the representation of any minority party that can win close to 20 percent of the vote in a five-seat district, but, as we have seen, it produces great difficulties for larger parties, which must take care in each district not to run more candidates than they have the votes to elect and must also attempt to distribute their votes fairly evenly between these candidates. For example, it would be disastrous for a party to niminate five candidates in a five-man district in which it had the votes only to elect three. To do so would be to spread out the votes so thinly that not three but only one or two candidates might be elected. A particularly attractive candidate could also so bunch the votes as to produce the same unfortunate result. These are serious problems for a large party, but not for a small one which cannot hope to elect more than one candidate and therefore runs only one.

The Japanese multi-seat system does, however, contribute to the stability of Japanese electoral politics. Shifts of a few percentage points in popular votes in the American one-seat system can bring changes of landslide proportions. In Japan they might bring at most the change of one seat between the majority party and the opposition in a five-seat district, and it would take a shift of votes of well over 20 percent to bring a change of two seats out of five. As a result, electoral politics in Japan changes more slowly and generally more predictably than in the United States.

One weakness of the system has been that there is no automatic method of bringing electoral districts and numbers of seats in line with population changes, and the ratios, which were equitable when established in 1947, have become greatly imbalanced since, creating discrepancies in extreme cases of almost four to one in the vote required for election to the lower house between the most and least populous districts. In the 1976 election ten candidates failed to gain seats although each received more than 100,000 votes, while nine others were elected with less than half as many votes. The result of this situation has been a gross underrepresentation of big cities, where almost all the postwar population increase has occurred, and an overrepresentation for rural areas which have seen a steady erosion of population.

Up until 1976, the Japanese relied on political action in the Diet to ameliorate this situation as best it could, but here the majority elected from overrepresented districts was not willing to permit any reduction in seats from their own districts, and the smaller parties blocked any serious consideration of a complete electoral reform along the lines of the Anglo-American small district system, because this would cut drastically into the number of seats they would win. All that happened was a slow and entirely inadequate increase of seats for the bigger cities. Between 1947 and 1976 such increases, together with additional representation for the Amami Islands and Okinawa when these were returned to Japan, brought the number of seats from the four hundred and sixty-six established in 1925 merely to five hundred and eleven. In any case, the unwieldiness of an overly large Diet puts limits on this sort of piecemeal reform by adding additional seats for more populous areas.

This situation, however, gave signs of basic change when on April 14, 1976, the Supreme Court ruled the present electoral system unconstitutional, since it did not provide the political equality promised in the constitution. This could be a decision analogous to the "one-man, one vote" ruling of the American Supreme Court, but as of the present writing it is not at all clear just how or when this decision will be translated into political action or even that any specific action will result from it.

Elections for governors and mayors produce only a single victor, but most other elections in Japan show the multi-seat, semi-proportional characteristics of the lower house elections. Village, town and small city assemblies are elected at large and metropolitan and prefectural assemblies from multi-seat districts. One of the two constituencies of the House of Councillors is the nation at large and the other the individual prefectures, which elect more than one person at a time, except for the two-seat prefectures, in which only one person is elected every three years. The larger number of seats for the more populous prefectures—eight in the case of Tokyo as opposed to the two for each of the least populous prefecture—still leave the metropolitan prefectures inadequately represented in the upper house too, with discrepancies in the number of voters per seat of up to five to one, but this is far less extreme than in the American Senate, where they reach seventy-five to one.

The prefectural constituencies in the upper house produce electoral results not unlike those of the lower house, and the persons elected are commonly rising politicians hoping in time to make it into the lower house or else are older men who have found this beyond their political strength. The fifty members elected every three years from the nation at large, however, include persons of a different type. Even a relatively small pressure group, if organized well enough, can elect a representative. Thus various professions may have their representatives, and even the armed forces, though viewed with suspicion and disdain by most Japanese, have enough supporters to elect two or three former military men. Popular television personalities or popular authors are in a particularly advantageous position, and quite a few of these so-called "talent" candidates (the English word is used) have been elected, though, as with the professional candidates, as members of one party or another. An attempt in the 1974 elections to have certain large business firms support their own candidates, however, proved a dismal failure.

ONE OUTSTANDING feature of electoral politics in Japan is the survival into recent years of the strongly rural flavor it had before World War II. Japan was a predominantly agrarian society when the electoral system first developed in the 1880s and 1890s. It was not until the 1920s that urban populations began to balance rural and not until after the war that Japan became an overwhelmingly urban society. Moreover, the vote was at first limited by tax qualifications largely to rural land owners, and it was not until after 1925 that the bulk of city people, including most white collar workers as well as industrial laborers, won the franchise. For these reasons, the traditional Japanese parties in their formative years were fundamentally oriented toward the rural vote, and this tendency has been maintained to a certain degree after the war by the overrepresentation of the rural areas.

Rural Japanese thus have had a longer experience with elections than have their urban compatriots, and they tend to be more involved in local issues. As a result, even today they vote in higher proportions than do city people—at rates of five out of six as compared to two out of three. The composite average of around 70–75 percent far outshines the American average of 50–60 percent. Local elections, at least in the less urban areas, also draw more voting interest than do national elections. Voting for local assemblymen is highest, followed by the lower house of the Diet and prefectural governors, and the lowest voting percentages are for the members of the upper house.

Another feature of Japanese electoral politics, closely associated with the multi-seat electoral district system, is its strongly personal flavor. Since the larger parties run more than one candidate in an electoral district, these candidates are inevitably in competition with one another for the vote. Thus each, instead of relying merely on the party and its organization, must develop his own personal voting appeal and his own electoral organization. He cannot be some worthy of the central party assigned to a safe district, as in the English system, but must be a genuine native son—either a bonafide local resident or at least a home town boy who has made good in the big city. Since he will be competing with his fellow party candidates primarily for the votes that their party would normally expect, and not for the votes that go to other parties, which are probably lost to him in any case, it is important that he have his own financing and his own machine. The resulting personal flavor of politics in Japan is much like that of the United States and contrasts with the less personalized politics of the United Kingdom and most other Western European countries.

Japanese electoral politics started in the nineteenth century with rather small leader-follower groups, largely rural in makeup and typically Japanese in style. Itagaki and Okuma had their personal followings made up of local leaders who in turn had their own personal supporters. Village groups, led by local "men of power" (*yuryokusha*), as the Japanese call them, tended to vote as blocs on the old assumption of village solidarity and for the rational reason that split votes would cancel each other out and thus dissipate local political leverage. Congeries of such blocs would be put together to elect local assemblymen and pyramids of such bloc groupings to elect a member of the House of Representatives. Blocs or groups of blocs might swing as a whole in their loyalties between candidates or even between parties. A strong political figure, however, might develop from these blocs a solid "base," called a *jiban*, which would return him without fail election after election and might be passed on to his political heir, possibly a son, after he had died. In return, he was expected to produce benefits for the area, for example, in the form of favorable locations for schools, bridges, railways, and the like. Electoral "bases" were usually concentrated in one part of an electoral district, which would vote overwhelmingly for its favorite son, while relatively few votes would come from other parts of the district, which were expected to support some other candidate of the same party.

This system has eroded seriously over time, especially since the war. Even farming communities no longer vote so much as blocs as they once did. The great numbers of farm residents who work as industrial laborers and the ever growing presence of outside influences in an age of mass communications have made even rural Japanese much more diverse in their political interests and attitudes. Candidates no longer count on a relatively solid bloc of votes from one particular area and therefore have had to spread their electoral net more widely throughout the district. As the Japanese put it, the old "vertical" political base has had to become steadily more "horizontal." One result of this has been the development by most politicians of large and complex personal support organizations, known as *koenkai*, which attempt to appeal to women, young people, and various interest groups throughout the electoral district.

The nature of the *koenkai* is influenced by the extreme restrictions placed both on the financing and conduct of elections. These restrictions are usually justified on the grounds that they discourage corruption and unfair competition for votes between rich and poor candidates, but they are in a sense survivals from prewar legislation which was designed at least in part by men who viewed democracy with suspicion and were desirous of making it hard to operate. Campaign funds are limited for each candidate to a modest sum, currently around $16,000 in the least populous districts and around $55,000 in the most populous, but periodically revised upwards because of inflation. These figures are entirely unrealistic, and a cynical popular saying had it that a hundred million yen ($333,000) was necessary for a successful campaign, and a mere seventy million ($233,000) would result in defeat. (Again the figures are regularly raised upwards to conform with inflation.) There is considerable hyperbole in this saying, but it does suggest the problem posed by unrealistically low financial restrictions.

There are in addition serious limits placed on the manner of campaigning. Voting campaigns are permitted only for the three to five weeks after the date for the election has been announced—always for a Sunday. No door to door soliciting or telephone calls are allowed—the Japanese are felt to be too susceptible to such personal pressures. There can be no parades and no wining or dining of voters. Only a limited number of posters, advertisements, postcards, brochures, and brief radio and television appearances are permitted. A blaring sound truck is the only overt campaigning freely allowed—with disastrous results for peace and quiet.

All these restrictions mean that there is always a tremendous number of petty infractions of Japanese election rules. They also force the *koenkai* to pose as "cultural" groups, rather than as election organizations. They operate around the year, holding "educational" meetings for their various women's, youth's, and other branches and sponsoring "educational" speeches by the candidate himself and his backers. In addition, the politician is endlessly busy cultivating the good will of his clientele, in ways that are only too familiar to his American counterpart. He makes himself constantly available for appearances in his district, receives his constituents at his office in Tokyo, administers as best he can to their personal needs, and drops them endless postcards from his travels abroad.

The larger cities do not lend themselves to personalized political organizations of this type. This was true even before the war and has become more markedly so since. In fact, more modern ways of life are eroding the old personalized politics even in small towns and rural Japan. The opposition parties of the left from their very beginnings in the 1920s based their appeal more on ideologies and programs than on personal contacts. Even for conservative politicians, the modern *koenkai* system cannot be operated very effectively in a heavily urbanized area, where competing distractions are greater and people do not know each other or live in self-contained communities. Many men are likely to reside and vote in one electoral district but have most of their social and intellectual contacts in another, where their factory or business is located. A more intellectual and less personalized appeal must be made to the various constituencies and pressure groups that make up the electoral district—labor unions, agricultural cooperatives, women's organizations, youth organizations, and professional groups. Ideological issues and political labels tend to take the place or at least supplement personal appeal. As urbanization and more modernized conditions of life continue to grow, the old personalized politics goes on eroding steadily, and the policy-oriented politics characteristic of the cities increasingly becomes the norm.

The Communist party comes closest to fitting the ideal Western picture of a party constructed around principles, not personalities, and enlisting in its formal organization those who believe in these principles. Its core is solidly constructed of the party faithful, who actually constitute a larger body of official party members than any other party has. The Komeito similarly has a solid party base but one less determined by political ideas than defined by loyalty to Soka Gakkai, the new religion that spawned the party. Both the Socialists and the Democratic Socialists also rely more on clear party platforms than do the conservative Liberal Democrats, and the core of their organizational strength is made up of labor unions—those of the largely white collar and government worker Sohyo federation in the case of the more leftist Socialists and those of the more blue collar Domei federation for the more centrist Democratic Socialists. Socialist and Democratic Socialist politicians, however, often have their own *koenkai*, while many Liberal Democratic politicians are striving to create, through a clearer party ideology, a "new conservatism" to supplement personal political appeal. Still, one can make a general three way division between the personalized politics and *koenkai* of the old system, the labor union basis of the two socialist parties, and the clearer party structures of the Communists and Komeito.

Parties

28

IN PREMODERN Japan, as in China, "party" was a concept looked upon with stern disapproval. It suggested disharmony or even subversion. Commoners were supposed to have no role in politics and samurai were to serve their lords obediently. Rival bureaucratic factions, however, had come to be a feature of the politics of both the shogunate and the daimyo domains by late Tokugawa times, and the Meiji Japanese took quickly to the concept of popular parties, though some lingering misgivings did survive about their legitimacy all the way up to World War II.

As we have seen, Itagaki in 1874 started his first party, which quickly burgeoned into the "freedom and peoples' rights movement," and Okuma followed with a second party movement in 1882. From these two original political currents stemmed the two major traditional party lines, which dominated Diet politics until the war. The Itagaki line dominated the early Diets under the name of Liberal party (Jiyuto, which literally means Freedom party) and then in 1900 joined with Ito's bureaucratic following to form the Seiyukai (Political Friends Society), which went on dominating Diet politics and produced in 1918 the first full party prime minister in Hara. After the war it was revived under the name of Liberal party.

The other line had more frequent changes of name, accompanied by repeated reorganizations, defections, and amalgamations. Called at various times the Progressive or Constitutional party, among other names, it became after 1927 the Minseito (Peoples' Government party). In most early elections, its vote was second only to the Itakagaki party line, which was always the plurality party, until finally in 1915 the Okuma line won a plurality and thereafter tended to alternate with the Seiyukai in that position, producing its first party prime minister in Kato in 1924. It was revived after the war as the Democratic party (sometimes called the Progressives). In 1955 it and the Liberals finally merged to form the Liberal Democratic party, a name that reveals its double origin.

In 1901 an effort was made, largely by Christian idealists, to found a socialist party, but it was immediately suppressed by the authorities. The Communist party in 1922 was the first of the so-called proletarian parties to be successfully launched but not for long. Two years later it was banned, and police pressure on its supporters steadily mounted. Starting in 1925, several short-lived socialist parties were founded, and these groups, insofar as they were tolerated by the police, consolidated into the Social Mass party in 1932. Both it and the more conservative parties, however, were dissolved in 1940 and entered the officially sponsored Imperial Rule Assistance Association.

After the war the Communist party was revived by its few remaining members, who were released from prison or returned from exile in China or the Soviet Union. The Social Mass party was also resurrected as the Socialist party, and its popular vote of 19 percent in the 1946 election and 26 percent in 1947 showed a clear extension of its rising popularity before the war, when it won 5 percent of the vote in 1936 and almost 10 percent in 1937. It also showed its prewar divisiveness over ideology, which might be described in simplified terms as the division between those who emphasized socialism over democracy and those who had the reverse priorities. The party split into right and left wings between 1951 and 1955 and then split again in 1960, with the seceding moderates forming the Democratic Socialist party.

Most of Japan's present parties, thus, have clear prewar antecedents, despite a welter of new parties which sprang up immediately after the war. The largest of these, the Cooperatives, merged with the Democrats in 1949, but most of the rest had disappeared even earlier. Among existing parties, only the Komeito (sometimes called the Clean Government party), which was founded by the Soka Gakkai in 1964 after a decade of dabbling in elections, is a purely postwar phenomenon.

IN PREWAR politics, which was dominated by rural voters who were less concerned with national politics than with local issues, personal knowledge of a candidate naturally meant much more than his party label. In fact, most local politicians did not bother to take a party label but ran instead as independents. There is a strong carry-over of these conditions even today in local politics and in the structure of the Liberal Democratic party. The smaller and more rural the electoral unit, the higher the proportion of politicians elected as independents. Conversely, the larger and more urban the unit, the more the party label is used, and the general urbanization and industrialization of Japanese society is producing at all levels a clear drift toward increasing use of party labels. Village and town assemblymen are still largely independents, though there are very few independents among assemblymen in big cities. Independents in prefectural assemblies once numbered almost a third but are now down to only a few, if any, in most prefectural assemblies. Only a handful of persons are elected as independents to the Diet, and most of these, when once elected, do not remain independents.

Governors and mayors are a separate case. In the early postwar years, when the two conservative parties had a strong majority between them, almost all governors and mayors were conservatives, though most preferred not to take a party label. Since then the number using the party label has increased until now more than half of the governors use it. However, as the combined vote for the opposition parties gradually increased and surpassed the conservative vote in the major urban areas, the governors and mayors of most metropolitan areas and even some of the middle-sized cities have come to stem from the opposition side, which the Japanese usually call the progressives or reformists. For example, the opposition parties have had a majority in the Tokyo assembly since 1965, and Minobe, who is the Socialist son of the controversial prewar interpreter of the constitution and like him was a professor at Tokyo University, has been governor of Tokyo since 1967. Progressive candidates, however, must have the support of two or more of the opposition parties to win elections, and consequently they too tend to call themselves independents.

The overwhelming hold of independent but conservative politicians on local politics in the more rural areas helps account for the rather curious structure of the Liberal Democratic party. It is in essence a political club made up primarily of Diet members and secondarily of their supporters and would-be successors among members of the local assemblies and governors and mayors. In other words, it is basically a club of professional politicians and has little mass membership or even much of a grass roots organization. This situation has induced some observers to call it an inverted pyramid, or a ghost party, in that it has a head but no feet. Both terms, however, are misleading. The political machines of local politicians and the *koenkai* of Diet members give the Liberal Democrats an extremely broad and vitally alive grass roots base, even if few Japanese voters think of themselves as belonging to the party.

The great majority of Japanese, in fact, eschew enrolling as members or even becoming avowed supporters of any party, clinging firmly to the pose of being independents in politics. The chief exceptions are the core supporters of the Communist and Komeito parties and the leaders of the labor unions that support the two socialist parties. Otherwise, most Japanese strongly prefer to consider themselves as independents, a stance that is becoming increasingly popular in the United States. In reality, however, the party preferences of Japanese voters are perhaps more consistent and therefore predictable than is the case with American voters.

THE LIBERAL Democratic party, ever since its founding in 1955, has had a majority of the seats in the Diet and the support of a majority, or close to a majority, of the voters. As the ruling party and by far the largest one, it deserves particularly close attention, especially since much that can be said about it applies at least in part to the other parties as well.

The heart of the Liberal Democratic party is its Diet membership. The coordinated voting of this group to elect the prime minister and support a program of legislation is fundamental to the effectiveness of the party's rule and to its very existence. Everything depends on strong party discipline in Diet votes. That the Japanese achieve this is remarkable considering the personalized basis of local politics and the reliance of each Diet member in elections more on his own *koenkai* and personal supporters than on the party machinery. In the United States the relatively independent personal political bases of the members of Congress lead to a situation in Washington in which individual preferences in voting clearly take precedence over party discipline, while the party discipline of most European parliamentary systems is associated with the weak personal bases of most European politicians. The Japanese demonstrate their sophistication and skill in group organization by their ability to combine local political bases that for most politicians are even more personalized and independent than in the American case, with a party discipline in the Diet and local assemblies that is as strong as in any European democracy.

The Liberal Democratic party achieves this solidarity in Diet action despite the fact that it is not held together by any clear ideology. Its members are simply the inheritors of the two main prewar political streams, which themselves never had sharply defined ideologies. In their early days the two were united in the fight to wrest more power for the Diet from the government—a battle now long since won—and they were differentiated from each other more by personal rivalries than by issues. The rising vote of the so-called "progressive" parties forced the two to join in 1955 to consolidate their strength, but this was only a marriage of convenience. The Liberal Democratic party does tend toward more conservative positions than the progressive parties, but it embraces among its various members a wide spectrum of views on almost any issue. In this regard it is quite unlike most European political parties and very much like the Democratic and Republican parties of the United States. But there is also a profound difference: the American parties are largely labels and organizations under which people get elected to office and to Congress, where they then operate more or less independently, while in Japan the party is less important for elections but provides an organization through which those elected make the parliamentary system and the local assemblies operate with reasonable efficiency.

One important feature of the Liberal Democratic party is the division of its Diet membership into factions. These are usually criticized as being divisive forces within the party, but actually they are one of the chief mechanisms through which the party produces a closely coordinated effort in the Diet. The factions in typical Japanese fashion are made up of followers and a leader or in some cases a small leadership group acting in the name of the leader. At most times there are about three or four major factions, with between forty and eighty members each, and perhaps a few more smaller ones. If the large factions were much larger they would be likely to split, and if the small ones were too small, they would not be very effective. Each normally has a clearly recognized faction leader, who is obviously one of the strong men of the Diet and party. When he dies or retires, the faction may break up or else undergo some difficulties before a new leader emerges.

It is sometimes asserted that the Liberal Democratic party is merely a coalition of factions. This certainly is the situation operationally, but it is not true in a more basic sense. The factions, unlike the parties in a coalition government in European parliamentary systems, are not entities which have any existence other than as elements within the Liberal Democratic party. They have even less ideological identity than the party itself. Sometimes vague policy leanings are attributed to them, and they are frequently lined up by political analysts on a left to right spectrum, but these generalizations are not very accurate. Any large faction includes members of very disparate views, and the various clubs and committees formed from time to time to push some particular political point of view always draw members from a variety of factions.

The dual origin of the Liberal Democratic party at first played a part in factional alignments, but this factor has now faded away almost completely. Many analysts have emphasized a supposed cleavage between factions headed by ex-bureaucrats and those under long-time politicians, but such a division never concerned most rank and file members—only 16 percent were of bureaucratic background in1966—and it was basically only a passing historical phase. Just as the founding of the Seiyukai in 1900 and the growing power of the parties in the 1920s induced ambitious bureaucrats to join the parties, the complete supremacy of the Diet after the war brought another influx of ex-bureaucrats to positions of party leadership, where they performed efficiently as men experienced in running Japan's bureaucratic machinery. All the long-lived postwar prime ministers have been of bureaucratic origin—Yoshida, Kishi, Ikeda, and Sato. The present prime minister, Fukuda, elected on December 24, 1976, is an ex-bureaucrat from the Finance Ministry. But Tanaka, who was prime minister from 1972 to 1974, was in origin no elite bureaucrat but a self-made businessman and politician, and Miki, who followed him from 1974 to December 1976, was the last of the prewar politicians. The younger men, who some day will succeed the present aging leadership, are mostly life-time politicians or at least left the bureaucracy early in their careers to go into politics. The wave of ex-bureaucrat leaders was a product of its time, which is now passing, and in any case was only a minor factor in producing the factional phenomenon.

The factions thus are not ideological subdivisions of the party but are functional components of it that, in typical Japanese fashion, are personalized leader-follower groupings. They have a clear value for both the leaders and the followers. They give a Diet strong man a personal base from which to launch his effort to win the party presidency or other high office. For the run of the mill Diet member, they offer a way for meaningful participation in Diet activities and psychological support of the sort most Japanese crave. Frequent factional meetings afford the members, particularly the junior ones, a valuable education in Diet politics and the issues. Joining a faction also offers the average Dietman a better chance than he would have on his own to achieve a high post as a committee chairman in the Diet, a parliamentary vice-minister, and eventually a member of the cabinet. Only a very few hardy individuals among Liberal Democratic Diet members refuse to join a faction.

Factions also play a role in the selection of Liberal Democratic candidates for the Diet. Candidates in one sense are self-selected because they either must be the successor as son or protege of a retiring or deceased Diet member or else must first develop their own local support and personal election machine before they can be considered for nomination. It still remains a function of the central party, however, to determine just which of the promising local aspirants will get the party label as an official party candidate. As we have seen, it is essential in electoral politics to nominate no more candidates than the party has the votes to elect. Party endorsement therefore is given only charily, and to win it the new candidate would probably need the support of some faction leader, whose faction he would then join if elected. He might also get supplementary financial support from the faction, which naturally is eager to have its members elected. Each official candidate receives some financial support from the party to be added to his own personal resources, but extra funds from his faction leader can give him the edge over the other candidates of his party in the district. To be able to raise funds for this purpose is obviously a prime requisite for a faction leader. The importance of factionalism in the selection and election of Diet members can be seen in the fact that the Liberal Democratic Diet members from any electoral district are normally factional rivals, and only rarely do two belong to the same faction.

Many would-be candidates for the Diet fail to win the official endorsement of the party, and some of these decide to run anyway, without the party blessing, as ostensible independents. This the party disapproves of strongly, but it is sometimes suspected that factional backers of these candidates give them clandestine support. If such independents win, usually at the expense of endorsed candidates, they almost invariably rejoin the party and, of course, their factional groups.

Factions have always been roundly condemned by almost all commentators on the Japanese political scene, and the Liberal Democrats themselves periodically announce their determination to do away with them. Factional competition does lead to considerable wastage of electoral funds and to bitter fighting within the party. But factions are not likely to disappear, because they are functional to the whole operation of the system. They not only have a role in the selection and election of candidates for the Diet, but they also function in the decision-making process and the selection of leadership. As we have seen, the selection of prime ministers and the passing of legislation depends on a unified Liberal Democratic vote in the Diet. This requires a party consensus, which is obtained through the interaction of factions operating as blocs of votes. It is obviously easier to work out a consensus between eight or nine factions than between more than four hundred party members in the two houses of the Diet. It has been on the whole a more orderly system than the wild scramble to decide presidential nominees every four years in the United States and the continual jockeying to line up votes for legislation in the American Congress. Thus the Liberal Democratic party, far from being emasculated by its factional divisions, as is usually claimed, is actually made into an effective, flexible political organization by their interplay.

THE PARTY convention is the central event in determining Liberal Democratic leadership. It is held annually, but every third year (until 1971 every second year) or whenever the prime minister has resigned, it must elect a new party leader. The membership of the convention reveals the basic nature of the party as a club of Diet members. Each Liberal Democratic member of the two houses has a vote, for a total of more than four hundred, in addition to which there is only one vote for each of the forty-seven prefectural party organizations, often divided into fractional votes for women, youth, and other electoral elements. The convention elects the party president (*sosai*), who subsequently is automatically chosen by the party's Diet majority as the prime minister. The choice may be made in open battle between factional coalitions on the floor of the convention. The winning coalition is informally known as the "main stream" and the losers as the "anti-main stream." Or else the selection of the president may be by private agreement between the faction leaders, as in the traditional American "smoke-filled room." A president, according to the rules adopted in 1971, can be elected by a simple majority vote for two successive three-year terms, but a third term requires a two thirds majority, which, it was assumed, would limit any candidate to a maximum of six years as prime minister.

Since the prime minister is chosen by the majority party's Dietmen through a system of factional bargaining and is not "the people's choice," as in the presidential system, he can hardly expect the popular support commonly accorded the president in the United States. Usually after a brief honeymoon period of popular enthusiasm, which may give him a slight majority of general approval in popular polls, his support measured in these terms is likely to fall to less than 30 percent, since even voters for his party feel no personal commitment to him and may prefer other faction leaders.

The choice of the other chief party officers depends upon the identity of the president, because they must be chosen in such a way as to maintain a balance between the factions, so that loyal support from all will be assured. The second most important figure is the secretary general (*kanjicho*), who makes the decisions on parliamentary vice-ministers and Diet committee chairmen and controls the relatively small party bureaucracy and the crucial Election Policy Committee, which determines which candidates for the Diet receive party endorsement. Other major posts include the chairmen of the Executive Council and the Policy Research Committee, whose functions in the decision-making process we shall consider later. On occasion a party vice-president is also elected. All these posts as well as the membership of the various party committees and the makeup of the cabinet chosen by the prime minister, must carefully maintain a factional balance. Faction leaders may themselves occupy some of the main party and cabinet posts, but sometimes they are represented only by some of their faction members. Once a geographic as well as a factional balance was considered necessary, but this, while very important in American politics, has become decidedly secondary to the factional balance in Japan.

All the other parties have the same general structure as the Liberal Democratic party. They regularly hold party conventions that elect the chief party officers, but only the Socialist party is big enough to have genuine factions. While these do not entirely lack the personal element of the factions of the Liberal Democratic party, they tend to be basically ideological groupings and, as a result, are much more bitterly contentious.

The Socialists hold annual party conventions, at which, until 1962, all the party members in the Diet automatically were delegates, but since then they too have had to be chosen by the local party organizations. Since Socialist Diet members are less than half as numerous as Liberal Democrats, they constitute a much smaller proportion of the delegates at the party conventions, and instead labor union leaders elected by the local party organizations are the largest element, constituting around 40 percent of the delegates. The party convention elects the chairman of the Central Executive Committee (who corresponds to the Liberal Democratic president) as well as the secretary general of the party and the other officers. It also elects all the members of the Central Executive Committee, which actually runs the party. The top officers of the party are virtually all members of the Diet and their choice represents the same sort of factional battles and efforts to achieve a factional balance as in the Liberal Democratic party.

The Decision=
Making Process

29 ↙

THE DIET is at the heart of the political decision-making process in Japan, and the parties and their electoral support are the keys to its composition. The whole system, however, operates in some ways quite differently from the political process in the United States or even in the parliamentary democracies of Europe. There are in fact clear overtones of the consensus system that we have already encountered in the Japanese business community.

The contrast with the United States is clearest because of the fundamental differences between the parliamentary and presidential systems of democracy. Since the prime minister is elected by a Diet majority, there is never any difference in party or any policy conflict between the legislative majority and the executive, as in the American system. Moreover, though legislation may be proposed by members of the Diet, including members of the opposition parties, the great bulk of the bills passed are submitted on behalf of the ruling party by the cabinet and are the product mainly of the ministries operating under the cabinet's control.

This is the manner in which most parliamentary democracies work, but the Japanese system begins to deviate from the others in the way the majority party decides on its legislative program. In other parliamentary democracies the party in power is likely to have a clear ideology and program, on the basis of which its members in parliament have been elected, but this is not true of the Liberal Democratic party. Its members have been elected more on their own personal appeal, and they do not come to the Diet with a fully worked-out party program. Nor does the prime minister, who has probably been elected through factional bargaining, have a mandate to carry out his own policies. The basic decisions are still to be made through a complex process of establishing a party consensus.

The Liberal Democratic party has a variety of mechanisms for this purpose. Each faction, for example, holds regular meetings to discuss policy matters, at which the leader educates his followers on the problems and his point of view, while gaining in turn from them an idea of what stands they would be willing to support. On particularly large and controversial issues, such as those of foreign policy, there are also supra-factional groupings that are formed to push some specific point of view. Typical examples are the Asian-African Study Society, which flourished a few years ago and leaned toward a slightly leftist emphasis on third world affiliation for Japan, and more recently a group of ultra-conservative young Turks who call themselves the *Seirankai*.

More central and important to the decision-making process, however, is the work of the Policy Research Committee (abbreviated to *Seichokai* in Japanese), whose chairman is one of the chief party officers. It is divided into fifteen committees, which correspond to the chief ministries and agencies and their corresponding Diet committees. There are in addition some thirty subcommittees and at any one time around twenty special committees or task forces. The committees have a few staff members and can call on specialists but are made up of the party's members in the Diet. Each Diet member is a voting member of one committee of his choice, but all can attend the sessions of any committee and participate in the debate. The committees thus serve as the chief area for the initial melding of the differing views held by the party's Diet members and for the coordination of their views with the expert opinion of the ministerial bureaucracy that normally drafts legislation. Back of the committee sessions, of course, there will often be extensive consultations among Diet members especially interested in the specific legislation and between them and the concerned ministry bureaucrats.

For relative routine decisions, the subsequent procedures are reminiscent of the *ringi* system of business and the bureaucracy. A committee decision goes to the Deliberation Commission of the Policy Research Committee, which itself represents a factional balance. When cleared there, it is forwarded to the Executive Council (*Somukai*) of the party, which has both a factional and regional balance in its membership. The Executive Council gives it formal party approval and sends it to the Legislative

Bureau of the cabinet for processing. After a final clearance from the technical point of view by the Council of Vice-Ministers, made up of the vice-ministers who are the real operating heads of the various ministries, it is then ready for formal adoption by the cabinet and submission as a government bill to the Diet. After this lengthy procedure, in which individual Diet members interested in the legislation and the various factions have both had ample opportunity to have their say, the party members are quite ready to vote for the bill in the Diet without further debate.

For controversial issues, the course may not be as smooth. When the Policy Research Committee cannot come up with a consensus decision, the problem may be referred to the Executive Council, or to an ad hoc meeting of the faction leaders, or possibly to the top party officers, namely the president and prime minister, the vice-president, and the chairmen of the Executive Council and the Policy Research Committee. These various groups represent a factional balance and therefore can serve as the means of achieving a consensus among the factions that will be binding on the party vote in the Diet.

Occasionally even these measures do not produce a consensus, in which case the decision may be up to the prime minister to make. In this case he will also have to live with the political consequences, including the possibility of subsequent repudiation by some of the members of his party. An alternative course in theory would be to call a caucus of the party's membership in both houses of the Diet, though this procedure is more likely to be of use in winning support for a decision already taken than for making the decision itself.

The procedures for achieving a party consensus in the Socialist party are basically similar to those of the Liberal Democratic party. Operating under the leadership of the chief party officers, a Policy Planning Committee and other committees work out party stands, which the party's members in the Diet then hold to faithfully. While ideological divisions within the party make some decisions difficult, on the whole the decision-making process is simpler than with the party in power, because there is no need to have detailed positions on most matters of legislation, and only a few issues can be selected for determined opposition, though not necessarily for specific alternative legislation.

WHILE the political decision-making process centers around party organs, it is by no means limited to politicians. A very large role is taken by the ministerial bureaucracy. In fact, some scholars view the ministries as being the basic decision-making bodies and the party organs and the Diet as merely ancillary. Actually some 70 percent of the bills submitted to the Diet are drafted by the ministries, and the great majority of these are passed, while only a small fraction of the remaining 30 percent submitted by the members of the Diet are adopted. Some of those that do pass are actually ministry drafts given for some political reason to a Diet member to present. Bills submitted by opposition members almost never pass. The ministry bills, moreover, represent in large part long term policies of the various ministries as hammered out through consensus decisions between various subdivisions of the ministry and its factional groupings.

The budget illustrates the procedure very well. Each ministry drafts its own budget, being allowed to make requests for something more than its current budget—frequently around 125 percent. Within each ministry there is an effort to maintain a balance in expenditures between the various bureaus, sections, and programs that does not depart much from the existing balance. The Finance Ministry in making up the final budget attempts to maintain the same sort of balance between ministries. Thus the established budgetary categories have a strong momentum, and changes in the budget are likely to be marginal rather than drastic. Such changes as are made may be largely in response to the bureaucracy's own perceptions of national needs and of popular desires.

At the same time, the budget like all other legislation must receive the approval of the majority party and is therefore subject to its strong influence. This can occur at a number of different levels. Stated objectives of the prime minister and his cabinet are likely to help determine the original drafting of budgets and legislation in the ministries, and the preliminary negotiations between the subcommittees of the Policy Research Committee and the bureaucrats can not only educate the politicans on technical matters but may show the bureaucrats which political objectives they must meet. And at every stage personal consultations can produce a two-way flow of influences between politicians and bureaucrats.

The bureaucrats also have a large decision-making role as the implementers of policy, as we have seen in the discussion of Japanese business. Legislation often is in general terms and depends on a great number of administrative rulings by the bureaucracy for its specific application. This is true in any country, but in Japan the area for bureaucratic rulings is on the whole broader than in the United States, and thus the bureaucrats exercise wider powers. An example is the detailed control the Ministry of

International Trade and Industry (MITI) has had over the development of Japanese industry and Japan's international economic contacts on the basis of a few broad authorizations. Naturally the bureaucrats must be careful in these rulings not to run counter to the general wishes of the party in power, but most of the specific decisions are theirs to make and are not dictated by politicians through the sort of close presidential and cabinet control that exists in the United States.

The ministries thus are far more powerful than the corresponding American departments, but they do not operate in a vacuum. In addition to their close interaction with the party in power, the bureaucrats are also in touch with the many pressure groups in the various fields of their activity. The farmers cooperatives and other agricultural bodies are of prime importance to the Agriculture Ministry, just as the Japan Medical Association is to the Welfare Ministry or the Japan Teachers Union to the Education Ministry and the federations of labor unions to the Labor Ministry, though in these two latter cases the relationship is more that of adversaries than collaborators. The various ministries connected with economic activities are closely associated with the business world, which is highly organized into federations of one sort or another, making the exchanges of opinion and influence between government and business a much more orderly and effective process than in the United States.

Much of this coordination with pressure groups is achieved through informal consultations, but the ministries have attempted to strengthen the process further by creating a great number of *Shingikai*, or Advisory Boards. In 1972 the number of such bodies was two hundred and forty. Only the Foreign Ministry lacked them for substantive fields of concern, perhaps feeling that foreign policy was too arcane, too sensitive, and certainly too explosive a subject for useful popular participation. As viewed by the bureaucracy, the *Shingikai* are probably seen as ways to create popular understanding and support for ministry policies, and they can also be utilized in factional disputes within the ministries, but at the same time they are at least capable of serving as channels for popular influence on ministry decisions.

THE POLITICAL decision-making process in Japan might best be viewed as being essentially three-sided. The ministries provide the expertize and administrative continuity. The Diet, which means specifically the party in power, provides the final political decisions through its decision-making procedures and its majority vote in the Diet. But both the bureaucracy and the party in power ultimately depend on the third angle of the triangle—the general public—which as the electorate determines the party in power and puts broad limits on the policies it can work out with the ministries. While the other two sides are relatively fixed entities—the bureaucracy is permanent and the party in power has not changed since the formation of the Liberal Democratic party in 1955—the public is diverse and changeable. It is first of all the electorate divided into a shifting vote for the various parties. Beyond that it is made up of countless pressure groups, which also wax and wane—farmers, fishermen, doctors, dentists, various ad hoc groups of concerned citizens or local residents, labor unions, trade associations, and business federations.

Coordination is necessary between these three sides of the political triangle. It is particularly close between the party in power and the bureaucracy, but the ministries also attempt to maintain contact with the public and its pressure groups, and the party has even closer ties with them. The central party organization is in direct touch with many of the pressure groups, while each member of the Diet, through his electoral organization, tries to maintain contact with the pressure groups and as much of the public as he can reach within his electoral district. The pressure groups for their part work through the individual members of the Diet but also attempt to exert direct influence on the ministries concerned and on the party in power.

The Liberal Democratic party, the portion of the public and its pressure groups that support it, and the bureaucracy are commonly lumped together in Japan as the political establishment, while the opposition parties and their supporters among the public and pressure groups are then seen as the anti-establishment. The division between the parties is obvious, but it is not as clear with the public and the pressure groups. Many voters split their votes between the parties, and still more constitute a floating vote which moves from party to party. And many if not most of the pressure groups are not to be characterized as either for or against the Liberal Democratic party. Still a general pro- and anti-establishment division does run through Japanese society.

Some observers picture a more restricted establishment consisting of a triumvirate of the politicians of the Liberal Democratic party, the bureaucracy, and big business as the one element representing the public side of the political scene. There is some reason for this interpretation, because big business did play an extremely significant role in decision making for much of the postwar period. Rapid industrial growth was the major policy of both the bureaucracy and the party in power, and, since industrial expansion was primarily in the hands of businessmen, bureaucrats and Liberal Democratic politicians naturally have cooperated closely with them in seeking to achieve this primary national goal.

Big business has also been the main source of funds for the Liberal Democratic party. Business does contribute lesser amounts to the other parties, but the Socialists and Democratic Socialists depend heavily on support from labor unions, while the Communists and Komeito derive substantial income from their publications and in the case of Komeito from the religious organization that stands behind it. Both business firms and labor unions are permitted to contribute to political parties, though a new Political Financing Law in 1976 greatly restricted the amounts allowed. Political contributions by individuals are relatively insignificant because there is not much personal wealth.

Businessmen, bureaucrats, and the leaders among the Liberal Democratic politicians, all of whom are heavily concentrated in Tokyo, also come for the most part from the same prestigious universities and are likely to have close personal and sometimes family relationships. Moreover, the bureaucrats, who are forced to retire early, occasionally make a later career for themselves with the party or more commonly accept positions as advisers in big business. The latter type of career is popularly called *amakudari*, or "descent from heaven," indicating the greater prestige of the bureaucracy. The three thus form a far more close-knit establishment than is to be found in the so-called Eastern establishment of the United States, though it does not differ as much from leadership circles in some European countries.

The Japanese have often described the symbiotic relationship between politicians, bureaucrats, and business leaders in terms of *janken*, the paper-scissors-stone game of Japanese children. The conservative politicians depend on the money of business; business depends on the administrative rulings of the bureaucracy; and the bureaucracy depends on the political decisions and Diet votes of the politicians. During the period when decisions on industrial growth policies were the major ones being made by the Japanese government, the particularly powerful pressure group of big business did indeed have a specially significant role in the political process.

However, the concept of a narrow triumvirate of leadership including big business is at best only part of the picture and is in any case now losing much of the validity it once had. It leaves out the crucial rural base of the Liberal Democratic party and the party's need to have a wide appeal throughout Japanese society in order to maintain its majority position. In the last analysis, the popular vote is a more basic necessity for the politicians than business money. The picture also applies better to the first two decades after the end of the occupation, when there was general agreement that industrial growth should be the cardinal policy, than it does to the 1970s, when other issues have begun to loom larger than economic growth, and the interests of politicians and bureaucrats have become less compatible with those of businessmen.

THE PLACE of the opposition or anti-establishment in the decision-making process should not be overlooked. Democratic systems usually lack clearly defined roles in decision making for minority political groups, though usually they do make some concessions in actual practice. The filibuster in the Senate and the Southern hold on committee chairmanships were long recognized in the United States as means through which minority Southern points of view had influence. In Japan the general desire for consensus decisions and therefore the popular dissatisfaction with narrow majority decisions on important matters give the political minority an even stronger position. If the Liberal Democratic party were to use its narrow Diet majority to ram through great numbers of bills against determined opposition, as it theoretically could, it would be seen by the public as acting undemocratically and would run the risk of organized demonstrations to the point of civil disorder and possible repudiation by the public at the next election. The intense political excitement and near breakdown of order in Tokyo in 1960 over a single issue, the revision of the Security Treaty, is a good illustration of the limits of majority power in the Japanese system.

This situation makes it imperative for the party in power to limit the number of controversial bills presented in the Diet as much as possible. Less controversial matters are carefully tailored to avoid any serious controversy, and the important controversial issues are made as palatable to the opposition as possible and are strictly limited in number. For many years, for example, there has been a Liberal Democratic consensus on upgrading the Defense Agency to the status of a Defense Ministry, but year after year the measure has been shelved as more symbolic than substantive and therefore not worth the political price that would have to be paid for it. It is commonly felt that three or four important controversial issues are all that can be handled in any one session of the Diet.

All this means that negotiations must be held with opposition parties and also with the pressure groups that are likely to oppose the policies that have been worked out between the party in power and the bureaucracy. The bureaucracy, which sees itself as technically expert rather than politically aligned, has informal contacts with anti-establishment as well as establishment groups. The party in power in its deliberations from the committee level in the Policy Research Council to the cabinet and in the subsequent operation of the Diet, takes into consideration opposition points of view and maintains close though usually informal contact with the opposition parties for this purpose. The extent and effectiveness of this cooperation with the opposition can be seen in the statistic that close to two thirds of legislation adopted by the Diet is passed unanimously. The legislative program of the Liberal Democratic party thus is subjected to considerable influence by the opposition before it ever has been presented to the Diet, and even after submission bills are often further modified to meet the objections of the opposition.

Since the vote of virtually every member of the Diet has already been determined through the achievement of a consensus in each party and since the stands of the various parties are known to each other and may even have been the subject of negotiations, there is little purpose to debate in the Diet. Debate, in fact, is only pro forma and without influence on the outcome. If shifts in party stands are to take place, these will be achieved through informal inter-party negotiations, not by public debate. Somewhat the same situation exists in the British parliament, but the British put great store on forensic skills and love to display them in parliamentary debate. The Japanese have little respect for verbal skills, and as a consequence there is less extensive debate on the issues in the Diet.

The Diet is seen by the party in power as simply the last and most difficult hurdle that decisions must clear. To the opposition parties it is the place where they can obstruct the passage of legislation. Their aim is not rational debate but obstruction. This can be carried out at two levels—at the preliminary Diet committee hearings and at the final plenary sessions. While the committees are sometimes used to modify legislation in order to make it more acceptable to the opposition, their more important use is as a first line of resistance for the opposition parties against legislation they have decided to oppose.

The need to have the budget passed by the beginning of the fiscal year in April and the limited length of the Diet sessions help the opposition parties carry out their obstructionist efforts successfully. Often the fight in the Diet is transferred from the issues to a contest over the extension of the Diet session needed by the Liberal Democrats to get their legislative program passed. An essential tactic of the opposition is to attempt to slow down or block the procedures of the Diet. The questioning in committees of a cabinet minister is often aimed at tricking him into an unwise statement that might then be used as a diversionary issue to slow down action on the legislation under consideration. Those undergoing such interrogations counter by attempting to be as taciturn as possible. Roll call votes in which each member must cast a vote before the speaker's rostrum may be insisted on and then prolonged by a leisurely "ox walk" on the part of the opposition members. Frequently the opposition threatens to boycott sessions and thus put the party in power in the position of seeming to ram through legislation without adequate consideration of opposing views. In extreme cases, the speaker of the house may be bottled up in his office by force or otherwise prevented from conducting sessions. In response to such strategies, the party in power can respond with trickery by suddenly calling sessions or votes before the opposition can marshall its forces. All of these more devious or violent practices of confrontation, however, though common in the 1950s, have decreased in recent years and are no longer characteristic of Diet activities in the 1970s.

THOUGH neither side in the Diet has much hope of influencing the other through debate at the committee level or in the plenary sessions, they both are very conscious that what they say and how they act will be widely reported to the public and may affect subsequent elections. Thus the public has a major, even if unseen, role at the Diet level of decision making, and this role tends to push the politicians toward compromise. Just as the party in power pays a heavy political price for giving the impression of ramming legislation through without due consideration of opposition points of view, the opposition pays a heavy price if it appears to be merely obstructionist. As a result, both sides have good reason to compromise on most issues and to be very selective about those they either decide to oppose to the bitter end or ram through against determined opposition.

The game in the Diet is played before the public audience, with the mass media serving as the eyes and ears of the public. Spokesmen for the parties present their respective cases through the media, and the newspapers in particular monitor all political developments with meticulous care and report them in detail. Since they have huge staffs, each newspaper can assign one or more specialists to follow each of the many aspects of Diet activity, all the ministries and major agencies of the bureaucracy, and, not just the parties, but their individual factions and faction leaders.

The reporters from the various newspapers assigned to a ministry or a faction leader constitute themselves formally into a press club, which establishes a curious symbiotic relationship with the organ of government or politician. The press clubs have officially assigned space within ministry buildings; they have press interviews virtually daily with the minister or vice-minister; and informal late evening meetings with them at home may be the normal wind-up of a politician's day. The press clubs are a ready-made channel through which the government bureaus or politicians can propagate views they wish to spread, and at the same time they serve as a source of intelligence for them and a means through which public opinion can be brought to bear on them.

The mass media, especially the newspapers, are so large and influential that they should probably be regarded as a separate element in the Japanese political process. They help shape popular responses to political issues and thus have a profound influence on political results. Since the press on the whole leans more to the anti-establishment side, it can be seen as another channel through which this side of the political spectrum does have an influence on political decisions. Certainly the newspapers keep as close and determined a watch on the government and politics as in any country. As a result, the Japanese people are probably as well informed on the inside workings of their government as are the people of any other democracy. At the same time, the feeling of intimacy and confidentiality established between press clubs and their respective government organs or politicians inhibits the type of hostile detective work and exposures by newsmen that has at times proven an important element in the American political process, though cases of this type of reporting have increased in Japan in recent years.

In summary, one can conclude that the political decision-making process in Japan, though extremely complex, is reasonably effective and seems well adapted to Japanese styles of interpersonal relations. It is flexible, careful, and thorough but moves very slowly. It probably accords more veto power to minority opposition elements and therefore produces more compromise decisions than in most other systems. Its most basic procedures are conducted largely out of sight in negotiations between bureaucratic groups, committee work in party organs, and endless informal consultations. What is most clearly visible may not be very attractive, at least to Westerners with their concepts of how a democratic government should work. Instead of the enlightening debate that one hopes for in parliaments, there is more brute confrontation over issues that have not been resolved through negotiations and consensus. The part of the public's participation in the process that is most visible is not the endless informal consultations that go on with pressure groups or the ultimate sanction of the voter but demonstrations in the streets over still unresolved matters. It should be noted, however, that confrontations in the Diet do help dramatize issues and stir up public interest, while demonstrations in the streets contribute a sense of popular participation in the political process. Both are good theater and, with the aid of the mass media, help involve the people more closely in the working of government—which is no mean achievement in a country once so thoroughly authoritarian. Superficial observers, concentrating on what is most visible in Japanese politics, have drawn uncomplimentary conclusions about the quality and effectiveness of the system. A deeper look, however, will reveal that it is reasonably efficient, does fit Japanese styles of operation, has great vitality, and has a certain attractiveness of its own.

Issues

30

THE JAPANESE political scene since the end of the occupation has been characterized by a very strong division between the majority Liberal Democrats and the opposition parties, collectively called the progressives or revisionists. On the right stand the conservatives, on the left parties largely of Marxist background. The division runs deep and has been exacerbated by the frustrations of the opposition at its seemingly permanent minority status and denial of a share in power.

This sharp dichotomy was clearest in the early post-occupation years and has blurred considerably since then. Divisions within the opposition run deep, though they are less in the spotlight of the mass media than is the basic left-right split. The voting support for both right and left also is diverse and spreads over a wide range of opinions. The Liberal Democratic party has only a rather vague ideology and has depended more on the personal appeal of its individual politician members, who have differing viewpoints. The voter support for the opposition parties taken together is about equally broad and vague and overlaps to a considerable extent with that of the conservatives.

At first what divided left and right most sharply was history. The parties of the left stemmed from the prewar Marxists, who were the chief victims of suppression and thought control by the prewar government. As a consequence, they wanted a complete break with the past and viewed with great suspicion the conservative parties, which had compromised themselves more fully with the militarists and included in their own postwar leadership a number of prewar and wartime bureaucrats. Kishi, for example, who was prime minister from 1957 to 1960, had been a member of Tojo's wartime cabinet. The left quickly adopted a pose of absolute and total opposition to everything the conservatives did or stood for. Even today political slogans carried by demonstrators often include the phrase *zettai hantai*, "absolute opposition," whatever the issue may be.

The conservatives varied from frank defenders of what they considered were the good aspects of prewar Japan to flexible pragmatists who simply wanted to make things work. To the true conservatives, the progressive groups, with their revolutionary Marxist rhetoric, seemed dangerously "un-Japanese." To the pragmatists, they seemed impractical ideologues who might wreck the system. Both types of conservative were afraid that militants engaged in direct political action would ruin the economy. Faced with the "absolute opposition" of the progressives, they dug in their heels in a determined and often uncompromising stand.

A sense, not of normal democratic process, but of total confrontation built up, which still lingers on in part today. Even seemingly small or technical issues were fought over with a fury that baffled the outside observer. To one side they were seen as the opening wedge for a wholesale restoration of prewar controls, to the other as the beginning of the destruction of Japan. Proposed new police powers for the control of public demonstrations were blocked by bitter opposition in 1958 on the grounds that they would open the door for a return to the prewar type of police control. The introduction in schools of courses on ethics was bitterly fought over in the early 1960s for fear they might lead to the prewar type of indoctrination. Furious struggles over the means of selecting school boards or approving textbooks stretched over the years. As a result of the bitterness of the fight between the left and right, the confrontation over specific issues often engendered more heat than light, and the issues themselves did not always emerge clearly. The violence of feelings in Japan in the early postwar years and even today is much greater than that between Democrats and Republicans in the United States, though the division on issues sometimes remains almost as obscure.

Since the Liberal Democratic party is clearly the party supported by big business, and three of the four opposition parties are of Marxist origin, one might assume that issues of class struggle, the redivision of wealth, and the socialization of industry might stand out most clearly, but this is not the case. In the early postwar years both left and right took Marxist theory more or less literally and assumed a basic confrontation on these issues. The ideological concepts of the left, however, never had much meaning for the Japanese public, and the confrontation in the long run has proved much less clear in reality than it seemed in theory.

Marxist rhetoric and categories of thought, however, have sunk deeply into Japanese intellectual life, dominating some academic disciplines and influencing the thinking and speech of conservatives as well as leftists. In the early postwar years, Marxism had the appeal of being the most daring new ideas of the liberated 1920s and the forbidden fruit of the 1930s. Since the Communists and some of the Socialists had courageously resisted domination by the militarists during the war years, their ideals were seen by many people as the obvious alternatives to the false gods of the prewar leadership.

The Marxist appeal to class interests, however, never caught on with the rank and file to the same degree as in some Western democracies. As we have seen, the Japanese are a very homogeneous people. They do not think of themselves in class terms, and if they are forced to specify their class, some four fifths or more now will opt for the middle class. They simply do not respond to class voting appeals or to slogans like "the dictatorship of the proletariat," which has the distasteful ring of authoritarian systems of the past.

The Communist leaders and many of the Socialist leaders too have always shown considerable ideological purity and zeal, but their ideologies have tended to be an albatross around their necks when they approached the voters. At conventions of the Socialist party, which are conclaves of the leading Socialist politicians and the heads of the more leftist unions, there has usually been a discernible shift to the left in rhetoric and ideas, but when it comes to elections the party tends to shift back toward the center. The pull of the center is well illustrated by the "vision" for Japan that the right-wing Socialist leader Eda, inspired by Italian Communist concepts of structural reform, put forth in the early 1960s. It called for a fourfold goal—British parliamentarianism, Soviet social welfare, American affluence, and the Japanese peace constitution. Although Eda lost out in the contest for party leadership in 1962, the Socialists re-

Facing page: A street in Tokyo closed to Sunday traffic. Such measures, as in other countries, are part of an effort to improve the quality of life for ordinary citizens. The crowd is characteristically young. Isetan is one of Tokyo's major department stores. (*Maryknoll*)

mained torn by the conflicting pulls of ideological purity and a more centrist voting public. The divisiveness of these conflicting pulls has not been much helped by the party's eventual compromise definition of itself as a "class-based mass party."

Somewhat the same struggle has gone on in the Communist party over the years, but here the conflict has been not only among the Japanese Communist leaders but also between them and their foreign mentors. In the 1949 election, the Communists, dropping their earlier militancy and proclaiming themselves a "lovable" Communist party, won almost 10 percent of the vote. When, on Moscow's orders, they returned to extreme militancy, their vote dropped and remained for more than a decade below 3 percent. In the 1960s, however, they gradually threw off their allegiance first to Moscow and by the mid-1960s to Peking as well. They softpedaled class, emphasized nationalism, and eventually came out in 1970 with a definition of their political goal as being "a multi-political party system under socialism designed to defend parliamentary government." In part because of this broader appeal, their popular vote rose above the 10 percent mark for the first time in the 1972 election.

The opposition parties have found proposals for the socialization of the economy no more useful than an appeal to class interests. The smashing success of the Japanese economy since the war has nullified the attraction of such issues. The parties of the left are seen as leaning more toward a socialized economy than the conservatives and as favoring a more equal division of the economic pie among the various elements of society, but they put forth no great vision of a socialized economy or even proposals for government ownership or control of specific industries. Few people believe that they could do better or even as well as the Liberal Democrats and their big business supporters in bringing prosperity to the Japanese people. Instead the progressive parties skirmish with the Liberal Democrats over a variety of side issues. They champion what is called "medium and small enterprises" against big business, but here they are siding with the status quo in favor of a declining aspect of the economy, which in any case should be labeled petty bourgeoisie rather than proletariat. They tend to favor greater emphasis on trade with the Communist countries, especially China, which is a concept with considerable appeal in Japan but which has severe practical limitations. In short, broad economic issues have simply not proven to be important in postwar political controversy in Japan—until Japan's extraordinary economic success began in the late 1960s to raise questions about continued economic growth, but these questions concerned new types of problems rather than the classic Marxist economic issues.

THE OPPOSITION parties have had more success with issues involving the defense of the individual rights guaranteed in the constitution. Since the two main possible infringers of these rights are obviously the government and big business, with both of which the party in power is identified, the Liberal Democrats are naturally vulnerable on a wide front to attacks on these issues. The whole war experience left the public extremely suspicious of all authority and deeply resentful of any acts, such as the acquisition of land for roads or airports, that might indicate government insensitivity to the interests of ordinary citizens. The party that exercised government authority always appeared to be on the wrong side in any controversy of this sort.

One specific area of conflict has been over the powers and prerogatives of labor unions, which are important supporters of the Socialist, Democratic Socialist, and Communist parties. The blue collar unions in private industry, which predominate in the Domei federation, have on the whole found it more advantageous to use their bargaining muscle in direct negotiations with industry, striking if necessary in the manner of American unions. No one disputes their right to such actions, and as a consequence the Democratic Socialist party, which Domei supports, has not been brought into conflict with the party in power over this issue. The situation with regard to the unions of government workers, many of them white collar, which predominate in the larger Sohyo federation, is quite different, for these unions are perennially in battle with the government over their right to strike. Since Sohyo supports the Socialists and some of its unions the Communists, these two parties are brought into sharp conflict with the party in power over this matter. The right of public workers to strike, however, is politically a two-edged sword. An inconvenienced public may react against the unions, as happened in the general strike of transportation and communication workers from November 26 to December 5, 1975.

On many other social problems there is often no clear division between right and left. The "progressive" parties may be critical of government policies but usually offer no clear alternative programs. The problem area of the universities is a good case in point. The opposition parties will play up to those elements that are dissatisfied with government innovations, but this tends to make them supporters of the status quo, and they themselves put forward no clear practical proposals on such key issues as the financial crises of private universities or the examination problem.

A growing area of social issues is the imbalance in growth between industry and social welfare and the increasing problems resulting from the breakneck rate of economic growth and its accompanying crowding and pollution. In order to maximize the reinvestment of profits for further growth, private housing, public facilities, and social benefits were seriously neglected up through the 1960s, and the effects of crowding and pollution became constantly more severe. Endless specific issues arose, mostly local in nature, that could be successfully exploited by the opposition, such as the asthma of the industrial city of Yokkaichi near Nagoya and the mercury poisoning at the fishing village of Minamata in southwestern Kyushu. New issues appeared all the time, as in the case of "sound pollution" from planes and trains, photochemical smog from exhaust fumes, and a nationwide panic in 1973 over the pollution of fish, which constitute the chief source of protein in the Japanese diet. The "right to sunshine," which tall buildings might deny their lower neighbors, also became a major issue, since sunshine is considered important in Japan for the general quality of life, for winter heating, and for drying laundry (washing machines are common in Japan but dryers are rare).

Reflecting the worldwide rise in sensitivity to problems of the environment, pollution, and the quality of life, Japanese concern over "public injury" (*kogai*) mounted rapidly in the late 1960s and early 1970s, but became diffused as an interparty issue. The concern was greatest in the metropolitan areas, where the ills were most evident. This produced a rapid rise in the metropolitan protest vote against the existing system, which helped the parties of the left capture the positions of governor and mayor and to dominate the local assemblies in most metropolitan and big city areas. However, the largest opposition party, the Socialists, did not attract much of this vote, which went instead to the Communists and the Komeito, since they seemed more effectively organized for protest and in the case of the Komeito was made up largely of the most disadvantaged urban elements. Thus this issue helped spread out the opposition vote among the four opposition parties, weakening the largest of them, and it brought to the Communists and the Komeito an electoral support that had little interest in the more central Communist or Komeito concerns.

Most of the agitation over public injury problems has not taken on clear political coloration. It is made up of a mass of "local residents' movements" (jumin undo) concerned with purely local issues, such as a polluting factory, a plan for a local nuclear plant or industrial zone, or the noise of a local airport. The various "citizens' movements" (shimin undo) of the 1950s and 1960s had usually involved foreign policy issues, such as American bases or the Vietnam War, and thus had been susceptible to manipulation by the opposition parties, but most local residents' movements resisted involvement in national politics and in this sense remained apolitical. Problems of public injury did help the opposition parties gain control over the local governments in many urban areas, and they did bring a new significance to local government, but in a highly centralized land like Japan the national government is in the best position to handle problems of this sort, and the party in power, by turning its attention to them, managed on the whole to defuse them as interparty issues.

A good case in point is the skill and speed with which the government faced the pollution problem, once it as well as the public became thoroughly awakened to it. As a result, Japan has come to stand not only in the forefront among the nations suffering from pollution but also in the forefront in dealing with it. A series of court decisions between 1971 and 1973 established the principle that the polluter should pay for the damages or inconvenience to individuals. Spurred by these decisions, the government moved rapidly ahead with administrative countermeasures. It created an Environment Agency in 1971 and established emission standards on pollution, which are among the strictest in the world and had achieved quite visible results already by the mid-1970s. Between 1968 and 1975 Japan cut sulphur dioxide pollution in the air by more than half, while more than doubling the consumption of the fuels that produced it. Japan also has established a system of compensation administered by the government, in which a specific polluting industry pays, when it can be identified, and categories of industries or other polluters, such as operators of motor vehicles, are taxed to provide the compensatory funds when specific blame cannot be assigned. Japanese industry has also come to show a willingness to accept responsibility for pollution and to negotiate privately over compensation payments. Japan today is investing in pollution controls and compensation a percentage of the GNP two or three times higher than that of the leading industrial nations of North America and Europe. Under these circumstances it is not surprising that most local residents' movements prefer to deal with the government and business rather than make their cause part of a political battle in behalf of opposition parties that have never been in power.

STRICTLY political problems loom largest among the issues dividing the conservatives and progressive parties in Japan, far overshadowing both economic and social issues. While foreign policy has normally been the focus for the greatest controversies, there are some political problems which are essentially domestic. The most important of these is the mutual fear of both the right and left that the other might subvert the political system established by the 1947 constitution.

The left at first believed that the conservatives meant to whittle away at the occupation reforms and the constitution, eventually destroying them. There were some grounds for these fears for a while, as the conservatives established the Self-Defense Forces in 1954, reconsolidated central control over the police in 1954 and over education in 1956—all against frantic opposition from the left—and united in 1955 into the Liberal Democratic party, many of whose members had the clear objective of revising the constitution in order to return theoretical sovereignty to the emperor and do away with article 9, which renounces war and bars the maintenance of a war potential. Significant revisions of the occupation reforms, however, went no further, and the conservatives, lacking the necessary two thirds majorities in the two houses of the Diet, eventually gave up all thought of constitutional reform. While some of the most conservative elements within the party probably still disapprove of aspects of the postwar political system, the only active opposition to it from the right comes from tiny bands of fanatical ultranationalists with whom no active politician would wish to be associated.

The right's fears of political subversion by the left are easy to understand because of the revolutionary Marxist rhetoric of the Communist and Socialist parties and the readiness of the whole left to resort to mass demonstrations on all issues from foreign policy to wage negotiations. But, as we have seen, even the Communist party gradually shifted to proclaimed support of Japan's democratic system, and it even shelved its demands for getting rid of the emperor. Most demonstrations have lost their revolutionary ardor and have become simply a part of the process of bargaining. Conservatives still fear, very probably with reason, that the leadership and hard core support of the Communists and the extreme left wing of the Socialist party, which often seems more radical than the Communists, do not sincerely support democracy and would subvert the system if they got the chance. Still the great bulk of the voters for all the opposition parties give unequivocal support to the constitution and its democratic procedures, and open opposition from the left has shrunk to a few small student bands, which as a result of their violent militancy have lost all touch with the rest of Japanese politics.

The history of the student movement is illustrative of the decline of leftist revolutionary sentiment in Japan. The organized student movement in Japan, like that of most other nations, has always inclined to the left. This was true of the earliest student movement following World War I and was even more clearly the case after World War II. Relatively small groups of leftist activists got control of the student organizations on most campuses, and their national federation, the Zengakuren, became almost synonymous with Japanese political radicalism. Much larger groups of students might at times be activated by these radicals over specific issues, but the bulk of the students remained politically apathetic most of the time, being more interested in other activities, such as sports, mountain climbing, music, and even their studies.

Student leftists were an important part of the political scene for the first decade and a half after the war and proved to be the core of the great demonstrations that shook the nation in 1960 over the ratification of the revised Security Treaty. But thereafter the student movement began to drift away from the center of the political stage. It broke up into a number of battling sects of Trotskyites and various obscure ideologies, with names like the Red Army (*Sekigun*) or Revolutionary Marxist (*Kakumaru*) or Nucleus (*Chukaku*) factions. These came into increasingly lethal combat with one another and looked with contempt and hatred even on the Communists as being hopelessly old-fashioned and conservative.

As political excitement rose in the late 1960s over the Vietnam War, the return of Okinawa, and the possibility of repudiating the Security Treaty in 1970, militant student groups, armed with staves and decked out in colored workmen's helmets identifying their sect, became increasingly prominent. Such student groups provided the backbone of the opposition forces in the battles over the new Tokyo airport at Narita northeast of the city, which started in 1966 and culminated in a deadly fracas in 1971. The students, taking advantage of an opposition movement to the airport among local residents in the Narita area, attempted to turn it into a general attack on the whole political system and Japan's foreign policy, claiming that the airport would be used to supply the American army in Vietnam. But their violence—they butchered three policemen in one clash—appalled the public and even their allies at Narita, though it was to be a few more years before the Narita dispute was finally settled.

Since the early 1970s the political role of the students has continued to fade, as the radical student movement moved further off to the far periphery of Japanese politics. No party or politician wishes to be associated in any way with these radicals. The Minsei, the student organization dominated by the Communits party, served almost as the law and order faction during the university troubles of the late 1960s and since then has got back control of many of the campus organizations. Meanwhile the student sects of the far left have sunk further into internecine warfare, executions of their own disloyal members, and senseless acts of terrorism, such as the gunning down of twenty-six chance victims at the Lod Airport in Israel in 1972 and the bombing of the Mitsubishi Heavy Industry headquarters in Tokyo in 1974, in which eight persons were killed and three hundred and sixty-four injured. Thus the successors to the once influential Zengakuren are now completely out of the political picture and are viewed with outrage and contempt by almost all sectors of the public.

While open opposition to the existing political system has shrunk on both the right and the left to an insignificant "lunatic" fringe, dissatisfaction with the way the system operates is widespread and is naturally focused primarily on the party in power. Desiring harmony and consensus, the public is disgusted that the most visible parts of the decision-making process are demonstrations in the streets and confrontations in the Diet over unresolved issues. Those who support the opposition parties are frustrated and indignant over the seeming permanence of Liberal Democratic rule, which they mistakenly interpret to mean denial of any role to them. Some are distressed that the electoral process as well as party organizations are closely tied up with personal relationships and do not seem to be determined by issues. Most are unhappy that the strict electoral rules are constantly flouted or at least circumvented by strategies of dubious legality. There are always charges of corruption and a strong feeling that politics is dirty.

The cries of corruption are often misunderstood by foreigners and therefore need some explanation. Political corruption is not widespread in Japan, as compared with many countries and is probably much less than in local government in the United States. There is little vote buying in Japan, because the secret ballot and a huge electorate—it normally takes upwards of 50,000 votes to win a lower house seat—make vote buying impractical and not worth the political risks. The national bureaucracy has been entirely untarnished by scandal, though politicians and local bureaucrats are sometimes suspected, not of stealing public funds, but of receiving bribes for political favors. In the case of politicians, such payments are probably taken not so much for personal gain as for campaign purposes.

The chief problem in Japan, as elsewhere, is the vagueness of the line between legal and illegal political contributions. The lavish entertainment of politicians and bureaucrats by businessmen well provided with expense accounts can have an unsavory odor, as can also the Japanese propensity for giving gifts, even though these are considered merely customary. More serious is the fact that almost all politicians receive and expend vastly greater funds for elections than they are allowed to by law. As we have seen, both business firms and labor unions are permitted to make political contributions, but nonetheless the line between legal political contributions and payoffs remains indistinct, leaving much room for suspicions of corruption.

Some other charges of corruption seem to be more marginal, as when a politician is felt to be using his official position improperly to benefit his electoral district or his own electoral chances. For example, in the "black mists" election of 1967, so named for the "black mists" of corruption, one cabinet minister was charged with having improperly located in his district an express stop on a main railway line and the director of the Defense Agency was accused of having used a Self-Defense Forces band for his own political purposes.

Two famous recent cases of "corruption" are worth specific mention. Both involved Tanaka, who was prime minister from 1972 to 1974. Tanaka is a self-made business magnate who was felt to be too free and easy in his acceptance of political contributions and the use of his own money to exert political influence. A magazine expose of this "money politics," inspired by the Watergate case in the United States, led to his resignation as prime minister in December 1974. To restore the image of the Liberal Democratic party and to avoid a big battle between Fukuda and

Ohira, the two chief candidates to succeed Tanaka, a lesser faction leader, Miki, was chosen for the prime ministership and was subsequently termed the "Mr. Clean" of the party.

The other case started with allegations made in Senate hearings in Washington in February 1976 that high Japanese officials had received huge bribes from the Lockheed Corporation to influence their decisions on plane purchases. The scandal, the worst in Japan's postwar history, produced a prolonged crisis in the operation of the Diet. Miki, living up to his "Mr. Clean" reputation, insisted on having the case vigorously investigated, and, though many of his fellow Liberal Democrats wished to force him out of office and cover up the scandal, the public gave him enthusiastic support. Tanaka and some other leading politicians, as well as a number of businessmen, were indicted and temporarily jailed until released on bail. Tanaka and the other indicted Diet numbers resigned from the party to save it embarrassment, but all but one of them were reelected to the Diet as so-called independents in the December 1976 elections. Although Miki was replaced by Fukuda as prime minister the same month, the independence and integrity of Japanese prosecutors and their high record of convictions suggest the likelihood of ultimate convictions in at least some of these cases.

Major corruption cases like the two involving Tanaka are rare, but there is a widespread feeling that politics is dirty. This has been a constant feature of postwar political controversy and has had a particularly adverse impact on the Liberal Democratic party as both the party in power and the party of big business, which is seen as the usual source of corruption. Efforts are being made to make the laws on corruption clearer, again under the inspiration of similar post-Watergate attempts in the United States. The Political Financing Law of 1976 was designed to put limits on political contributions, but there also seems to be need for reforms which will realistically allow greater legal expenditures for elections and more volunteer help but will demand a clear accounting of all political funds.

THE CLEAREST and largest of the controversies between the left and right in postwar Japanese politics have been over foreign policy and have always been seen as centering around relations with the United States. This situation naturally grew out of the tremendous role of the United States in Japan during the occupation. Historically the great cleavage over foreign policy started with the disillusionment of the left with the American occupation, when its emphasis shifted between 1947 and 1949 from further reforms to economic recovery and stability. The left saw the occupation as having changed from patron to enemy, and from then on it viewed almost all controversial issues in Japan as involving the relationship with the United States. Marxist theoreticians still sometimes argue over whether the chief enemy of the Japanese people is domestic "monopoly capitalism" or "capitalist imperialism," meaning the United States, to which they attribute the power of domestic "monopoly capitalism."

Since I shall consider Japanese foreign relations more fully in the final section of this book, I shall outline here only briefly the main foreign policy issues in postwar Japan. The Japanese emerged from the war thoroughly revolted at its horrors and fully convinced of the impracticality of their earlier attempt to carve out their own economic *Lebensraum* through military conquest. There was a deep and genuine passion for peace and a determination on the part of most Japanese to eschew any form of militarism and to remain neutral in all conflicts anywhere in the world. They espoused complete pacifism and embraced with enthusiasm article 9 of the constitution repudiating war. Such attitudes fit well the early postwar international status of Japan as a powerless, crippled, pariah nation.

The more conservative elements in Japan, however, rightly saw that the nation's only chance for recovery was through industrial growth, and they believed that, for such industrial growth, American cooperation, the great American market, and the open worldwide trading system the United States was sponsoring were all essential. A close alignment with the United States was therefore felt to be necessary after the end of the occupation.

The conservatives also felt that, however much they might themselves decry the cold war, Japan could not afford to be unprotected in a divided world. They thought that, despite article 9, Japan had a right to self-defense. They embodied this concept, against determined leftist opposition, in the Self-Defense Forces, which eventually won general acceptance, though at a modest level. Since strategic, economic, and above all domestic political considerations placed strict limits on Japanese self-defense, the conservatives also favored a commitment by the United States to Japan's security. The concept was first proposed by the conservative prime minister Ashida during his incumbency in 1948. It became embodied in the Security Treaty with the United States, which went into effect with the Peace Treaty in the spring of 1952. The original Security Treaty was more restrictive on Japan than Ashida or his successor, Yoshida, had wished, but the revisions in 1960 brought it in line with the original Japanese hopes.

While the conservatives were extraordinarily successful in their economic policy of close alignment with the United States, and Japan, under the Security Treaty, remained both safe and uninvolved in foreign wars, the treaty did expose the conservatives to incessant political attack at home. It was seen as flouting article 9 of the constitution and as trampling on the pacifist yearnings of the people. It seemed to stand in the way of a full rapprochement with the Chinese, which was deeply desired by most Japanese. Moreover, Marxists interpreted it as endangering Japan rather than giving it security. They argued that alignment with a "capitalist imperialist" America, which despite its verbal blandishments was seen to be the true "warmonger," would invite attack by the Communist "peace camp" and threaten involvement of Japan in American military adventurism abroad, as in Korea or Vietnam. More practically, the Security Treaty committed the party in power to the naturally distasteful presence of a foreign military, with its military bases and the economic and social problems that inevitably surrounded them.

Japanese politics, particularly in the early years after the occupation, seemed to revolve largely around the American connection. The Security Treaty was the biggest of all issues, and its renegotiation in 1960 occasioned the greatest mass protest movement in Japanese history. America's Vietnam War, the return of Okinawa, and the possible repudiation of the Security Treaty were the main issues of the late 1960s. Endless problems involving the bases were seized upon by the opposition and sometimes blown up into political *causes célèbres*. Almost any issue, however far removed from foreign policy, was likely to be linked in some way with the American relationship.

This was thus the one clear issue that divided the Liberal Democrats from the opposition parties. The party in power stood firmly for the alignment with the United States, though, realizing its vulnerability to attack on this issue, it attempted to avoid debate over it. Quite frequently it posed as not liking the Security Treaty but as having been forced to accept it in order to have the necessary economic association with the United

States, which was more generally understood and approved. All the opposition parties opposed the Security Treaty, usually in absolute terms.

Gradually, however, even this issue began to fade. The decrease in the number and size of the American bases in Japan and the growing affluence of the Japanese reduced problems surrounding the bases. The seeming decline in the danger of general warfare in East Asia in the 1970s reduced the anxieties of both supporters and opponents of the treaty. The Soviet Union and the People's Republic of China shifted from determined opposition to the Security Treaty to tacit approval of it because of their bitter animosity for each other, and this development punctured the arguments of Marxist ideologues in Japan. As the possibilities for sharing power with the Liberal Democrats came closer, the opposition parties also began to adopt less extreme and more realistic foreign policy positions. They slowly lessened their antagonism to the treaty. The most moderate of them, the Democratic Socialists, eventually in 1975 moved to open approval, and in the election in December 1976 none of the parties made a special issue of the Security Treaty. Thus, the stand of the Liberal Democrats, who themselves favor a gradual reduction of American bases and a downplaying of the treaty, and that of the opposition parties gradually began to converge. During the 1970s, moreover, foreign policy issues came to be seen as involving much more than the question of neutrality or alignment with the United States. Questions of the global availability of raw materials and the maintenance of international trade were becoming much more important, and attitudes toward these problems did not divide into the old left-right cleavage on foreign policy.

Trends

31

JAPAN in the early 1950s was a country that had been through two decades of traumatic experiences—the years of shrinking personal freedoms and fanatic indoctrination as the military took over in the 1930s, the physical and spiritual devastation of the war, and the sweeping reforms under alien rule during the occupation. Soon it plunged into the most rapid rate of economic growth and social evolution that any major country has ever experienced. One would expect from this that Japanese politics would have been fast changing and even erratic. Instead it has been relatively stable and extraordinarily predictable.

This stability can be attributed to a number of factors. The most fundamental though least provable may be the underlying stability of Japanese society, which I have described in an earlier section. Another factor is the division of the opposition at first into two or three parties and since 1964 into four, which has contributed to the long lease on power of the Liberal Democrats. Still another is the multi-seat electoral district system, which produces a slower change in the parliamentary strength of the parties than does the Anglo-American system. But the most important factor may be the steadiness of Japanese voting habits.

The stability of the Japanese vote is best illustrated by the vote for the lower house of the Diet, which from year to year and even decade to decade has shown remarkably consistent trends, traceable back into the prewar period. In 1932, shortly after the Manchurian Incident, the two traditional parties together won over 94 percent of the vote. Subsequently, under pressure from the left as well as the right, their share fell to

77.6 percent in 1936 and 71 in 1937. Then came the interim of the war years and the early postwar confusion, but by 1952, shortly after the end of the occupation, the conservative vote was back up to 66 percent, not far below where it had been before the war. Thereafter it resumed the downward course it had already shown in the 1930s, but at a very slow and steady pace. Between 1952 and 1976 the vote fell election after election from 66.1 percent to 41.8—a rate of almost exactly 1 percent per year. It would be hard to match such a slow but steady rate of decline anywhere in the world.

Unchanging partisan votes elsewhere are often associated with regional preferences, like the former Democratic vote of the South in the United States or rigid class voting habits in the United Kingdom. But neither of these characterize Japan. There are no discernible regional preferences, and while farmers tend to vote conservative and organized labor progressive, there are rural areas which vote Socialist, and blue collar workers as well as white feel no compulsion to vote for a party because of their class or even if they belong to a union which supports it. The steadiness of Japanese voting habits, I believe, is basically the result of a quite different factor—the individual support machines which most candidates have and which tend to hold on to their personalized support regardless of the issues and the political crises in Tokyo. The slow steady change in the vote then is to be attributed, not so much to the rise or fall of political ideologies, as to sociological shifts, such as the movement of population from the countryside to the city and the increase in affluence and physical mobility of the Japanese, which wear away these personalized support groups and put voters in a new social context.

The Liberal Democratic party is correctly called the party of the farmers and big business, but of course it is much more than this. Still, the heavy rural vote for the Liberal Democrats, which has been made even more important by its overweighting in the electoral process, has been one of the chief reasons for the party's long hold on power. The left, in frustration, often views farmers as the stupid, "feudalistic," peasant captives of the conservative politicians, but the preference of the farmers for the Liberal Democratic party is the natural product of the normal conservatism of rural people, the strong bond between the traditional parties and rural Japanese ever since the 1880s, and the Liberal Democrats' record of generous agricultural price supports, which have given farmers a reasonable share in Japan's postwar industrial affluence.

Rural society in Japan, as in most parts of the world, is fundamentally conservative. Desperate economic conditions in the 1920s produced some agrarian radicalism, which was exploited in the 1930s by the militarists, but the sweeping land reforms carried through by the American occupation between 1946 and 1949 helped restore rural contentedness and conservatism. The reforms limited the ownership of agricultural land to local residents and holdings to two and one half acres beyond what the individual farmer cultivated himself, for a total of seven and one half acres for any one holding. (The figures varied according to local agricultural productivity, but these are national averages.) All land above these limits had to be sold to the actual cultivators at prices that amounted to virtual confiscation. Tenancy plunged from 46 percent to between 5 and 10. These land reforms were followed by the great economic upsurge of postwar Japan, in which the farmers participated through politically determined high price supports for rice and protection of their market from foreign imports. As a result, most rural Japanese remained essentially conservative and maintained their old ties with the traditional parties and their modern successor, the Liberal Democrats.

The farm vote, however, accounts for only a fraction of Liberal Democratic electoral support, and big business provides even less. It simply has very few votes to deliver. Even when big business ran candidates in the upper house elections of 1974, these fared badly, as we have seen. But big business is important to the Liberal Democrats in other ways besides votes. Its cooperation with the party and bureaucracy in working out economic policies has been vital, and it is the chief source of party financing.

Usually a specialized agency is set up by big business to allot assessments and funnel the funds to the party. Individual corporations also make contributions directly to one or more factions and quite commonly to some of the opposition parties as well, presumably in the spirit of spreading one's bets. Despite the Liberal Democratic party's dependence on big business money, however, business magnates usually do not attempt to dictate party policies. They were influential in bringing the conservative politicians together in 1955 and perhaps in the choice of Sato for prime minister in 1964 over Kono, his chief rival, who was seen as less favorable to big business. But for the most part they exert their influence only on economic issues of direct interest to them, in the manner of any other pressure group.

The bulk of the Liberal Democratic votes come neither from farmers nor big businessmen, but from citizens of all types who become involved in the support machines of Liberal Democratic politicians or merely happen to incline toward conservative views or to have greater faith in the leadership skills of the Liberal Democrats over their rivals, particularly in the crucial economic area. Conservative voters are to be found overwhelmingly in the smaller cities, towns, and countryside, where personalized support machines can be maintained, and they are notably fewer in the great metropolitan areas, where such organizations cannot easily operate. This situation ties in with the demographic reasons for the decline of the conservative vote and explains the rather frantic efforts of some younger Liberal Democratic politicians in recent years to devise a new conservative ideology which might better attract the metropolitan voter.

THE VOTE for the opposition parties shows the reverse picture from the Liberal Democratic vote. It is heavily metropolitan and has increased steadily even if slowly. Since the occupation the total opposition vote has risen slightly with each election, moving from 29.5 percent in 1953 to 48.3 percent in 1976, which comes out on average at a little less than 1 percent per year, almost the exact amount of the Liberal Democratic loss. There has normally been around a 5 percent vote for independents, mostly conservatives, and in 1976 a dissident conservative group, the New Liberal Club, won 4.2 percent of the vote, thus accounting for the rest of the percentage points and giving the conservatives even in 1976 a slight popular edge.

The opposition vote seems to be of two kinds. One is attracted by the leftist ideologies of the three older opposition parties. These cover a wide range from the revolutionary doctrines espoused at times by the Communists and the left wing Socialists to the strongly parliamentarian and mildly socialistic views of the Democratic Socialists. As in most other industrialized nations, such leftist concepts have more appeal to intellectuals, to younger people, and to union-organized blue and white collar workers. All these groups are heavily concentrated in metropolitan areas and are growing in numbers.

The other type of opposition vote, which is also to be found mostly in metropolitan areas, might be called the nonideological protest vote. The crowding, pollution, and other ills resulting from rapid economic growth fall most heavily on metropolitan districts, and as a consequence many of their residents are disenchanted with a government that seems more attuned to the interests of big business and rural folk than to those of urban dwellers. As we have seen, much of this vote in recent elections has gone to the Communists and thus comes from people who have no particular interest in the traditional Communist goals, but the Komeito has also received a large part of the protest vote.

The Komeito is a curious party that is the political wing of the new religious movement known as Soka Gakkai and, like its mother religion, is made up largely of urban people who have banded together in religious fellowship to compensate for their lack of other meaningful group associations or to make up for other handicaps. They are almost by definition disadvantaged urban dwellers, and therefore their party is a natural nucleus for a protest vote. As an opposition party, the Komeito has taken on much of the rhetoric and political coloration of the other opposition parties, which are of Marxist origin, but it seems improbable that these ideas have much hold on either its leadership or voting support. What the Komeito would actually stand for if it had a share in power is not easy to say, but, judging from its membership, one might expect it to lean toward old-fashioned nationalism and conservatism, and its leaders quite understandably show a strong interest in social welfare problems.

The most significant fact about the opposition is its deep division into four parties. At one time it seemed to be more or less united, consisting primarily of a Socialist party with only a small fringe Communist party. This was true in 1947 when the Socialists won 30.7 percent of the seats in the lower house and as late as 1955, when the two wings of the party, shortly before their reunification, won 33.4 percent, providing exactly the one third needed to block any revision of the constitution. Time seemed to be on the Socialist side, and it appeared predictable that before long they would win a majority and become the party in power. But since 1955 this dream has gradually gone glimmering. The opposition has broken up into four more evenly matched parties, and by 1976, when the combined opposition vote at 48.3 percent had almost become a majority, the Socialist share of 20.7 percent was considerably less than half of the total.

The image of a once promising movement that has faded, and frustration over their apparent inability ever to come to power, have contributed to the decline of the Socialist party. But it can also be attributed to the deep ideological divisions within the party and the constant internecine battles that result. Another reason for their decline is probably because the Socialists, with their longer history, are more dependent on old-fashioned personalized support machines than are, for example, the Communists and the Komeito and thus suffer from the same sort of attrition that besets the Liberal Democrats. For all these reasons the Socialists appear less effective as a protest movement than do the more tightly organized Communists and Komeito, and therefore they lose out on this vote as well.

While not many votes appear to switch between the conservatives and opposition parties, votes do fluctuate quite widely between the opposition parties themselves, as can be seen in the drop in the Socialist vote between 1947 and 1949 from 26 to 13.5 percent and the corresponding rise of the Communist vote from 3.7 to 9.7 percent. The Socialists had been discredited by their participation in two successive coalition cabinets in 1947 and 1948, the first under a Socialist prime minister, Katayama, at a time when Japan was still in a pitiful economic condition and no cabinet could be more than the handmaiden of the occupation. As a consequence, many leftist voters temporarily switched their allegiance from them to the Communists in the 1949 election. The rather abrupt fall of the Socialist vote again between 1967 and 1968 from 28 percent to 21.4 can similarly be linked with the rise of the Komeito vote from 5.4 percent to 11. Many protest voters had obviously decided that the Komeito was a more attractive medium of protest.

ONE MAY wonder why, if the conservative side of Japanese politics is able to organize itself effectively through the ideologically amorphous, faction-ridden Liberal Democratic party, the opposition side, made up of Japanese with the same social characteristics and organizational skills, cannot do the same for the left. One explanation for this failure may be that the progressive parties have become the prisoners of their own ideologies. Founded originally by intellectuals in the 1920s, they still have a tendency toward divisiveness and philosophical hair splitting.

The Communists have had endless internal battles, though the clear and firm control of Miyamoto since the mid-1960s has given them more unity and cohesiveness in recent years. The Socialists carried over their prewar ideological divisions into the postwar scene. Their first postwar leader was Nishio, a labor union leader of moderate leanings. The Protestant Christian element in the party, dating back to the first stirrings of the socialist movement, was also moderate. At the other extreme were revolutionary radicals hard to distinguish from the most extreme Communists. Inevitably the party tended to split, usually over key foreign policy issues. As we have seen, attitudes toward the 1952 Peace Treaty precipitated a complete rupture from 1951 to 1955 between the right and left wings of the party, and once again in 1960 a part of the right split off, this time permanently, to form the Democratic Socialist party. The remaining Socialists have continued to be divided into ideological factions which constantly feud over party leadership. The left has usually won, though the extreme left has declined in electoral strength in recent years, probably because of the rise of the Communist vote.

In recent years Marxist ideology has faded somewhat. It never was more than a borrowed coloration for the Komeito, and it has come to mean almost nothing to the Democratic Socialists, whose hold on roughly 7 percent of the voters is based on the relatively moderate blue collar unions of the Domei labor federation and on moderate white collar and intellectual supporters. Many of the less radical Socialists are similarly indifferent to Marxist theory, and the party as a whole has tried to play down ideological issues in its appeal to the electorate. The Communists have gone even further in declaring their loyal support of the multi-party parliamentary system, and during the student unrest of the late 1960s they studiously adhered to a moderate line and kept their student movement under careful control.

Ideological differences, however, still run sufficiently deep in feelings, if not in stated policies, to preclude cooperation across the opposition board. The Democratic Socialists and probably the Komeito could never cooperate with the Communists, or possibly even with some left wing Socialists. Some right wing Socialists might also find cooperation with the Communists impossible, and even the left wing has such a history of bitter conflict with the Communists over control of the labor movement that collaboration would be difficult. Even within the Socialist party, it is not clear that there could be effective cooperation between the left and right wings if they faced the responsibility of producing positive policies rather than merely negative stands. The opposition thus is not only split into four parties but also has a deep ideological fault line within it, running through the middle of the Socialist party and dividing it into two possibly irreconcilable halves.

The organization of the opposition parties also militates against any one of them getting dominant power. The Socialists and Democratic Socialists depend heavily on financing from their respective labor federations, Sohyo and Domei, and as a result are under strong labor influence. This reduces their appeal to nonunion voters and in the case of the Socialists helps account for their tendency to lean further to the left than the mass support they would need to become a majority party. In the case of the Komeito and the Communists, the firmness of their organizations has given them an advantage in attracting the urban protest vote, but it also carries with it political liabilities. The Komeito has always had slightly totalitarian overtones in the manipulation of its faithful religious support by a closely organized leadership. This situation tends to repel the general public. For example, the drop in the popular vote for the party from 11 percent to 7.3 between 1969 and 1972 is usually attributed to adverse publicity when Soka Gakkai tried in 1970–71 to suppress a book that was critical of it. The organizational firmness of the Communist party, its relatively large mass base of devoted adherents, its ability to form a successful and disciplined student movement, and its very successful party newspaper, *Akahata*, or "Red Flag," are all much admired, but such tight organizational skills are also frightening to the average Japanese, who sees signs in the party of Japan's own authoritarian past. Strong centralized party structures have helped carry the Komeito and Communist party up over the 10 percent mark in the popular vote but may be inhibiting to further growth.

All in all the opposition is considerably weaker than it appears on the surface. It wins an overwhelming proportion of the votes in metropolitan areas and is thus able to elect governors and mayors, usually supported by two or more progressive parties, and assembly majorities. But these progressive politicians in local government, though constituting an effective symbol of protest, can do very little to affect basic political decisions, since these are made by the central government, which is under Liberal Democratic control. Much of the opposition vote also is an urban vote of protest against the failures of the Liberal Democrats but is not necessarily a vote for the ideologies of the left. In fact, two of the opposition parties themselves, the Democratic Socialists and Komeito, do not really support these goals. And many people who vote Communist or Socialist would think twice if they felt that there were any possibility of Communists or Socialists coming to power and putting into effect traditional Communist or Socialist policies. Actually progressive governors, mayors, and assemblies in metropolitan Japan are much less doctrinaire in their policies than the platforms of the parties that elected them might suggest.

One reason why leftism in Japan seems to loom larger than life, particularly in the eyes of foreign observers, is because it is so heavily concentrated in the great urban centers, especially Tokyo, which are most in the news and best known to outsiders. Here Minobe, the well-known Socialist governor, heads the local government. Here takes place the visible clash between the opposition and the party in power in the Diet and the bulk of popular protest demonstrations. Here are congregated the intellectuals who lean heavily to the left. And here the great mass newspapers, again tilted slightly to the left, hold sway.

Between a leftist leaning urban intellectual environment and the general revulsion against the ultra-rightist concepts of the past, there has been in Japan ever since the end of the war a sort of McCarthyism of the left. While even the most outrageous attacks on conservatives or conservative ideas have always been accepted as intellectually respectable, even moderate, reasoned criticism of leftists or leftist ideas has run the risk of being condemned as bigotry. The United States and its allies are considered fair game for criticism of any sort, but the Communist world, especially China, is treated with kid gloves, and its problems or failures are often either ignored or glossed over. These attitudes may be changing at last, but only very slowly. The foreigner listening to intellectuals, following the Japanese press, or observing the surface manifestations of confrontation politics can still be misled into believing that the Japanese lean far more to the left than they actually do.

WE ARE now ready to consider what is likely to happen in Japanese politics when the Liberal Democrats eventually lose their majority, as seems probable in the not distant future. In the lower house elections of December 5, 1976, they actually came out with a minority—only 249 out of a total of 511 seats—though subsequently a number of successful independent candidates joined the party, pushing its membership over the needed 256 and allowing it to select Fukuda as prime minister when the Diet reconvened on December 24. The Liberal Democratic majority has become so thin that it seems likely that it will be lost in the next election, say in two to four years, or at least by the one after that in five to eight years. The Supreme Court decision in the spring of 1976 in favor of a more equitable division of seats between city and countryside may make this outcome all the more certain.

The Liberal Democratic majority in the upper house is virtually certain to be gone still earlier. The party entered 1977 with the smallest possible majority—a mere one seat—and, unless there is some unexpected reversal of voting trends, the party will undoubtedly find itself in a minority position after the next election for half the house in June 1977. Under these circumstances, the Liberal Democrats will have control over only one of the two houses, and the constitutional provision in article 59 for joint committees of the two houses on points of difference between them may then become an important element in the legislative process.

In the meantime, the Liberal Democrats have already lost the complete control they once enjoyed in both houses, since they no longer can muster a majority in all the committees. Membership in the committees in both houses is in accordance with the number of seats each party has in that house. If there is an even number of members of a committee, the Liberal Democrats, with their present numbers in both houses, are entitled to no more than half the committee members, and if one of their members were selected as chairman, then they could be outvoted by the opposition.

Since the conservatives have ruled without interruption since the end of the occupation, many people are nervous about what will happen now that their majority is slipping. Some even predict a creeping or galloping leftist revolution and others a rightist counter *coup d'état*. A common assumption once was that the end of the Liberal Democratic majority would lead at once to a coalition government of the opposition parties, but this seems unlikely, as the preceding discussion has shown. If a coalition of all the opposition parties or enough of them to constitute a Diet majority were attempted, it would almost certainly have only a brief, stormy career and might possibly trigger a temporary swing back toward the right. The fear, however, remains that a loss of the Liberal Democratic majority in the Diet will lead to a prolonged period of political turmoil and possibly chaos.

In my judgment none of the above developments are likely. What is much more probable is a coalition government between the Liberal Democrats and one or more of the centrist parties, or a less formal alliance between a minority Liberal Democratic government and some of the centrist parties, which, while not joining the government, as evidenced by the acceptance of posts in the cabinet, would agree to support it on nonconfidence votes, in return for a larger say in the legislative program. Such arrangements might not be difficult to make with the Democratic Socialists, whose pragmatic views are not very different from those of the more liberal elements among the Liberal Democrats, or even with the Komeito, whose actual leanings as a government party might be found to parallel some conservative as well as liberal trends within the Liberal Democratic party. If this sort of coalition or alliance were created, the result in a sense would be no more than the addition of one or two new factions to an expanded Liberal Democratic party, and it would extend the party's dominance for a considerable time.

An even more obvious ally for the Liberal Democrats than the Democratic Socialists or the Komeito would be their own dissident splinter group, the New Liberal Club, which broke away after the Lockheed scandal in the spring of 1976, under the leadership of Kono Yohei, the son of the now deceased unsuccessful candidate for the prime ministership in 1964. The phenomenal success of this group in the 1976 elections, however, may encourage them to aspire to more ambitious goals. They started with only five lower house Dietmen, but they increased their membership in this election to seventeen, winning 4.2 percent of the total vote, even though they ran candidates in only twenty-five of the one hundred and thirty electoral districts. Obviously their appeal of youth, honesty, and a fresh even if conservative idealism attracted a significant part of the urban vote. The New Liberal Club may presage a more basic realignment of political forces, which has long been hinted at by the uneasiness of the more moderate Socialists over their association with the leftwing radicals in their party, and the restiveness of some of the younger and more metropolitan members of the Liberal Democratic party, who have chafed at the old-fashioned, old-man image of their party. Even Miki threatened to bolt the party before his choice as prime minister in 1974.

The 1976 elections seem to have strengthened the center of the political spectrum against the two ends. The Liberal Democrats declined significantly in both seats and popular votes; the Communists, through poor luck, fell drastically in seats from thirty-eight to seventeen, though only declining from 10.5 percent of the popular vote to 10.4; the Socialists declined somewhat more from 21.9 to 20.7 percent of the vote, though they got their share in the increase of Diet seats—five out of twenty. In the center the New Liberal Club did spectacularly, and the Komeito increased from twenty-nine to fifty-five seats, as their popular vote bounced back from 8.5 percent in 1972 to 10.9, where it had stood in 1969, and even the Democratic Socialists, through good luck, increased their seats from nineteen to twenty-nine, even though their popular vote slid off from 7 percent to 6.3.

It does not seem at all impossible that over the next several years a new centrist party might emerge, centering around the New Liberal Club, the Democratic Socialists, and the Komeito and attracting substantial portions of the Liberal Democrats and even the Socialists. If this were to happen, this new party might achieve prolonged dominance over the remaining diehard conservatives on the one side and the Communists and left Socialists on the other. Made up like the Liberal Democrats of factions, which at least at first would be defined by their party origin, a centrist party might well prove to have the same capacity for stable and effective rule in the future as the Liberal Democrats have displayed in the past.

The two possibilities outlined above are not mutually exclusive: a coalition or alliance under Liberal Democratic leadership might in time develop into a more basic realignment and the emergence of a new dominant centrist party. In either case, the political system and the government's domestic and foreign policies are likely to continue with little basic change. Government decisions would remain a carefully balanced consensus of the various groups that participate in the new party or coalition, with the same sort of cautious consideration paid to opposition viewpoints. The transition would in reality be quite small. There might be a time of heightened conflict if the Liberal Democratic majority for a while were extremely thin and the opposition parties attempted through parliamentary maneuvering to force it to give up its power, while it continued to cling stubbornly to its old position. But in actuality the transition has already been under way for some time. As Liberal Democratic majorities have shrunk, the party has been forced to increase negotiations with and concessions to at least some of the opposition parties, most often the centrist ones, in order to keep the Diet running efficiently and get necessary legislation passed. It is only a small step from this situation to one in which centrist parties give tacit support to the cabinet on crucial issues or themselves join the cabinet or even a more centrist coalition of forces becomes the new party in power.

In terms of policies, too, the shift from purely conservative to coalition cabinets or a new centrist party would mark no great change. The once clear dividing line on foreign policy and the defense relationship with the United States is fading. Coalition cabinets or a centrist party would certainly maintain the close economic relationship with the United States and probably accept its nuclear umbrella, while pressing quietly for a continuing diminution of American bases in Japan, as has been the Liberal Democratic policy for a long time. There would also be little change in social and economic policies. The Liberal Democratic party, like the public in general, has already given up the policy of economic growth at any price and is paying more attention than before to social welfare and the quality of life. As we have seen, it is as much concerned with problems of public nuisance as is the opposition and has tackled them with alacrity. The inclusion of centrist elements in the cabinet or a centrist party in power would probably do no more than speed up the trend toward the welfare state, which is already clear in Japan as in most industrialized nations. Since the big business supporters of the Liberal Democrats do not view government with distrust, as is the case with business in the United States, and are less concerned with corporate profits than with their own role as managers of the economy in behalf of national interests, they are not as likely as business elements in the United States to resist bitterly a drift in this direction.

Seen in this light, the long and portentously heralded loss of the Liberal Democratic majority appears likely to be less of a shock than many have supposed. While it may bring modifications in detail in some of the ways the political system operates and a continuing shift of domestic economic policies toward the center or left, it is not likely to bring any sharp shifts in political structure or basic policies. The new government would in large part be made up of elements that constituted the old, and policies would be merely a continuation of trends that are already under way.

Political
Style

32

THE FOREIGN observer of the Japanese democratic system is often surprised when he fails to find in it things he is accustomed to, such as brilliant parliamentary debate, as in the British system, or Congressional drafting of legislation and probing committee work, as in the United States. He may be dismayed by much that he does find that is unfamiliar, such as the strong-arm measures of confrontation in the Diet, the continual recourse to mass demonstrations by the opposition, the incessant charges of corruption, and the much publicized factional divisions of the party in power. He may react with scorn or ridicule, especially since he is likely to be quite unaware of the less visible aspects of decision-making procedures in Japan. The weaknesses of the system in his eyes, when combined with the realization that democracy has a relatively short history in Japan and did collapse once already in the 1930s, can lead to the judgment that Japanese democracy is at best a "fragile blossom" or is even a travesty perpetrated by people who have no understanding of it.

If, however, one takes the Japanese political system on its own terms and does not insist that it approximate closely American, British, or continental European models, it appears to measure up quite well as an effective system of democratic rule, not notably inferior to those of the West and perhaps stronger in some respects. There is little cogent public debate over issues in the Diet or elsewhere but probably a great deal more formal and informal consultation than occurs in the West. Parties are somewhat differently constituted than in the West but probably are as effective as channels between public opinion and ultimate political decisions. The services provided by government to the people are certainly as efficient as anywhere and are reasonably responsive to public interests.

The greatest potential weaknesses of Japanese democracy seem to lie in the people rather than the system. They probably have less of a strong "gut" feeling for democracy than do the English speaking nations. Democracy's roots obviously do not run historically as deep. Japanese therefore may not have the passion for democracy of the English speaking peoples, who see it as part of their sacred heritage.

At the same time, the commitment to parliamentary government in contemporary Japan and specifically to the constitution that embraces it is extremely strong. The Japanese do have almost ninety years of experience with democratic forms of government, and the disastrous course of the 1930s and the war years has soured them on any form of authoritarianism. They are convinced almost to a man that parliamentary rule is the only tolerable system. The 1947 constitution attracts the impassioned loyalty of all but a few at the two extremes of the political spectrum. For most, any alternative system of rule seems almost inconceivable. The fact that the first draft of the constitution was largely written by Americans is considered of no consequence. In fact, the somewhat anti-American left is strongest in its loyalty to the constitution. The document's verbiage, which at first sounded odd, has become through usage commonplace and standard. Most people are adamantly opposed to any revision of the constitution, however small, for fear that this might open the lid to more important changes.

Another possible weakness of democracy in Japan is the relative subordination of the individual to the groups to which he belongs. In the West, democracy has always been closely associated with the strength of individualism. But the balance in recent years between individualism and group identification has been shifting somewhat toward the individual in Japan, while it may be going in the opposite direction in the West, and, in any case, there is no reason why a people made up of a great number of diverse groups cannot operate a democratic system as well or perhaps even better than a people divided up into solitary individuals.

Another related problem is the longing of the Japanese for harmony and their abhorrence of an open clash of opinions, which put an added strain on the democratic system in Japan by making close majority decisions less acceptable. Open conflict of views and the resolution of differences of opinion by simple majority votes are both at the heart of any democratic system, but the Japanese would prefer more subtle ways of adjusting conflicts and achieving consensus decisions. The result is a relatively cumbersome system of decision making, which, some argue, produces a slower pace in resolving problems. It is even alleged that the Japanese system is not capable of reaching effective decisions on some issues and that this situation, in time of crisis, could produce grave dangers.

Such interpretations, however, should be accepted with reserve. It is not at all clear that other democracies are any better at making swift or difficult decisions. The Japanese system, moreover, is not as likely as some to produce a quick alternation of policies based on shifting political majorities, which would nullify the decisions made. On the whole, the Japanese democratic system may be as capable as any of making effective decisions with reasonable speed. Although the Japanese have hung back from some international decisions Americans or others would like to see them make, they have been extraordinarily quick and efficient in making the decisions that concern them most, such as those involved in economic growth or more recently problems of pollution.

One thing, however, is certain. Japan even at a time of crisis is not likely to come up with the sort of charismatic leadership that is commonly sought for from the presidency in the United States or that Churchill provided for wartime England. On the other hand, the strong group orientation of the Japanese seems to make them capable of pulling together in times of stress even without such leadership. And, in any case, charismatic leadership, or at least the need for it, might better be regarded as a weakness than a strength in democratic societies.

On the positive side, it seems clear that the sharpness of political divisions on both foreign policies and domestic issues is decreasing in Japan. Whereas the polarization of political opinion seems to be increasing in some democratic lands, in Japan, where such polarization seemed severe only a few years ago, it clearly is on the wane. Nor does Japan face in as severe form the types of problems of modern urban, industrial life that have caused some scholars to wonder about the ultimate governability of democracies elsewhere. In their drift toward the welfare state, the Japanese have not mortgaged their future to present benefits. There is scarcely any national debt, and both as individuals and a nation they seem prepared to forgo present consumption in the interest of future advantages. They have no sizable ethnic minorities, large disadvantaged groups, or regional animosities such as plague the politics of some Western democracies. They remain relatively law abiding and free of crime. Accustomed since Tokugawa times to bureaucratic rule and deeply imbued with their borrowed continental European legal system, the Japanese fit much more easily into the growing legalism and omnipresent bureaucratic supervision of modern times than do Americans, who have a traditional distrust for government and long for the freedoms of a not distant American past. The great skills in crowded, group living that the Japanese have developed over the centuries serve them well in this complex modern age.

While unresolved political issues do produce open confrontation both in the Diet and in the streets, this for the most part is kept within bounds and becomes simply part of the system—a way of appealing to the public through the mass media. Occasionally there has been unacceptable violence, particularly in the early postwar years. As late as 1959 Asanuma, the chairman of the Socialist party, was spectacularly stabbed to death in front of television cameras by a fanatical rightist youth. On the whole, however, one is more struck by the rarity of serious violence, despite the bitterness of political feelings. The massive street demonstrations over the years have produced phenomenally little carnage. Most demonstrations are directed toward symbolic, not practical, ends, and the police are trained to contain violence, not to beat it down. The great number of huge demonstrations protesting the ratification of the revised Security Treaty in 1960 resulted in only one fatality—a woman university student who was accidentally trampled to death. Subsequently, the activities of radical students produced more casualities, but in the process of becoming more violent the radical students moved completely off the political spectrum, becoming a social rather than a political problem.

When one looks at the Japanese political scene, it is hard to find clouds, whether political, economic, or social, that really threaten the parliamentary democratic system. The political process, though differing in many respects from the democratic systems of the West, appears to embrace almost everyone and to be thoroughgoing and tolerably efficient. Its intricate procedures transfer individual voting preferences into acceptable decisions about as effectively as in the Western democracies. The political system has operated successfully under the 1947 constitution for three full decades—a long time for constitutions in some parts of the world—and the people overwhelmingly support the constitution and take great pride in it as "the peace constitution," so named for its most controversial paragraph renouncing war. All in all, both Japanese society and its democratic system of government seem sound and healthy.

The Japanese adjustment to the oil crisis of 1973 and the following world depression from 1974 to 1976 illustrates the point. The threat of the oil embargo to the nation's livelihood was greater and the impact of skyrocketing oil prices far more severe than in any other major county. In the succeeding depression, growth rates fell from around 11 percent to a minus 2 percent, producing a more abrupt economic deceleration than elsewhere. Runaway inflation at first outpaced even huge wage increases, before both were reduced to lower figures. As a consequence, there was problably an overall loss of income for most Japanese in real terms. But all this was stoically accepted by the Japanese with no visible political or social tremors. Meanwhile the political system ground out countermeasures as quickly and effectively as anywhere in the West, and soon Japan resumed its economic growth, at a slower rate than before to be sure but still more rapidly than in most other large industrial nations.

The domestic Japanese system does seem to be operating well, but if one enlarges one's focus to include the world, the prospects for Japan are less reassuring. The Japanese are entirely dependent on a huge flow of goods in and out of the country, and this could be destroyed either by war or a serious deterioration of the international trading system. No one could guess what political changes in Japan might follow a shock of this sort. The two times in modern history when the Japanese were forced to swerve sharply from their established course were both basically the product of foreign problems and pressures. One was the opening of the country and the great Meiji transformation that followed it in the nineteenth century. The other was the China and Pacific Wars and the resulting postwar changes in the twentieth century. If the Japanese were to be much deflected from the course they are now pursuing, the motive force for this change would almost certainly come from outside the country. In any case, foreign relations are the most uncertain element in Japan's future as well as the dominant one, and it is therefore to this final aspect of the study that we now turn.

JAPAN
and the
WORLD

PART FIVE

The Prewar
Record

33 ↙

THE IMPORTANCE of Japan's relations with the outside world—
or lack of them—has been a recurring theme that has run through
the whole of our story, sometimes just as a background melody but
becoming a crashingly dominant leitmotif in recent times. Some 115 million Japanese—or even half that number—can live in their narrow islands only if there is a huge flow of natural resources into Japan, a corresponding outward flow of manufactures to pay for these imports, and the conditions of world peace and global trade that permit this vast exchange of goods. All their other skills and accomplishments will avail the Japanese little if these conditions do not prevail. A suitable world environment and satisfactory relations with other peoples thus are overwhelming necessities for Japan.

International relations, however, are the area in which the Japanese feel the least confidence. Their past experience has not prepared them well for foreign contacts. Their very strengths and virtues, such as their strong self-identity, their extraordinary homogeneity, and their close-knit society, are sometimes handicaps rather than assets when they face the outside world. Their language, which is radically different from all others, is a barrier of monumental size between them and other peoples. They are like a sportsman who has had an extraordinary record of successes but suddenly finds himself in a new game for which his equipment and skills are ill adapted. This situation developed quite suddenly and unexpectedly for the Japanese. In fact, they became aware of it for the most part only during the past decade. Throughout most of Japanese history foreign rela-

335

tions have either not been very important for them or else have proved manageable with the skills they did possess. We might start with a brief review of this record.

Before the clear dawn of history in Japan in the sixth century, there had been large movements of people into Japan from Korea and, probably connected with this, Japanese military involvement in the peninsula. But thereafter for almost a thousand years the Japanese had only minimal contacts with outsiders. The peaceful importation of elements of Chinese culture was a major theme of Japanese history, but not foreign wars or the migration of people. Trade gradually increased and with it came some Japanese piratical activities, starting in the fourteenth century on the coasts of the nearby continent and spreading later as far as Southeast Asia. The Portuguese and other Europeans appeared in Japan as traders and Christian missionaries in the sixteenth century, but they were forced out in the seventeenth, and their religion was obliterated from the islands. Japan then settled into two centuries of artificially enforced isolation, except for tiny and closely regulated trade contacts with the Chinese, Koreans, and Dutch. During this whole great sweep of history from the sixth to the nineteenth century, the only foreign wars or invasions the Japanese experienced were the two attempted invasions of Japan by the Mongol rulers of China in the thirteenth century and Hideyoshi's attempted conquest of Korea between 1592 and 1598. No other major nation has a record remotely this free of invasions and foreign military adventures.

Foreign relations first posed a truly serious problem for the Japanese in the middle of the nineteenth century, when the Western world, now far ahead of an isolated Japan in technology, beat on Japan's closed doors, demanding entry and trade. The Japanese were forced to open up and to scramble hard to protect themselves from superior Western military and economic technology by acquiring it for themselves. In the process, they found it necessary to make revolutionary changes in their society and political system, but, drawing on their traditional characteristics of homogeneity, hard work, and skill in cooperative enterprise, they succeeded in this task in a way no other people did when first confronted by Western technological superiority.

It was a dangerous and rapacious world, however, that Japan had been forced to join. The late nineteenth century witnessed the height of the age of imperialism. The strong devoured the weak and fenced with one another for strategic advantages. Military strength appeared to the Japanese as essential as industrial power to win security and a place in the sun. This basically was the reason why they put great emphasis on developing a strong army and navy and embarked on expansion abroad. Korea was perceived as a dagger pointed at the heart of Japan if it were in the hands of a hostile power. Japan fought two wars over its control and won both, the first with China in 1894–95 and the next with Russia in 1904–05. Out of these wars, a Japanese Empire emerged, embracing Taiwan, Korea, the southern tip of Manchuria, and the southern half of Sakhalin. By World War I Japan was the paramount military as well as economic power in East Asia, and during that war it was able to extend its economic predominance over large parts of China. It also acquired through the war settlement the German islands of the North Pacific and the German holdings in the coastal Chinese province of Shantung.

A subtle change came over Japanese perceptions of foreign relations at about this time. Military strength and expansion had in one way brought Japan security, but in another it had brought a new vulnerability. The industrial base and increased population on which Japan's military might stood had made Japan dependent for the first time in history on foreign sources of supply. Iron ore and other key minerals came from abroad, oil, on which the army and navy ran, largely from Indonesia (then the Dutch East Indies) and the west coast of the United States, soybeans, which were important as a source of protein for humans and fertilizer for agriculture, from Manchuria, and some rice from Korea and Taiwan. This was a problem without end. As industry and population grew further so also would Japan's dependence on the outside world.

World conditions, however, had become less favorable to imperial expansion. The Western powers, exhausted by World War I, had called a halt to foreign conquest and sought security in international cooperation. Any Japanese expansion would henceforth draw the condemnation of the world rather than its admiration. The spirit of nationalism also was growing in the less developed countries, particularly China, where Japan's best hopes for future expansion lay. Trade boycotts and popular resistance threatened to make imperialist expansion more costly and uncertain than it had been in the past.

In these circumstances it is not surprising that the party cabinets of the 1920s, under strong influence from businessmen who disliked high taxes and feared damage to their international trade, turned away from military expansion, withdrew from Shantung and a military adventure in Siberia, reduced military expenditures greatly as a proportion of the national budget, and agreed at the Washington Conference in 1921–22 to a limitation on capital ships that would give the more concentrated Japanese navy a proportion of three to five with the two-ocean fleet of the Americans and the worldwide fleet of the British. While maintaining their military dominance in the Western Pacific, the Japanese sought security for their expanding economy through reliance on international trade and a peaceful world order, as symbolized by the ideals of President Wilson and the League of Nations.

We have already seen how elements of the Japanese army reversed this policy in 1931 by starting the conquest of Manchuria and plunging Japan back into a course of imperial expansion. We need not reexamine here in detail the reasons for this rapid about-face. Certainly internal dissatisfaction, especially on the part of the military, with the foreign policies of the party governments was a major factor. So also was the world depression that struck in 1929, greatly heightening political and social tensions within the country and frightening the Japanese with the prospect of being shut out of most of the world by restrictive trade policies. Some felt that the Western powers, satiated with imperial expansion and relatively secure from world depression because of the size of their holdings, had hoodwinked Japan into giving up its expansion before it had acquired an adequate base to maintain its economic and military power. In addition, they saw the white race as having seized for its own use the attractive open lands of the world, such as North America and Australia, and as excluding the Japanese from them on arrogant racial grounds, thus bottling the Japanese up, as it were, in their own narrow islands.

The Manchurian Incident led to further expansion into China, more clashes with Chinese troops, and eventually the China War, when in 1937 the Nationalist Government of Chiang Kai-shek, under pressure from the Chinese Communist regime in the northwest, finally stood up against further Japanese encroachments. While the Japanese army won an almost endless string of battles and campaigns, seizing control of much of China, both the Nationalists and Communists continued to resist from their bases in the deep interior of the huge land, and the Japanese war machine bogged down in the quagmire of Chinese nationalism. Japan kept expanding the war in order to find a way to knock out Chinese resistance, but its alignment with Germany and Italy and the association in American minds of Japan's bid for hegemony over East Asia with the Nazi attempt to establish hegemony over Europe aroused the United States to increase its economic pressures against Japan. A virtual ban on oil shipments in the summer of 1941 forced the Japanese government to choose between war with the United States or backing down. It elected to attack, winning spectacularly at first but ending in 1945 in total collapse, as Japan for the first time in its history came under the rule of a foreign conqueror.

Neutrality
or Alignment

34

T
HE POSTWAR Japanese found themselves in an entirely new
situation. At first they were a demoralized and destitute people and
an outcast nation in world society. They had no military or economic power, and the military might they once possessed had become
completely outclassed by the emergence of nuclear superpowers. Their
chief concern was merely survival as individuals and as a nation. Then,
when they finally did regain their independence and gradually grew prosperous and economically strong, they discovered that their increased
numbers and greater reliance on industry had made them far more dependent than ever before on the resources and trade of the world. But
they no longer had an option between differing methods in seeking to
solve this problem. Imperial expansion was clearly out of the question,
and only peaceful trade remained as a road that could lead Japan to a
viable future.

Japan had been stripped by the victors of its small empire in Korea,
Taiwan, Manchuria, and Sakhalin, and even some of its integral
parts—the Kurile Islands and for a while the Ryukyu Islands, or Okinawa.
Moreover, the spirit of nationalism had become still more powerful everywhere in the world, and imperial rule, to say nothing of fresh conquests,
had become quite impossible. The remaining imperial powers soon found
that they could not hold on to the colonies they already had, even though
they had ruled some of these regions for centuries. While great land
powers were able to maintain their grip on contiguous territories inhabited by subject peoples—the Soviet Union and China are the chief ex-

amples—all maritime empires melted rapidly away. Sometimes the colonial powers fought to keep their empires, as the Dutch did in Indonesia, the French in Indochina and Algeria, and the Portuguese in Africa, but most were given up voluntarily in recognition of the new realities. Under these circumstances, no Japanese, no matter how old-fashioned, could think in terms of imperial conquest.

It was obvious that the only alternative for Japan was a peaceful world of relatively open trade. At first the bitter anti-militarism and enthusiastic pacifism of the Japanese was largely an emotional reaction to the horrors of war and the tribulations it had brought them, but gradually these attitudes became a matter of rational conviction as well. As postwar emotions faded and new generations grew up with no memory of the war, the strong intellectual conviction remained that world peace was a necessity for Japan. As a result, ever since the end of the war peace has been the key concept in the minds of most Japanese. Their pacifism is deep and sincere, being supported by both emotion and rationality.

As long as Japan was powerless and under foreign occupation, it had no problems of foreign relations, and most Japanese could agree simply on the need for world peace. But as Japan regained its independence and in time economic power, questions arose as to what stand it should take for its own safety and in behalf of world peace in a world that was in actuality divided into hostile military camps. No one doubted that Japan should stay out of any sort of war and seek to avoid involvement in international disputes as much as possible. The government, with general approval, sought to do this through adopting a "low posture," as the Japanese described it, and concentrating on Japan's economic recovery and growth. But beyond this a deep controversy arose over whether Japan should seek its own security through close alignment with the United States or should cut itself free and maintain strict neutrality in world affairs. As we have seen, this became the largest issue in Japanese politics for the next two decades.

The issue was forced on the Japanese by the United States when it decided to go ahead with a separate peace treaty with Japan in 1951, without the participation of the Soviet Union or China, and to parallel the peace treaty with a Security Treaty between Japan and the United States, permitting the retention of American military bases in an independent Japan and committing the United States to Japan's defense. From the point of view of the United States, both decisions seemed inevitable. The occupation had already outlived its usefulness, and its further continuation threatened to do harm to the accomplishments already achieved. But a peace treaty including all parties seemed impossible. It was difficult to invite China because there was disagreement between the United States and its allies as to which Chinese regime really represented China. The United States recognized the Nationalists and the United Kingdom and some of the other allies the People's Republic in Peking, with which the United States was then at war in Korea. It also seemed clear that Moscow, as well as Peking, would not agree to the peace terms the United States felt to be necessary. This was particularly true of the maintenance of American bases in Japan, which appeared essential to Americans both as a backup to the American military position in the war in Korea and for the defense of an otherwise defenseless Japan, situated in a dangerously exposed position.

Japan's conservative political leadership understood this reasoning and shared it. Ashida as prime minister first advocated a continuing defense relationship with the United States, and Yoshida who succeeded him supported this policy. Even the more moderate Socialists accepted the necessity of a "separate peace treaty" and split with the left wing over this issue. The remainder of the opposition groups, however, were bitterly opposed. In their eyes the Americans had shifted from liberators to enemies by stopping further reforms in Japan in their wish to foster economic recovery and a stronger position in the cold war and had thus ruled out the possibility of socializing the Japanese economy. Their sympathies lay more with the Communist nations, which they felt were the real "peace camp," resisting the capitalist aggressors. They felt that the Security Treaty and the American bases it permitted endangered Japan rather than giving it security, for these bases, they feared, would inevitably involve Japan in America's wars and would serve as a magnet drawing retaliation from the other side. The Security Treaty and the bases, they also felt, trampled on Japan's constitutional renunciation of war, in which most Japanese took great pride, and on their ardent desire to remain neutral in international conflicts.

Such attitudes had great popular appeal and were shared at least in part by many supporters of the conservative parties. While the economic record of the Liberal Democratic party was to prove its chief strength, its foreign policy of alignment with the United States always remained its greatest weakness. Neutrality appeared far more attractive to Japanese than even a passive sort of alliance with either side. Extensive American bases, particularly around Tokyo, were a thorn in the side of Japanese pride and a constant social irritant. Inevitably unpleasant incidents and crimes occurred involving American military personnel, who at first were subject only to American military courts in a system reminiscent of the hated extraterritoriality of the nineteenth century. The bases occupied choice land desired for other purposes, and proposals for extending their air strips, as at Sunakawa at the American airbase in Tachikawa near Tokyo in 1954, raised violent and protracted demonstrations. The rest of the world might be distressed by Soviet military actions or political pressures in Czechoslovakia, Hungary, or Berlin, but such matters seemed far away to Japanese, to whom American bases and men in uniform in their own land were the chief reminders of the hated militarism of the past.

There was a particular sensitivity in Japan to the nuclear weapons of the Americans. Japanese had been the victims of the two atomic bombs that helped bring World War II to an end. When in 1954 fallout from an American atomic test at Bikini in the mid-Pacific showered down on a Japanese fishing boat, the Fukuryu-maru, resulting in the death of one crewman, there was a vast public uproar over what was called with some hyperbole the third atomic bombing of humanity. Mass memorial meetings, held each year in Hiroshima on August 6, the anniversary of the first bombing, became huge demonstrations of protest against the United States and the Security Treaty, though in 1961 these public festivals began to break up between the various opposition parties and then to lose their anti-American focus as concern rose in Japan over Soviet and Chinese nuclear armaments.

The nuclear sensitivity of the Japanese, sometimes called their "nuclear allergy," was not limited to weapons but included nuclear power and propulsion. In the course of the 1960s, Japan cautiously moved into the commercial production of electricity through nuclear power. Such a development appeared particularly necessary for this energy-poor nation, but there was always intense opposition, at first largely political in motivation but in time more from local residents who simply did not welcome nuclear power plants as neighbors. Nuclear powered vessels of the American navy were also a special target for protests. Only after years of careful negotiations to insure their absolute safety, were nuclear powered submarines finally allowed in 1964 into naval bases in Japan, at first in the face of massive demonstrations. These in time died down, but in 1968, when excitement over the Vietnam War was running high, the visit by a nuclear-powered aircraft carrier occasioned even greater protests. Japan's own experiment in an experimental nuclear-powered vessel, the *Mutsu*, also ended in fiasco in 1974 when no Japanese port community would agree to serve as home port for it.

Throughout the 1950s and well into the 1960s much of Japanese politics focused around base problems, anti-base and anti-nuclear demonstrations, and opposition to the Security Treaty. The revision of the treaty in 1960 led, as we have seen, to Japan's greatest postwar crisis. The revision was necessary because the treaty had certain features that did not befit a fully independent nation of Japan's stature. It permitted the use of American troops in Japan to quell civil disturbances, if requested by the Japanese government. It provided for no Japanese control on American nuclear weapons, which were such a sore point to the Japanese public. And it had no terminal date or means of termination. The 1960 revision dropped the possible use of American troops in Japan and set a ten year limit on the treaty, after which either side could renounce it on one year's notice. On the nuclear problem, the new treaty and some attached agreements established that the United States would not make major changes in armaments in Japan without prior consultation with the Japanese government. This in more direct language meant that the United States would not mount or stockpile nuclear weapons or even bring them into Japan without formal Japanese approval, which most people felt would never be given. The same stipulations about prior consultation, which implied a Japanese veto, were also applied to the use of American bases in Japan for direct military action abroad, as in Korea.

These changes were naturally to the liking of the Japanese leadership, but the opposition forces, with the exception of those Socialists who split off to form the Democratic Socialist party, decided to fight the ratification of the treaty on the grounds that the earlier treaty, though worse, had been forced on a Japan that was not yet free, while a new treaty, even though an improvement was being voluntarily agreed to by a now independent Japan. Various extraneous factors stirred up public excitement —the U-2 incident in which an American spy plane was shot down over the Soviet Union, the resulting cancellation of a summit meeting between Eisenhower and Khrushchev, and Kishi's forcing through of the treaty's ratification in the lower house so that it would go into effect by the time of a planned visit to Japan of Eisenhower on June 19. The opposition maintained that this amounted to anti-democratic acts by the prime minister and American intervention in Japanese domestic politics. The result was a tremendous popular outburst.

ONCE THE ratification of the new Security Treaty went into effect, however, the political situation calmed down, and for the next few years the debate over neutrality or alignment became less violent, as the new prime minister, Ikeda, adopted a "low posture" in domestic politics and drew attention to Japan's growing prosperity through his ten year "income doubling" plan. Another defense issue also began to lose its edge at this same time. This was the clash over the creation by the government, in seeming defiance of article 9 of the constitution, of an army, navy, and air force under the name of the Self-Defense Forces.

When in 1950 the remaining American ground troops in Japan were hastily dumped into Korea to stem the North Korean advance, MacArthur ordered the Japanese to create a national police reserve to take their place in Japan. This the government reorganized and expanded at the end of the occupation and in 1954 further expanded and renamed the Land, Sea, and Air Self-Defense Forces, placing them under a Defense Agency.

The conservative politicians clearly felt Japan should have some defense capabilities of its own, but at the same time they wished to keep these small for financial and political reasons. Yoshida and his successors cleverly resisted American pressures for a more rapid military build-up or a wider regional role for the Self-Defense Forces, on the grounds of the constitution and popular attitudes. Eventually the American government came to accept the Japanese view that, given the political climate in Japan, a very limited military posture for Japan was all that could be expected and probably was the wisest course in any case, because of the fears of Japan's neighbor about restored Japanese military power. The present overall size of the three Self-Defense Forces taken together is 277,000 persons, only a little more than the limit of 250,000 set in 1954.

Since the occupation Japan has kept to a very modest defense budget in relative terms. At first it amounted to a little over 1 percent of Japan's GNP, but, as GNP grew, it declined and in recent years has been only between 0.7 and 0.9 percent. This compares to around 3 to 5 percent for major Western European countries, some 7 percent for the United

States, and probably 10 percent or more for China, the Soviet Union, and some other countries. On the other hand, the present huge size of the Japanese economy means that the military budget is in reality one of the larger ones in the world—actually the seventh largest—and it supports well-paid, well-equipped, and excellently trained land, sea, and air forces, which would loom large in some parts of the world. Its air force, in fact, is one of the best in Asia. But Japan's military power is completely outclassed by the United States and the Soviet Union, and it has under arms scarcely more than a twentieth as many men as China and far less than half as many as Taiwan or either of the two Koreas.

The opposition parties in Japan from the start bitterly opposed the creation of the Self-Defense Forces, fearing a restoration of prewar militarism and pointing out that they clearly transgressed the constitution. Public opinion at first also ran strongly against them. They outraged the anti-militarist and pacifist feelings of most Japanese, who yearned for an unarmed neutrality in which other nations would respect Japan's high pacifist ideals and not attack it. MacArthur had somewhat anachronistically held out the ideal of Japan becoming "the Switzerland of Asia," and many Japanese aspired to being a nation that like Switzerland had its neutrality honored by others. They seemed to be quite unaware that the Swiss maintained a heavy military burden in order to help produce this result. Unarmed neutrality was always a slogan of the Socialists, though the Communists more realistically believed in national military power, so long as it was under their own control. Opposition to the Self-Defense Forces, as we have seen, has prevented the upgrading of the Defense Agency to a ministry, and public attitudes always remained suspicious if not downright hostile. The Self-Defense Forces have had difficulty in finding an adequate number of recruits and usually are below authorized strength. Conscription, of course, has been utterly unthinkable in the strongly pacifist atmosphere of postwar Japan.

The opposition to the Self-Defense Forces, however, has slowly waned. Few people any longer fear that they might lead to the revival of the militarism of prewar days. The Self-Defense Forces for their part have conducted themselves throughout in exemplary fashion, maintaining a low profile, avoiding all involvement in politics, and doing their best to be of service to the public in times of natural calamities, such as typhoons and earthquakes. Supreme Court decisions made in 1959 and later accepted the obvious reinterpretation of the constitution by the Diet that is implicit in the concept of self-defense. The public too seems to have accepted this reinterpretation. For some years now, public opinion polls, while strongly rejecting any expansion of the Self-Defense Forces and any role for them abroad, have given overwhelming support to their maintenance at current levels.

DESPITE the relative calm of the early 1960s, the dispute over neutrality or alignment came to a boil a second time in the latter half of the decade. The heightened American involvement in Vietnam after 1965 raised again the spector of a Japan threatened with becoming embroiled in war because of its association with the United States. Detailed television and newspaper reporting made vivid the horrors of the war. The sympathies of the Japanese, as of most other peoples in the world, were with those Vietnamese who were fighting against the alien American interlopers. The Japanese equated the war with their own misadventure in China and as recent victims of American bombing identified with the North Vietnamese sufferers from American air attacks. Citizens' movements against the Vietnam War and organized student demonstrations became intense, and some local authorities of opposition leanings, such as the mayor of Yokohama, took actions to block the use of American bases in Japan to supply the American forces in Vietnam.

At much the same time excitement arose over continued American military rule over Okinawa, which began to loom as a Japanese irredenta. Okinawa prefecture, named for its largest island, had been before the war the southernmost Japanese prefecture, occupying the southern two thirds of the Ryukyu chain of islands. The Ryukyus are inhabited by a branch of the Japanese people, who speak a very distinct form of the language and show some cultural differences from other Japanese, deriving from their close trade contacts throughout history with China. They had their own kings but in 1609 were conquered by Satsuma, the great southern Kyushu feudal domain, and thereafter were a tightly held sub-fief of Satsuma, although their "kings" were allowed to continue to pay "tribute" to China as a means of maintaining a clandestine foreign trade with the outside world in Satsuma's behalf. This anomalous position led in the nineteenth century to controversy between China and Japan over their conflicting claims to the islands. This was settled in Japan's favor when China agreed in 1874 to pay an indemnity to Japan for the killing of some Okinawan seamen by aborigines on Taiwan and for the Japanese military expedition sent to chastise them.

The United States, which seized Okinawa in bloody fighting in the closing months of World War II, decided to keep the whole of the Ryukyu chain to serve as its chief military base in the Western Pacific but soon discovered that the frequency of typhoons reduced its value, especially as a naval base. In 1954 the United States returned to Japan the northern Amami islands of the chain but continued to hold on to Okinawa prefecture, which took on increased military significance as the Vietnam War led to a build-up of American military power in the Western Pacific and anti-base demonstrations interfered with the free use of American bases in the main islands of Japan. It became American military dogma that, since Japan had put restrictions on the use of American bases in Japan and a victory of the opposition parties there might lead to their total elimination, American bases in Okinawa must be maintained at all costs.

At the end of World War II, the attitude of the Okinawans had been at first somewhat ambivalent toward both Japan and the United States. They were full of resentments toward other Japanese because they had been treated by them as inferior country bumpkins. Okinawa had also been the only part of Japan which had actually been fought over in the war, and they had therefore suffered more than other Japanese. But American military rule, which only grudgingly opened the way to local autonomy, gradually persuaded the Okinawans by its alienness and arrogance that they were Japanese after all. A movement for the restoration of Okinawa to Japan developed in the islands and finally in the late 1960s began to draw an ardent response from other Japanese, who had by then become so well restored in their own pride and affluence as to become exercised over the plight of close to a million compatriots in Okinawa still living under foreign rule. Such sentiments tugged at the hearts of nationalistic conservatives as well as anti-American leftists. Okinawa thus became a major new issue in Japanese-American relations, and American rule over the islands threatened to impair, if not destroy, Japan's alignment with the United States.

A third issue joined Okinawa and the Vietnam War to create a crescendo of political excitement as the 1960s drew to a close. This was the approaching date of June 19, 1970, when the new Security Treaty would complete its first decade and thereafter be open to change or abandonment. Remembering the 1960 treaty crisis, the various opposition groups looked to 1970 as the year for the next great effort to terminate the Japanese alignment with the United States.

The expected crisis never materialized. Neither government proposed any change in the treaty and thus there never was any need for ratification by the Diet of a new treaty, which would have provided a specific target for the opposition. In fact, it was the realization of the difficulty of winning ratification that persuaded the two governments not to make any changes, though both probably would have preferred to see some modifications.

The Okinawa issue also melted away before reaching crisis proportions. Aware of the strength of nationalistic sentiments over Okinawa and the significance of the year in the minds of the opposition, the American side yielded on this issue and promised to return the islands within a few years. This decision was announced in a communique issued by President Nixon and Prime Minister Sato on November 21, 1969. It was also agreed that, once the islands had reverted to Japan, the extensive American bases there would fall under the same restrictions that applied to the bases in the main islands. The United States made these concessions because it realized that the Okinawan situation endangered general Japanese-American relations and that, if these turned sour, irredentist feelings in Okinawa would probably undermine the utility of the bases there as well.

The American side, however, did wish some assurances from the Japanese that in the event of a military crisis in Korea or Taiwan the Japanese government would permit the United States to use its Okinawa bases. For this purpose Sato made vague references in the 1969 communique to Japan's special concern over the security of these two areas. The opposition forces, interpreting these statements as a Japanese commitment to the defense of these areas, launched a prolonged attack on them, renewing old charges that the United States was forcing Japan to join actively in NEATO, meaning a "Northeast Asia Treaty Organization," a name analogous to SEATO, or the Southeast Asia Treaty Organization. SEATO, however, was moribund by this time, and NEATO had never existed. The term, though often referred to by Japanese leftists, was actually unknown to the American leaders of the time. Thus the communique of 1969 stirred up a small political storm within Japan, but it put an end to the Okinawan problem. The islands were finally returned to Japan on May 15, 1972, and gradually political tensions in Okinawa shifted from the United States and its bases to the treatment by the Japanese national government of this most remote and economically backward of its forty-seven prefectures.

Even the Vietnam War faded as an issue as the United States stopped increasing its forces in Vietnam in 1968 and then started a slow withdrawal, which was completed in 1974. Thus all three issues that had threatened a crisis in Japanese-American relations in the late 1960s disappeared in the early 1970s.

The whole question of neutrality or alignment, in fact, began to lose much of the passion that had once surrounded it. It remained as a major formal issue dividing the opposition parties from the Liberal Democrats, and occasionally some special problem would arise to heat up the old feelings. For example, in October 1974, a statement by a retired American admiral raised excitement over the issue of whether or not American naval vessels putting into Japanese ports or transitting Japanese waters had nuclear weapons on board and thus were transgressing the agreement not to introduce nuclear weapons into Japan. This was an old issue which hung on the meaning of the word "introduce." The Japanese public obviously interpreted it in a much more restrictive sense than did the American government. The two governments, however, chose to remain silent on this ambiguity, and the furor soon calmed down. The American alliance simply did not raise the political passions it once did. Finally in 1975 the Democratic Socialists openly came out in support of the Security Treaty, and in the 1976 elections the treaty for the first time was not used by any party as a major campaign issue.

THE CHIEF reason why the issue of neutrality or alignment began to lose its central place in Japanese politics in the 1970s was that changing international conditions and new problems made it appear in an entirely new light. The American alliance was now more than two decades old but had not involved Japan in American wars, and in any case further American military adventures in East Asia now seemed much less likely than before. The alliance also had drawn nothing more than verbal attacks from the Communist powers, and even these were diminishing. The rift between China and the Soviet Union had deepened, and both sides were desirous of gaining support in this rivalry from Japan as well as the United States, or at least of denying this support to the other side. The Russians, in contrast to their usual harshness, began to pursue what the Japanese called a "smiling diplomacy" toward Japan, and Moscow and Peking gave up their condemnations of the Security Treaty. Both feared that a Japan without this alliance might drift into the other's orbit or else build up its own military power to major proportions. Leftist critics of the Security Treaty in Japan found the ground cut from under their feet by the moderation of Chinese and Soviet attitudes toward it.

The Chinese, noting the waning of the American military threat in Southeast Asia, also moved for a rapprochement with Washington. This was heralded in the stunning announcement on July 15, 1971, that President Nixon would visit China and was consummated during his visit there the next February by the establishment of informal relations between the two countries. The United States continued to recognize Taiwan and keep its ambassador to China in Taipei, but the People's Republic and the United States set up missions in each other's capitals. This move opened the way for the Japanese government to set at rest one of the hottest and most divisive of all domestic political issues—namely, Japan's relations with China.

Yoshida in 1952 had been forced by the United States against his will to recognize the Nationalist Government on Taiwan as the real China. Representatives of the American government had made clear to him that otherwise ratification of the peace treaty with Japan would encounter difficulties in the Senate. From the start, however, the opposition parties pushed for recognition of Peking, and most Japanese sympathized with their stand. But the Liberal Democrats hung back even when the People's Republic gained in power and most other nations shifted their recognition from the Nationalists to Peking. Their reluctance was in part because of respect for Chiang Kai-shek and his generous attitude toward Japan after the war, in part out of interest in Taiwan as their own former colony and an important area for trade, but mostly because of fear that recognition of Peking might anger the United States and threaten Japan's alignment with it. Nixon's actions in 1971 and 1972, however, removed this restraint, and the Japanese happily hastened to establish formal relations with Peking. In a visit by Prime Minister Tanaka in September 1972, Japan went a step beyond the United States in according the People's Republic full diplomatic recognition in place of Taiwan. Hitherto Japan had traded with the People's Republic and had had other informal relations with it but had recognized the Nationalist government on Taiwan as being China. Now it reversed its relations with the two.

In both the American and Japanese communiques with China in 1972, the problem of Taiwan was in a sense set aside for future solution. The Americans and Japanese both stated their recognition that Chinese on both sides of the Taiwan Straits felt that Taiwan was part of a unitary China, while the Chinese, by not objecting to the American defense commitment to and continued recognition of Taiwan and Japanese trade and other contacts with the island, tacitly agreed to let the actual separation of Taiwan from China continue for the time being. Chinese feelings about unity, however, remain strong, as does the determination of the fifteen million people on Taiwan, and particularly the native Taiwanese five sixths of this population, not to be incorporated into a Communist China. Since Taiwan has proven to be a very successful economic unit and has strong military forces as well as an American military commitment of sorts, an early resolution of the problem does not seem at all likely. But in any case, by the mid 1970s the Taiwan issue seemed considerably less menacing to peace in East Asia than it had ever since the separation of the island from China in 1949.

Other threats to peace in East Asia also seemed to be declining. Few believed that the Sino-Soviet rift would lead to actual conflict between the two, and it seemed instead to make both Peking and Moscow more cautious about becoming embroiled with the United States or with each other in conflicts and disputes in other lands. Korea, divided into two extremely hostile and heavily armed states, remained a danger point, and the deployment of American troops near the border and an American defense commitment to South Korea threatened to involve the United States and possibly the other major East Asian powers if war broke out again in the peninsula. But both the Soviet Union and China refused to support the North Korean Communist dictator in adventuristic moves when he sought to stir up a crisis in Korea in order to take advantage of the supposed American failure of will following the disaster in Vietnam. The Americans for their part did their best to calm the situation and, embarrassed by the harshly repressive policies of the South Korean president, gave thought to a gradual withdrawal from the peninsula, though it was made clear that the United States would take into consideration Japanese interests in the matter, since the American position in Korea was considered to be in large part for the security of Japan. Korea did remain a worrisome problem, as did continuing instabilities in Southeast Asia, but not so much so as when the United States had been actually involved in fighting in East Asia and tensions between it and China and the Soviet Union had been more severe.

Another significant shift in the international situation in the early 1970s was a rise in doubts about the reliability of the American defense commitment to Japan. Hitherto both Japan and the United States had more or less taken the other for granted. Americans had a certain carry-over of patronizing attitudes developed during the occupation. The Japanese tended to feel that the United States had assumed the role of a big brother, to which it would have to measure up, regardless of what Japan did. Suddenly neither side felt as confident of the other as before. Although the Sino-American rapprochement has been a political boon to the Japanese, it had at first been carried out in such a way as to cause consternation in Japan. The United States government had for many years urged close consultation and cooperation between Washington and Tokyo on China policy, but when it decided to make a spectacular shift in its own policy it failed even to notify the Japanese in advance, much less consult with them. To the Japanese it seemed that the faithfulness of their government to America's China policy, despite intense domestic pressures to change, had been rewarded by this callous disregard of Japan. In dismay they dubbed the July 15, 1971, announcement of the presidential visit to China the "Nixon shock." Many feared that the United States had decided to abandon its alignment with Japan in favor of one with China.

This worry, combined with the American withdrawal from Vietnam and considerable confusion in American society over foreign policy, made the Japanese wonder if the American defense alignment was any longer of much value to Japan. The emphasis of Secretary of State Kissinger during his early years in office on balance of power problems with the Soviet Union, at the expense of the American alliances with Western Europe and Japan, and the feeling of the Japanese that Kissinger disliked and ignored them strengthened this anxiety. Talk by Kissinger and others about a five-sided balance of power in the world, in which Japan was to constitute one of the sides, was also worrisome, however unrealistic. Most Japanese today, whether rightly or wrongly, have little worry about Japan's security—the country has not been the victim of unprovoked aggression since the thirteenth century—but, insofar as they do have such concerns, their anxieties shifted somewhat from the fear that Japan might become embroiled in American military adventures to the worry that the United States might not live up to its defense commitments to them. This shift in attitudes in a sense turned the debate over neutrality and alignment inside out.

STANDS on the Security Treaty remained during the mid-1970s a formal point of difference between most of the opposition parties and the Liberal Democrats, but actual opposition to the treaty has relaxed greatly, and few Japanese expect much change in it even if the opposition parties were to get a share in power. The irritations and problems of the American relationship have also declined a great deal. Japanese feel a much greater sense of equality with the United States, and the American government has learned to be meticulous in treating the Japanese government as a full equal and consulting it on all problems of common interest. American bases no longer loom large in Japan, and both sides in any case expect a continuing decline in their number and size. An eventual transfer of the control and operation of the bases to the Japanese military and provisional use of them by the American military seems a possible final solution to the problem. Most Japanese have also come to realize that an American nuclear umbrella is greatly preferable to Japan's development of nuclear weapons and that an American commitment to Japan's defense, however vague or dubious, is probably the best form of security for Japan.

There is also general agreement on the maintenance of the Self-Defense Forces at the existing modest levels as a supplementary element of security, even though it is not clear how they could ever be actually used. An attack on Japan of small enough proportions for these forces to be of any significance seems entirely improbable. Such an attack would not be made by the Soviet Union or tolerated from any source by the United States because it would threaten the balance between the two superpowers and thus might trigger a nuclear holocaust. The Self-Defense Forces also are clearly incapable of defending Japan's vital interests, and a military of sufficient size to do so is unthinkable. A navy that could defend Japan's oil life line from the Persian Gulf and its other vital life lines for necessary imports would have to be of unimaginable size and cost. Any attempt to create any appreciable part of such a navy would stir up such animosities among Japan's neighbors and such anxieties among the major military powers as to greatly worsen Japan's security rather than enhance it. Even lesser forces which could be regionally significant would run these same dangers without being able to protect Japan's vital interests, which are global rather than regional.

The Self-Defense Forces thus have no very clear military role. Conceivably they could be used in peace-keeping activities in behalf of the United Nations, though the Japanese, in their determination to keep out of international quarrels, are not as yet ready to countenance even this. The Self-Defense Forces do in a sense constitute a local defense sector in a general American military posture in the Western Pacific, contributing particularly to anti-submarine defense. And most Japanese probably derive a certain sense of security from the fact that these forces do exist and Japan therefore is not exclusively dependent on American arms and attitudes for defense. But whatever their utility, the Self-Defense Forces are now generally accepted by the Japanese public and are no longer a bone of serious political controversy.

While many problems in the development of nuclear-generated electric power remain as active political issues, almost no one in Japan now advocates that Japan should develop nuclear weapons. The country is so small and its population and industry so concentrated that is has no chance of surviving a determined first strike. All it could possibly do is to mount a post mortem retaliation from nuclear-armed submarines already at sea. This would be of small comfort and certainly of less utility than an even dubious American nuclear umbrella. At one time the one conceivable argument in favor of nuclear weapons for Japan was that they seemed to be the badge of great power status. This was because the United States, the Soviet Union, China, the United Kingdom, and France—the five nations which, as the chief victors in World War II, had been accorded permanent membership and the veto in the Security Council of the United Nations—happened to be the five nations which possessed nuclear weapons. As the United Nations declined in influence, however, and nuclear arms seemed on the point of spreading to lesser countries, even this prestige value lost its shine, and Japanese came to believe all the more strongly that they could win more prestige as a nuclear-free great power than as an inadequately armed one.

Japan nevertheless has maintained the option of becoming a nuclear power. It has ample technological skills and financial power. It has maintained its nuclear science and has developed at least slightly the delivery power of rocketry in connection with weather and communication satellites. But it seems most unlikely that Japan will decide to become a nuclear power. After years of delay, in which it sought to induce concessions by the nuclear powers, it finally ratified the nuclear anti-proliferation treaty in the spring of 1976. The Liberal Democratic government has also made clear that its own position on nuclear weapons is fully in accord with popular sentiments. Over the years it has repeatedly proclaimed that Japan's three basic nuclear principles are not to make nuclear weapons, not to possess them, and not to allow them into the country.

In these various ways the nuclear issue and the other issues of national security, including the whole debate over neutrality or alignment, have dwindled in intensity. They sometimes remain as formal points of difference between the opposition parties and the party in power, but they have lost much of their meaning and most of their passion, while other issues of foreign policy, not closely tied to problems of military defense, have become far more important.

International
Trade

35

THE SECURITY TREATY and the whole alliance with the United States have loomed so large in political controversy in postwar Japan that they are often considered to have constituted Japan's basic foreign policy, but actually a more fundamental foreign policy has lain behind them. This was the determination to pursue trade as vigorously as possible with all foreign countries and through it to restore Japan's economic strength. Japan has carried out this policy with brilliant success, using the American alliance skillfully to support it. While the alliance at times may have inhibited trade with some countries, it relieved Japan of costly military expenditures, reduced the possibility that Japan's own military power might frighten off prospective trading partners in East Asia, and permitted Japan to take shelter behind a strong American military and political stance, avoiding direct involvement in international controversies and concentrating on its own economic growth. This policy of priority for trade was so taken for granted by almost all Japanese that it usually was not even perceived as being Japan's foremost foreign policy.

Early in the occupation the American authorities abandoned impractical efforts to extract from a bankrupt Japan reparation payments for the countries it had despoiled, but, once restored to independence, the Japanese sought to reestablish trade with their neighbors on the basis of reparation payments, which they now were able to make and which could be designed in a way to develop markets for Japanese manufactures abroad. Starting in 1954 with Burma, Japan made a series of reparation settlements with the countries of Southeast Asia, and these in time led to a great flow of trade with this region. The Nationalist regime on Taiwan, with which Japan had established treaty relations in 1952, demanded no reparations—the great Japanese economic investment in its Taiwan colony was considered adequate recompense—and trade between Japan and Taiwan also grew to significant proportions.

The last of the reparation agreements, though it was not so called, was with South Korea in 1965. This required years of difficult negotiations because of a number of factors. The Koreans were extremely bitter against the Japanese for thirty-five years of oppressive colonial rule. There were also conflicts over fishing rights in the seas between the two countries, where the South Koreans laid claim to exclusive rights over waters marked out by defense zones originally established by the American forces in Korea. In addition, the leftist opposition in Japan opposed a settlement with South Korea when there was none with the Communist North, and large numbers of restless and sometimes unruly Koreans in Japan, who for the most part sided with the North, further complicated the situation. However, once relations with South Korea were normalized, trade boomed, the Korean economy began to surge forward, and economic relations between the two countries became very close, in fact so close that many Koreans began to fear that Japan might reestablish an economic form of colonial domination over them.

In the meantime Japan had also been restoring its trade with the rest of the world. Americans had rapidly lost their animosity toward the Japanese because of their close association with them as the occupying power and their interest in Japan's economic success under their tutelage. Thus the American market was open to Japan from the start and took at once the same dominant position it had held in Japan's trade during most of the prewar period. In the early post-occupation years, trade with the United States amounted to about a third of Japan's total trade, and even in the 1970s it still was more than a fifth—a reasonable percentage in view of the fact that the United States accounted for about a quarter of the world's productivity. In the early postwar period, a great flow from the United States to Japan of industrial technology, in which the Japanese had fallen behind during the war years, and substantial amounts of American banking capital also contributed critically to Japan's economic recovery and the restoration of its world trade.

The markets of the developing countries all over the world were also open to cheap Japanese industrial products, and some regions, particularly Latin America, became quite important to Japan. The Australians, who at first had harbored deep hatreds because of Japanese wartime atrocities, also came to realize that Japan was becoming the best market for their exports of natural resources, and as a consequence they developed friendlier attitudes toward the Japanese and close trade relations. Most of the countries of Western Europe, however, being further removed from Japan, remained less interested in Japan's friendship and trade, continuing to place special restrictions on imports from Japan, though in recent years these have been relaxed.

Trade with the Communist countries was a different matter, because Japan at the end of the occupation had no treaty relations with them, and they, in any case, strove for an autarkic sort of economy, with foreign trade kept to a minimum. Japan from the start, however, made clear its desire to trade with all nations, regardless of their internal politics or defense alignments. In 1956 the Soviet Union finally agreed to normalize its relations with Japan, and thereafter economic relations gradually developed between the two countries and also in time with the Communist countries of East Europe, especially as they began to assert their economic independence of the Soviet Union.

Since Japan is in need of raw materials and the great natural resources of Siberia await development and exploitation, it may seem inevitable that a huge economic relationship will some day develop between Japan and the Soviet Union, but, though pursued from both sides, this has not as yet materialized on a large scale. Oil and gas in Sakhalin, once owned by Japan, and lumber resources on the eastern Siberian littoral have been extensively developed in Japan's behalf but not the huge oil and gas reserves in the Yakutsk and Tyumen regions in the more central parts of Siberia. These would require the building of extensive transport facilities in remote and forbidding terrain. They would also call for huge investments and raise many uncertainties. They might draw a hostile reaction from the Chinese, which the Japanese would like to avoid. Japanese businessmen also have doubts about entering into such mammoth undertakings without the participation of American businessmen to help bear the financial burden and to assure a greater likelihood that the Soviet Union would live up to the bargain. But such tripartite cooperation has not as yet developed.

Japan and the Soviet Union also have not yet signed a full peace treaty, though one has been under negotiation for years and is desired by both sides. The sticking point has been Japanese claims to certain northern territories under Soviet rule. At the end of the war the Soviet Union took the Kurile chain of islands from Japan, including some small offshore islands of Hokkaido known as Habomai and Shikotan, and ejected the sparse Japanese population from all these barren territories. Japan, which has valid rights to all the Kuriles, has decided to press claims only to the two southernmost, Kunashiri and Etorofu, as well as to the small offshore islands. During the late 1960s, the Japanese government began to place special stress on the return of these islands, possibly as a means of diverting public attention from the American-held irredenta in Okinawa to the Russian-held irredenta in the north. The Soviet Union, however, has proved adamant. Opening up territorial claims of any sort would prove extremely embarrassing for it, because China in Asia and the Communist satellite states in Europe all have their potential claims on Russian-held areas. Thus the "northern territories" remains a thorn in the side of Japanese-Soviet relations.

Economic relations with China seem even more important to most Japanese than those with the Soviet Union. The prewar expansionists had created the strong impression that China was Japan's most natural and largest trading partner—its economic promised land. In actuality, trade with China had been only a fraction of the trade with the United States, except for the 1930s when for strategic reasons Japan put a large economic investment into Manchuria. Since the war the China trade has until quite recently lagged behind trade with Taiwan and has never exceeded 4 percent of Japan's total trade, though it constituted around a quarter of China's much smaller foreign trade. Most Japanese, however, have had a firm belief throughout in the potential importance of the China trade, which may not be surprising when one considers that Americans too have persistently held to unrealistic concepts of the possibilities of trade with China. For the Japanese, the China trade was always a burning political issue, and it combined with a sense of cultural closeness to the Chinese to make Japanese of both the left and right unhappy that relations with their great continental neighbor seemed to be constrained by the hostility between the United States and China.

The Japanese government and businessmen pursued trade with China as best they could, avoiding on the one side the strategic exports banned by American policy and meekly conforming on the other side to the specific patterns insisted on by the Chinese and, in the case of businessmen and opposition politicians, mouthing the standard Chinese condemnations of the United States and of Japanese-American relations. Throughout, the Japanese government sought to establish the principle that economic matters should be considered as being separate from politics. Specifically this meant that, although Japan recognized the Nationalist government on Taiwan, it would trade with both Taiwan and the People's Republic. The Chinese on the other hand insisted on the inseparability of economics and politics. In the long run the Japanese won out on this issue. A small amount of trade between Japan and China did develop during the 1950s. In 1958 China suddenly cut it off, ostensibly because of the tearing down of a Chinese flag by a Japanese youth at a trade fair in Nagasaki, but actually in an effort to exert pressure on Japan. This effort, however, met with no success, and trade was gradually restored and then mounted rapidly after the Chinese rapprochement with the United States and Japan in the early 1970s, finally growing to roughly the same size as the very considerable trade Japan had already established with Taiwan. By this time, of course, the Japanese principle of the separation of economics and politics had come to apply in reverse, with Japan now recognizing Peking diplomatically but trading extensively with both the People's Republic and Taiwan.

Trade with China never lived up to the extravagant expectations many Japanese had for it. China did not open its markets to foreign consumer goods and insisted on restricting trade to carefully controlled channels. It also did not have available for export many of the natural resources the Japanese needed. The one exception was oil, which in the 1970s the Chinese began to export to Japan on a modest scale, perhaps in an effort to make the Japanese less eager for Siberian oil. If China's oil production were sufficiently developed, it could perhaps lead to a very sizable Sino-Japanese trade, but the Chinese have shown no desire for this, and the Japanese themselves have appeared reluctant to build facilities to process the paraffin-rich Chinese oil in addition to their extensive facilities for handling the sulphur-rich oil of the Persian Gulf. There are also limitations to the degree Japan would be willing to become dependent on Chinese oil, because of the fear that Peking might cut it off suddenly for political reasons. In any case, Chinese oil so far has not exceeded 2.5 percent of Japanese oil imports in any year.

A S T H E Japanese restored their trade with the whole world, they also won back a position for themselves in the family of nations. At first the Soviet Union regularly vetoed their application for membership in the United Nations, but, after the Soviet-Japanese normalization of relations in 1956, Moscow permitted Japan to join that world body. This the Japanese did with tremendous enthusiasm, for the United Nations seemed to embody their hopes for world peace. Both the public and the government always gave it great respect and hearty support. To the political left it appeared to be the guarantee that "unarmed neutrality" could be a practical policy. For the government, complete support for the United Nations was a useful way to play down Japan's alliance with the United States and to conceal the fact that Japan's only policy on virtually all contentious international issues was strict noninvolvement. However, as we have seen, complete support for the United Nations did not include participating in its peace-keeping missions. This remained true even after Japan had regained its self-confidence and world esteem, but by that time, of course, hopes that the United Nations would play the leading role in maintaining world peace had dimmed in Japan as elsewhere in the world.

In the course of the 1960s, attitudes toward Japan on the part of its neighbors altered sufficiently to permit Japan to play a leading role in certain attempts to build regional cooperation and solidarity, as in the short-lived Asian and Pacific Council and the more lasting and significant Asian Development Bank, both established in 1966. But much more important than these regional groupings or membership in the United Nations was Japan's admission into the worldwide economic groupings largely made up of, or at least dominated by, the industrialized nations of the West. Already in 1952 Japan became a member of the International Monetary Fund and the International Bank for Reconstruction and Development. In 1955 it joined the GATT, the General Agreement on Tariffs and Trade, which in the 1960s, under the name of the Kennedy Round, fostered a general lowering of duties on industrial goods that was of great significance for Japanese trade. In 1964, with strong American backing and against general European reluctance, Japan was allowed into the OECD, the Organization for Economic Cooperation and Development, which is in a sense the economic club of the industralized trading nations and has been in recent years an increasingly important locus for international economic negotiations for Japan as well as the nations of the West. Bit by bit Japan won recognition as being one of the leading industrialized powers. By the 1970s it was quite naturally included together with the United States, the United Kingdom, West Germany, France, and sometimes Italy and Canada, when summit conferences of the leading industrial trading nations were held. Japan, in other words, became recognized as an integral part of the so-called "first world," which hitherto had also been commonly called the West, but because of Japan's membership, was now sometimes known as the trilateral community of North America, Western Europe, and Japan.

JAPAN'S postwar foreign policy has undoubtedly been a great success. Not only has Japan won its way back into the community of nations, but its emphasis on foreign trade above all else and on divorcing trade insofar as possible from political or strategic considerations has helped make it far more prosperous and economically stronger than ever before. Under these policies, trade soared and the economy boomed. Japan became the "economic miracle" of the postwar world. Its industry moved from labor intensive light goods to capital intensive heavy goods and chemicals and then on to various technically sophisticated products. World markets were inundated first with Japanese textiles, then cameras and electronic equipment, then ships, giant tankers, steel, and chemical fertilizers, and then automobiles and a host of other consumer goods and machinery. Finally the emphasis in Japanese exports began to move to computers and other technologically sophisticated wares. For the future Japan has its eye on developing what it calls the knowledge-intensive industries—that is, those with a high component of technical skills, which Japan has in abundance, and with comparatively little pollution or consumption of energy or raw materials, in which Japan faces serious limitations.

Japan's booming industry and soaring trade, however, produced new problems. We have seen how urban crowding and pollution and the imbalance between investment in industry and in public facilities and social overhead had created by the late 1960s grave domestic difficulties, which dampened Japanese enthusiasm for economic growth at any price. Japan's triumphs in trade also led to difficult new international problems. Its rate of economic growth had been around 10 percent per year in real terms, which was considerably faster than in almost any other nation in

A steel plant on the Inland Sea. Depending on imported iron ore and coking coal, the Japanese steel industry is among the largest and most efficient in the world. This factory stands on land reclaimed from the sea, and both it and the plants in the background are so placed as to benefit from cheap oceanic transportation. (*Embassy of Japan*)

the world, and was roughly twice as fast as the world as a whole. Japan's trade had grown even more rapidly and had risen from less than 2 percent of total world trade in 1953 to about 7 percent by the early 1970s. This discrepancy in growth rates between Japan and the rest of the world was a factor in causing disequilibriums in the world economy and new tensions in Japan's relations with other countries.

Japan had become the economic colossus of Asia and as such revived old fears and created new resentments in neighboring lands. By the 1970s Japan was in most cases the first or at least the second largest trading partner of all its neighbors, including the Communist nations. A third or more of the exports of Australia, the Philippines, and South Korea went to Japan. Japanese businessmen overran all the non-Communist countries of East and Southeast Asia, sometimes driving hard bargains or resorting to underhand measures in countries where these seemed necessary. In their avid search for the natural resources Japan needed, they were seen as despoiling the natural wealth of other lands or at least as taking advantage of the economic naiveté of the natives. Japanese goods flooded all markets and neon signs advertising them dominated the night skies of cities. Clannish and preferring to stick together behind their language barriers in their own clubs and hotels, Japanese businessmen seemed arrogant and threatening and were perhaps resented even more than American or European businessmen just because their physical resemblance to the native populations suggested that they should somehow be less alien. Many people feared that Japan might be creating through economic means the Greater East Asia Co-Prosperity Sphere that it had failed to establish through conquest in World War II. Such fears were felt with particular strength in countries like South Korea and the Philippines, where the Japanese were remembered as ruthless colonial masters or cruel wartime conquerors.

To such anxieties there was added the resentment that the Japanese were remiss in giving aid to their poorer neighbors. Japan, of course, had joined the other industrialized countries in providing aid. By 1975 over 20,000 persons from developing countries, largely in Asia, had recieved training in Japan at Japanese government expense and over 10,000 Japanese experts had been sent to help in these countries. Though smaller on a proportionate basis than the efforts of some Western countries, these activities were not inconsiderable. The statistics on Japanese economic aid also seemed comparable to those of the West. However, when examined more closely they proved to be largely supportive of Japanese trade activities, and outright government grants were much smaller and the terms for loans stiffer than in the case of most other providers of aid. Japan's neighbors felt that this was poor treatment from the one fellow Asian nation which was affluent and industrially advanced.

Grumblings against the Japanese grew over the years. The popular term "ugly American" for the foreign exploiter was shifted to the "ugly Japanese." The Japanese were not unaware of these sign of discontent, but at first, in their concentration on their own goals, they paid them scant heed. The seriousness of the situation was brought home to them with crashing force when a good will trip to Southeast Asia by Prime Minister Tanaka in January 1974 turned into a debacle of anti-Japanese protests and rioting. While there were internal political tensions involved in the particularly serious outbreaks in Indonesia and Thailand, there could be no mistaking the depth of the hostility toward Japan. The Japanese as a result began to take the complaints of their neighbors more seriously and to attempt to shape their trade tactics and aid policies to meet them.

A similar crisis also built up in Japan's relations with the industrialized countries, particularly the United States. As we have seen, the American market was from the first entirely open to Japan for exploitation, except for occasional restrictions misleadingly called "voluntary restraints." In fields such as textiles, in which a generally stagnant American industry felt threatened by Japanese imports, the American government, wishing to avoid the appearnace of putting restraints on trade, would persuade the Japanese government to place so-called "voluntary restraints" on it from the Japanese side. But such American restrictions were inconsequential compared to the general Japanese policy of restricting all imports into Japan that might significantly compete with native products. Japan also exercised close restrictions on all foreign investments. The United States at first accepted this imbalanced economic relationship, because it was seen as necessary for a weak, impoverished Japan, which seemed at the time to offer no serious economic competition to the United States. It was fortunate that the United States took this liberal attitude, because otherwise the Japanese economic recovery would probably have been much slower and, if Japan had been open from the start to foreign investment, the resultant American ownership of much of Japan's industry might have produced intolerable political tensions between the two countries.

As Japan prospered, however, and its economy grew strong, this imbalanced situation brought mounting American dissatisfaction and demands for reciprocity in economic treatment through Japan's liberalizing of its trade and investment policies. Australia and the countries of Western Europe also demanded that Japan liberalize its trade policies before they would give up their own restrictions on imports from Japan. Japan was seen on all sides as a selfish nation, intent only on its own immediate economic gain, insensitive to the economic needs of others, and unconcerned with the noneconomic problems of the world. It came to be condemned as an "economic animal," and DeGaulle is said to have described Prime Minister Ikeda as a "transistor salesman." Americans complained bitterly of the "free ride" Japan was taking at American expense, meaning not only that Americans paid the heavy military bill that gave Japan security but also that trade relations were slanted in Japan's favor.

In the early postwar years Japan's economic growth had been constrained by difficulties with the balance of trade and the balance of payments, but by the end of the 1960s both had turned clearly in Japan's favor. Japan began to have huge trade surpluses and built up great holdings of foreign exchange. American businessmen and politicians reacted to this situation with resentment. It seemed clear that the Japanese yen was seriously undervalued and that steps should be taken to redress the economic balance. The Japanese recognized the general validity of these positions but argued that Japan needed more time to adjust to them. They pointed out that Japan was already making moves, even if slowly, toward liberalizing its trade and investment policies, and they maintained, with some justification, that Japan, because of its lack of space and resources, was a poorer country than its economic statistics might suggest. But basically the problem seems to have been that the Japanese people and government had been so conditioned by the trauma of Japan's postwar poverty that they were reluctant to abandon the controls that had helped bring affluence to the nation.

In this impasse, President Nixon suddenly announced on August 15, 1971, a new American economic policy, suspending the convertibility of the dollar into gold and establishing a temporary 10 percent surcharge on imports. These measures were both aimed primarily at Japan, and, coming exactly a month after the "Nixon shock" on China policy, they were dubbed by Japanese the "second Nixon shock." This American action did not immediately clear up the problem—in the next year, 1972, Japan ran a record four billion dollar surplus in its trade with the United States alone—but it did put an end to the postwar monetary system, established at Bretton Woods, which was based on the dollar at a fixed gold value, and it eventually produced a new system of floating exchange rates. The Japanese yen, which ever since the occupation had been pegged at three hundred and sixty to a dollar, rose in value for a while to two hundred and sixty-five to the dollar and thereafter floated closer to three hundred. The Japanese were also shocked into speeding up the liberalization of investments and industrial imports, and within the next few years they got rid of most restrictions on both, without any serious repercussions in the Japanese economy.

Japan, like many other nations, does retain strict controls on the importation of many agricultural products, since without these most Japanese agriculture would not be economically viable. American rice, can be delivered at Japanese ports at about half the cost of Japanese rice, the chief Japanese agricultural product. The reasons for these restrictions are, of course, more social and psychological than economic. Economically it would be advantageous for Japan to import almost all of the agricultural products it needs, but the resultant destruction of rural society and the specter of almost complete dependence on foreign sources for food would produce unbearable problems.

Some foreign experts feel that, even after the thorough-going liberalization of investments and industrial imports, Japan still maintains invisible but effective restrictions that are the product of the language barrier, the complex administrative controls exercised by the bureaucracy, and tacit collusion among the Japanese against foreigners. The Japanese reply that the problem is rather the failure of the foreigners to learn the Japanese language and familiarize themselves with the Japanese system of operation. They point out that they themselves could never have penetrated foreign markets without careful study of foreign languages and economic systems. Charges are also often made that the Japanese are engaging in dumping practices or are illegally subsidizing exports, but such allegations are as difficult to prove in Japan as in other countries. As Japanese exports to Western Europe increased markedly in the 1970s, an imbalance in trade in Japan's favor of around four billion developed, creating by early 1977 strong pressures in Western Europe for retaliation against Japan, and American anxieties were once again aroused over a large gap in the trade balance with Japan.

There are thus continuing economic frictions between Japan and the outside world, though on the whole these are perhaps a little less acute than only a few years ago, and the Japanese are clearly more aware of the need to take quick countermeasures to alleviate them. Japan is now a well-established and responsive member of the group of industrialized trading nations, and it is in mutually beneficial economic contact with most of the rest of the world. As its growth slows down to a rate closer to that of the world as a whole, as appears probable, it seems likely that economic tensions with other countries will gradually lessen to levels well below those of the late 1960s and early 1970s.

Interdependence

36

THE VAST expansion of Japan's industry and trade since the war not only brought it new problems but also greatly increased its dependence on the outside world for raw materials and foreign markets to pay for them. This has been Japan's most basic problem ever since the conflict over policies of trade or empire in the 1920s and 1930s, but it is now many times more acute. A measure of the huge increase in Japan's dependence on the outside world can be seen in the figures on oil imports. The quantity of foreign oil needed in the 1930s to operate Japan's navy and army for two years—that is, the amount of oil which when Japan was threatened with its denial in 1941 forced it to take the desperate gamble on war with the United States—comes to only a six day supply of oil imports in the 1970s. All nations are now more or less dependent on the rest of the world, but some are much more so than others and are thus more vulnerable to the vagaries of international politics and trade. Japan is certainly one of these—in fact, the leading example among the major countries of the world.

Some statistics at first glance may seem to contradict this statement. Japanese exports and imports each account for only about 10 percent of Japan's production and consumption—that is, for about 10 percent of GNP. These percentages are only about twice those for the United States, with its high degree of self-sufficiency, and about half those of most of the lands of Western Europe. Many small countries throughout the world have even higher proportions. One reason for this situation is that the smaller the geographic and population base of a country, the less likely that it can meet its various economic needs domestically and therefore the higher the rate of its foreign trade. For example, the three million people of New Zealand or the five million of Denmark cannot possibly support an independent automotive industry. Japan, on the other hand, with close to 115 million, has a large domestic market that lies behind her industrial success and makes self-sufficiency easy in virtually all industrial goods. As one of the most populous countries in the world, its ratios of imports and exports should be relatively low.

Two other factors are more significant than the gross ratios of international trade. These are the nature of imports and where they come from. The bulk of international trade in Western Europe is within the European Economic Community and therefore is not unlike interstate commerce in the United States, and most of it consists of goods which conceivably could be produced domestically, even if at a higher price. Western Europe taken as a unit has a lower level of economic dependence on the rest of the world than does Japan. Even in the case of the United States, its largest trade is regional, being with Canada, a nation with a close symbiotic economic relationship with the United States. Japan, in contrast, has relatively little regional trade of this sort. Its economic relations with South Korea and Taiwan, both parts of its former empire, might qualify for this category, but together they add up to only a very small portion of Japan's trade—little more than a twentieth. Even Southeast Asia is some 1,500 to 3,000 miles away and certainly forms no regional economic community with Japan. All areas within 3,000 miles of Japan, including China and western Siberia, would account for less than a third of Japan's trade.

The makeup of Japan's foreign trade makes the country even more clearly dependent on the global economy. Most of the energy and raw materials on which Japan operates and a large proportion of the food on which the Japanese people live comes from distant parts of the world. Foreign trade may involve only 10 percent of Japanese production and consumption, but without this 10 percent most of the rest of the economy would not work at all, nor could the majority of the Japanese people even survive. Japan is absolutely dependent on trade relations with remote areas, many of them on the opposite side of the world or not far from it. In this sense, no major country is more dependent on global trade than is Japan.

The theme of Japan's dependence for life on foreign raw materials and international trade has appeared repeatedly in this book and need not be spelled out in great detail here, but we might remind ourselves of some illustrative examples. Japan has to import virtually all its oil, iron ore, lead, wool, and cotton. It is the largest importer in the world of all these items as well as of coal, copper, zinc, lumber, and many other raw materials. Around 85 percent of the energy on which it runs is derived from foreign fuels, mostly oil. In fact, over 60 percent of its total energy depends on oil from the Persian Gulf, more than 7,000 miles away by sea.

Counting feed grains used for the production of meat within Japan, the country is more than half dependent on foreign imports for food. Practically all of Japan's feed grains, almost 95 percent of its wheat, and even more of its soybeans are imported, mostly from the United States. The Japanese are self-sufficient in their main staple, rice—in fact, they had surpluses for a while—but this is only because they have cut down on the quantity of rice they eat as their diet has become more varied, and they have maintained rice production, as we have seen, only through a system of strict import restrictions and heavy price supports at levels far above world prices. With only about 3 percent of the world's population, Japan absorbs about 10 percent of all the foodstuffs in international trade and more than half of what goes to all of Asia.

FOR SEVERAL years after the war, raw materials were in plentiful supply through the world and were of declining cost as compared with the industrial goods Japan produced. It was a buyers' market in raw materials. Japan's very lack of raw materials as well as the wartime destruction of its cities appeared ironically almost as economic blessings in disguise. The Japanese were free to buy the resources they needed anywhere in the world at the most advantageous prices and were not tempted, as many countries were, to try to utilize domestic sources of inferior quality or higher price. They pioneered in the construction of giant tankers and ore carriers, which made oceanic transportation costs plummet to relative insignificance as compared to overland transportation. They had few obsolescent factories and machines to slow the rise of productivity and could start afresh with completely up-to-date plants and machinery. When bulky fuels or ores were involved, they located these factories at seaside, thus eliminating overland haulage. Japan's poverty in natural resources and the destruction of its industrial facilities during the war were thus turned to advantage in its rise to industrial power.

The euphoria resulting from Japan's economic success during the 1960s blotted out for a time anxieties over its utter dependence on the outside world for its means of livelihood, but in the 1970s a series of events brought this dependence very much to the fore again. The oil crisis, precipitated by the Arab-Israeli War of October 1973, was the most important of these events. The resulting oil embargo by the Arab states threatened to destroy the Japanese economy. Even Americans were fearful, though imported oil was only a small fraction of their energy resources and was used mostly for peripheral and therefore partially curtailable purposes, such as private automotive transportation and domestic heating. By way of contrast, imported oil provided the bulk of Japan's energy and was used mainly to power its industries. The Japanese suffered a truly traumatic shock. For them the world would never seem the same again.

Even though the Arab oil embargo was soon lifted and was found in retrospect to have not had serious effects, the threat of economic strangulation has remained ever since a real possibility in Japanese minds. They, like people elsewhere, wonder about other commodities, such as copper and bauxite for aluminum, which are in worldwide demand but are produced in only a few countries. Moreover they had already had their worries aroused over their dependence on foreign supplies of food. In the summer of 1973, just before the oil embargo, the United States government, fearful that heavy Soviet purchases of soybeans would create a shortage, suddenly declared an embargo on soybean exports to all countries, including Japan, even though it had long been America's chief export market for soybeans and these constituted a major source of protein for the Japanese diet. The embargo was soon lifted, and Japan was able to procure all the soybeans it needed, but this third "Nixon shock" reminded the Japanese of their dependence on foreign sources for crucial supplies of food and showed them that even as friendly a country as the United States could act in callous disregard of vital Japanese needs.

The Arab oil embargo had proved more of a fright than an economic blow, but the subsequent hiking of prices by the oil cartel of the OPEC nations led to a quadrupling of oil costs. Prices of many other raw materials also shot up at much the same time, while food costs also soared, in part because of the increased price of energy, in part because of drought conditions that had led to heavy food imports in the Soviet Union and other parts of the world. This vast increase in the cost of Japan's major imports from 1974 on seemed to mark a major turning of the tide in the terms of trade for Japan.

The Hakozaki Maru, a modern container vessel. Container ships together with giant oil tankers and bulk carriers for ores have greatly reduced the costs of oceanic transportation. This port scene is typically busy, with many ships both dockside and in the offing. Maru (of uncertain meaning) is traditionally the last component of the names of all commercial vessels. (*Embassy of Japan*)

Japan's essential imports are nonrenewable raw materials, which are in finite supply in the world, or agricultural products, which are limited by the finite amount of agricultural terrain and the constraints of weather. As the population of the world continues to grow and living standards to rise, the demand for these finite resources will inevitably increase. World population already stands at around four billion and has been doubling roughly every thirty-five years. As the developing world grows both in population and economically and the industrial nations continue to move ahead economically, the number of consumers and per capita consumption will both increase. Thus the demand for the limited supplies of the products Japan must import will inevitably grow and at a rapid pace. But the industrial goods and sophisticated services that make up Japan's exports can be produced almost without limit, except for those imposed by the limitations of raw materials and agricultural goods. And inevitably a growing proportion of the world's population will become capable of producing these industrial goods and services. Their value as compared to the value of nonrenewable raw materials and agricultural products will undoubtedly fall. Thus Japan may find it harder to sell sufficient quantities of its exports to pay for needed imports.

Over time, thus, the terms of trade are likely to turn against Japan, and it may become increasingly difficult for the Japanese to achieve sufficient technological superiority over most of the rest of the world to maintain their present position of relative affluence, much less increase it. The halcyon postwar decades, when energy and raw materials were cheap and technological skills in short worldwide supply, are not likely to be repeated.

It is true that Japan has adjusted well to the oil shock and the explosion of raw material prices and has successfully come out from the worldwide depression they produced, which bottomed out for the Japanese in 1975 and 1976. For a few more decades Japan is likely to be an economically faster growing nation than are most of the others among the already industrialized countries or even among the developing nations, though the average rate of growth in Japan will probably be in the range of 5 to 8 percent rather than the 10 to 11 percent of a few years ago. Over a longer time span, however, the picture may be more gloomy. If the Japanese are to maintain their relative position in the world or even avoid a substantial or perhaps catastrophic decline, there must be a steady or even rapid growth in world trade, which itself is only possible if there is continued world peace and a marked improvement in the handling of international tensions and global problems.

ALL NATIONS have a stake in a peaceful world system, growing global trade, and the successful management of human affairs within the confines of "spaceship earth," but none more so than Japan. The prophets of doom describe many scenarios through which destruction may come to all mankind. If any of these predictions are right, there is no hope for Japan or any other country. But, far short of such worldwide doomsday predictions, Japan faces possible catastrophe in situations in which most other countries would be merely inconvenienced or temporarily depressed. The close to 115 million Japanese, crowded into the narrow flat lands of their small islands, are like a party of Alpinists clinging to a narrow ledge and therefore more threatened by the storms of international conflict than are most other peoples encamped on broader bits of terrain.

This is not the place to go deeply into the many threats to world peace, the global ecology, or world trade, but we might consider very briefly the effects on Japan of a few of the many possible developments. It is doubtful that much of present world civilization would survive a general nuclear holocaust, but certainly Japan as it now exists would not. As nuclear weapons proliferate, as seems probable, even localized wars, if they prevented Japan's access to food supplies or oil resources, would probably bring the country tumbling down. Unlimited population growth in the developing countries or growing frictions between them and the industrialized countries might lead to such disorders as to impair world trade. There is also a growing capacity for acts of international terrorism to produce chaos in an ever more closely and intricately knit world. Any of these developments would have particularly serious consequences for Japan's finely tuned economy and worldwide economic dependence.

Problems of global ecology would affect Japan as much as any country and probably more than most. Severe pollution of the world's oceans or simply over-exploitation of its fish resources would seriously affect the Japanese, who depend for their protein resources heavily on fish, three quarters of them from distant seas. Slight shifts in climate resulting from global pollution of the atmosphere or even from purely natural phenomena might drastically reduce agricultural production with calamitous results for Japan as well as for the agricultural lands affected. In all these eventualities, Japan would inevitably be among the chief sufferers and would lack effective countermeasures.

Major wars or ecological disasters may be improbable, but one possible catastrophe for Japan is all too likely. This is simply the decline or merely the stagnation of world trade. It takes no great insight or morbid imagination to see this as a possibility. International economic relations are becoming ever more complex and difficult to handle. The industrialized nations find themselves increasingly affected by trade policies, exchange rates, and inflation in other countries. Multinational corporations, balancing themselves between economic conditions in many countries and free to some extent from the control of any, are constantly growing in their roles, raising difficult new problems and creating new international tensions. Resentments and frictions between the industrialized providers of machine production and capital and the developing countries, which have little to export but raw materials and light manufactures, become constantly more severe. Growing economic nationalism on the part of both industrialized and developing nations would not be surprising, and this could lead to increasingly restrictionist policies and trade wars. In these, Japan, because of its poor hand in natural resources, would almost certainly be the loser. A sharp shift in attitude toward international trade on the part of the United States alone could set off a chain reaction that would leave the United States perhaps impoverished but Japan in ruins. The decline or stagnation of world trade would have serious consequences for all countries, even for huge and resources-rich lands like the United States and more so for the countries of Western Europe, but for Japan it might well be fatal. The internally strong and healthy Japan I have described in this book might not survive even this all too possible next phase of history.

To state the case in positive terms, Japan has as great an interest as any nation in the maintenance of world peace, the expansion of world trade, and the solution of the global problems that mankind faces. As a major consumer of nonrenewable raw materials, it has a prime interest in the orderly exploitation of the oceans, Antarctica, and other unexploited areas of the world. The current efforts to find agreement on an international convention of the seas is perhaps of greater concern to Japan than any other country, because of its dependence on the waters of the world for a significant portion of its food and on global sea lanes for its economic survival. The recent unilateral extension by many countries of territorial jurisdictions to twelve miles and claims to the produce of the waters and what lies below them to a distance of two hundred miles are matters of grave concern to Japan. So also is whaling, which in recent years has raised worldwide concern over the possible extinction of these great mammals. Japan takes 40 percent of the global whale catch and as late as 1970 got from it 9 percent of its meat consumption. Global problems of pollution and ecology involve the Japanese as much as any people, because they are among the chief polluters and have a worldwide dependence on nature.

The problems of world trade, however, are probably the most complex and immediately pressing for Japan. Much must be achieved if world trade is not to stagnate and restrictive policies and trade wars are to be avoided. First come the problems of economic cooperation between the industrialized trading nations of North America, Western Europe, Japan, and Australia. These countries provide more than 40 percent of Japan's imports and also markets. They also come closest to sharing the same economic interests with Japan and the same values. There is need for constant improvement in the cooperation between these countries, not just in trade relations but in their monetary policies, controls over inflation, and the handling of problems of unemployment, pollution, and the regulation of multinational corporations. A fine balance must be achieved between the mutually advantageous ideal of free trade and the political necessity of avoiding sudden upsurges of imports into a country that might cause local economic difficulties and resulting international tensions. The involuntary "voluntary restraints" in Japanese-American relations of a few years ago may have to be developed into a more general but also truly voluntary system of "orderly international marketing." Here is a huge and complex area of needed effort, in which Japan is in many ways central, as still the fastest growing country among the industrialized trading nations and the one which the others regard with some suspicion as being the most different and difficult to comprehend.

Beyond this primary economic relationship for Japan are three other lesser but still very important ones. All require hard and imaginative efforts. Trade with the Communist nations remains relatively small—5 percent for imports and 8 percent for exports in 1975, for example—but some day it might be much more important, particularly with the Soviet Union. Japan shares with the other industrialized nations the difficult problem of relations with the oil-rich lands of the Middle East and the recycling of the vast monetary holdings their oil wealth has brought them. Something like a quarter of all Japanese imports come from this region, almost entirely in the form of oil. A breakdown of effective economic relations with the Middle East would bring disaster to most of the industrialized countries, but first of all to Japan.

The relationship between the so-called industrialized North, of which Japan is a major part, and the developing South, which contains the bulk of the world's population, is probably the gravest problem facing mankind, even overshadowing in the long run the problems of the nuclear balance. The South holds much of the world's resources, but it also has the fastest growing populations. Economic growth in many countries hardly outstrips population growth. The economic gap with the industrialized North is increasing, as are also frictions and resentments. The problems are manifold and often seem overwhelming. The long term threat to world stability is severe. A dissatisfied South or even a desperate fraction of its population might be able to disrupt the whole world and its trade. It can be questioned whether the industrialized nations can maintain their stability and affluence if the developing countries do not achieve much greater stability and affluence than they now enjoy. Here are vastly complex and serious problems for all industrialized nations, but for none more than for Japan. Its location puts it closer to the great centers of population of the developing world, and it does more of its trade with them than do the other industrialized countries—in fact, more than half of Japan's trade, both exports and imports, is with these lands, if one includes the Middle East and China with the other developing countries.

A NATION'S security was once measured in terms of its ability to fend off military attack. But under existing conditions in the world there seems little likelihood that any nation would attack Japan, and its somewhat vague defense relationship with the United States probably gives it all the security it needs on this score. The real front line of defense for Japan is not on any military perimeter. It is the maintenance and healthy growth of international cooperation. For this, world peace is, of course, necessary but so also is the solution of endless economic and political problems in Japan's relations with the various countries of the world. Once Korea, if it were in unfriendly hands, was seen as a strategic dagger pointed at the heart of Japan. Changed military technology and world conditions now make such a concept an anachronism. A more apt figure of speech would be to describe stagnation or decline in world trade as a sword of Damocles hanging precariously above Japan's head. The thread that supports it is threatened by a variety of breezes—major wars, global ecological damage, or, most probably, the inability of human beings to cooperate successfully in a situation of rapidly increasing complexity and growing tension.

One might expect that the vigor the Japanese once put into military defense would now go into the solution of the economic and other problems that stand in the way of effective world cooperation, for this is Japan's great strategic frontier. But such is hardly the case. In fact, the Japanese seem remarkably passive, more like spectators at the great drama of world history than like participants in it. They tend to wait for others to take initiatives and then merely to react to these. In part this may be a natural continuation of a strategy that was necessary for them in the early postwar years and served them well at that time. In part it seems to be an expression of their traditional isolationism. They still seem to see Japan as somehow separate from the world. They do their best to fathom what the world may have in store for them but do not think of Japan as being a major force that will help shape the world. To other peoples they seem ready to take advantage of whatever others might develop in international relations, but unwilling to take any risks themselves. The American concept of the Japanese desire for a "free ride" has not been entirely off the mark. The Japanese seem slow to realize that, while Japan is undoubtedly dependent on the rest of the world, what that world will be is in no small degree dependent on Japan's role in it. It is indeed an irony—perhaps even a tragedy—that the Japanese, while possessing the world's most global economy, should at the same time be among its psychologically most parochial peoples. As they themselves are fond of saying, they have an "island country mentality" (*shimaguni konjo*).

A decade ago the Japanese seemed little aware of the needs of the situation, but there has been a great awakening since the various oil, price, and Nixon shocks of the early 1970s. The Japanese, however, still have a long way to go to muster their skills and energies to meet this problem the way they did earlier problems, foreign and domestic, when once they perceived them. A great language barrier lies between them and the rest of the world, far greater than for any other industrialized nation and even greater than for most developing countries, where relatively small elites have often been forced to learn foreign languages well just because of the technological backwardness of their own cultures. The Japanese are renowned for being silent participants in international conferences and smiling but inarticulate visitors in the offices of their counterparts abroad. Accustomed to their own socially tight little isles, they find it difficult to feel at ease with others and make others feel at ease with them. Doubting their skills in international relations, they hang back all the more in nervous diffidence.

These difficulties can be overcome, as the Japanese have fully demonstrated in the skill, vigor, and success with which they have developed economic relations with the whole world—the one aspect of international relations which they early perceived as being crucial for them. Attitudes toward the outside world are also changing fast among younger Japanese, who show less of the self-doubts and offishness of their elders. Now that all Japanese are beginning to comprehend the nature of Japan's international problems, one can expect considerable progress in meeting them. But in the meantime many of the old problems persist, and it is to these problems that we turn next.

Language

37

L ANGUAGE is a fundamental tool in international relations, and the Japanese language is also a major subject in itself. It is what defines the Japanese more distinctly than any other feature in their culture. At the same time it is a major problem in their relationship with the outside world. Thus it deserves our detailed consideration.

Few people in Japan or elsewhere fully realize how great the language barrier is in Japan's international contacts. In most of the rest of the world differences of language with other countries seem not to raise serious problems but to be only minor complications or irritants. Even in non-Western countries, where the language of international communication is usually English but sometimes French, the education of the elite leadership is likely to have been largely in one of these two languages. In such countries as India, for example, the problem of understanding is not so much between this leadership and the outside world as between it and the less educated populace. This is a far graver problem than the one Japan faces, but it is a domestic rather than international problem.

In most of the world, foreign language skills seem to have been developed sufficiently to meet the needs, and, on the surface, the same seems true of Japan. Almost all Japanese study English for six years in junior and senior high school and many for further years in university. The Japanese government in its Foreign Office and other ministries has sufficient officers with adequate foreign language skills to conduct Japan's official business with the outside world in a satisfactory manner. The Japanese business community has developed adequate language skills to conduct its huge international economic activities. Japanese scientists usually have enough language skills for meaningful contact with the world scientific community. Japanese mass media send back to Japan reams of copy on the outside world, and foreign books and articles are translated into Japanese and published in amazing quantities. The reverse flow of reporting, translations, and published materials put out by Japanese in English or other foreign languages is extremely modest by comparison but at least is much greater than a decade or two ago. Very few foreigners have learned Japanese, but here again the increase from virtually none a generation or two ago has been spectacular. Someone has calculated that, whereas in 1934 there were only thirteen scholars in the United States capable of making substantial use of the Japanese language, by 1969 there were five hundred.

There can be no doubt that improvements have been made and the language barrier has been reduced a little, but not nearly enough to meet the needs. The situation might be more accurately described in negative terms. Despite the huge amount of effort put into the teaching of English in Japan, the results are extremely meager. For reasons we shall go into later, it is more difficult for Japanese to learn English than it is for many other peoples, and language teaching in Japan is extraordinarily poor. Although in the bureaucracy, the business world, and science the Japanese have developed at least minimally adequate foreign language skills, in most other fields they have very little. Outside the natural sciences, only a tiny sprinkling of scholars can take meaningful part in international conferences. While almost all Japanese have studied English in school, few can even read English with sufficient speed and accuracy to make English reading more than a painful process of decipherment. All Japanese know hundreds of English words which have been incorporated into the Japanese vocabulary, but these are so distorted in Japanese pronunciation as to be for the most part quite unrecognizable to foreigners and these same words usually cannot be understood by Japanese when spoken by a native speaker of English. Millions of Japanese can assay a few phrases of spoken English—"Hello" (Haro), "My name is . . ." (Mai neimu izu . . .), "Goodbye" (Gudo-bai)—but not many would be able to understand the response, much less enter into a meaningful conversation in English.

It is not that the Japanese know other Western languages or those of their part of the world instead of English. The use of Chinese characters in Japanese writing and a little study in school of classical Chinese permits them to read Chinese names and signs and simple bits of classical Chinese, so long as these are not written in the new abbreviations used in the People's Republic of China. There are also thousands of names and terms in Japanese which have been borrowed from Chinese or are based on Chinese words, but the Japanese and Chinese pronunciations of these have strayed so far apart that they are not mutually recognizable. For example, the name for the Yellow River is Hwang-ho in Chinese but Kōka in Japanese, and "economics" is *ching-chi* in Chinese but *keizai* in Japanese. Actually only a tiny number of Japanese can read or speak modern Chinese, and still fewer know any Korean, even though Korean is a language closely related to Japanese and Korea is Japan's nearest neighbor. Once German was considered the foreign language for medicine, philosophy, and law and French for the arts, but the number of Japanese who really know these or any other foreign languages is infinitesimal. In fact, a knowledge of foreign languages other than English is largely limited to a few specialized groups of businessmen, diplomats, scholars, or expatriates.

One could point out that some of the English-speaking peoples, notably the Americans and Australians, are no better than the Japanese in their command of foreign languages. But in their cases, they fortunately speak the international language of our times, and the rest of the world therefore crosses the language barrier to them. In fact, this situation accounts at least in part for their own linguistic failings. But this is hardly the case for the Japanese.

Once the Koreans and Taiwanese, as subjects of the Japanese empire, were forced to go to school in Japanese and did learn it well, but the younger generations in these countries have grown up with no knowledge of the language. In the early twentieth century many Chinese went to Japan for their higher education, but now, except for a few aged remnants of this phase of history, almost no Chinese know any Japanese. Knowledge of Japanese in the rest of the world is even less. There is only a handful of scholars and diplomats in Europe who know the language and even fewer in South Asia, the Middle East, Africa, and Latin America. In parts of Australia Japanese is now quite extensively taught, and it has spread to many American universities, but even then university students of the Japanese language in the United States number only a twenty-fifth as many as students of French. The number of Westerners who have scrambled from their side far enough across the language barrier to be able to engage in intelligent discourse in Japanese may not much exceed a thousand.

Translation is the main pass through the language barrier, and there can be no doubt that it has improved greatly in recent years. The art of simultaneous interpreting of a speaker while he is still speaking, which is extremely difficult between Japanese and English because of their very different structures, has permitted a great speeding up of conference discussions. Translation, however, remains an uncertain reed. Even assuming a perfect knowledge of both languages on the part of the interpreter, which is rarely the case, English and Japanese both suffer a radical transformation in being converted into the other. Word order is in large part reversed; clear statements become obscure; polite phrases become insulting; and a remark, even though accurately translated in a literal sense, may take on an entirely different thrust. Simultaneous interpreters, for all their wizardry, often can cover only about two thirds of the original statement. And simple errors of translation are all too common. I have often observed an inquiry by an American slightly mistranslated into Japanese and the Japanese answer then in turn mistranslated. Surprised at the probably irrelevant answer he has got, the American may conclude that Japanese mental processes are different from his own.

Even written translations leave much to be desired. Over the past century the Japanese, in their eagerness to learn about the West, have come to accept "literal translations" (*chokuyaku*) from Western languages into rather barbaric Japanese, but these "literal translations" are all too likely to distort the thrust of the original, miss its subtler meanings, and contain many simple errors where the translator's knowledge of the foreign language wore thin. The Japanese, through a huge effort in published translations, do keep up with cultural, social, political, and intellectual trends in the West, but Japanese perceptions of these trends are definitely colored by the transformation of the translation process and still more by the lack of intellectual interchange on these matters with the outside world.

However unsatisfactory the translation process from foreign languages into Japanese, the reverse flow is much weaker. Foreign audiences for the most part have little interest in Japan—the importance of the country in the world is still not widely appreciated—and no tolerance for literal translations from Japanese or even for more skillful translations of materials written for Japanese audiences. The assumptions as to what the audience already knows and is interested in as well as the whole style of presentation is too unfamiliar to make the effort to read such materials seem worthwhile. The result is a paucity of translations from Japanese into foreign languages. The one exception is modern Japanese literature, some of which, in the masterful hands of a few scholars, mostly Americans, has been rendered into excellent English translations of wide appeal. But literature tells about only one corner of modern Japanese intellectual life. For the rest, Japanese ideas are transmitted abroad only very weakly and through the filter of a few foreign "experts" on Japan and a handful of Japanese scholars who have developed an adequate command of English. Japanese intellectual life for the most part goes on behind a language barrier, quite separate from the rest of the world. It is influenced by a vast flood of translated materials from abroad but has almost no return impact. Scarcely any outsiders take part in it to correct its misunderstandings of the outside world, to subject its concepts to broader international scrutiny, or to pass on to others its results.

Japan, as we have seen, is the second largest of the industrialized, trading democracies and a key country in the "first world's" relations with the Communist "second world" and the developing "third world," but the language barriers with all three of these worlds are greater for Japan than for any other major country. In all the other first world countries, the majority of leaders of all types have a command of English and often share other languages as well. Most cabinet ministers, government officials, and business and intellectual leaders can talk face to face, without the interposition of interpreters, who in any case have a far easier task in translating between the Indo-European languages of the West than to or from Japanese. In contrast, almost no Japanese politicians and relatively few government officials, businessmen, or intellectual leaders can speak with their counterparts in other countries beyond the level of a few social pleasantries and possible the discussion of golf scores. Of the many dozens of cabinet ministers I have known in Japan over the past two decades, I can think of only three who could conduct a truly serious intellectual discussion in English. Of the hundreds of professors of history, including Western history, I have known over the last four decades, I can think of not very many more.

In some ways the situation is worse than it was seventy or eighty years ago. A study of cabinet officers reveals that between 1885 and 1912 the percentage of those with significant foreign experience was 61, but for the pre-1945 period it was down to 21, and for the postwar period, reflecting prewar educational conditions, it was a mere 16.6 percent.* The better Japan's own educational system became, the less was the foreign experience of its leadership. As long as such conditions persist, the intimate and detailed cooperation needed between the industrialized trading democracies will be much more difficult to achieve in Japan's case than for any of the other first world countries.

Japan's relations with the other countries of the world face as severe a language barrier. In most of these countries, the language of communication for the Japanese is English, though in some it is French and in Latin America Spanish or Portuguese. The uncertain command of the Japanese over these languages greatly compounds their difficulties, easily causing misunderstandings. In international meetings, moreover, Japanese ability in the language of the conference, which usually is English, is likely to rank at or near the bottom among the participants. Inevitably the voice of Japan seems less loud and distinct than it should be. Even given the will to make a positive contribution, the Japanese are likely to have less impact than they would wish. This is a sorry state of affairs for a country so great in economic size and so overwhelmingly dependent on its international relations.

JAPAN's language problems are in part her own making but in part the unfortunate result of linguistic realities. We might first examine these realities before turning to a consideration of what the Japanese might do about the language situation to better prepare themselves for the problems they face.

First let us dispose of one common canard about the Japanese language. Many foreigners, most of whom have precious little knowledge of Japanese, complain that the language is too lacking in clarity or logic to fit modern technological or scientific needs. Even some Japanese make this charge, but it is, of course, balderdash, as the extraordinary success of the Japanese in modern times has shown. All languages have infinite capacities for ambiguities and unclarities, and probably it is easier to be ambiguous and vague in Japanese than in most Indo-European tongues. Cer-

* Peter P. Cheng, "The Japanese Cabinets, 1885–1973: An Elite Analysis," *Asian Survey*, December 1974.

tainly the Japanese, with their suspicion of verbal skills, their confidence in nonverbal understanding, their desire for consensus decisions, and their eagerness to avoid personal confrontation, do a great deal more beating around the verbal bush than we do and usually try to avoid the "frankly speaking" approach so dear to Americans. They prefer in their writing as well as their talk a loose structure of argument, rather than careful logical reasoning, and suggestion or illustration, rather than sharp, clear statements. But there is nothing about the Japanese language which prevents concise, clear, and logical presentation, if that is what one wishes to make. The Japanese language itself is fully up to the demands of modern life.

Where the Japanese run into difficulty is in their linguistic contact with other peoples. It is commonly asserted that Japanese is extremely difficult for others to learn and that the Japanese are very poor at learning other languages. Unfortunately there is much truth to both evaluations, which are of course the two sides of the same coin. Japanese is very different from almost all other languages and therefore is difficult for others to learn. The Japanese conversely find almost all other languages very different from their own and so do not learn them with ease.

The languages of the world divide up into families which share basic structural similarities, phonetic resemblances, and also elements of basic vocabulary. Speakers of English not only have the advantage of speaking the language which is at present by far the most widely used for international communication but also belongs to the most widespread family of languages. This is Indo-European, which covers almost all of Europe, large parts of Asia in Siberia, Iran, Afghanistan, and the northern two thirds of the Indian subcontinent, and the great bulk of North and South America. Over these vast areas, the basic structure of languages is the same, and there are phonetic similarities and underlying shared morphemes, as seen in such key words as *mother*, *mutter*, *mère*, *mater* and the like, or *three*, *drei*, *trois*, and the *tri* of Latin, Russian, and Sanskrit. Any speaker of one Indo-European language has a long leg up on learning another, and the speakers of the specifically Western languages of this family have the further advantage of the huge borrowings of vocabulary between them, as in the vast numbers of words with Latin or Greek stems or the contemporary vocabulary borrowings, such as words like *Leitmotif*, *coup d'état*, or *siesta* in English and the flood of English words which recently have invaded French, German, and the other Western tongues.

Speakers of languages belonging to other families usually have the same sort of advantage within it. Let us take Chinese, for example, since it has been a language of particular significance to Japan. The Chinese of North, Central, and West China is the language with the greatest number of native speakers in the world, surpassing even English, Spanish, Russian, and the Hindi-Urdu of the northwestern part of the Indian subcontinent. Chinese is part of the Sinitic family of languages, which includes the other Chinese languages of the Southern coastal areas, usually called the Chinese dialects, as well as Tibetan, Burmese, Thai, and Vietnamese. The Sinitic languages are characterized by tones that differentiate words which otherwise are pronounced alike, a tendency toward one syllable words, a lack of inflections, which are so characteristic of Indo-European, and a resulting emphasis on word order as determining the relationship of words in a sentence. Since English has suffered (or perhaps one should say benefited from) a severe loss of its inflections, it too has become heavily dependent on word order for meaning and in a way which happens to be much like Chinese word order. In fact, the two are so much alike in this respect that it is possible for Chinese to speak in a restricted English vocabulary but using Chinese word order and still be understood by English speakers who know no Chinese. This is so-called Pidgin English as it was spoken on the China coast before World War II. This chance similarity between Chinese and English makes it easier for speakers of each language to learn the other.

The Japanese, in contrast, do not belong to a large or dominant family of languages or have any such chance linguistic advantages. In fact, the language cards seem mostly stacked against them. Japanese probably belongs to the Altaic family of languages, named for a mountain range in Mongolia. The Altaic languages include Turkish, Mongolian, the Manchu of the last semi-nomadic conquerors of China, and Korean, and they bear resemblances in structure to other languages of Asian origin such as Hungarian and Finnish, and possibly the Dravidian tongues of South India. The structure of Japanese is very close to Korean and quite similar to Mongolian, but, if it is really related, it has strayed far from these others. It takes a specialist to recognize any underlying similarities of vocabulary or phonetics. Japanese do have some advantages in learning Korean and possibly even Mongolian and Turkish, but at best this is a minor asset in the modern world as compared to the huge advantages of speakers of Indo-European tongues.

Though first Chinese and later English have been the two most important foreign languages for Japanese, it would be hard to imagine languages that differ more from Japanese in both structure and phonetics. Japanese, next to Polynesian, is phonetically one of the simplest languages in the world. It has only the five standard Latin vowels, *a, e, i, o,* and *u*, all pronounced as these are in Italian, Spanish, or German, while Chinese has many more and English a still more bewildering variety. Japanese consonants also are quite restricted in number—*l* and *v* among the common ones are entirely missing—and consonants do not occur in clusters or at the end of syllables, except for *n*. Chinese is somewhat richer in consonants, and English has a huge array of consonants and consonantal clusters both at the beginning and end of syllables. Some of the problems Japanese have with English consonants can be illustrated by the way they would pronounce two English words: *valorous* becomes *barorasu* and *script* becomes *sukuriputo*. Chinese moreover depends heavily on tones and English on stress accent, both of which are lacking in Japanese. Thus even a simple Chinese or English sentence constitutes a nightmare of unfamiliar sounds and accents for a Japanese. The problems English speakers face in French *u* or German *ü* or *ö* are multiplied many times over for Japanese attempting to speak almost any foreign tongue. (By way of contrast, the only really difficult phonetic problem in Japanese for English speakers is the difference between long and short vowels and consonants, as in *koko*, "here," and *kōkō*, "senior high school," or *kita*, "north," and *kitta*, "cut," since these distinctions are absent from English.)

In structure, Japanese is radically different from both Chinese and English. Like Chinese, it lacks the distinctions between singular and plural and between "a" and "the" as well as the gender of most Indo-European languages. Japanese does not specify the subject of a sentence if this can be otherwise surmised by the context or the degree of politeness of the verb. And quite unlike Chinese, it is highly inflected, though in a way entirely different from the Indo-European languages. Verbs and adjectives tie on at their end through agglutination, as it is called, a series of inflections that specify mood, voice (such as passive or causative), the perfect or imperfect tense, negative or positive, and degrees of politeness. Examples based on the word *kaku*, "to write," are *kakanakatta*, "did not write," and the unlikely but grammatically possible *kakaseraremashitaraba*, "if it were (politely) caused to be written." To frame a sentence in English, Japanese thus must restructure their word patterns and remember to take account of a variety of unfamiliar things—number, most tense forms, whether to use "a" or "the," and a host of difficult phonetic problems. It is little wonder that they have to struggle harder than most nonnative speakers to learn English and seem to achieve less.

M A N Y people confuse languages with writing, but these are, of course, entirely distinct. The Latin alphabet is used in most of Europe, all of North and South America, and large parts of Africa and Asia, including Indonesia, Malaysia, the Philippines, and Vietnam in Southeast Asia. Other phonetic systems of writing are used in all other parts of the world except for East Asia, where the use of Chinese characters still prevails in China, Korea, and Japan. Originally pictographic, Chinese characters developed thousands of years ago beyond simple pictographs, but they remained a system of unique symbols for each monosyllabic Chinese word. There are thousands of them, and many are extremely complex. This system of writing is very difficult to learn, and it could not be used easily for other languages, particularly unrelated ones like Japanese, for which the Chinese characters provided no adequate way to indicate inflections. Japanese can be easily transcribed into almost any phonetic system of writing, but the Japanese had the bad luck of learning about the Chinese writing system first and becoming so deeply steeped in it that they have never been able to extricate themselves fully from this cumbersome mode of writing.

From the sixth to the ninth centuries, when the Japanese first took over much of Chinese civilization, they did so through the Chinese written language. They used written Chinese to run their own government and other affairs, just as the people of North Europe made use of Latin, which was a much simpler matter, since the writing system was easy and the language closely related to their own. In the eighth and ninth centuries and then again from around the fifteenth to the nineteenth centuries, when influences from China were particularly strong, Japanese scholars and men of affairs wrote tolerably good Chinese and read it with some ease, but it is doubtful that many of them were ever able to speak it well or understand it by ear. Certainly today a Japanese who can speak Chinese is a rarity.

As Japan developed, the need grew to write the native language that all spoke. From the beginning, geographic and personal names and Japanese poems were spelled out in characters used phonetically for individual syllables. From this practice there evolved in the ninth century a writing system, called *kana*, in which certain characters written in simplified form were used phonetically to represent the sounds of specific syllables. Actually two forms of such syllabaries developed, the one called *katakana*, in which the original character was abbreviated by selecting some element in it, the other *hiragana*, in which the whole character was written in extremely cursive, abbreviated form. The two have existed ever since, though neither was fully standardized until the nineteenth century. Today *katakana* is ordinarily used for foreign names and words (other than Chinese or Korean), somewhat in the way we use italics, and *hiragana* for everything else that is written phonetically.

A great native literature appeared in the tenth and eleventh centuries, written entirely in *kana*, and it has been perfectly possible ever since to write Japanese this way, but the prestige of China and its writing system remained so strong that the Japanese continued to use written Chinese for official or scholarly purposes or inserted Chinese words written in Chinese characters into texts in Japanese. At times, their written Chinese was so corrupted by Japanese that it bcame almost a bastard language of its own, half way between the two, with Japanese inflections added to the Chinese characters and with certain symbols used to indicate the reordering of the Chinese words to fit Japanese grammar. The result is something that is only understandable if one knows the original meaning of the Chinese characters and the Japanese grammar that is made to accompany them, but this is still the way Japanese are taught to read classical Chinese texts in their schools.

Over the centuries the Japanese naturally incorporated into their own vocabulary huge numbers of Chinese words, particularly for technical and scholarly terms, but they did not go as far as the Koreans, who actually took over Chinese type names for themselves and for most place names. Chinese words as used in Japanese, however, involved a problem. Since the richer Chinese phonetic system was reduced to a much smaller number of sounds in Japanese, a great many Chinese words which sounded quite different in Chinese were pronounced alike in Japanese. For example, some twenty Chinese syllables, running from *kao* to *kuang* and *hsiao*, each theoretically divisible into four tones for a total of eighty distinct syllables, reduce to the single syllable *kō* in Japanese, and well over a hundred words of Chinese origin pronounced *kōka* are listed in Japanese dictionaries. This is why the Japanese stuck to writing most borrowed Chinese words in characters rather than *kana*.

From badly corrupted written Chinese and Japanese texts larded with Chinese characters evolved the modern mixed writing system, in which most nouns and other uninflected words of both Chinese and Japanese origin and the stems of most verbs and adjectives are written with characters, and the inflections and other things that cannot be written in characters are recorded in *kana*. This system of writing is probably the most complex and difficult of any in common use anywhere in the world. Even the absurd irregularities of English spelling, which are nothing short of a tragedy for the world's leading international language, fall far short of the difficulties of the Japanese writing system.

The *kana* offer no great learning problem, because there are only forty-eight of them in each system and only two diacritic marks. Some 1,850 Chinese characters, however, must be learned in the nine years of compulsory education, and more are needed for specialized fields of study. Each character not only has a pronunciation derived from the original Chinese pronunciation (sometimes there are two) but in addition is usually equated with one or more Japanese words of corresponding meaning. In an extreme case, the character for "to give birth to," seven entirely distinct Japanese words are written with this one symbol. Only the context indicates which of the multiple readings for a character is the correct one.

That the Japanese have achieved such high educational standards despite this horrendous system of writing is a tribute to their zeal for education. Actually the need to conquer this great barrier to literacy may help account for the good study habits and discipline the Japanese have developed, though some have suggested that the rote memory work required for learning characters has cut into the originality of Japanese thought and tended to inculcate blind obedience. Certainly the difficulty of the writing system is one of the reasons why so few foreigners have mastered Japanese.

Many people, both Japanese and foreign, have advocated that the Japanese should abandon their cumbersome mixed script for a purely phonetic one. *Kana* is usually thought of as the natural substitute. However it is not as satisfactory for this purpose today as it was when used with such brilliant literary results in the eleventh century, because since then long consonants and vowels and certain new consonants (*cha* and *sha* would be examples) have become important features of the spoken language, and none of these are handled well by *kana*. Actually the Latin alphabet would be far more satisfactory. With only nineteen Latin letters and one or two diacritic marks one can write Japanese perfectly, and anything that can be understood by ear can be read with ease in this form with just a little practice. Most Japanese do not believe this, but I made this discovery to my own great surprise during World War II when I was working on the breaking and translating of Japanese codes.

In the early days of the occupation some people thought that the Americans would insist on a shift to Latin letters, or *rōmaji* ("Roman characters") as they are known in Japanese, but this did not happen, and now, except for a few linguistic experts, there is scarcely any interest in the idea. The Japanese strongly resist the thought of abandoning Chinese characters, for a number of reasons. Almost all people who have learned the Japanese writing system, be they Japanese or foreigners, stubbornly reject the idea that the language can be written in any other way. Perhaps they have made too great an effort in learning it to be willing to give up the advantages of their investment. Characters also have an esthetic value, at least for those who know them, that are not to be found in phonetic scripts. They have an almost magical quality too. They seem to have more substance then words written phonetically and to have a life of their own, quite distinct from the words they are used to represent. Technical and scholarly words written in characters always clearly reveal their component elements and in a way are self-explanatory. Any sixth grader can have some concept of the word *hyōga*, because it is "ice river," or *kōkogaku*, which is study antiquity science." The meaning of the corresponding English words, "glacier" and "archeology," are not at all as self-evident to the American child. Characters also lend themselves to easy abbreviations in the writing of names and to pithy slogans. The arts of newspaper headlines and political sloganeering, as these now exist in Japan, are unimaginable without the use of characters. They also help in speed reading or in scanning a text, because key terms stand out more recognizably.

A still more important reason for the continued use of characters is that Chinese characters have always lain at the heart of what cultural unity East Asia has had. As late as a century and a half ago well-educated men in Japan, Korea, Vietnam, and the various language areas of China all could read and write the same classical Chinese. Even today names, titles, and slogans written in characters are mutually intelligible to Japanese, Koreans, and Chinese. For example, a book entitled, let us say, "The Decline and Fall of the Han Empire," which involves no inflected words in Japanese and Korean, would be almost identically written in the three countries. There is also a huge common vocabulary in Chinese, Korean, and Japanese, derived from classical Chinese and also from modern words coined in Japan from classical Chinese elements. These are mutually intelligible in writing even though they are almost never recognizable by ear.

This cultural bond of the written word, however, is in the process of dissolving. The Vietnamese have abandoned characters entirely. The abbreviations used for many characters in the People's Republic of China are largely not recognizable to Koreans and Japanese. The Koreans have their own very efficient phonetic script, *han'gul*, and it is gradually replacing characters. In Japan the number of characters used has been quite strictly limited, many of these are abbreviated in ways different from those in use in China, and the use of *kana* is slowly rising, while the use of characters is correspondingly falling. In another generation or two the once great East Asian cultural link of Chinese characters may be largely gone.

The main argument in favor of the continued use of characters is that their abandonment would cut off the contemporary Japanese from an understanding of their heritage. It certainly would constitute a much greater cultural break than did the shift in writing from Latin to the local languages in Europe, which even then took centuries to accomplish. It would require the jettisoning of a huge number of words that cannot be adequately identified by sound, though these words are already of marginal utility. The break between the contemporary Japanese and their written heritage, however, is slowly coming in any case, as Japanese knowledge of characters declines, and modern life makes ancient ways seem remote and strange. A sudden shift in writing systems in Japan is not likely, unless some dreadful catastrophe overtakes Japan, but I suspect that over a space of a few generations the Japanese will gradually shift for most purposes to a purely or at least largely phonetic system of writing.

ONE OF THE reasons for the growing use of *kana* in Japanese writing is the large number of words that have been borrowed from English. The

Japanese have always been ready to borrow foreign words. I have already mentioned the borrowings from classical Chinese and the many modern words the Japanese have coined out of Chinese elements, in the same way as Europeans have shaped new words out of Latin and Greek. These then spread to Korea and China, much as imported raw materials were made into machine goods in Japan and then re-exported.

The Japanese borrowed words from Portuguese in the sixteenth century—*pan* for bread is an example still in use—and from Dutch in the Tokugawa period, as in the case of *buriki* from *blik* for "tin." The opening of Japan in the nineteenth century brought in quantities of new European words. German words became common in medicine, law, and philosophy, and French words prevailed in the fields of fashion and the arts. But English words predominated, since Britishers and Americans were the most numerous instructors in the new sciences and technological skills and also dominated trade and most of Japan's other foreign contacts. English almost at once became the chief language of communication for Japanese with the outside world. Fukuzawa, the early Meiji popularizer of knowledge about the West, tells the pathetic story of how he, as an eager young student of the Dutch language, rushed to the new port of Yokohama in 1860 to get in touch with the foreign community just becoming established there, only to make the crushing discovery that he had learned the wrong language. English was the *lingua franca* of Yokohama, as it already was in most of the other ports of Asia.

In the new Japan created by the reforms that followed the Meiji Restoration, medical doctors, some government officials, and scholars in certain fields of learning took up German or French as their primary foreign language, but for all others it was English, and its predominance grew as the United States became an increasingly important force in the Western Pacific and Japanese immigrants to Hawaii and the mainland of the United States became another source of linguistic influence on Japan. Gradually the American brand of English came to predominate over British. The Japanese, especially in their teaching of English in schools, have usually insisted that they were following the King's English, but Japanese pronunciation of English is so bad that the accuracy of this assertion normally cannot be ascertained from pronunciation, and in the adoption of English words for use in Japanese it obviously is not correct. In almost every case in which American and English usage differ, the American word has been adopted, as in *erebētā* ("elevator") instead of "lift" or *torakku* ("truck") instead of "lorry."

The real flood of English words into Japanese started in the liberal 1920s, following World War I, not with the American occupation, as most people think. During this period came such now standard words as *takushi* ("taxi") and *rajio* ("radio") as well as coined terms like *sarariman* ("salary man") for white collar workers. During the 1930s and war years, the militarists frowned on the use of English words in Japanese and insisted that the worst offenders be replaced by native words. These substitutes, however, were commonly made up of borrowed Chinese lexical elements as in *yakyū*, which still is used together with its English counterpart, *bēsubōru* ("baseball"). The American occupation swept away all remaining dikes, and the flood of English words entering Japanese has remained high ever since. Linguistic purists sometimes raise objections, but there seems no stopping scholars from introducing new concepts through new English terms, developed largely in the United States, or the entertainment world, advertising, the mass media, and the general public from appropriating words and phrases from English with complete abandon.

Some of the new English vocabulary serves no useful purpose, since it simply replaces perfectly good Japanese words. *Raion* ("lion") has virtually driven out the original word *shishi*. This happened already before the war, I suspect because of a popular brand of toothpaste called *Raion* (perhaps inspired by "Dr. Lyon's" toothpaste), which had a lion on its trademark and thus established the connection with the sound *raion* in the minds of children. Since the war, even English words for colors—*pinku, orenji, guriin, burū*—have replaced or come to parallel perfectly good native words. Many English words are used simply to be stylish, as in the case of French words in English. This would apply to the prevalent use of English and also French names for cafés (*kafue*), or coffee shops (*kōhi-shoppu*) as they are often now called. In most cases, however, English words constitute the addition of a new thing, concept, or connotation into the Japanese language. To create words for these purposes from strictly Japanese lexical elements would be even more confusing and artificial than the Nazi effort to replace international words with German ones. To create words out of Chinese lexical elements, as was previously the custom, would be very unsatisfactory, because words of this type usually sound much like other words and are therefore not clear when spoken. English words obviously make much better neologisms in Japanese, and actually great numbers of English technical terms are used in spoken Japanese simply because their character counterparts are not usually distinguishable.

The massive vocabulary borrowings from English have greatly strengthened and enriched Japanese with clearly identifiable new words as well as a host of new concepts. And they do not really threaten the integrity of the Japanese language. It is so unique a language that no matter how much vocabulary it borrows, it will remain entirely distinct from English and completely itself. The Japanese people therefore have been very wise to pay language purists no heed. The capacity to absorb new vocabulary from other languages is in a sense one of the glories of Japanese, as it is of English.

One might suppose that the tremendous number of English words used in Japanese would be a great aid to Japanese in learning English. Of course, it is in a way. Many English words are already familiar to them. But in other ways these borrowings are actually an additional handicap. I have cited above a number of English words as borrowed in Japanese to illustrate how greatly their pronunciations are distorted in order to fit them into the simple Japanese phonetic system. Thoroughly entrenched in these mispronunciations, the Japanese finds it all the the harder to pronounce these words in a form recognizable to English speakers. And English words in Japanese often take on their own meaning, quite distinct from English. *Handoru* ("handle") is a "steering wheel," *kurakushon* (from "claxon") the "horn," *mashin* a "sewing machine," *guriin ka* ("green car") a first class carriage on a train, *naitā* ("nighter") a night game in baseball, *kūrā* ("cooler") an air conditioner, and *rinchi* ("lynch") almost any act of group violence to a person—a true case of lynching, so far as I know, has never occurred in Japan.

The Japanese also often use English in quite creative ways, though with mystifying results for the native speaker of English. I remember my own puzzlement a few years ago when I encountered the word *bēya* as a headline abbreviation in a newspaper. On reading the article, I discovered it was an abbreviation of *bēsu-appu*, derived from "base up," which in Japanese means an across the board raise of the wage base—surely a very useful term but one unknown to English. *Zene-suto*, is an abbreviation of "general strike," but *pan-suto* stands for "panty stocking," or what we would call "panty hose." The common witicism that the United States and England are two countries divided by a common language might better be applied to "Japanese English." It is pathetic to see the frustration of Japanese in finding that English speakers cannot recognize, much less understand, many of the English words they use. English words in Japanese have greatly strengthened the Japanese language but have not helped much in overcoming Japan's language barrier.

HARD linguistic realities are fundamentally responsible for the high linguistic barriers between Japan and the outside world, but it is surprising nonetheless that the Japanese have not done more to try to overcome them. English language teaching in the Japanese school system, as mentioned earlier, is on the whole poor and out of date. Actually it is concerned mainly with the grammatical analysis and reading of classical English texts and is aimed not at practical use so much as at preparing students to pass university entrance examinations. The reading of contemporary materials is usually slighted, and almost no effort is made to teach speaking or comprehension by ear.

The failure adequately to improve and modernize English teaching stands with the failure to improve the university system as two of the very few areas in postwar Japan in which tradition and apathy have been allowed to prevail in an otherwise much changed and very dynamic society. Clearly the Japanese leadership has not fully appreciated the importance of language skills for Japan today and the consequent need to improve the teaching of English.

There are a number of reasons for this blind spot. One is that Japan has traditionally thought of contact with other cultures as being through the written word. This was true of their early borrowing of Chinese culture, and since the opening of Japan in the 1850s they have seen themselves as needing to learn about the West through things and through written texts, but not as dependent on two way communication. It seemed adequate to import foreign knowledge through writings which could be deciphered and translated at leisure and to train a few experts for this purpose and for necessary dealings with foreigners. There even seemed an advantage in not communicating much with foreigners and in keeping them from learning much about Japan and what was in the minds of Japanese. In this way, Japan would have the advantage of operating out of sight of the foreigners, while they would be fully revealed to Japanese. Thus, the Japanese have a long tradition of learning to decipher a foreign language but not of speaking or communicating with foreigners.

Since the great majority of Japanese leaders never really mastered a foreign language, a certain contempt grew up for those who did. People who knew English well and gained some advantage from this skill were suspected of being superficial in other matters. They were in any case likely to be people who had achieved this special facility largely outside the standard Japanese educational system and were therefore probably regarded as semi-outsiders. A pejorative term developed for them—the *eigo-zukai*, or "English users."

There was also the fear—largely unspoken—that, if many Japanese learned a foreign language too well, this might impair their command of the Japanese language or at least some of their identity as Japanese. This was, of course, an irrational feeling. Dutch children can learn English and German, two closely related tongues, with no loss of their own language, and millions of Europeans master foreign languages with no worry about losing their national identity. In Japan, however, this fear has been tied up with the broader problem of national identity, which we will discuss in the next chapter, and thus it has had a large even if not clearly expressed influence on Japanese attitudes toward the teaching of foreign languages.

Since the great majority of Japanese, including the leadership, lives largely behind their linguistic walls, they have little appreciation of the drawbacks of this situation. They are not aware that Japan is as intellectually isolated as it is or that to others it sometimes appears to be a tongue-tied giant or a sinister outsider on the edges of world society. Only slowly have they begun to realize the need for others to understand Japan better and for Japanese to know more about the rest of the world. For both of these purposes a great improvement in language skills is mandatory.

This is a two way problem, involving foreigners as well as Japanese. But even assuming a great increase in the learning of Japanese by other peoples, the major effort will still have to be made by the Japanese. Because of its difficult writing system, because of its sharp differences from most of the other languages of the world, including all the more important ones, and simply because of recent history, it is most unlikely that Japanese will become one of the major international languages. Even students from developing countries who have gone to Japan to acquire technical knowledge are frequently reluctant to learn the language, because it takes such great time and effort and is of little use to them once they have returned home. Even for these foreign students in Japan, instruction by Japanese experts through English often seems the best solution to the problem.

The Japanese in recent years have greatly increased their efforts at learning English. Enthusiastic youngsters do their best to supplement their inadequate school instruction, and many go to the United States during summer vacations to study at language institutes for foreigners. The English Speaking Society is an important social group on most university campuses and usually puts on plays in English. Special English language schools have sprung up in great numbers throughout Japan, and some offer reasonably good language instruction, though many are scarcely more than money-making schemes. Business firms employ native speakers of English to teach their officers who are being sent to overseas assignments. But the real solution to the problem lies in the improvement of the vast efforts in English instruction that are already part of the regular school system. A little imagination and capital is all that is needed—neither on a scale at all comparable to the tremendous investments the Japanese have devoted to meeting many other less important needs.

The chief problem is the more than 50,000 teachers of English at present in Japanese schools, most of whom are not actually able to speak English themselves. An effective program for retraining them would be necessary and early replacement of those unable to be retrained by teachers with more adequate skills. In retraining old teachers and training new ones, Japan could afford to send many of them abroad for prolonged periods of study or to bring young native speakers of English to Japan to work at special English language institutes and perhaps to participate in the actual teaching in the schools. Thousands of young Americans or Britishers would be happy to go to Japan for these purposes at minimal salaries.

English teaching at the same time should be divorced as much as possible from university entrance examinations and focused on practical use, such as the reading of contemporary written English and on speaking English and understanding it by ear. For developing oral and aural skills, full use should be made of electronic equipment in language laboratories in schools and better language instruction by radio and television. Perhaps most important, the learning of English should start, not in the seventh grade, but at an earlier age, when children are still able to learn with ease to make new sounds and appear to be generally more capable of language learning. Formal instruction could start in the first or second grade, and television programs could be aimed at still younger children. If these measures were taken, the language barrier might be overcome within a decade, at least for the rising generation of Japanese, even if not for their elders.

Separateness and
Internationalism

38

WHILE THE language barrier is relatively easy to define and therefore perhaps to deal with, another barrier in Japan's relationship with the outside world is more amorphous, subtle, and therefore probably more difficult to overcome. In treating it I must be more intuitive and personal. The barrier I have in mind is the Japanese sense of being somehow a separate people—of being unique. The line between the "we" of the Japanese as a national group and the "they" of the rest of mankind seems to be sharper for them than for most peoples who participate much in international life. They appear to have a greater feeling of group solidarity and a correspondingly stronger sense of their difference from others.

These attitudes are not surprising. They are probably a natural product of Japan's distinctive language, its relative isolation geographically and throughout early history, and its unique position in modern times as the one major industrialized country that is not of Western cultural background or the white race—the country that does not quite fit into either the Western or Eastern worlds. It also probably derives from the emphasis throughout Japanese society on group identification. The line between those inside and outside any group has always been sharply drawn, and the biggest and today the most important Japanese group is the Japanese people themselves.

A sense of separateness is not easy to measure. Most people have no idea how their own feelings would compare with those of other peoples. Nationalism runs rampant throughout the world and quite naturally is particularly strong among new and developing nations, not very sure of their own identity. Unconscious racial and cultural arrogance and disdain for others is pronounced throughout the West. Chinese feelings of cultural superiority are monumental, deriving as they do from a three thousand year tradition. But the Japanese sense of distinctiveness—not necessarily of superiority or even of nationalism but of just being different—is itself very distinctive.

Many Japanese might be hurt or at least puzzled by this assertion. They feel themselves to be extremely international, and in some ways they are. Their schools probably teach more broadly about the world than do those of any other country. In addition to ample attention to Japanese history and culture, knowledge about the West, its history, and culture form a major part of Japanese education, and Chinese history and culture also come in for considerable attention. In contrast, the school curriculums in Western countries venture little beyond the confines of Occidental history and culture, and even in the United States, which may have developed furthest in this regard, non-Western cultures receive only very peripheral treatment in a few parts of the country. Developing countries are likely to pay some continuing attention in their educational systems to their former colonial masters but may not have developed adequately the study of their own cultural heritage and probably pay no heed to neighboring lands or other parts of the world. Japanese education does ignore vast stretches of the world, but still it is probably more international than that of any other country in its coverage in considerable depth of at least some other distant and greatly different cultural traditions.

Life in Japan also is in some ways as international as anywhere in the world. Newspapers and television give good international coverage. In fact, on average the Japanese probably receive more world news than any other people. Japanese scientists are on the frontiers of science, and their scholars are well aware of the intellectual trends of the West. World fads, styles, and fashions sweep Japan as fast and fully as anywhere. The music of the West is available in as great quantity and as high quality as in the West itself, and the art of the whole world is well known and appreciated. The cuisine of the various countries of the West, of China, and of much of the rest of the world is available in rare excellence in the cities of Japan. Japanese life styles approximate the international norms of the West.

No people have committed themselves more enthusiastically to internationalism than the Japanese or have so specifically repudiated nationalism. They have repeatedly proclaimed their devotion to the United Nations, and "international" has become the sort of word for them that "motherhood" has traditionally been for Americans. Particularly in the early postwar years, the Japanese turned away from all symbols of nationalism, such as the national flag and anthem, and avoided the word itself. Even today the flag is used much more sparingly than in most other lands, and the national anthem, the *Kimigayo*, is so little heard that small children sometimes call it the *"sumō* song," since it is played before televized bouts of *sumō* wrestling, much as "The Star-Spangled Banner" is sung before baseball or football games in the United States. The traditional word for "nationalism," *kokka-shugi*, is still little used—its composition from Chinese lexical elements meaning "country-family-ism" has a particularly outdated, "feudalistic" ring—and "patriotism" (*aikoku* "love country") is used only by extreme rightists.

One can see why Japanese would think of themselves, not as less international than others, but as more so. One need only scratch the surface, however, to discover the superficialities of their internationalism and the strong sense of separateness the Japanese still feel. Most Japanese so strongly identify themselves with their country and their fellow Japanese that they have no need for the word "patriotism" or for patriotic symbols to build up this feeling. In avoiding the word *kokka-shugi*, they have either adopted the more neutral sounding English word *nashonarizumu* or such terms as *kokumin-shugi* ("country-people-ism") or *minzoku-shugi* ("race-ism," which to me has a more sinister ring than *kokka-shugi*). Even at the height of the postwar Japanese reaction against nationalism and the authority of the state, all Japanese remained so completely nationalistic in a basic sense that no one ever dreamed of the sort of problems that arise in some other countries where there is insufficient identification of the individual with the nation.

The strength of the Japanese feeling of separateness becomes more clear-cut when one considers Japanese attitudes toward other peoples. Japanese seem to have a sharp awareness at all times of themselves as being Japanese and of others as being first of all "not Japanese." Again such attitudes are hard to measure, but the Japanese seem to feel them more strongly than do other peoples—except for persecuted minorities or simple tribal peoples. The first answer of a Japanese to the question "Who are you?" is likely to be "A Japanese."

Any person who goes abroad is probably surprised at the strength of his own nationalistic feelings, but Japanese are less able than most others to lose consciousness of their national origins even momentarily and are more likely to see themselves always, not just as representing themselves, but as somehow being exemplars of the whole Japanese nation. A Japanese who distinguishes himself in the world is much less likely to think of himself or be thought of by his friends and acquaintances as little Taro Yamamoto who made good, but as *a Japanese* who became famous. In the Olympics, with its raising of national flags and playing of national anthems, the nationalism of all participants is fanned, but at least those from the Western democracies usually feel a sense of personal achievement much more and the burden of national honor much less than do Japanese participants.

The strength of these Japanese attitudes has created special problems for those Japanese who migrate abroad. When Japan went to war with the United States in 1941, the problem became acute for the Japanese in this country—the first generation *issei* who, because of racial discrimination, had not been allowed to acquire American citizenship and their second generation *nisei* children who were Americans by birth. They could have no fuzzy mixture of loyalties, because if they were still to be Japanese they must be completely so. The great majority opted for complete identification instead with the United States. Those on the West Coast submitted meekly to grossly unfair treatment in being removed from their homes, with serious financial losses, and being incarcerated in "relocation centers." The young Japanese men of Hawaii, together with some from the "relocation centers," also formed an all *nisei* military unit, which fought for the United States with extraordinary heroism, suffering the highest rate of casualties and winning the most decorations of any American unit. Immigrants from other countries, less bound by such exclusive claims by their motherland, have found they could maintain a mix of loyalties longer. The contrast between Japanese and Chinese in the United States is particularly sharp. The Japanese, despite their racial difference from most other Americans, have lost their language and been absorbed into the mainstream of American life almost as fast as any immigrant group. On the whole, the Chinese, held more by cultural than nationalistic bonds, have maintained their language and their traditional ways of life much longer.

The Japanese sense of solidarity and exclusiveness is clearest in their attitudes toward foreigners in Japan. They take it for granted that foreigners are and always will remain foreign—that is, outsiders. The contrast with American attitudes is sharp, for Americans stand at the other end of the spectrum in taking for granted that any foreigner in the United States, no matter how outlandish he may seem, would like to become an American citizen and probably will. Japanese visitors to the United States are startled to discover that they are not treated in the way Japanese would treat foreigners but are expected to know English and the way things operate in this country. I can remember an official cultural conference between the United States and Japan in which on one side of the table sat the Americans, including American residents in Japan, Americans of Japanese origin, and even one Japanese resident of the United States, while on the other side sat only Japanese residents of Japan.

The foreigner in Japan, so long as he is not thought to be a permanent immigrant, is treated very politely, but always as an outsider. If he speaks any Japanese at all, no matter how badly, he is praised for this remarkable accomplishment, as though he were an idiot child who suddenly showed a streak of intelligence. If he is knowledgeable about Japan, he may be asked deferentially his opinions and told he knows more than they do themselves, but his opinions are regarded always as those of an outsider, not an insider.

In a sense, all this makes the foreigner's position easy in Japan. He is never in doubt about his own identity—he is a foreigner, no matter how long he lives in Japan or how deeply he may be involved in its life. For a person like myself, born and raised in Japan and thereafter always concerned in its study, this attitude has proved an aid to me in keeping clear my own American identity. It was particularly helpful in the years of confrontation and war between the United States and Japan, for it precluded any possible emotional conflict.

Many long-time foreign residents of Japan, however, find it infuriating to be always regarded as *gaijin*, or outsiders. In my youth shortly after World War I, the term was the fuller *gaikokujin*, "outside-country-person," but Westerners were usually called *seiyōjin* "West-sea person," and the pejoratives for them of *ijin*, "strange people," and *ketō*, "hairy barbarian," were not unknown. But, whatever the term, the foreigner was almost always treated courteously. Even in the hypernationalistic and anti-Western 1930s, he was never in danger from anyone, except perhaps

the overly zealous police. But he was always an "outside person." Even
the few who became Japanese citizens through marriage or naturalization
were not really accepted as such by other Japanese.

Other East Asians in Japan are not quite as much outsiders as are Westerners and people from the other parts of the world. In fact the word
gaijin actually is not much used for them. They are called simply
Koreans, or Chinese, or Taiwanese. But Japanese attitudes toward them
illustrate my point even better. Most Koreans and Chinese in Japan are
permanent residents, many of them having been born there and speaking
no other language but Japanese. Visually and often in their living habits
they cannot be distinguished from Japanese. But the Japanese do their
best to keep them separate, making it difficult for them to acquire Japanese citizenship and commonly discriminating against them. Intermarriage is rare and is looked down upon. Few successfully pass, not the color
line, but the national consciousness line. I have known one successful
bureaucrat of recent Chinese origin, and there are a few well-known baseball stars of Taiwanese or Korean origin, but most are still held at arm's
length outside of Japanese society.

A tragic incident in August 1974 typified the situation. A young man of
Korean origin who, though born in Japan and speaking no Korean, had
been denied acceptance into Japanese society and therefore was confused
as to his own identity, tried to shoot the South Korean president and
killed the president's wife instead. This caused an international stir, but
the real culprit was a Japanese society that refuses to accept young men
like him. There is little wonder that the 600,000 persons of Korean origin
living in Japan but denied full membership in Japanese society continue
to constitute a difficult "Korean problem" for Japan.

I recall an incident which well illustrates the distinction the Japanese
feel between themselves and other peoples. A Japanese leader in Fukuoka
in Kyushu was horrified to learn that the next American consul in his city
was to be a man of Japanese ancestry. When it was explained to him that
this was considered normal in the United States and that the American
ambassador to Poland, for example, was a man of Polish origin, he ex-
ploded in indignation, saying that if we thought that this was the same
sort of situation, then we did not know anything about Japan. In actuality,
he proved wrong, and the new consul was well received and very successful, but the man's attitude shows how different the Japanese feel

themselves to be. In fact, they almost glory in the thought that they are
somehow unique.

A SENSE of national distinctiveness is usually associated with attitudes
of superiority and contempt for others, but this is not necessarily the situation in Japan. At times in the past the Japanese have asserted their superiority, as when in late Tokugawa times they placed much emphasis on the
divine descent of the imperial line and on Japan as being "the land of the
gods" or again, in the period leading up to World War II, when some of
them saw Japan as the champion and liberator of Asia and the chastizer
of a corrupt West. A mystical term much used at that time but actually
drawn from ancient Chinese philosophy was *hakkō ichiu*, "the eight
corners of the world under one roof," which signified vaguely a Japanese
moral predominance over the world. Such occasional bursts of asser-
tiveness of national superiority, however, are less surprising than the
Japanese readiness at most times to admit the superiority of at least
some other country or countries.

The Japanese sense of differentness has never precluded the use of
foreign models and the tacit admission through their use of the superiority of a foreign country, at least in some respects. China was this model
throughout most of Japanese history, but in modern times it has been the
leading countries of the West. Consciousness of the model and the degree
of borrowing from it has tended to vary from time to time. In fact, one
can discern a pendulum-like swing—a rush of learning followed by a
period of assimilation and reassertion of traditional characteristics. In
modern times, we have seen the enthusiasm for almost everything Western in the early Meiji period, followed by a more nationalistic phase
starting in the 1880s, followed in turn by a new craze for Western things
in the early years after World War I and then by the militarist reaction of
the 1930s, and finally the great new surge of foreign influences under the
American occupation, which has been giving way in recent years to a
gradual reassertion of some of the more traditional Japanese values.

These pendulum-like swings may be a part of a broader pattern of history, affecting other non-Western countries which have undergone influences from the West in modern times, and they may be discernible in
comparable situations in earlier history. In the case of Japan, however,

the swings seem to be decreasing. Despite the particularly heavy flood of innovations from abroad produced by the unusual features of the postwar situation—the total defeat of Japan and the presence of a foreign army of occupation—the swing back has been very mild. Perhaps Japan, having caught up with the West, is beginning to get beyond these emotional swings between attraction to and rejection of a foreign model.

The conscious use in Japan of foreign models in the past, however, has given rise to the theory that the Japanese suffer more from an inferiority complex than from a superiority complex. The two, though seemingly antithetical, actually do not seem to be very far apart. Traditionally the most blatant assertions of national superiority have usually been associated with obvious fears of inferiority. The early stirrings of nationalism in North Europe were probably produced in part by a sense of historical and cultural inferiority to the older lands of the Mediterranean area. Early American "spread-eagle" nationalism was obviously linked with the country's position as a raw and still weak frontier of the Western world. Nationalism throughout the non-Western nations seems clearly tied up with the recent colonialism or semi-colonialism of these lands. In Japan, too, the early expressions of nationalism were largely in reaction to a Japanese sense of inferiority to China. China might be huge, old, and the traditional home of civilization and the Confucian sages, but only Japan could be "the land of the gods." Modern nationalism in Japan has been largely couched in terms of catching up with the West and then surpassing it. But, to return to the theory of a Japanese inferiority complex, I doubt that they have more of one than do most other peoples, and in any case the concept is a little too slippery to be of much use.

The traditional consciousness of cultural borrowings from China and of catching up with the West in modern times, however, has helped make the Japanese very self-conscious in their dealings with foreigners. Self-consciousness also grows quite readily out of the nature of traditional Japanese society, in which conformity to the group and the acceptance of the judgment of others have taken precedence over individualism. Modern Japan has had to be self-conscious about measuring up to Western norms, and the individual Japanese has always been keenly sensitive to what other people, especially Westerners, might think of them. The opinions of foreigners, most too ignorant about Japan to have an opinion worth knowing, are constantly sought by newspapermen or private citizens. One is reminded of self-conscious American newspapermen not so long ago asking visiting Britishers as they descended the gangplank in New York what they thought about American women. Japanese going abroad, or taking up a new sport, or engaging in some other new activity are likely to be meticulous about having the correct garb and displaying the approved style in the activity, whether it be golf, tennis, or cocktail sipping. Their very insistence on appearing to do things right often gets in the way of their doing them well. Certainly their self-consciousness is no aid in learning to speak foreign languages, which requires a certain degree of reckless abandon rather than tongue-tied perfectionism. Their self-consciousness also is likely to make others feel awkward and thus become an added barrier in their dealings with them.

The Japanese in modern times have also had a special anxiety which Westerners have not had, though it has been common in much of the non-Western world. This is the fear that Japan will lose its identity in the flood of influences from the West. The Meiji Japanese were forced to conform to Western concepts of an international system and to borrow Western technology and institutions in order to protect themselves. For most of the last century the Japanese have been trying to catch up with Western technical skills and in the process have been deeply influenced by Western culture in many other ways. The first generation of modernizers in the Meiji period were so securely anchored in their own Tokugawa upbringing as to have had no fears that they would lose their Japaneseness, but the products of the new and largely Western educational system did have doubts. We see them already in literary figures of the turn of the century like Natsume Soseki, and they have grown ever since. The popular novelist Mishima, who killed himself in a spectacular *harakiri* in 1970, was still seeking the "true Japan." Temporary reassertions of traditional Japanese ways and values have been swamped in the next surge of catching up with the West, which then in turn would produce increased doubts as to whether Japan was still really Japan.

The early 1970s saw a new cresting of these fears. A spate of books and journal articles appeared asking what it meant to be a Japanese and what was Japan's distinctive role in the world. The Japanese called it the *Nihonjin-ron*, which might be translated "the debate over being Japanese." Fear that the Japanese might further lose their Japaneseness is probably one of the major, though unspoken, reasons why the Japanese have not really tried to reform the teaching of English and why some people advocate that foreign languages should be taught less in Japan rather than more. Their argument is that a few should be taught English better but that most Japanese should be spared the time and effort that now goes into learning it inadequately. Hidden in the argument is the feeling that this would also spare them the corrupting influence of a foreign language which might further erode their Japaneseness.

One can comprehend Japanese anxieties without agreeing with them. If one defines all modern technology as being culturally Western, then very little remains in Japan that has not been affected by it. But there is very little in the West too that has not been influenced by modern technology. We are almost as far from our eighteenth century forebears as the Japanese are from theirs. The industrial revolution and modern technology originated in the West, to be sure, but like technological advances throughout history they inevitably belong to all people. The spread of agriculture and the use of bronze and iron did not make all cultures part of the ones where these innovations started. The spread of Chinese inventions like paper, printing, gunpowder, and porcelain did not make other lands culturally Chinese. Modern technology and industrial society belong as much to the Japanese as to the peoples of the West. Looking back from our present historical vantage point, the Japanese can be seen to have had even the steam engine more than half as long as British or Americans. The time gap in later technological innovations becomes less and less, until it finally vanishes in our own day. With a still longer view of this history in the future, the Western lead in modern technology will appear only a minor detail.

If one does not identify modern technology with Western culture, then the picture looks very different. Among the leading cultural traits of the West are Christianity and individualism, but less than 1 percent of the Japanese have embraced Christianity, and their attitude toward individualism separates them sharply from Western peoples. On the other hand, they share with the West many institutions and values—modern education, mass democracy, mass media, mass sports, and the like—that are not features of traditional Western culture but are typical modern developments in keeping with modern technology. The Japanese have given to these modern institutions and values their own special flavor. These institutions belong to them as much as they do to the rest of us. Young Japanese seem to sense this and therefore to be less concerned with the danger of losing their Japanese identity. These attitudes are changing rapidly, almost year by year. As a result, fears about Japan becoming West-

ernized or losing its identity are mainly problems for the older generation and as such will inevitably fade away. In fact, a much more serious
problem for the Japanese in the contemporary world of complex and intimate international relationships is that they still feel too Japanese, not
that they are not Japanese enough.

THE JAPANESE concept of their difference from other peoples is not
so much a matter of superiority, that is, of quality, but a difference in kind.
They see themselves as being different not because they are better or
worse than others but simply because they are different. In essence it is a
deeply racist concept, almost as though Japanese were a different species
of animal from the rest of humanity. Conditions as they existed only a
little over a century ago lent credence to this feeling. All the people in the
world who spoke the distinctive Japanese language and lived in the distinctive Japanese way were to be found in the sharply drawn and isolated
Japanese national unit, and, except for a handful of Ainu and still fewer
Chinese, Korean, and Dutch traders, there were no other people of any
sort in Japan. Even up to World War II the average Japanese was not
likely to have ever had contacts of any significance with a foreigner. Contemporary conditions, however, are far different. The Japanese way of
life is no longer so very distinctive. Foreigners of all sorts stream through
Japan, and Japanese wander the globe. People of Japanese origin have
fitted into foreign societies, and when their descendants visit Japan,
speaking only broken Japanese or none at all, they have had to be
regarded as outsiders. Some have even become senators or congressmen
in the United States or Brazil. The old concept certainly has been
shaken, but it is not gone completely.

Americans often feel that racism is particularly an American problem.
Naturally it is a more evident problem in countries where different races
live together, but racism is a worldwide attitude and is perhaps strongest
in areas where, because of little contact with other races, it has neither
been brought to the surface or challenged. Certainly in East Asia, the part
of the world I have studied most, racist attitudes run strong—in my judgment far stronger than in the United States. When the Japanese first
came into frequent contact with Caucasians in the nineteenth century,
they found them strange and revolting. Their big noses and curious col-
oring—blue eyes and red hair—made them seem more like mythical

goblins than human beings, and they were distressingly smelly because of their richer diet of animal fats and their heavy woolen clothing. *Bata-kusai*, meaning "stinking of butter," once was a common pejorative for Western. Such attitudes have long since been outgrown, and the problem of smell has probably been alleviated by the richer Japanese diet and the increase in bathing and dry cleaning in the West. The sense of racial difference, however, still remains strong among the Japanese. In the many cases of interracial marriages I have known between Japanese and Caucasians, I cannot think of one in which, if there were family opposition, it was not stronger, or at least as strong, from the Japanese side compared to the Western.

Japanese attitudes toward the black race are far worse. Having had almost no contact with blacks before the coming of the American army of occupation, the Japanese still tend to view them with some wonderment and revulsion. During the racial troubles of the late 1960s in the United States, the Japanese were appalled by the American race problem. Some younger Japanese of the left could sympathize intellectually with the blacks, but the basic Japanese reaction, unlike that of the developing world, was one of commiseration with the whites, with whom they could more easily identify. It was not the injustices to blacks in the situation in the United States that struck them as much as the difficulty of the problems the whites faced.

The racist attitude of East Asians is clearest in their treatment of children of mixed racial parentage. In Korea and Vietnam the abandoned offspring of American soldiers and native women, usually of low class, have usually been rejected by the local society or at least subjected to discrimination. The situation has been worse for the half-blacks than for the half-whites. The best hope of either group has usually been to find adoption into so-called racist America. Somewhat the same situation existed in early postwar Japan. A worthy Japanese lady who was much praised for founding an orphanage for such children could only hold out the hope that they might in time find a life for themselves on the frontiers of civilization in the Amazon. As these children of mixed race grew up, however, some of them, with their half-Western looks, became stars in show business. And a few mixed children of good families have been accepted into normal Japanese society and have had successful careers. But many mixed children have found it more comfortable to emigrate if they could, most frequently to the United States.

The strong racist feelings of the Japanese and other East Asians apply to other Asians, such as the racially close Southeast Asians and, more strongly, to the very different Indians and Middle Easterners. Racist feelings—or at least something very akin to them—also exist between the racially very similar peoples of East Asia. Most Japanese, Koreans, and Chinese view marriage with each other with almost as much distaste as marriage with a Caucasian. In fact, more Japanese parents today would probably accept an American son-in-law with better grace than a Chinese or Korean.

The contrast is marked with the West, where international intermarriages have always been common, particularly among the aristocracy. Class was more important than nationality. The Queen of England, for example, is German in origin, even though the family name has been changed in a fit of nationalism from Hanover to Windsor and that of her consort from Battenberg to Mountbatten. Kaiser Wilhelm and his cousin Nicholas, the last of the czars, were both grandchildren of Queen Victoria and incidentally talked English together. East Asia had no comparable tradition of international mixing of the aristocracy. Insofar as intermarriages occurred in premodern times, they were mostly between sailors or pirates and the social scum of port cities.

ASIDE from their racial feelings, the Japanese with their emphasis on hierarchy within their own society, tend to think of countries in a hierarchical order. All people do this to some extent, but the Japanese more frequently and more consciously than most. Just as the word *Nippon-ichi*, "the first in Japan," is constantly on Japanese lips, so also is *sekai-ichi*, "the first in the world." Although, now that they feel they have caught up with the West, they are not as concerned as they once were over national rankings, they do remain surprisingly conscious of their relative world standing in a number of statistical categories. They are fully aware that they are third in the world in GNP, first together with Sweden in longevity, first in the production of ships, second or third in the production of some other things, and fifteenth, let us say, in per capita income. (A number of small affluent countries like those of Scandinavia, Switzerland, Iceland, and New Zealand give them a lower rank than one might expect.)

The Japanese are constantly ranking other countries too in terms of how much they are liked or disliked by Japanese. This is an indoor sport unknown elsewhere but a regular feature of Japanese public opinion polls. In these the distant countries of the West tend to come out on top on the favorable side and Japan's near neighbors on top on the unfavorable side. Because of the broad relationship with the United States, it appears high in the liked column—it was highest for a long time—but also fairly high on the disliked side too. The clear winner of this international popularity contest in recent years has been Switzerland, which has the advantage of being little known by Japanese but of seeming somehow to embody the ideal of world peace. England and France and to some extent Germany, remembered as being models for Japan in modern times, also get reasonably good ratings.

The prize for most disliked country is usually fought out between North Korea, South Korea, and the Soviet Union, which receive few if any favorable votes. China ranks relatively high among liked countries but also usually draws a considerable negative vote. India in the years of Nehru's glory appeared modestly among liked countries—again as a symbol of peace—but in recent years it has been more likely to appear, if at all, in the negative column, because Japanese tend to look on India as very alien and somewhat repugnant. Most other countries in the world are too little in the Japanese consciousness to draw significant favorable or critical notice.

On the whole, thus, the Japanese show strong preferences for the Western democracies over the Communist states or the various countries of the non-Western world. An unfavorable comparison of Japan with Western nations is more likely to be accepted by Japanese without resentment than a favorable comparison with non-Western lands. They feel demeaned that anyone would even make the comparison with such, to them, backward countries. These attitudes are not surprising in light of the West's dominance in modern times and Japan's development of an industrial and democratic society that closely parallels that of the West. But there is at the same time some uneasiness among many Japanese as to whether Japan really belongs in the "first world" or will be accepted by the other members as belonging. There is the fear of a racial or at least cultural blackball.

Despite the usual preference for the West, the periodic swing back of the pendulum toward traditional values in Japan has been accompanied each time by a rise of pan-Asian feelings. Around the turn of the century

Okakura, the philosopher–art historian, declared sententiously and quite inaccurately that "Asia is one." In the 1930s the militarists claimed to be liberating Asia from Western corruption and exploitation. The upsurge in the 1970s of the *Nihonjin-ron*, the search for Japaneseness, was accompanied by much talk about Asian roots and cultural solidarity. Actually these pan-Asian sentiments were never supported by much substance. The pan-Asian sentiments of the Japanese themselves were felt largely for Chinese and applied little to other Asians. And the other Asians, particularly the Chinese, usually looked on the Japanese with distrust or open hostility. They may themselves have had pan-Asian sentiments, but if so these were not at all like those in Japanese minds. Thus the periodic flare-up of pan-Asian feelings in Japan has had little positive content and has been more a negative reaction against the West.

POPULAR attitudes in Japan toward foreign countries are most fully developed with regard to the United States, China, the Soviet Union, and Korea. Many Japanese are quite knowledgeable about some of the other leading Western countries, particularly the United Kingdom, France, Germany, Australia, and Canada, but the United States looms so large in the popular imagination that all others tend to be submerged in its popular image. Any Westerner in Japan is almost automatically assumed to be an American unless he can prove the contrary—a situation that some find intensely irritating. Because of considerable Japanese emigration to and huge economic contacts with Brazil, some Japanese know something about that country, but otherwise Latin America figures little in the popular imagination. Some non-Western countries, particularly those of Southeast Asia, have large economic relations with Japan, and others are much in the world news, but even these stir little popular interest, and the whole non-Western world, except for China and Korea, exists merely on the fringes of the Japanese consciousness.

Korea in language, in some underlying cultural traits, and in its modern institutions as a former Japanese colony, is the country most like Japan, but there is no feeling of closeness and warmth between Japanese and Koreans. The latter, remembering Japan's past colonial exploitation of them, nurture a hatred for Japan, which is passed on to the next generation through the educational system. These deep resentments, however, are paralleled by unspoken admiration. Koreans pay Japan the ultimate compliment of using it as a model. The Japanese for their part tend to be contemptuous of Koreans. They think of Korea as a backward country they once ruled and Koreans as a troublesome minority in Japan. Koreans in Japan do have more than their share of crime and dubious business practices, but this is only natural for a new, underprivileged group inserted at the bottom of society and denied full membership in it. Korea is to Japanese a problem—a place where political instability and military tensions might threaten Japan's own security, and the source of a minority group in Japan which, because the Japanese have refused to accept it fully, has been turned into a semi-permanent irritant. Fortunately, however, younger people in both countries are losing the old attitudes and are showing themselves to be ready for friendlier relations between these two geographically and culturally close countries.

The Soviet Union is the one country for which the Japanese have a traditional hostility. It started with rivalries with czarist Russia in the late eighteenth century over the northern islands of Hokkaido, Sakhalin, and the Kuriles. The Japanese border with Russia is the only one ill defined enough to have produced for Japan the traditional sort of border rivalry, and the four disputed northern islands are still a bone of contention. These feelings of hostility over disputed territory were greatly strengthened by the Russo-Japanese War of 1904–05 and again at the end of World War II, when a defeated Japan sought Soviet aid in arranging a surrender, and Moscow replied by invading Manchuria. The Japanese believe that the Russians allowed about a third of their Japanese prisoners to die after the war in prison camps in Siberia, and for four years after the end of the occupation a Soviet veto did keep Japan out of the United Nations.

The Soviet Union to all but a few pro-Soviet Communists is seen as a land which has most of the undesirable features of the West and few of its attractive qualities. At the same time, Japanese are very much aware of the Soviet Union's strength, and they are intrigued by the possibility of the exploitation of Siberian natural resources in Japan's behalf. They are determined to have correct relations with the Soviet Union, keeping these as much as possible in balance with their relations with China, for which they have much warmer sentiments.

Popular Japanese attitudes toward China are intense and extremely complex. There is a strong sense of admiration and closeness, deriving from the long use of China as a model for Japan. The Japanese are much aware of the Chinese roots of their culture in the writing system, their vocabulary, their arts, and many of their traditional values. China is their Greece and Rome. Before the war they were fond of describing their relationship with China as being one of *dōbun-dōshu*, "the same culture and same race." China has never been seen as constituting any sort of menace to Japan, nor do Japanese today have any fear of it. But they do tend to overestimate the importance of trade with China, and all of them feel that it is absolutely essential that Japan should be on friendly terms with this close neighbor which happens to be the largest of all countries.

Most Japanese sentiments about China reflect a memory of things past, but contemporary China also has a fascination, as it does for so many people in the world. The Japanese see China as having been boldly independent where they themselves have been too subservient in their relationship with the United States. They see the Chinese as remaining true to their Asian roots where Japanese have allowed them to wither. This concept is a little curious, since, despite obvious cultural continuities, communism has amounted to a complete repudiation of many if not most traditional Chinese values, but it remains nonetheless a common attitude in Japan. On top of this, Japanese ever since the war have felt a sense of guilt toward Chinese for having despoiled their country and a feeling that somehow Japan must make amends to China for these transgressions of the past.

These various attitudes have produced a remarkable deference on the part of Japanese toward China. They feel they must retain Chinese good will at all costs. They avoid criticism of China and accept meekly Chinese criticism of Japan, no matter how harsh or unfair. Trade missions and opposition politicians sign their names to joint statements condemning Japanese policy. Newspapers avoid printing things that would offend China, claiming that otherwise they would not be allowed to report from China. There are signs in the late 1970s of Japanese comments about China becoming franker and bolder, but there is still the tendency to consider any criticism of China as being bigoted or at least unwise.

There is another side to the picture, however, which makes it more complex. For one thing, the Chinese have never reciprocated the warm feelings of the Japanese, viewing them with distrust and more than a little contempt. The Japanese nostalgia for China has been a classic case of unrequited love. Moreover, Japan and China in fact were culturally very different countries already in the early nineteenth century, and since then they have followed quite different courses of development, drifting even farther apart. Thus the Japanese feeling of cultural closeness to China is not based on much reality. Japanese, especially younger ones, cannot imagine themselves living under the prevailing conditions of life in China, which when actually encountered by Japanese prove extremely distasteful to them. Trade with China is also not likely to loom large in Japan, at least so long as China remains an autarkic Communist country. Nor for that matter are Japan and China likely to become serious economic rivals. Their economies operate on such different planes as not to come into much competition with each other.

Japan, moreover, maintains strong economic ties with Taiwan, and the native five sixths of the island's population, in sharp contrast with the Koreans, have relatively warm feelings toward their former colonial masters, to which the Japanese naturally respond. Perhaps the Taiwanese attitude is a subtle way of showing opposition to the Nationalist government of mainlanders that rules over them. In any case, Taiwan stands as something of a barrier to the development of a close Japanese-Chinese relationship—just as it does in American-Chinese relations. Japan will do its best to maintain correct and formally amicable relations with China, but it is not likely to become as important to Japan, either in a friendly or hostile way, as many people have imagined.

Popular attitudes toward the United States are even more complex than toward China. I have already discussed them quite fully in earlier parts of this book and need only briefly review them here. Up until the early twentieth century, the United States was regarded as the most generous and friendly of the Western nations that Japanese were using as models. Thereafter it became Japan's chief strategic rival, though economic and cultural relations with it remained larger than with any other country. The postwar occupation involved the United States intimately in all aspects of Japanese life, making it Japan's model *par excellence* but also creating the conflict over alignment or neutrality that has been the central theme of political controversy ever since. Japanese attitudes toward the United States show much of the love-hate syndrome. It is easy to interpret the intellectual debate in Japan and the statements of opposition politicians as indicating a deep anti-Americanism in Japan, and in a sense this is correct. At the same time, there is a much stronger pro-American sentiment, not just on the part of the "establishment" but also at a grass-roots level.

Criticism of the United States is felt to be easy because it is in a sense within the family. As Japanese sometimes point out, there is no use in criticizing the Soviet Union or China, but it is worthwhile with the United States, since more can be expected of it. Insofar as Japanese still seek outside models, it is largely to the United States they look. They take for granted a huge continued flow of American cultural influences and now a considerable reverse flow from Japan to America. They feel themselves familiar with American life from having seen many American films and television programs. Advertisements mention that a product is popular, not in London and certainly not in Moscow or Peking, but in New York. Americans are the foreigners Japanese know best and feel most at home with. When they go abroad, the United States is their most common target. In 1973 some 650,000 Japanese visited the United States, which was almost twice the number for any other land, including even nearby Taiwan, while American visitors to Japan were at least five times as numerous as those from any other country. Japanese frequently state that they feel more at home in the United States than in Europe, to say nothing of the rest of the world. It would not occur to them in this context even to mention countries like Indonesia, India, Egypt or the Soviet Union, which are obviously vastly more foreign to them. If the Japanese have achieved a sense of true fellow feeling with any other people in the world, it is with Americans.

FOR A PEOPLE who had virtually no outside contacts only a little over a century ago, the Japanese have developed extraordinarily diverse and close international relations with most of the world. But if we look at them as a nation that is entirely dependent for survival on the continuation of world peace and a growing global trade, then their contacts seem thin and inadequate. They have developed enough skills to handle specific economic and other relations with the outside world but not to make a contribution to the solving of world problems that is commensurate with their size and skills. Most other peoples would see the Japanese as being a silent participant in the world order others have fashioned, contributing perhaps in a negative way by themselves eschewing military power but not contributing much positively. In fact, their high economic growth rates, combined with their seeming secretiveness and insensibility to others, make them appear to many people as potentially disruptive to world trade and world order rather than as contributing to a smoothly operating world system.

Japan in its own interest needs to do better. The world faces grave problems, ranging from technical matters of global ecology and resources to complex problems of world trade and international tensions. Japan, with its great potentialities, should be attempting to maximize its contribution to the solution of these problems. To do this, Japanese would have to have not only greater skills in language communication on the specific problems but also a much stronger sense of mutual trust and cooperation between themselves and others. Without a greater sense of fellow feeling on the part of Japanese for other peoples and, perhaps more difficult, of other peoples for the Japanese, there may not be enough mutual trust and understanding to permit the solution of these grave problems mankind faces.

The needs go much deeper than the enthusiasm for the United Nations and the formal "internationalism" that the Japanese have espoused. They must overcome their sense of separateness and, to put it bluntly, show a greater readiness to join the human race. They must really identify themselves with the rest of the world and feel a part of it. Foreign language skills are not needed just by experts for specific negotiations but by all Japanese in order to help them establish contacts with others and develop these feelings. That is why the problem of English teaching in Japan concerns *all* Japanese, not just the expert few. Of course, such problems are not exclusively Japanese. All peoples need to develop a truly international spirit. But the need is greatest for those who are most precariously dependent on the outside world and those who because of their strength and skills are the potential shapers of the future. Japan ranks at or near the top in both categories.

It is fortunate that the Japanese government and people in the 1970s have both shown a growing awareness of this problem. Japan has increased its efforts in international cooperation and has begun to take more positive stands in international debate. The government established the Japan Foundation in 1972 to further cultural contacts with the outside world, particularly foreign understanding of Japan. The United Nations University was induced to make its headquarters in Japan, though this institution probably illustrates better, not accomplishments, but the distance yet to be traversed.

The United Nations University, as a conglomeration of research institutes throughout the world, is more a symbol of internationalism than an effective organ for internationalizing Japanese. Its creation still leaves Japanese universities probably the least international in the world. The national universities, which are the cream of the system, cannot by law employ foreigners as regular professors. Foreign professors, in fact, can be found only in small numbers in a few peripheral institutions largely of Christian missionary background, and even then mostly as teachers of English. Except for a handful of special programs set up in a few private universities, there are virtually no foreign students at any Japanese universities. Statistics reveal a few, but on examination these prove to be mostly Koreans and Chinese permanently resident in Japan and speaking Japanese as their mother tongue. In most other countries such people would not be considered foreigners. Even Japanese who have not gone through the regular Japanese high schools but have studied abroad are either not allowed into Japanese universities or find it next to impossible to pass the entrance examinations. They are virtually forced to study abroad and are then likely to be excluded as educational outsiders from a normal career in Japan. Thus, in a Japan desperately in need of becoming more international, everything seems organized to keep universities as little international as possible and Japanese students confined to a narrowly national educational system.

Japan obviously has much to overcome in its search for internationalism, but perhaps I have made the picture too dark. I have been writing basically about the older generation and their problems. Young Japanese are often quite different. They seem almost a new breed, unconsciously contradicting many of the old stereotypes. They are largely free of the old prejudices and fears. What improvement in foreign language skills there has been has resulted perhaps as much from their enthusiasm for learning English as from improved teaching. They are avid for experiencing life abroad. They approach other peoples with easy openness. It is refreshing to see Japanese teenagers come for summer visits to the United States and fit in, despite their linguistic disabilities, with no apparent sense of strangeness or self-consciousness. They are entirely ready to be members of an international society of shared interests and problems and seem no more separate or self-conscious than any other people in the world. It could be pointed out that, while young Japanese start out this way, they eventually are shoved back into the more self-conscious Japanese mold. But perhaps youth will eventually crack the mold. In any case, the solution of Japan's problem of shifting from an overly strong feeling of separateness to a true sense of internationalism is likely to be achieved more by a change of generations than by reforms of the system.

The
Future

39

![signature mark]

A NY VIEW into the future depends basically on the accuracy of one's understanding of the past. If past trends have been correctly identified, then one can assume some continuity of these trends into the future. But not as straight line developments. Some trends contradict others, and all are likely to curve upwards or downwards depending on the situation. Moreover the one certainty, we know from the past, is that many entirely unpredictable things will happen, perhaps drastically changing these trends. The future most certainly is not clear, but peering ahead into its haze, one can discern certain great problem areas.

One such area lies in the field of natural disasters, of which Japan has always had its full share. The terrible Tokyo earthquake and fire of 1923 etched itself deeply into the Japanese consciousness. With much greater concentrations of population now, high rise buildings, elevated roads and railways, subways, and virtual underground cities, some lying below sea level, great earthquakes or even storms might be far more destructive than before. The Japanese nervousness on this score was illustrated by the great popularity in the early 1970s of a best seller named simply *The Sinking of Japan*, which described in lurid detail the swallowing up of the whole country by the Pacific Ocean. But natural catastrophes of sufficient magnitude to affect Japan's future seem very improbable and far less threatening than a variety of possible man-made disasters.

A major problem area for all countries is the internal organization of society, particularly a large one like Japan. Modern industrial society is so extremely complicated to operate that it shows signs of becoming

unmanageable and breaking down from the weight of its own intrica-
cies. Modern democracies, which require the selection of leadership
and decisions on vastly difficult problems by huge masses of people, are
particularly cumbersome and difficult to operate, and these difficulties
raise questions as to their ultimate governability under modern conditions. More authoritarian regimes, which place the control of society and
the economy in the hands of a few, usually prove even more inefficient.
In this particular problem area, however, Japan seems relatively well
off—possibly the best off of all the larger countries. As we have seen, it is
handling this sort of problem quite well. Possibly growing individualism
and affluence will cut into some of its present skills. An aging labor force
and growing labor unrest may reduce some of its present efficiency. But,
on the whole, the Japanese can look ahead with some confidence to
problems of this sort.

A third great problem area concerns world ecology and global
resources. Here all countries ultimately face the same difficulties, but
some are more immediately threatened than others. Japan may well be
the most threatened among the larger countries. Population growth,
however, is not a serious part of the problem, as it is in many lands.
Japan's population is growing at only a little over 1 percent a year and is
predicted to level off completely at about 135 million around the year
2,000. This rate of increase is insignificant compared to Japan's rate of
economic growth, though Japan's problems of ecology and resources
would naturally be far easier to solve if its population were not already as
large as it is. Even without population growth these problems are serious
enough for Japan. At first the Japanese were slow to recognize them, but
recently they have responded to them with vigor and show signs of bringing them under control within Japan. But the problems of global pollution
and worldwide resources cannot be solved by the Japanese alone. These
depend on the willingness of the various peoples of the world to cooperate
in their solution and on international skills in achieving this goal.

This leads us to the fourth great problem area, which is international
cooperation not only about world ecology and resources but also about
world trade and world peace. These matters are all absolutely crucial for
Japan. Other nations might survive widespread disorders and prolonged
warfare short of a nuclear Armageddon, but probably not Japan. Others
might be little damaged or at least survive a prolonged decline of world
trade or failure of it to grow, but again not Japan. International cooper-

ation depends on the attitude of other peoples, but this is an area in which the Japanese themselves have not performed as well as they should. They are becoming aware of this failure, but may not realize that the root cause is their own sense of separateness and uniqueness. Insofar as the questions about Japan's future lie in the hands of the Japanese themselves, this is the biggest of the problems they face. My personal guess, based on the attitudes of young Japanese, is that over the long run they will meet the challenge well and that, if catastrophe does come to Japan, it will at least not be of their own making.

The Japanese in their self-consciousness keep asking themselves what is Japan's role in the modern world. It is probably not a healthy sign that they have such a concern for finding a unique role for themselves, and the answer they commonly come up with is certainly neither accurate nor healthy. Since they see Japan as the one "Eastern" country that has fully industrialized itself to become like the industrial West, they frequently imagine that Japan should be the interpreter between East and West. But even if there is a West—a rather doubtful proposition—there is most certainly no single East. In any case, Japan, with its difficulties in being understood by the countries of both East and West, is hardly cut out for the role of interpreter between the two. Perhaps Japan does serve in this capacity for a few small areas that are somewhat like it, such as the pieces of its former empire in South Korea and Taiwan, but scarcely for areas like Africa, the Middle East, India, and even Southeast Asia, which have more understanding of at least parts of the West than they do of Japan and with which the Japanese have less intimate relations than do some Western countries.

There are, however, potential roles for Japan of great significance over and above its position simply as one of the larger and stronger national units. As the one great and wealthy country that has renounced war and maintains only a very modest Self-Defense Force, Japan may help all nations find their way past the crushing burdens of military rivalries to a more peaceful and prosperous age.

Toward non-Western peoples the Japanese can also play a very significant role of inspiration in a number of ways, as they have at times in the past. Asian nationalism in the early years of this century was to a large extent triggered by the Japanese ability to stand up to the nations of the West in military power and, more specifically, to defeat the Russians. More recently the Japanese achievement of affluence has shown that economic strength and wealth need not be limited to the Western world. The even more remarkable Japanese achievement in developing a fully open, democratic society and a successful parliamentary system could have an even greater impact, if it were better known and understood abroad, but so far it has had little influence beyond the democratic elements in South Korea and Taiwan. The success of the Japanese in adopting so much from Western culture while maintaining their own strong cultural traditions and thus producing a dynamic cultural mix which is entirely their own, again if comprehended by others, could both comfort and inspire non-Western peoples, who fear that in becoming modernized they will lose their cultural identity.

For the industrialized countries, Japan also has a special role. As the only industrialized power stemming from a non-Western cultural background, it has brought to the solution of the problems of industrial, urban life and mass democracy attitudes and skills quite distinct from those the others have. We have already seen the vast impact of Japanese artistic skills and esthetic concepts on the United States and, to a lesser extent, on some other Western lands. A comparable influence could come in time in these other fields, and Japan, instead of being just a follower and borrower, might make a greater proportionate contribution to the solutions of the problems of modern times than its mere size might warrant.

The Japanese might also lead the way toward the development of the global fellow feeling that mankind needs for survival. This book has emphasized their traditional isolation and their continuing sense of separateness. They do appear at present further from the goal than are some other peoples. At the same time, however, they have probably made greater progress from their starting point a century and a half ago. It has been a long uphill road for them against great language difficulties and a deeply ingrained sense of separateness. If now they clearly see the problem they face, they could well come from behind to win the race—to put it in the competitive imagery in which they themselves might think, but which, it is to be hoped, will someday seem outdated. The relationship Japan has already developed with the United States and to a lesser extent with the other Western industrialized nations is the first example in world history of broad and deep cooperation on the basis of equality across the major cultural and racial lines that divide the world. This relationship is far from perfect or complete, but it is the beginning of a type of relationship that some day must embrace all the peoples of the world.

The Japanese sense of unease in their past relations with foreign nations and their insensitivity and obtuseness in dealings with others may seem to be poor preparation for Japan to play a leading role in developing international fellow feeling, but because of accidents of geography and history they may be forced into a leading role in this effort. The openness of young Japanese to the outside world does hold out hope that they can rise to the challenges. The twenty-first century may not be "the Japanese century," as some non-Japanese have grandiloquently proclaimed, but Japan may well be among the leaders—possibly even the preeminent leader—in finding solutions to the problems that mankind will face in the twenty-first century.

Suggested
Reading

Index

Suggested Reading

THERE ARE MANY excellent books for those who would like to do a little more detailed reading on some of the aspects of Japan treated in this book. For an overall view of modern Japan, Frank Gibney's *Japan: The Fragile Superpower* (New York, Norton, 1975) makes good and reliable reading, and Richard Halloran's *Japan: Images and Reality* (New York, Knopf, 1969), Zbigniew Brzezinski's *Fragile Blossom: Crisis and Change in Japan* (New York, Harper and Row, 1972), and Masataka Kosaka's *100 Million Japanese: The Postwar Experience* (Tokyo, Kodansha, 1972) can all be recommended. Jack Seward's *The Japanese* (New York, Morrow, 1972), though using the same title as mine, treats the subject in a more casual, anecdotal way from the point of view of the foreign resident in Japan.

Many books deal with Japan's relations with the outside world and particularly with the United States. Among the better ones are John K. Emmerson, *Arms, Yen and Power* (New York, Dunellen, 1971); Priscilla Clapp and Morton H. Halperin, eds., *United States Japanese Relations: The 1970s* (Cambridge, Harvard University Press, 1974); Gerald L. Curtis, ed., *Japanese American Relations in the 1970s* (New York, The American Assembly, 1970); F. C. Langdon, *Japan's Foreign Policy* (Vancouver, University of British Columbia Press, 1973); James W. Morley, ed., *Forecast for Japan: Security in the 1970s* (Princeton, Princeton University Press, 1972), Lawrence Olson, *Japan in Postwar Asia* (New York, Praeger, 1970); Henry Rosovsky, ed., *Discord in the Pacific: Challenge to the Japanese-American Alliance* (New York, The American Assembly 1972); and Martin E. Weinstein, *Japan's Postwar Defense Policy 1947–1968* (New York, Columbia University Press, 1971).

There are a number of small books describing Japanese government and politics, of which the following are among the better and more recent ones: J. A. A. Stockwin, *Japan: Divided Politics in a Growth Economy* (New York, Norton, 1975); Ardath W. Burks, *The Government of Japan* (New York,

Crowell, 1972); Nobutake Ike, *Japanese Politics: Patron Client Democracy* (New York, Knopf, 1972); Theodore McNelly, *Contemporary Government of Japan* (Boston, Houghton Mifflin, 1972); Robert E. Ward, *Japan's Political System* (New York, Prentice-Hall, 1967); Frank Langdon, *Politics in Japan* (Boston, Little, Brown, 1967); and Warren M. Tsuneishi, *Japanese Political Style* (New York, Harper and Row, 1966). In addition there are some excellent studies on certain specific aspects of the Japanese political scene. Particularly worthy of mention are Gerald Curtis, *Election Campaigning Japanese Style* (New York, Columbia University Press, 1971); Haruhiro Fukui, *Party in Power: The Japanese Liberal-Democrats and Policy Making* (Berkeley, University of California Press, 1970); Nathaniel B. Thayer, *How the Conservatives Rule Japan* (Princeton, Princeton University Press, 1971); and Ezra Vogel, ed., *Modern Japanese Organization and Decision Making* (Berkeley, University of California Press, 1975).

In connection with Japanese society, two books have already been mentioned in the text: Takeo Doi's, *The Anatomy of Dependence* (Tokyo, Kodansha, 1971), and Chie Nakane's, *Japanese Society* (Berkeley, University of California Press, 1970). In addition note should be taken of Tadashi Fukutake's *Japanese Society Today* (Tokyo, University of Tokyo Press, 1974), Takeshi Ishida's *Japanese Society* (New York, Random House, 1971); R. P. Dore's *City Life in Japan: A Study of a Tokyo Ward* (Berkeley, University of California Press, 1958); Herbert Passim's *Society and Education in Japan* (New York, Columbia University Press, 1965); Ezra Vogel's *Japan's New Middle Class: The Salary Man and His Family in a Tokyo Suburb* (Berkeley, University of California Press, 1963); and the classic analysis of Japanese personality by Ruth Benedict in *The Chrysanthemum and the Sword: Patterns of Japanese Culture* (New York, Meridian Books, 1946).

For Japanese economics and business there is a wealth of fine works. *Asia's New Giant: How the Japanese Economy Works* (Washington, D.C., The Brookings Institution, 1976), edited jointly by Hugh Patrick and Henry Rosovsky, is not only the most recent authoritative work but also the biggest. Other valuable recent works are Saburo Okita, *Japan in the World Economy* (Tokyo, Japan Foundation, 1975); Isaiah Frank, *The Japanese Economy in International Perspective* (Baltimore, Johns Hopkins University Press, 1975); Eugene J. Kaplan, ed., *Japan: The Government-Business Relationship* (Department of Commerce, Washington, D.C., 1972); R. P. Dore, *British Factory, Japanese Factory: The Origins of National Diversity in Employment Relations* (Berkeley, University of California Press, 1973); and Nakayama Ichiro, *Industrialization and Labor-Management Relations in Japan* (Tokyo, Japanese Institute of Labour, 1975). James C. Abegglen's *Management and Worker: The Japanese Solution* (Tokyo, Kodansha, 1973) and M. Y. Yoshino's *Japan's Multinational Enterprises* (Cambridge, Harvard University Press, 1976) are among the several excellent studies of Japanese business by these two authors.

For the historical background, my *Japan: The Story of a Nation* (New York, Knopf, 1974) gives fuller coverage than is to be found in this book, and a still more detailed treatment is to be found in Fairbank, Reischauer, and Craig, *East Asia: Tradition and Transformation* (Boston, Houghton Mifflin, 1973). Basically the same text also appears in Reischauer and Craig, *Japan: Tradition and Transformation* (Boston, Houghton Mifflin, 1977). There is also John Whitney Hall's *Japan: From Prehistory to Modern Times* (New York, Delacorte, 1970). On premodern Japanese history there are Sir George Sansom's classic work, *Japan: A Short Cultural History* (New York, Appleton-Century, rev. ed., 1944); his massive three-volume *History of Japan* (Stanford, Stanford University Press, 1958, 1961, and 1963); and Bradley Smith's gorgeous *Japan: A History in Art* (New York, Simon and Schuster, 1964). On modern history there are many good works, including W. G. Beasley, *The Modern History of Japan* (New York, Praeger, 1963); Hugh Borton, *Japan's Modern Century* (New York, Ronald, 1970); and Richard Storry, *A History of Modern Japan* (New York, Penguin Books, 1960). Charles E. Neu's *The Troubled Encounter: The United States and Japan* (New York, Wiley, 1975) and William L. Neumann's *America Encounters Japan: From Perry to MacArthur* (Baltimore, Johns Hopkins, 1963) are two broad accounts of the history of Japanese-American relations, and two general studies of the American occupation of Japan are to be found in Kazuo Kawai's *Japan's American Interlude* (Chicago, University of Chicago Press, 1960) and in my *The United States and Japan* (Cambridge, Harvard University Press, 1950, 3rd ed., 1965). The story of the political convulsions that swept Japan in 1960 is well told in George R. Packard, *Protest in Tokyo: The Security Treaty Crisis of 1960* (Princeton, Princeton University Press, 1966).

I have listed above only a small sampling of some of the more general books on Japan. They in turn can lead to more detailed and narrowly focused books, which exist in profusion. And wholly outside this range of writings on Japan are the great numbers of beautiful books on Japanese art and the wealth of fine translations of Japanese literature.

Index

433